BEST AMERICAN
CRIME WRITING
2004

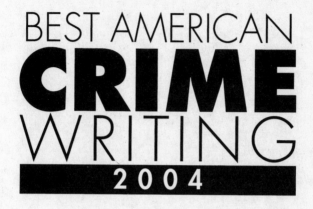

BEST AMERICAN CRIME WRITING 2004

INTRODUCTION BY
JOSEPH WAMBAUGH

EDITED BY **OTTO PENZLER**
AND **THOMAS H. COOK**

PANTHEON BOOKS
NEW YORK

ISSN 1542-0558

ISBN 0-375-42165-3

www.pantheonbooks.com

Book design by Debbie Glasserman

Printed in the United States of America
First Edition

CONTENTS

PREFACE

Once again, American crime writing rose to the highest level of journalistic excellence, and as always, it was difficult to select among such an embarrassment of riches. And yet selections had to be made, and we made them with an eye to the depth of the research, the sheer excellence of the writing, and as always, with an occasional nod to the quirky and the humorous. We sought variety in length and subject matter as well but always held to our firm conviction that the quality of the writing is what matters most.

As editors, we have tried never to be swayed by the fame of an author, but solely by the quality of that author's submission. As a result, many lesser-known writers have been included in our collections. This year, however, a great many Big Names made prominent entries into the field of crime writing. More important, their articles demonstrated the intellectual depth and literary style that have gained these writers the reputations they enjoy. As a result, this year's volume is a bit more star-studded than previous ones. Included in it are Scott Turow's thoughtful consideration of capital punishment, James Fallows's analysis of the death of Mohammed al-Dura, Jon Krakauer's account of peculiarly Mormon murders, and James Ellroy's melancholy meditation on a girl named Stephanie.

This year several writers contributed essays that were highly personal, and by their intimacy provided a unique glimpse into their own lives. Brendan Riley's "Megan's Law and Me" approaches this controversial legislation from the perspective of a sex offender, while Cecilia Balli's haunting "Ciudad de la Muerte" takes readers into the heart of her own stark fear.

Other writers chose to portray elements of the criminal justice system. In "A Miscarriage of Justice," Robert F. Kennedy Jr. portrays a defendant tried and convicted by the media, while John H. Richardson's "Not Guilty by Reason of Afghanistan" offers the specter of an absurd defense.

Crime lives not only in the act but also in its aftermath, a subject explored from four different directions in Robert Draper's "Night of the Bullies," Luke Dittrich's "Possessed," Sabrina Rubin Erdely's "Who Is the Boy in the Box?" and Pat Jordan's "CSC: Crime Scene Cleanup."

Crime in high and protected places is scrutinized in Clara Bingham's "Code of Dishonor," Charles Bowden's "Lord of the Drug Ring," and Elisabeth Franck's "The Professor and the Porn."

It is the prevention of crime that is the subject of Heather Mac Donald's "Chief Bratton Takes on LA." In "Watching the Detectives," Jay Kirk focuses on solving crimes, while Mark Bowden explores "The Dark Art of Interrogation."

And what anthology of crime writing would be complete without a dip into the absurd, the geriatric bank robber in David Grann's "The Old Man and the Gun," for example, or the wildly fraudulent escapade recounted in Mark Schone's "Unfortunate Con."

To our relief, there was no awesomely monstrous outrage in 2003, at least not one on the scale of September 11. For that, and by way of conclusion, we wish to express our continuing gratitude to all those throughout the globe who are laboring with such skill and determination to protect the civilized world from the enemies of human freedom and cultural diversity who would otherwise destroy it.

In terms of the nature and scope of this collection, we defined American crime reporting as any factual story involving crime written by an American or a Canadian and published in the United States or Canada during the calendar year 2003. We examined a very wide range of publications, which included all national and regional magazines and nearly two hundred so-called little magazines, reviews, and journals.

We welcome submissions by any writer, publisher, editor, or other interested party for *Best American Crime Writing 2005*. Please send a tear sheet with the name of the publication in which the submission appears, the date of publication, and if available, the address of the author. If first publication was in electronic format, a hard copy must be submitted. Only articles actually published with a 2004 publication date are eligible. All submissions must be made by December 31, 2004, and should be sent to Otto Penzler, The Mysterious Bookshop, 129 West 56th Street, New York, NY 10019. Those wishing verification that their submission was received should provide a self-addressed, stamped postcard or envelope. Submitted material cannot be returned.

Thomas H. Cook
Otto Penzler
New York
January 2004

INTRODUCTION

When Otto Penzler asked me to write an introduction to this volume I was reluctant, even though I was eager to work with a man who has meant so much to practitioners of my craft. I hesitated because the subject of lawsuit dangers to true-crime writers has been well covered, and I didn't want to rehash the subject, crucial though it is. Otto prevailed upon me to expand on this vital topic because of my extensive experience with the bottom-feeding, strange fish who thrive in the litigation tanks of America. I do so now in the hope that together we might pull the plug and drain a bit of that miasmic water.

I have written five nonfiction crime books about some very bad people. Not surprisingly, bad people tend to seek the counsel of other bad people in their relentless hunt for prey and profit. On five separate occasions I've been sued, but spurned legal blackmail, i.e., settlement offers, choosing to swim with those strange fish whose rows of needle teeth have taken chunks from my hide, but from whom I've always managed to escape.

Once, I even had the experience of facing a Los Angeles jury during the trial of another writer of true crime, Joe McGinnis, author of *Fatal Vision*, who was being sued by Dr. Jeffrey MacDonald, a man convicted of murdering his family on a U.S. Army base while serving with the Green Berets. I was there in that courtroom because Joe's excellent New York lawyer, Dan Kornstein, wanted writers with nonfiction experience—Jimmy Breslin, William F. Buckley Jr., and others—to testify about common practices in nonfiction interviews. Moreover, I was in the unique position of having "auditioned" for Dr. MacDonald prior to his decision to do the book with Joe McGinnis. I could tell the jury how MacDonald told absurd lies about his meeting with me, a meeting witnessed by my wife as well as by a companion of MacDonald's, a cop with whom I'd served in the LAPD, who could corroborate my testimony.

When I finished that court appearance this old detective was sure of two things: The jury saw us writers as members of the hated "media," and they didn't want to believe that the attractive, articulate Princeton physician could have committed the atrocity for which another jury had convicted him. After all, he didn't look like a killer, did he?

In the end, one key juror remained stubbornly on Joe's side, reportedly locking herself in a bathroom until the others gave up. A mistrial was declared, and Joe McGinnis, who'd spent months living on the other side of America from his family, struck a deal to avoid another litigation nightmare that would have bankrupted him economically and emotionally, like so many victims of the American litigation industry.

All of this was much on my mind some years later when I was sitting before my own jury, fighting a lawsuit filed by someone who I had been certain would like his depiction in my book, a man whom I considered a friend. That is one of the hard lessons of nonfiction: You must never think you know friend from foe when you write a true story. As in a whodunnit, where a good detective must consider everyone to be a potential suspect, a true-crime writer should consider everyone he or she interviews to be a potential litigant. When I was staring into the impassive faces of my jury, those people with the power to impoverish me, I kept wondering what I might have done better.

Of course I had written the truth, but notwithstanding myths you may have heard, truth is not a powerful defense. Indeed, I had even secured a signed waiver from the person who was suing me! It was a standard release supposedly protecting me from precisely what I was facing. It said that anything I'd written, whether fact or fiction or a combination thereof, would be acceptable to the undersigned who had received money for his signature. But how many angels can dance on the head of a pin? We writers don't know, but lawyers do. An appellate court decided that the "or" in "fact or fiction" was nebulous, and that a jury had to decide what the legal waiver really meant to the person who'd signed it.

I did prevail in the lawsuit, and the routed plaintiff and former friend actually offered me a jaunty farewell that said, "Well, you can't blame me for seeking a windfall, can you?" I, who had just suffered through an ordeal that stole at least five years from my longevity on this earth, could not respond. I was too busy breathing in a bag.

Here's what I most remember about that particular lawsuit. One evening prior to trial I happened onto one of the lawyers who'd earlier won the appeal of my initial summary judgment, thus forcing me into that jury trial. I was at a Chinese restaurant, and what I shall never forget is this: The lawyer, a crocodile in sensible shoes, was awaiting her moo goo gai pan takeout and seemed perplexed that I wasn't chummier. True, she and her colleagues were trying to take every dollar that my family and I would ever have, but after all, she was just doing a job, and her job was to help to destroy me whether I was right or wrong, but why should I take that personally? Sammy "the Bull" Gravano had a similar work ethic.

Among the horrors of defamation lawsuits, in which plaintiffs attack a writer's honesty, integrity, and everything that defines our profession, you should never forget this: Judges are black-robed lawyers, and many of them love those litigation tanks swarming with bottom-feeders. Many do not want the American legal system to be brought in line with the rest of the civilized world.

Only one of my nonfiction books, *The Blooding*, did not result in a lawsuit or even a threat of one. And why not? Simple answer: The story of the discovery of genetic fingerprinting and its first use in a murder investigation took place in England. And although there were people in the book who were not thrilled with their depictions, they did not dare to sue me, for in England, as in every other industrialized nation except ours, there is a potential penalty for filing a failed lawsuit. The loser will usually be required to pay all or part of the winner's legal fees, thus assuring that their system is not overwhelmed by worthless litigation—as is ours. In the United States anybody can make a deal with a contingency-fee lawyer by agreeing to divide whatever is recouped and then by filing any sort of action, hoping to terrorize defendants into paying go-away money.

Now, disingenuous denizens of the courts will call my characterization unfair, and claim that there is an avenue of redress for victims of frivolous lawsuits, a countersuit for "malicious prosecution." They will not tell you that it is virtually impossible to prove "malice" in such matters because the courts do not want to curtail the litigation by which they all prosper. Ask trial lawyers to list the successful malicious prosecution lawsuits they have ever heard of, let alone tried.

With respect, I quibble with one aspect of last year's Pileggi introduction, concerning the writer-interviewee relationship when someone is paid money to talk. Checkbook journalism is always spoken of disparagingly, but writers should not think of monetary payment to nonfiction interviewees as having anything to do with what will be said in the interview; it is all about avoiding lawsuits. Whenever possible, writer and publisher should be eager to pay for a signature on a meticulously worded, bulletproof waiver. You are buying peace of mind, knowing that you will never have to live for months, far from home, facing ruin as Joe McGinnis did, or sit in a Chinese restaurant facing a Junior Leaguer with a law degree and a Hannibal Lecter smile.

Be aware that even if a publisher has defamation insurance purporting to cover a writer's legal fees, almost all policies have an escape clause stating that if a verdict for the plaintiff still stands after all appeals are exhausted, then it is the defendant writer, not the publisher, who will pay the judgment and the legal fees. Try taking that thought to bed with you for several months, or years. I guarantee that you will become an expert on which antacid works best at bedtime, but nothing else will work at bedtime, that's for sure.

So, other than securing a safety-net waiver from true-crime interviewees — other than corroborating any information that purports to be the truth, other than being wary of those you interview, who after seeing themselves on the printed page can monster-morph faster than any midnight traveler bitten by *Canis lupus* under a late and lonely moon — is there wolfsbane you can nail to your door? Yes, if we fight for it.

Curtailing litigation should be a nonpartisan issue. It is crucial that you badger your state and federal representatives until our nation is brought in line with the rest of the world, by the passage of "loser pays" legislation, wherein all or part of a prevailing party's legal fees will be paid by the loser. And don't let trial lawyers try to tell you that such legislation would penalize the poor — all of those "little Davids taking on corporate Goliaths." In defamation cases, you are Goliath, according to their definition, regardless of how small and powerless you might be. The "poor" are judgment-proof by virtue of being poor, thus they will be always free to sue with impunity. We can't do anything about contingency-fee lawsuits from indigent plaintiffs, but most plaintiffs do have assets that can and should be put at risk along with the defendant's.

Publishers, insurance companies, other media outlets, and all nonfiction writers must be willing to face the emotional and financial hardship of battling back and never submitting to legal extortion. We must defend each and every lawsuit as an attack on our constitutional guarantees, and we must never forget that it is our duty to continue writing the truth, come what may.

But a brave defense is not enough; we must be proactive at the ballot box and punish cynical politicians who love largesse thrown to them by trial lawyers, while knowing full well that all goods and services have punishing amounts built in to cover our nation's massive litigation costs. Demand that your elected representatives address two little words, the most terrifying words in the language to all those strange fish who feed and spawn in America's litigation tanks. The two little words are *tort reform*.

Joseph Wambaugh

BEST AMERICAN
CRIME WRITING
2004

CIUDAD DE LA MUERTE
CECILIA BALLI

Do you know what happens to a human body in the desert? If it's fresh, the intestines eat themselves out. The body swells, the lungs ooze fluids through the nostrils and mouth, and the decaying organs let out a cocktail of nauseating gases. Sometimes, scavengers leave their mark: a gnawed leg, a missing shoulder. Eventually, all that is left is a pile of white bones. But there is a cruel trick the dry weather will sometimes play on a corpse. It will dehydrate the skin before the bacteria can get to it, producing a mummy—a blackened girl with skin dry as cardboard, baring her teeth like a frightened animal.

In February 1996 a seventeen-year-old girl named María Guadalupe del Río Vázquez went shopping in downtown Ciudad Juárez and vanished into thin air. Days later, her body was found in the desolate mountains of the Chihuahuan Desert—raped, strangled, her left breast mutilated. As girls continued to disappear, residents of the city formed bands and scoured the mountains for more bodies. The state police picked up the corpses—seventeen in all, an epidemic of murder—and quickly scurried away, leaving behind clothing, locks of hair, shoes curled like orange peels. The girls' hands were bound with their own shoelaces. All of the victims resembled each other: pretty, slim, medium to dark skin, long, straight dark hair. In a country that privileges men, whiteness, and wealth, these victims were female, brown, and poor. In a city that resents immigration and anything else from central and southern Mexico, these young women who had come to the northern border hoping to find work were social outcasts, strangers without names—especially now that they lay in silence in the sand, looking just like the ones before and the ones who would follow.

The deaths in the mountainous desert region known as Lomas de Poleo confirmed the worst fears of the women of Juárez: that something sinister had overcome their city. Beginning in 1993, there had been an unusual number of news reports in Juárez about the abduction and murder of women, an anomaly in Mexico. The grisly discoveries in the desert signaled that the worst crime wave in modern Mexican history had entered a new and more intense phase. Today, the toll of women who have been murdered in the past ten years is more than three hundred, staining the reputation of the country's fourth-largest city worldwide. Some of the women were murdered by their husbands and boyfriends. Other killings seemed to be random acts of violence. Around a third of the victims, however, were teenage girls whose deaths appear to be connected to a cryptic and chilling kind of serial killing. This crime is indisputably solvable: Evidence has been scattered like bread crumbs all over the crime scenes, but the state authorities have jailed no one who truly seems responsible. Be it incompetence or a cover-up, the lack of credible prosecution in these cases is perhaps the most blatant—and certainly the most baffling—illustration of the nearly flawless record of impunity that characterizes the Mexican justice system.

Who would commit such crimes? Juárez brims with rumor and suspicion. A serial killer with government protection is an obvious possibility. The indifference of the authorities charged with investigating the murders has focused suspicion on themselves. Maybe it's the Juárez police, some people say. They drive those white pickups with the campers, where they could easily hide a rotting body or a pile of bones, and they're always prowling around the shantytown of Anapra, on the edge of the desert, peering out their windows. The Chihuahua state police zoom about in sleek, unmarked SUVs capable of navigating the rugged desert terrain. Recently, federal investigators speculated that fourteen of the killings might be linked to an organ-smuggling ring.

Or maybe it's the drug dealers. The desert is, after all, their country, a frontier on the fringe of globalization. Between dips in the mountains, you glimpse El Paso to the north, its downtown towers gleaming like teeth. The Rio Grande cut through the mountains and created a valley that would in time birth the most densely populated border region in the world. But in Lomas de Poleo, there is only the sand and the desert scrub and a sea of trash—empty jugs, shabby toys, broken toilets, an unwound cassette of English lessons, plastic bags clinging to the brush like confetti. A frail man picks his way through a dumpster. An occasional small truck rattles off into the distance. They say that at night, this becomes the realm of gang members and drug runners, an army of men hauling their illicit goods into the United States. Rumor has it that if you wander far enough into the disorienting maze of primitive roads that have been scratched out of the sand, you will come upon a crude runway and a marvelous ranch with a swimming pool. If anybody sees you there, you should say you got lost and quickly turn around.

The obvious questions—who, why, how—remain unanswered. The abductions occur in mysterious moments, in quick, ghastly twists of fate that nobody seems—or at least wants to admit—to have witnessed. Most recently, they have transpired in the heart of the city in broad daylight. Some people believe the girls are taken by force, while others think it is more likely that the victims are lured by a seemingly innocent offer. A few mothers have said that their daughters disappeared a day or two after being approached about a job. Only one thing can be said with certainty, and it's that in Juárez, Mexico, the most barbarous things are possible.

The sun shimmers over downtown Juárez like white linen, but I have learned to march down its streets staring at the ground or ahead with icy, distant eyes. To do anything else is to acknowledge the lusty stares from men of all ages who stand at the corners of the city's busy thoroughfares waiting for nothing to happen. So begins the taunting. A skinny man with red eyes lets out a slow whistle through clenched teeth. Two young boys look at me, look at each other, and nod with a dirty grin. From among a group of men huddled on the steps of a shop, one calls out *"¡Una como esa!"*—One like her!—and the rest burst out laughing, their mustaches spreading gleefully across their faces as they watch me walk by. This is everywhere in urban Mexico, I remind myself, but knowing what I do about the fate of women in Juárez, their glares begin to feel more predatory. I watch my feet skitter on the pavement and, with every step, wish I could shed these hips, this chest, this hair. To walk through downtown Juárez is to know and deeply regret that you are a young woman.

Juárez, though, is a city of young women. They run its shops; they keep its hundreds of factories humming. In 1964 the United States terminated the Bracero guest-worker program with Mexico and deported many of its laborers, dumping thousands of men along the Mexican side of the border. In an effort to reemploy them, the Mexican government launched the Border Industrialization Program, which prodded American manufacturers to assemble their products in northern Mexico using cheap labor. The plan succeeded, but its main beneficiaries turned out to be women, who, it was determined, would make better workers for the new factories, or maquiladoras, because of their presumed superior manual dexterity. Word spread throughout Mexico that thousands of assembly-line jobs were cropping up in Juárez, and the nation's north quickly became the emblem of modernity and economic opportunity. In the seventies, factory-sponsored buses rumbled into the heartland and along the coasts and returned with thousands of hungry laborers. Among them were many single women with children in tow, who, aside from landing their own jobs in the *maquilas*, began to staff the throngs of stores and restaurants that proliferated to satisfy the new consumerism of Juárez's formerly cash-strapped population.

And so, if the working women of this border city had once earned reputations as prostitutes or bartenders, they now earned paychecks as factory workers, saleswomen, police officers, teachers—a few even as managers and engineers in the concrete tilt-ups that were constructed all around town to house around four hundred maquiladoras. For anywhere from $4 to $7 a day, they assembled automotive parts and electronic components and made clothing. Of the girls who couldn't afford to go to college—which is to say, the vast majority—some took computer classes, where they learned to use Microsoft Word and Excel so that they might become secretaries and administrative assistants. Juárez, after all, is a city that places a high premium on skills such as knowing how to use computers and speak English. Even in its most impoverished desert neighborhood, a dazed collection of impromptu homes stitched together from wood pallets, mattresses, cardboard boxes, and baling wire, I saw a tiny brick shack with a dozen mismatched chairs planted outside and a hand-painted sign that promised "*Clases de inglés.*"

But the migration was too fast, too disorganized. The population shot up to an estimated 1.5 million. Gone was the charm Juárez had possessed in the thirties, when its valley bore succulent grapes, or in the forties, when the music of Glenn Miller and Agustín Lara never stopped playing on Juárez Avenue, even as its neighboring country went to war. It was one of Mexico's biggest blunders to have planted its largest industrial experiment in the desert, in a city separated from the rest of the country not only symbolically, by its distinctly North American feel, but also physically, by the stunning but unforgiving Juárez Mountains. Cardboard shanties began to dot the landscape. Sewage spilled onto the streets. Power lines reproduced like parasites. Today, radio talk-show hosts ramble on about the ways in which immigrants ruined their beautiful community. I asked a well-bred young man what he felt were the virtues of his hometown, and despite a genuine effort, all he could name were the swank, cavernous clubs where the rich kids spend their weekends consuming alcohol by the bottle.

Even as the maquiladoras have begun relocating to China in the past two years, the reputation of Juárez as a city of opportunity lingers in impoverished rural Mexico. Inside the city, however, Mexico's economic vulnerability is exposed like raw flesh. The city is filled with broken people who crack open with the most innocent of questions. I met a woman from Zacatecas who lives in Anapra with her husband and three daughters in a minuscule house that they built out of wood pallets and thatched with black roofing material. They possess one bed, no refrigerator, and a tin washtub for bathing. State officials offered them this sliver of land, but the sliver is in the desert mountains, where life is not "beautiful," as the woman's brother had sent word home; it's shivery cold and always covered in a thin film of orange dirt. When I asked her how she liked living in this *colonia* along the city's northwestern frontier, the woman's smile quivered and a puddle of tears instantly dribbled to her chin.

Still, the worst part about Juárez, she told me, is the threat of violence that hangs over the sprawling city like a veil of terror. For just a short distance from her home, the bodies of girls who resemble her own sixteen-year-old Ana have appeared in the desert. Lured to their deaths—perhaps by promises of a job?—they lie abandoned like the heaps of trash that fleck this interminable sea of sand.

"Disculpe, señorita . . ." I turned toward the male voice that came from behind me and saw a dark-skinned, round-faced man in his thirties striding in my direction with a large basket of candies wedged between his neck and shoulder. He was heavyset, clad in light-brown slacks, a white, long-sleeved shirt with blue pinstripes, and a green windbreaker.

It was lunchtime, and I had walked out of a restaurant to return a call to a source on my cell phone, leaving behind three journalists with whom I'd been roaming the city. Diana Washington Valdez, an *El Paso Times* reporter who has been chronicling the Juárez women's deaths, had thought I should meet an attorney who is defending one of the government's scapegoats for the murders. But when we had rattled the wrought-iron gates of his office, there had been no reply. We had decided to wait at a small restaurant next door, and since a peal of music was issuing from a nearby television, I had gone outside to return the call. After I'd finished, I'd dialed my sister's number.

He looked rather humble, and this, I thought, was confirmed by the apologetic smile he wore, as if he were sorry to be intruding for something as mundane as the time or how to find a street. I half-smiled at him. "Hold on," I told my sister. I was about to save him the trouble of asking by telling him that I was not from around here when he spoke once more.

"Are you looking for work?"

Journalists and activists and sociologists trying to explain the loss of hundreds of women in such violent ways have constructed a common narrative. The story tells that when the immigrants came to Juárez from the countryside, they brought with them traditional Mexican ideas about gender. Women were to stay home, obey their husbands, and raise their children. But when wives and girlfriends and daughters began earning their own paychecks, they tasted a new independence and savored it. They bought nice things for themselves. They went dancing. They decided when bad relationships needed ending. In many cases, because unemployment rates for men were higher, women even took on the role of breadwinner in their families. The men saw their masculinity challenged and lashed out. Their resentment, uncontained by weakened religious and community bonds, turned violent, into a rage that manifested itself in the ruthless killing of women. This story has become so popular that when I interviewed the director of the Juárez Association of Maquiladoras, he recited it for me almost as though he were delivering a pitch at a business convention.

Yet the violence in Juárez—against men as well as women—is at its barest a criminal act and the direct by-product of the lack of rule of law in the Mexican justice system. Killers know that the odds are overwhelming that they can get away with murder. Nationally, only two in every one hundred crimes are ever solved, including cases that are closed by throwing a scapegoat in jail. There are no jury trials, and it is easy to influence a judge with money. If not one of the Juárez girls' cases has been properly resolved in ten years, only two explanations are possible: Law enforcement is either inept or corrupt. Most people believe both are true.

"I got to witness the inefficiency," says Oscar Maynez, the chief of forensics in Juárez from 1999 to 2002. Maynez has been involved in the cases of the murdered women of Juárez from the beginning. In 1993, as an instructor at the state police academy, he was skimming criminal files to use in his class when something disturbing grabbed his attention: In three separate cases, it appeared that three young women had been raped and strangled. Fearing that a serial killer might be on the loose, he created a psychological profile of the killer. When he approached his superiors with the report, however, every one of them, including the Juárez police chief and the deputy attorney general in the state capital of Chihuahua, dismissed its importance.

Maynez left his job a year later to pursue a master's degree in Washington, D.C. When he returned to reorganize the state crime lab, in 1999, he was greeted by a growing pile of women's remains, along with case records and forensic evidence, all of it hopelessly confused. Though some of the bodies still had vital clues embedded, the lab had never done any follow-up on those that had appeared between 1993 and 1999, including DNA analyses of the rapists' semen. Maynez was certain now—and the thought enraged him—that either a serial killer or a well-funded criminal ring was systematically targeting Juárez's youngest and poorest women. And yet, six years after his initial findings, neither the local nor the state authorities had made an effort to pursue an investigation according to Maynez's profile.

In early November 2001 eight female bodies were found in a cotton field across a busy street from the maquiladora association's air-conditioned offices. Five of them had been dumped in an old sewage canal, the other three in an irrigation ditch. Most followed a similar modus operandi: hands bound, apparently raped and strangled. Two days after the first corpses were found, Maynez and his crew began their work, dusting for evidence with tiny paintbrushes. As they did so, a man drove up in a bulldozer, saying that he'd been ordered by the attorney general's office to dig up the area to search for more bodies. Maynez sent him off to work elsewhere, preserving the crime scene.

Just a few days later, the police presented an edited videotape confession of two bus drivers who said they had killed the women, naming each of the eight. It seemed odd that the murderers would know the complete names of their victims—middle names, maternal and paternal names. When the accused were admitted to the city jail, it became obvious that they were scapegoats and had been forced to confess, for they showed multiple signs of torture, including electrical burns on their genitals. The cost of defending them turned out to be quite high. In February 2002 one of the two lawyers who were representing the drivers was shot and killed by state police officers as he drove his car; they say they mistook him for a fugitive. (An investigation was conducted, but the officers were never charged.) And a few days after the national human rights commission agreed to hear the drivers' cases, one of them mysteriously died in custody while undergoing an unauthorized surgery based on forged documents for a hernia that he had developed from the torture.

To date, eighteen people have been arrested in connection with the murders, including an Egyptian chemist named Abdel Latif Sharif Sharif, who arrived in Juárez by way of the United States, where he had lived for twenty-five years. He had accumulated two convictions for sexual battery in Florida. Sharif, who has been jailed in Mexico since October 1995, was accused by Chihuahua state prosecutors of several of the Juárez murders but convicted of only one. Though the conviction was overturned in 2000, a state judge ruled in favor of the prosecution's appeal, and Sharif remains imprisoned in Chihuahua City.

Judging from the lack of evidence, none of those eighteen individuals has been justly charged or convicted. The biggest testament to this is the fact that the murders continue unabated. At a press conference in jail in 1998, Sharif divulged information he had received from a police officer who claimed that the person behind the killings was Armando Martínez, the adopted son of a prominent Juárez bar owner. Sharif's source, Victor Valenzuela Rivera, said that he had overheard Martínez bragging about the murders at the Safari Club, one of his father's bars and a place frequented by police officers and *narcotraficantes*. Valenzuela insisted that Martínez, who also goes by Alejandro Maynez, had said he was being protected by government officials and the police and that he had bragged about his involvement in the trafficking of drugs and jewelry. The following year, Valenzuela repeated this account before several federal legislators and reporters; again, there were bloody repercussions. After Irene Blanco, the woman who had defended Sharif in court, demanded that the press investigate the allegations against Martínez, her son was shot and nearly killed by unknown assailants. The police say the shooting was drug-related; others blame police officers themselves. Martínez's whereabouts are unknown.

Valenzuela's testimony was not the only suggestion that the murders might be linked to the drug world. In 1996 a group of civilians searching for women's remains in Lomas de Poleo came upon a wooden shack and inside it an eerie sight: red and white votive candles, female garments, traces of fresh blood, and a wooden panel with detailed sketches on it. On one side of the panel was a drawing of a scorpion—a symbol of the Juárez cartel—as well as depictions of three unclothed women with long hair and a fourth lying on the floor, eyes closed, looking sad. A handful of soldiers peered out from behind what looked like marijuana plants, and at the top there was an ace of spades. The other side showed similar sketches: two unclothed women with their legs spread, an ace of clubs, and a male figure that looked like a gang member in a trench coat and hat. The panel was handed over to Victoria Caraveo, a women's activist, who turned it in to state authorities. Though the incident was reported by the Mexican papers, today government officials refuse to acknowledge that the panel ever existed.

As Oscar Maynez sees it, the problem with the Mexican justice system begins with "a complete absence of scruples among the people at the top." The criminologist says that the state crime lab has become merely an office that signs death certificates. In the case of the eight girls' bodies discovered in 2001, Maynez told the *El Paso Times*, "We were asked to plant evidence against two bus drivers who were charged with the murders." Though the drivers were prosecuted, their evidence file, Maynez says, remained empty. Frustrated, he resigned in January 2002. Because it has become his life's mission to save Juárez—or at least reduce its death toll—he is still intent upon getting his job back someday. The only chance of this happening is if the National Action Party (PAN) retakes control of the state.

But the PAN-controlled federal government isn't doing much to solve the Juárez murders either. Some of Chihuahua's top leaders a decade ago now sit in the highest ranks of President Vicente Fox's administration. In December 2001 federal legislators formed a committee to investigate the issue; it has yet to release a report. The bad blood between political parties and the long history of turf wars between state and federal law enforcement groups have prevented any sort of interagency cooperation, a key to solving difficult crimes in the United States. (On one of my trips to Juárez, I watched news footage of a mob of men pummeling each other—it was the state and federal police, fighting over who was supposed to protect the governor of Chihuahua when he flew into the city.) Early this March, the federal attorney general finally sent his investigators to the border, and in May they announced their intention to reopen fourteen of the murder cases as part of an investigation into organ smuggling.

Activists in Juárez and El Paso believe that the only way the murders can ever be solved is for Mexican federal officials to invite the American FBI to investigate, but historically, neither side has seemed eager for this to occur. Nationalism runs high in Mexico, and the country's leaders do not want Americans meddling in their affairs. In El Paso, officials like outgoing mayor Ray Caballero hesitate to offend their peers in Chihuahua. Caballero, who has had little to say publicly about the murdered women, told me, "For me to come out and make one pronouncement does not solve the problem." Perhaps circumstances are changing. This spring his office announced the creation of a hotline that will allow people in Juárez to report information to the El Paso police, who will then turn it over to investigators in Chihuahua. In late April, two deputies of the Mexican federal attorney general asked the FBI to collaborate with them on their investigations of the Juárez murder cases and the Juárez drug cartel. FBI agents have also been training Mexican prosecutors and detectives in Juárez and El Paso.

"Are you looking for work?"

My heart stopped. I knew that line, knew it immediately. My

eyes, frozen, terrified, locked onto his. "N-n-n-o," I believe I stuttered, but the man spoke again: "Where are you from?" His eyes crawled down my body and back up to my face. I was wearing leather boots, a black turtleneck, and fitted jeans—the last pair of clean pants I had managed to dig out of my suitcase that morning. And I regretted it immediately, because they might have been appropriate for trekking in mountains but not, I realized now, for walking around downtown. My heart was back, pounding furiously. Only then did I notice that as I had talked on the phone, I had absentmindedly paced half a block away from the restaurant's door. At that moment, there was nobody within sight, not even a single officer from the police station next door. I tried to envision the scenarios, tried to imagine some chance of safety. Would he ask me to follow him somewhere? Would someone drive up out of nowhere and force me into a vehicle? Did I have control of the situation or did he? If I darted toward the restaurant door, would I startle him, causing him to reach over and grab me? If I screamed, would my sister, who was now dangling by my thigh on the other end of a cell phone—listening, I hoped desperately, to this conversation—be able to help? Would Diana and the others inside the restaurant hear me over the music? If I was not able to escape, how much would I have to suffer before being killed? Was this it? Had I really—and the brief thought of this made me sad—gambled it all for a story?

For a few infinite seconds, nothing, and everything, was possible. But as my heart began to slow down and my mind sped up, I thought of another possibility. "I'm from El Paso," I said.

Irma Monrreal lives in a dust-tinged neighborhood known as Los Aztecas. The streets are unpaved, lined with tiny cement homes that peek out from behind clumsy cinder-block walls. Her home on Calle Grulla, which she bought on credit for $1,000, originally consisted of one room, in which she slept with seven children, but her eldest sons constructed another two rooms. Like so many immigrants in Juárez, Irma had hopped on a train and headed to the border with visions of prosperity flitting about in her head. In the fields of her state of Zacatecas, she had earned $3 a day hoeing beans and chiles. The big talk those days was of the factories in Juárez, where one could make nearly three times as much money. Since she and her husband had separated and her two eldest boys, who were thirteen and fourteen years old, would soon be needing jobs, she moved to Juárez and altered her sons' birth certificates so that they could immediately begin work in the maquiladoras.

Though Irma had a bundle of children to care for, she was closest to her third-youngest, Esmeralda, a blithe girl with a broad, round face and an unflinchingly optimistic attitude. At fifteen, she had completed middle school and was determined to keep studying so that someday she might work in a big place—like the airport, she told her mother—and earn lots of money. She was an excellent typist. She didn't date or spend much time with friends, but she was extremely close to her little sister Zulema, who was four years younger. The two pretended that they were television stars or models, and on special occasions they attended mass and treated themselves to lunch. When nighttime set in, they dreamed in bunk beds.

The only thing Esmeralda desired even more than an education was to have a *quinceañera* and to wear, like every other girl in Juárez who turns fifteen, a white gown to her rite-of-passage celebration. Her mother, who earns about $30 a week at a plastics factory, was saving up what she could to pay for the party, but Esmeralda felt the urge to pitch in. When an acquaintance asked Irma if she could borrow her teenage daughter to help around the house, Esmeralda pleaded with her hesitant mother to say yes, promising that she would work only up until the December 15 ceremony.

A week went by, and Esmeralda was excited, chatty. One evening she confided to her mom that a young man who was a few years older than she and who worked at the printshop where she had ordered her invitations had asked her out to lunch. She seemed deeply flattered that someone would notice her, but Irma admonished her not to take any offers from strangers. Her daughter promised that she wouldn't. A second week passed. Esmeralda would finish working at about four o'clock and head straight home, arriving well before Irma departed for her overnight shift at the maquiladora.

But a few days later, something went terribly wrong. At four-thirty, there was no sign of Esmeralda. Then it was five o'clock. Then six. At ten minutes to seven, Irma was forced to leave for work, but she asked her other children to watch for their sister. In the factory, she punched her time card and began talking to God silently.

The night dragged. When her shift was finally over, at seven in the morning, Irma rushed home to see her daughter's face, but her world imploded when her children opened the door: *Esmeralda no llegó.* The girl had vanished.

During the following ten days, Irma sometimes wondered whether her mind hadn't just taken a crazy turn. *Her* Esmeralda. How could this be happening? At night, she was overwhelmed with terror as she speculated where the girl might be, what she might be going through at that very moment. To lose a family member and not know what has happened to her is to live an existential anguish of believing fiercely and at the same time losing all notion of truth. I spoke with a psychologist at a Juárez women's crisis center who said that she finds it almost impossible to help the relatives of disappeared people heal because they are unable to discount that their abducted family member is either dead or alive. In El Paso I met Jaime Hervella, a Juárez native who runs a small accounting and consulting business as well as an organization for relatives of the disappeared on both sides of the border. "It's the worst of tragedies," he said, motioning with his waxlike hands over a cluttered desk. Then his bifocals fogged up, and he wept suddenly. "I just can't handle talking to the little old women, the mothers. Morning comes and they implore God, the Virgin, the man who drives the dump truck. Nighttime falls and they are still asking themselves, 'Where could my child be?' And the hours pass in this way, and the sun begins to disappear."

As she scavenged her memory for clues, Irma recalled the young man who had invited her daughter to lunch and immediately sent her son to look for him. But the owner of the printshop said he'd left his job. He refused to give any more information. After several visits herself, Irma finally persuaded the shop owner's son to tell her where their former employee lived. She found the little house, but it was locked; she banged on the door, the windows, screaming loudly in case her daughter was inside, listening. Esmeralda had told her mother that the young man had asked her for her schedule and that he had wanted to know whether her mom always walked her home from work. As Irma circled the house, the man arrived. She explained who she was and asked if he knew anything about her daughter, but he brushed her away, saying that he was married.

A few days later, a co-worker at the maquiladora asked Irma if she'd heard the news: Eight bodies had been found in a couple of ditches at the intersection of Ejército Nacional and Paseo de la Victoria. Could one of them be Esmeralda? Next came the phone call from the state prosecutor's office, asking her to identify the body. At the morgue, however, Irma was told it was too gruesome to view. She would have to obtain signed permission from the prosecutor's office. They offered to bring out the blouse that was on the corpse when it was found; Irma's heart collapsed when she glimpsed the speckled yellow, pink, orange, and white. It was the blouse that Esmeralda's older sister Cecilia had sent from Colorado, where she had moved to with her husband.

Yet there was still that lingering doubt, so Irma requested the permit to see the body. Fearing the shock would be too great for their mother to bear, her two eldest sons insisted on identifying it themselves. When they arrived home from the morgue, they were silent, their heads hung low.

"So?" Irma asked anxiously. "Was it your sister?"

But the response was hesitant, brittle: "We don't know."

"What do you mean, you don't know?!" Irma sputtered.

"It's just that . . . she doesn't have a face."

The words shattered on the floor like a Christmas ornament. She burst: "But what about her hair—was it her hair?"

"It's just that she doesn't have any hair," came the grief-stricken reply. "She doesn't have any ears. She doesn't have anything."

The corpse presumed to be Esmeralda's was one of the three found on November 6, a day before the other five were discovered a short distance away. All of the bodies were partially or wholly unclothed, some with their hands tied. But unlike the other girls, most of whom had been reduced to mere skeletal remains, Esmeralda's state of decomposition was particularly grisly and perplexing. She was missing most of the flesh from her collarbone up to her face. The authorities suggested that the rats in the fields had had their share, but Irma noted—and Oscar Maynez, the chief of forensics, concurred—that it would have made more sense for them to feast on the meatier parts of her body. The mystery deepened when the forensic workers took hair and blood from Esmeralda's mother and father and sent them to a laboratory in Mexico City. Even when DNA samples from the parents who had identified clothing were compared with those from the girls wearing the clothing, the results came back without a match. This opened up two possibilities: Either the samples had been grossly contaminated or, even more eerily, the murderers were switching clothes with other, as yet unfound, victims.

"Why?" Irma cried out as I sat with her one wintry afternoon in her tidy home, which is crammed with curly-haired dolls and deflated balloons and stuffed animals her daughter had collected—the last traces of happiness left in her little house. "Do they want to drive me crazy or something? Is it her or isn't it?" In a silver frame on top of a brown armoire, Esmeralda sat squeezed into a strapless red top, her shoulder-length hair dyed a blondish brown. She was laughing irresistibly—cracking up—but across from the photo, Irma slumped in her chair in blue sweats and a denim shirt, her body heaving uncontrollably as I listened, speechless. "Why does God let the evil ones take the good ones away? Why the poor, if we don't bring any harm on anybody? Nobody can imagine what this trauma is like. I go to work and I don't know if my children are going to be safe when I return. It's a terror that's lived day by day, hour by hour."

Like numerous stories I had heard from other victims' families, Irma's included the lament that her family has fallen apart as her children struggle to confront the tragedy of losing their sister and try to assign blame. Unable to channel their newfound hate, they have begun hating each other. Her eldest sons have stopped talking to her. Zulema, who refuses to sleep in her bunk bed now, attempted to kill herself and her eight-year-old brother with tranquilizers a doctor had prescribed for Irma. Defeated, the woman spoke with the shame of a child who has discovered that she has made an irrevocably wrong choice. She wished, with all her might, that she had never made that fateful decision to come to Juárez. "They've destroyed my life," she said with vacant eyes and a flat voice, once she had regained her composure. "I don't believe in anything anymore. There is a saying that one comes here in search of a better life, but those are nothing but illusions."

Irma eventually claimed the body, she says, so that she would "have somewhere to cry." Instead of determining whether more lab work needed to be done, the authorities instantly handed it over. They never interrogated the suspicious young man Irma had reported, and in a tasteless act of disregard for her daughter, they ruled that the cause of the young woman's death was "undetermined," even though it seemed apparent that she had been strangled. On November 16 Irma buried the corpse, using the *quinceañera* savings to pay for the $600 coffin.

"*Soy de El Paso*," I said to the man outside the restaurant. I held my breath. I remembered what Diana had told me when we first met to talk about the story: "They know who to leave alone. They leave the Americans alone. They leave the rich girls alone, because there might be trouble. The other girls? A dime a dozen." And yes, his interest faded instantly. "I'm sorry," he said, still bearing his apologetic smile, though somewhat more sheepishly. "I—I just saw you holding that piece of paper so I thought maybe you were looking for a job. Sorry." He turned around and began to walk away.

I was still frightened, but now that I felt a little safer, the journalist in me began to return. "Why?" I called out nervously. "Do you know of a job?" He turned around and stared at me. "I hire girls to work at a grocery store," he said. His eyebrows crinkled. "Where are you from?" Shaking my head, I stammered, "Oh, no—I'm from El Paso. My friends are waiting for me inside this restaurant." I brushed past him in a hurry, skipping up the restaurant's steps and to the table where the rest of the group was finishing their meal. Diana was gone. I took my seat. My legs, my hands, trembled violently.

"You'll never guess what happened to me," I said in a shaky voice. The others fell silent and looked at me with interest. "I just got offered a job." As the words spilled, one of the group nodded slowly. "You fit the profile," she said. When I described the man to her, she said that he had walked into the restaurant earlier, while I was on the phone. He had chatted with the woman who was cooking, taken some food, and left.

I jumped from my chair and stepped over to the counter. "Excuse me, *señora*," I said to the woman at the grill. "Do you know the man who just came in a few minutes ago?" "Not very well," she replied. "At night he guards the lawyer's office next door and by day he sells candies on the street."

At that moment, something blocked the light from the doorway. I turned around and found myself face-to-face with the same man from outside, this time without his basket. He looked nervous. "Let me buy you a Coke," he offered. "No, thanks," I replied firmly. Then I asked him, "Do you really have a store?"

"You're a journalist," he said, "aren't you?" His question caught me by surprise. I turned toward my table, then back to his intense gaze. "I—I'm here with some journalist friends," I stuttered. "No," he said forcefully, "but *you're* a journalist, aren't you?" It was obvious that he knew. "Well, yes, but I'm just here accompanying my friends, who are working on a story." His tone softened. "Come on, let's sit down. Let me buy you a drink. *En confianza.*" *You can trust me.* "No," I repeated, "I'm with my friends and we're leaving." I walked back to the table. Diana had returned, unaware of what had transpired. Later I would learn that she had gone to the lawyer's office, encountered the candy man, and told him she was with a group of journalists who wanted to see his boss. But with the man standing there, all I wanted to do was get away. We all gathered our belongings and hurried toward the door. "The lawyer says he'll be here tomorrow, if you want to see him," we heard the man call out to us. I never turned back.

That night, safe in El Paso, I stared at the ceiling in the darkness of my hotel room and replayed the afternoon's events over and over. My family had worried when I told them that I was going to write about the women of Juárez, even after I assured them that plenty of other journalists had done so safely. But *you*, they shot back, as if I'd missed the most obvious point, *you* look just like those girls. I thought of how much care I had taken not to go to Juárez alone, even if it had meant sacrificing my journalistic independence. And yet, in that one brief instant I had let my guard down, and I had been approached by someone mysterious. I will never know for sure if that was it—if, as I have told colleagues I felt at that moment, I really touched the story, my own life colliding with those of the girls whose lives I had been hoping to preserve. What I do know is this: that I had felt my heart beat, the way they must have felt it beat too.

As I thought this, warm tears spilled down the sides of my face and trickled into my ears. And I realized that I was crying not for myself, but for the women of Juárez—for the girls who had died and for the mothers who survived them. They say that whenever a new body is found, every grieving mother relives her pain. I was crying for the girls who had stayed on the other side of the border. For the ones who couldn't leave their reflections on paper and run far, far away, as I was going to do. I cried because I realized how easy it would have been to believe the man who approached me; because I understood that the girls were not naive, or careless, or, as a former attorney general of Chihuahua once said, asking for it. They were simply women—poor women, brown women. Fighters, dreamers. And they weren't even dreaming of all that much, by our standards: a secretarial job, a bedroom set, a fifteenth-birthday party. A little chance to live.

I cried because of the absurdity of it all, because it was possible for a life to be worth less than a brief taste of power. I cried thinking of how we had failed them.

━━━━━

A year after I first visited El Paso and Ciudad Juárez to report this story, I found myself returning with my car crammed with my belongings. I am now writing a book about the murders. It is not the kind of subject that makes you jump out of bed every morning; it is the kind that seizes you and pulls you in, not letting you go as long as there are more disappearances and more bodies and more questions than answers.

In just one year, the national rage and the international pressure on Mexico to resolve the girls' deaths has grown tremendously. In October 2003, four members of the U.S. Congress visited Juárez to learn more about the crimes, and so far seventy-eight House representatives have signed a resolution condemning the killings and urging American support in their investigation. A month after I arrived in Juárez, on Valentine's Day of 2004, close to three thousand protesters marched across the border in commemoration of the international V-Day, led by playwright Eve Ensler and the actresses Jane Fonda and Sally Fields. President Bush discussed the issue with President Vicente Fox at a March meeting in Crawford, Texas; on the same day their talks ended, a group of Chihuahua civil organizations held a symbolic mock trial in which a jury of human rights activists demanded a political trial of Governor Patricio Martinez and the firing of the state attorney general, Jesús José Solís.

President Fox has appointed a full-time human rights commissioner and a prosecutor to focus on the crimes, and although their budgets and jurisdictional authority are limited, there is growing hope in the idea that the murders have finally become a national priority. But as sexual killings of women begin to appear in other parts of the country and in Guatemala—and as evidence surfaces that Mexican police are deeply entrenched in protecting drug traffickers and aiding them with murder—there is also fear that the death of women could have a more intractable cause. In early March, The Dallas Morning News *published an article in which unnamed Mexican sources suggested that the girls in Juárez are being raped, tortured, and killed to celebrate successful drug runs.*

When I first began working on this subject, there were nights following long hours of work in which a group of us journalists gathered for drinks and talked about the day when the story would be over. We are still having that conversation.

FOR THE LOVE OF GOD
JON KRAKAUER

On June 5, 2002, in the middle of the night, fourteen-year-old Elizabeth Smart was abducted at knifepoint from her Salt Lake City bedroom while her parents slept in a nearby part of the house. Smart's alleged abductor—a forty-nine-year-old street preacher named Brian David Mitchell—reportedly took her to a secluded campsite in the foothills above her home, where he and his fifty-seven-year-old wife held a weird, self-styled wedding ritual in which Smart was "sealed" to Mitchell in "the new and everlasting covenant"—a Mormon euphemism for polygamous marriage. Immediately thereafter, the girl was forced to remove her red pajamas, prosecutors say, and Mitchell consummated the marriage with an act of rape.

Details of the audacious kidnapping were reported breathlessly and without pause by the news media, leaving much of the country aghast and riveted. When a massive investigation failed to locate Smart or her unidentified abductor by summer's end, people assumed the worst: that she had been subjected to some unspeakable ordeal and murdered. Then, nine months after she disappeared, she turned up alive, surprising almost everyone.

The astonishing reappearance of Elizabeth Smart occurred in the jittery days immediately before the invasion of Iraq. Most Americans, made fretful by the uncertainties of the impending war and a sputtering economy, were desperate for some good news, any good news, and rejoiced with commensurate intensity when the girl was reunited with her family.

Like so many of his countrymen, Dan Lafferty was spellbound by the Elizabeth Smart saga, which he monitored from a cheap television in a cramped cell, deep in the bowels of the Utah state prison, where he is serving two life sentences for murdering a young mother and her baby in 1984. Within hours of Smart's rescue, the media disclosed that her alleged abductor was an excommunicated Mormon. "With that small piece of information," Lafferty boasts, "I immediately guessed that he was probably a fundamentalist and that Elizabeth was somehow involved in a polygamy situation."

Lafferty's hunch was at least half true. Brian David Mitchell was indeed a Mormon fundamentalist, a religious zealot who believed that the Church of Jesus Christ of Latter-day Saints had made a ruinous blunder in 1890 when its leaders renounced polygamy, which until then had been promoted as "the most holy and important doctrine ever revealed to man on earth." Nineteen months before Elizabeth Smart disappeared, Mitchell received a divine revelation in which the Lord explained to him that he had been placed on earth to serve as God's mouthpiece during the Last Days. God also commanded Mitchell to take seven additional wives. Elizabeth may have had the misfortune to be the first.

None of Mitchell's reported behavior strikes fifty-six-year-old Dan Lafferty as surprising or particularly outlandish, because he himself is a polygamist and self-described religious zealot who receives frequent communiqués from God. In fact it was God, he explains, who commanded him to commit the murders that landed him behind bars for life.

Dan hasn't shaved or cut his hair since he arrived at the state prison near Draper, Utah. His beard, wrapped with rubber bands into a stiff gray cable, now descends to his belly. His hair has gone white and fans across the back of his orange prison jumpsuit. Although crow's-feet furrow the corners of his eyes, there is something unmistakably boyish about his countenance. His skin is so pale it seems translucent. A crude tattoo of a spiderweb radiates from Dan's left elbow, wrapping the crook of his arm in a jagged indigo lattice. His wrists are bound in handcuffs, and his shackled ankles are chained to a steel ring embedded in the concrete floor of the visitors room. On his otherwise bare feet are cheap rubber flip-flops. A large, powerfully built man who rarely ventures outside his cell, he cheerfully refers to the prison's maximum-security unit as "my monastery." Raised a devout Mormon, Dan says he has "always been interested in God and the Kingdom of God. It's been the center of my focus since I was a young child."

On July 24, 1984, Dan and his older brother, Ron, forced their way into the apartment of their youngest brother, Allen, in the sleepy white-bread town of American Fork, twenty minutes down the interstate from Dan's prison cell. Inside the brick duplex, Dan found his fifteen-month-old niece, Erica, standing in her crib, smiling up at him. "I spoke to her for a minute," Dan recalls. "I told her, I'm not sure what this is all about, but apparently it's God's will that you leave this world; perhaps we can talk about it later." And then he ended her life with a ten-inch boning knife.

After dispatching Erica, he calmly walked into the kitchen and used the same knife to kill the baby's twenty-four-year-old mother, Brenda. Dan insists, very convincingly, that he has never felt any regret over the deed, or any shame. He is absolutely certain that God intended for him to kill Brenda and Erica Lafferty: "It was like someone had taken me by the hand that day and led me comfortably through everything that happened."

These murders are shocking for a host of reasons, but no aspect of the crimes is more disquieting than Lafferty's complete and determined absence of remorse. How could an apparently sane, avowedly pious man kill a blameless woman and her baby so ruthlessly, without the barest flicker of emotion? What filled him with such certitude? Any attempt to answer these questions must plumb those murky sectors of the heart and head that prompt most of us to believe in God—and that compel an impassioned few to carry that irrational belief to its logical end.

Although religious devotion is commonly extolled in this country, it has a troubling element that is often ignored or denied. As a means of motivating people to be cruel and inhumane—as a means of inciting evil, to borrow the vocabulary of the devout—there may be no more potent force than religion. Men have been committing heinous acts in the name of God ever since mankind began believing in deities. When the subject of religiously inspired bloodshed comes up, Americans immediately think of Islamic fundamentalism, which is to be expected in the wake of the September 11 attacks on New York City and Washington, D.C. But Muhammad is not the only prophet whose words have been used to sanction barbarism; Christians, Jews, Hindus, Sikhs, and even Buddhists have also been propelled by scripture to butcher innocents. For every Osama bin Laden, there is a David Koresh, a Jim Jones, or a Dan Lafferty.

Outwardly, these religious zealots appear to be motivated by the anticipation of a great reward—wealth, fame, eternal salvation—but the real recompense may well be the obsession itself. As a result of his (or her) infatuation, the fanatic's existence overflows with purpose. Ambiguity vanishes. A narcissistic sense of self-assurance displaces all doubt. A delicious rage quickens the pulse, fueled by the sins and shortcomings of lesser mortals. Perspective narrows until the last remnants of proportion are shed from one's life. Through immoderation, the fanatic experiences something akin to rapture.

Faith is the very antithesis of reason, injudiciousness a crucial component of spiritual devotion. And when religious fanaticism supplants ratiocination, all bets are suddenly off. Anything can happen. Absolutely anything. Common sense is no match for the voice of God—as the actions of Dan Lafferty vividly attest.

. . .

Balanced atop the highest spire of the Salt Lake Temple, gleaming in the Utah sun, a statue of the angel Moroni stands watch over downtown Salt Lake City with his golden trumpet raised. This massive granite edifice is the spiritual and temporal nexus of the Church of Jesus Christ of Latter-day Saints. At last count, the LDS Church — which presents itself as the world's only true religion — harbored more than eleven million Saints the world over, making Mormonism the fastest-growing faith in the Western Hemisphere. In the United States, Mormons now outnumber Presbyterians and Episcopalians. On the planet as a whole, there are more Mormons than Jews.

The church's affairs are directed by a cadre of elderly white males in dark suits who carry out their holy duties from a twenty-six-story office tower beside Temple Square. To a man, the LDS leadership adamantly insists that Dan Lafferty should under no circumstances be considered Mormon — a member of a religious community that has earned a reputation for being chaste, optimistic, outgoing, dutiful. Although the faith that moved Lafferty to slay his niece and sister-in-law is Mormon fundamentalism, LDS leaders bristle visibly when Mormons and Mormon fundamentalists are even mentioned in the same breath.

Nevertheless, Mormons and those who call themselves Mormon fundamentalists believe in the same holy texts and the same sacred history. Both groups believe that Joseph Smith, who founded Mormonism in 1830, played a vital role in God's plan for mankind; both consider him to be a prophet comparable in stature to Moses and Isaiah; and both are convinced that God regards them, and them alone, as his favored children: "a peculiar treasure unto me above all people." But Mormon fundamentalists diverge from their Mormon compatriots on one especially inflammatory point: They passionately believe that Saints have a divine obligation to take multiple wives.

There are more than thirty thousand Mormon fundamentalist polygamists living in Canada, in Mexico, and throughout the American West. Some experts estimate that they may number as many as one hundred thousand. Even this larger figure amounts to less than one percent of the membership in the LDS Church, but all the same, the mainstream leaders are extremely discomfited by these legions of polygamous brethren. The LDS leadership has worked very hard to convince the American public—as well as the church membership—that polygamy was a quaint idiosyncrasy practiced by a mere handful of nineteenth-century Mormons. The religious literature handed out by the earnest young missionaries in Temple Square makes no mention of the fact that Joseph Smith—still the religion's focal personage—married at least thirty-three women, and probably as many as forty-eight. Nor does it mention that the youngest of these wives was just fourteen years old when Smith explained to her that God had commanded that she marry him or face eternal damnation.

In fact, polygamy was arguably the most sacred credo of Smith's church—a tenet important enough to be canonized for the ages in the Doctrine and Covenants, one of Mormonism's primary scriptural texts. The revered prophet taught that a man needed at least three wives to attain the "fullness of exaltation" in the afterlife. He warned that God had explicitly commanded, "All those who have this law revealed unto them must obey the same . . . and if ye abide not that covenant, then are ye damned; for no one can reject this covenant and be permitted to enter into my glory."

Joseph Smith was murdered by a mob of Mormon-haters in 1844. Brigham Young assumed leadership of the church and led the Saints to the barren wilds of the Great Basin, where in short order they established a remarkable empire and unabashedly embraced the covenant of "spiritual wifery." This both titillated and shocked the sensibilities of Victorian-era Americans. In 1856, recognizing the strength of the antipolygamy vote, Republican candidate John C.

Fremont ran for president on a platform that pledged to "prohibit in the territories those twin relics of barbarism—Polygamy and Slavery." Fremont lost the election, but a year later the man who won, James Buchanan, sent the U.S. Army to invade Utah and dismantle Brigham Young's theocracy.

The so-called Utah War, however, neither removed Brigham Young from power nor ended the doctrine of plural marriage, to the annoyance and bafflement of a whole series of American presidents. An escalating sequence of judicial and legislative challenges to polygamy ensued, culminating in the Edmunds-Tucker Act of 1887, which disincorporated the LDS Church. In 1890, with their feet held fast to the fire, the Saints reluctantly renounced the practice.

If LDS leaders were initially loath to abandon plural marriage, eventually they adopted a more pragmatic approach to American politics, emphatically rejecting the practice and actually urging government agencies to prosecute polygamists. It was this single change in policy, more than anything else, that transformed the LDS Church into its astonishingly successful present-day iteration. Having jettisoned polygamy, Mormons gradually ceased to be regarded as a crackpot sect. They acquired the trappings of a conventional faith so successfully that Mormonism is now widely considered to be the quintessential American religion.

Mormon fundamentalists, however, believe that acceptance into the American mainstream came at way too high a price. They insist that the church sold them out—that the LDS leadership abandoned one of the religion's most crucial theological tenets for the sake of political expedience. These present-day polygamists therefore consider themselves to be the keepers of the flame—the only true and righteous Mormons.

An hour down the interstate from Salt Lake City, the stolid city of Provo covers the flats between Utah Lake and eleven-thousand-foot

Provo Peak. Boasting a population of slightly more than one hundred thousand, it is the seat of Utah County and home to Brigham Young University—the Mormon world's flagship institution of higher learning, owned and tightly controlled by the LDS Church.

Most non-Mormons think of Salt Lake City as the geographic heart of Mormondom, but in fact half the population of Salt Lake is non-Mormon, and many Latter-day Saints regard that city as a sinful place that's been corrupted by outsiders. To the Saints themselves, the true Mormon heartland is here in Provo and in surrounding Utah County—the site of chaste little towns like Highland, American Fork, Orem, Payson, and Salem—where the population is nearly 90 percent LDS. This is the most Republican county in the most Republican state in the nation.

Robert Crossfield, a fundamentalist from Canada who calls himself the prophet Onias, arrived in the Provo area in the early 1980s and met the Mormon businessman Bernard Brady.* Onias was assembling an organization called the School of the Prophets, and he invited Brady to become a counselor. Modeling the school on an institution of the same name established by Joseph Smith, Onias preached many of the standard fundamentalist principles to his acolytes: the virtues of plural marriage, the divinely ordained supremacy of the white race, and the imminent return of Jesus Christ—on which date the devout would be lifted up and welcomed into the Kingdom of God while the unholy would be swept from the face of the earth in a hurricane of fire. But the main focus of Onias's school was instructing his followers in the sacred art of receiving divine revelation.

From the beginning, Joseph Smith had preached that if Mormons lived piously and obeyed God's commandments, He would

*Name has been changed.

communicate with each of them one-on-one. Mormons were instructed to seek "impressions from the Lord" to guide them in every aspect of their lives, and the concept proved to be immensely popular. Many people were drawn to the new religion because it gave them an uncommonly intimate relationship with God. It was like nothing they had experienced before, and it stirred their religious passions. Onias sought to rekindle this same passion through the School of the Prophets by resurrecting the practice of personal revelation.

Bernard Brady, energized by Onias's ideas, set out to recruit worthy candidates for the school. One of them was a fellow named Dan Lafferty. "Dan was unique in the strength of his desire to do what was meaningful," says Brady, "to do what was right. A white lie here and there—to most people that wouldn't be a big thing. But to Dan, it would be unthinkable."

Brady pauses for a minute, and a look of profound regret darkens his face. In a faltering voice, he adds, "So I introduced Dan Lafferty to Bob Crossfield. Looking back on it now, it's unfortunate that I was the catalyst who brought Bob and the Laffertys together. But it happened."

Dan Lafferty grew up in rural Utah County, just south of Provo, as a model Latter-day Saint, virtuous and compliant, "zooming down the highway to heaven." Polygamy never crossed his mind. After high school, he went on a two-year mission to Scotland, where he met Matilda Loomis,* the divorced mother of two girls. After Dan's mission, Matilda came to Utah, and they were sealed for time and eternity in the Provo temple. Then the newlyweds moved to California,

*Name has been changed.

where Dan studied for five years at the Los Angeles School of Chiropractors. One Sunday in California, they happened to hear a member of their local LDS ward give a talk about plural marriage. "During the talk, this guy said, 'Okay, let's see a show of hands from everybody who comes from a polygamous background,'" Dan recalls. "And there were only like four people who didn't raise their hands in the whole congregation. That really got my attention. I decided to learn everything I could about polygamy."

He began reading books about Mormon fundamentalism. Upon returning from California to Utah County, Dan went to the Brigham Young University library, where he unearthed a fifty-one-page booklet promoting polygamy titled *The Peace Maker*. Written in 1842 by an associate of Joseph Smith's, it offered an elaborate biblical rationale for polygamy, which the author proposed as a cure for the myriad ills that plagued monogamous relationships. Part of the cure was making sure that women remained properly subservient, as God intended. According to the tract, "the wife is pronounced the husband's property, as much so as his manservant, his maidservant, his ox or his horse."

The Peace Maker expressed Taliban-like views about the roles of men and women, and Dan began strictly enforcing those roles within his family, which had grown to include Matilda, her two daughters, and four children they had conceived together. Matilda was no longer allowed to drive, handle money, or talk to anyone outside the family when Dan wasn't present, and she had to wear a dress at all times. Dan forbade the family to receive outside medical care and began treating the children himself by means of prayer, fasting, and herbal remedies. In July 1983, when his fifth child, a son, was born, Dan delivered the baby at home and circumcised the infant himself. The Laffertys started raising their own food. Dan turned off the gas and electricity. No publications of any kind were allowed in the home except LDS books and magazines. Dan even got rid of all their watches and clocks, believing they should "keep time by the spirit."

When Matilda disobeyed Dan, he spanked her. If she continued to disobey him, he warned, she would be forced to leave the marriage without her children—who, according to the principles elucidated in *The Peace Maker*, were the father's property. Dan also announced that he would be taking plural wives. "It was a hellish situation," says Matilda. "There were no choices. Either leave the kids or accept his will." At first, Dan proposed taking as a plural wife Matilda's oldest daughter. He abandoned that idea, however, to marry a woman who looked after Robert Redford's horses on a ranch outside Provo.

Living according to the strictures in *The Peace Maker* felt good to Dan—it felt *right*, as though this was the way God intended men and women to live. Inspired, Dan sought out other texts about Mormonism as it was practiced in the early years. He learned that in the nineteenth century, Joseph Smith and Brigham Young preached about the righteousness of a sacred doctrine known as "blood atonement": Certain grievous acts committed against Mormons, as Young explained it, could only be rectified if the "sinners have their blood spilt upon the ground." In addition, Smith taught that the laws of God take precedence over the laws of men.

Dan's interest in legal theory started in California following a conflict with state and county authorities. At the time, Dan supported his family primarily by running a small sandwich business out of his home. "It was a very profitable little hustle," Dan says proudly. "Or it was until the board of health closed me down for not following regulations. They claimed I needed a license and that I wasn't paying the required taxes." Matilda had just given birth to a baby boy. Money was tight. Losing that income proved to be a pivotal event in Dan's passage to fundamentalism.

"After they shut me down," he recalls, "I didn't know quite what to do. It didn't seem right that the government would penalize me for being ambitious and trying to support my family—that they would actually force me to go on welfare instead of letting me run my little business. It seemed so stupid—the worst kind of government intrusion. In the Book of Mormon, Moroni talks about how all of us have an obligation to make sure we have a good and just government. When I read that, it really got me going. It made me realize that I needed to start getting involved in political issues. I saw that when it comes right down to it, you can't really separate political issues from religious issues."

Upon returning to Utah, Dan went to work for his father, who had opened a chiropractic office in the basement of his Provo home. Dan's younger brother Mark soon joined him. During breaks between patients, they engaged in heartfelt discussions about religious doctrine. Often, five of the six Lafferty brothers—Dan, Mark, Watson, Tim, and Allen—were present for these ad hoc conferences. Dan usually led the discussions, which inevitably concluded that the government was dangerously out of control. Buttressing his arguments by quoting scripture from the Book of Mormon, he patiently explained that the government had no right to require American citizens to obtain any kind of license or pay taxes or submit to the oppressive burden of a Social Security number. Although Dan had not yet allied himself with any established school of thought, his self-directed studies had transformed him into a de facto Mormon fundamentalist—an exceedingly ardent one. The impetus for most fundamentalist movements—whether Mormon, Catholic, Evangelical Christian, Muslim, or Jewish—is a yearning to return to the mythical order and imagined perfection of the original church. Dan was moved by this same desire. The more he studied historical documents, the more certain he was that the LDS Church had blundered off course in 1890 when then president and prophet Wilford Woodruff was coerced into abandoning the doctrine of plural marriage by the godless government in Washington, D.C.

Dan was intent on adhering unfailingly to God's "true" commandments, as determined by a literal interpretation of his church's most sacred texts. He was no less intent on adhering to the "true" commandments of his country's most sacred texts. To him, the Book of Mormon, *The Peace Maker*, the United States Constitution, and the Declaration of Independence are all of a piece. The authority that flows from their divinely inspired sentences is absolute and immutable. And it is the duty of righteous men and women to conduct their lives according to a stringently literal reading of those sentences.

After seeking guidance through prayer and receiving confirmation that he was acting in accordance with the Lord's wishes, Dan sent his driver's license back to the state of Utah, revoked his marriage license, and returned his Social Security card. He ignored posted speed limits and simply drove "wisely and carefully." And he quit paying taxes of any kind—which provoked frequent confrontations with the cashiers in local stores.

By early 1983, the Lafferty boys were meeting on a regular basis to discuss the merits of the principles advocated in *The Peace Maker*. When three of the brothers attempted to uphold their new beliefs in their homes, however, their wives refused, voicing their complaints to Dianna—the wife of the oldest brother, Ron.

Ron functioned as the emotional anchor for the greater Lafferty clan. His brothers and sisters looked up to him for counseling and emotional support. He and Dianna lived with their six kids in Highland, a small, prosperous semirural community tucked against the foot of the Wasatch Range, midway between Provo and Salt Lake City. In 1982, Ron was a Highland city councilman and a stalwart of the local LDS congregation, where he had been appointed first counselor to the bishop. By all accounts, he was a wonderful father to his children, and he and Dianna had an uncommonly solid marriage—a relationship envied by most of their acquaintances.

By mid-1982, it was apparent to Dianna that Ron's brothers were in acute need of guidance. In August of that year, she concluded that four of the other five Lafferty wives were miserable because of the fundamentalist strictures Dan was advocating, so Dianna pleaded with Ron to have a talk with his brothers, and he agreed to pay them a visit.

One evening when they were visiting at their parents' Provo home, Ron stopped by to join in the discourse. His brothers welcomed him warmly, even when he began to read from an essay published by the LDS Church warning of the evils of fundamentalism. As the evening progressed, Ron asked increasingly pointed questions and tried as hard as he could to persuade his younger brothers that Dan's nutty ideas were putting their eternal souls in jeopardy.

Conceding nothing, Dan argued with great passion that the LDS Church had taken a wrong turn when it abandoned polygamy and that the only way to put it back on course was to adopt the sacred tenets advanced in *The Peace Maker*. Ron tried to refute Dan's arguments, point by point, by quoting scripture from the Bible and the Book of Mormon. Dan countered with points of his own drawn from the same texts, as well as from the Constitution. "Ron wasn't at the meeting too awfully long," Dan remembers, "before he stopped trying to convince us we were wrong. 'What you guys are doing is right,' he admitted. 'It's everyone else who is wrong.'" In the space of a few hours, Dan had converted Ron from a dutiful Saint into a fire-breathing Mormon fundamentalist. When Ron returned home that night, Dianna told a friend, "a totally different man walked in the door."

Ron became a regular attendee at his brothers' meetings. He threw away his driver's license and removed the license plates from his vehicle. He quit his job operating heavy machinery for a construction company—an action that greatly heightened Dianna's concern, because the family was balanced on the edge of financial ruin. The economy throughout the Rocky Mountain region had just plunged into an abysmal recession. Ron was funding two after-hours building projects. He and Dianna had failed to make their loan payments. There wasn't enough money for groceries or for clothes for the kids.

Soon thereafter, Ron instructed Dianna to begin following the rules set forth in *The Peace Maker*. According to their friend Penelope Weiss, Ron expected Dianna "to be his slave. It was such a complete reversal. Before Dan brainwashed him, Ron had treated Dianna like a queen. He was one of the nicest men I've ever known. But he became one of the meanest."

As Ron became more controlling and more extreme, Dianna lost hope that she could change him back into the loving father and considerate husband she'd known. He began to talk with growing enthusiasm about polygamy, a practice that made her sick even to contemplate. When Ron announced that he intended to marry off their teenage daughters as plural wives, Dianna reached her breaking point. Desperate, she turned for help to Brenda Lafferty, who was married to Allen, the youngest of the six brothers.

After Dan persuaded his brothers to adopt his fundamentalist beliefs, all their wives acquiesced and submitted, to one degree or another, to the humiliations decreed in *The Peace Maker*—all their wives, that is, except Brenda Wright Lafferty. Intelligent, articulate, and assertive, "Brenda stood up to those Lafferty boys," says her mother, LaRae Wright. "She was probably the youngest of the wives, but she was the strong one. She told the others to stand up for their rights and to think for themselves. And she set an example by refusing to go along with Allen's demands. She told him in no uncertain terms that she didn't want him doing things with his brothers. And the brothers blamed her for that, for keeping their family apart. The Lafferty boys didn't like Brenda because she got in their way."

Brenda was one of seven children raised by LaRae and Jim Wright in Twin Falls, Idaho, an agricultural town forty miles north of the Utah state line, where Brenda enjoyed a storybook, assiduously pious Mormon childhood. Popular, and active in school government, she was an ambitious student who excelled at almost everything she tried. She was also beautiful, in the wholesome, all-American farm-girl idiom: In 1980 she was first runner-up in the Miss Twin Falls Pageant.

Brenda went to college at Brigham Young University, four hours down the interstate, where she met Allen Lafferty. According to her mother, Allen "had a lot of charisma. They hit it off, and they just started going together." On April 22, 1982, Allen and Brenda were sealed for time and eternity in the Salt Lake Temple. She was twenty-one years old. A year later, they had a baby girl, Erica.

At the university, Brenda majored in communications and anchored a television newsmagazine program on KBYU, the PBS affiliate broadcast throughout Utah on channel 11. After she married Allen, however, "she put her broadcasting career on the shelf," according to Brenda's older sister, Betty Wright McEntire. "Allen wanted her to be a traditional subservient wife. He wanted her to be totally reliant on him."

When Allen first became part of the family, Betty recalls, "there was this instant attachment. . . . He was like a wonderful big brother. At the time, we had no idea that there was all this other stuff going on in his family. Then we started to notice how fanatical they all were." For instance, Betty says, when the baby got sick, Allen "wouldn't let Brenda take Erica to the doctor. And it just kept getting worse and worse."

Life was growing harder for Dianna Lafferty, too, thanks to Ron's zealous embrace of fundamentalism. Because her home in Highland was just a few minutes away from the small apartment where Brenda lived with Allen and Erica, Dianna turned to her for help. Although Brenda held stubbornly to her belief that she could turn Allen around, she was convinced that Ron was too far gone. Both Ron and Dan had been excommunicated from the LDS Church. Ron was increasingly abusive to Dianna and talked with ever greater fervor about taking plural wives. Brenda urged Dianna to divorce Ron, for her children's sake and her own.

Leaving Ron was all but unthinkable for Dianna. As she later explained to the Utah County prosecutor, she had six children, hadn't graduated from college, had never held a job, and possessed no marketable skills. But at her core, she knew Brenda was right. Relying on Brenda and a few close friends, Dianna summoned the courage to initiate divorce proceedings.

The divorce was finalized in the autumn of 1983. Around Thanksgiving, Dianna packed up the kids and moved to Florida, putting as much space as she could between herself and the Lafferty boys. Ron was stunned.

Around this time, Bernard Brady introduced Dan to the prophet Onias, the Canadian fundamentalist. Dan, in turn, introduced Onias to his brothers, and soon thereafter Ron, Dan, Mark, Watson, and Tim Lafferty were inducted into Onias's School of the Prophets. Allen was eager to participate as well, but Brenda put her foot down.

Although standing up to Allen meant standing up to the entire Lafferty clan, Brenda did not shy away from such confrontations. Not only was she quite willing to argue theology, she also possessed an impressive command of LDS scripture that allowed her to more than hold her own when debating doctrine with Ron and Dan. They came to despise her for defying them and for her influence over Allen, whom they considered "pussy-whipped."

"Brenda was the only one of the Lafferty wives who was educated," Betty says. "Her education was what they were afraid of. Brenda was confident in her beliefs and her sense of right and wrong. She wasn't about to let anyone take that away from her. She felt it was her duty to defend the other women. She was their only hope." Reflecting on the load her little sister had shouldered, Betty pauses. "At that point she was still just twenty-three years old," she adds. "To be that young, and to be surrounded by all these people who were supposed to be more mature . . ." Betty pauses again. "My sister was an amazing woman."

When Bernard Brady brought the prophet Onias and the Lafferty brothers together, in the autumn of 1983, it seemed to be an auspicious union. There was an instant feeling of kinship and shared values, and the men talked excitedly until "the wee hours of the morning," according to Onias. Giddy with their sense of divinely empowered mission, they were convinced that collectively they were destined to alter the course of human history.

By early 1984, the School of the Prophets was meeting weekly, usually at the Laffertys' Provo home. Ron no longer had a job or a regular paycheck. He was regarded as a pariah by his church and community. He was reduced to living out of his 1974 Impala station wagon—the only asset of any value in his possession. The departure of his wife and children gnawed at him day and night. Over time his hurt was transformed into an implacable rage, mostly directed at three individuals: Richard Stowe, Chloe Low, and Brenda Lafferty.

Stowe, a neighbor of Ron and Dianna's, had presided over the High Council Court that excommunicated Ron from the church. In Ron's view, Stowe had offered crucial financial assistance, via the church, that allowed Dianna to continue with the divorce proceedings.

Chloe Low had been an uncommonly close friend of Ron and Dianna's for a dozen years, but as Ron's behavior grew increasingly monstrous, she came down firmly on Dianna's side. When Dianna was preparing to flee with her kids, Chloe was there to help pack up their lives. As Ron saw it, without Chloe Low's assistance, Dianna would never have had the wherewithal to leave.

Most of Ron's long-simmering wrath, however, was reserved for Brenda Wright Lafferty—Allen's smart, beautiful, headstrong wife.

Rejected by his own wife, scorned by his community, Ron poured himself into the School of the Prophets. It became his family, his life, his world. And the school's main thrust, as Onias had conceived it, was to teach the faithful how to receive and interpret revelations from God. As the winter of 1984 edged toward spring, Ron began receiving this instruction in earnest. On February 24, he became the first of Onias's students to take delivery of a commandment from the Almighty. Sitting at a computer borrowed from Bernard Brady, Ron closed his eyes and waited until he felt the spirit of the Lord cause a finger to depress a key, and then another and another. By and by, a message inched across the screen.

Throughout February and March, Ron received approximately twenty revelations. Some he recorded on the spot; others he kept in his head to better understand them before he committed them to print. The most disturbing of Ron's revelations occurred in late March, and he recorded it by hand on a sheet of yellow legal paper:

Thus Saith the lord unto My servants the Prophets. It is My will and commandment that ye remove the following individuals in order that My work might go forward. For they have truly become obstacles in My path and I will not allow My work to be stopped. First thy brother's wife, Brenda, and her baby, then

Chloe Low, then Richard Stowe. And it is My will that they be removed in rapid succession and that an example be made of them in order that others might see the fate of those who fight against the true Saints of God. . . . And great blessings await him if he will do My Will, for I am the Lord thy God and have control over all things.

Upon receiving this revelation, Ron showed it to Dan. "Ron was a little bit frightened by the things he was receiving," says Dan. "I told him, 'Well, I can see why you're concerned. . . . All I can say is, make sure it's from God. You don't want to act on commandments that are not from God, but at the same time you don't want to offend God by refusing to do His work.'" Over the days that followed, Ron had another revelation, in which he was told that he was "the mouth of God" and Dan "the arm of God." The brothers interpreted this to mean that Dan was to do the actual killing.

In the fundamentalist worldview, a sharp line runs through all of creation, dividing good from evil, and everybody falls on one side of that line or the other. After much praying, Ron and Dan decided that the four individuals God had commanded them to remove must be wicked—"children of perdition," as Dan phrased it—and therefore deserved to be murdered.

In May, Ron and Dan left Utah in Ron's dilapidated Impala wagon and began an extended sojourn, calling on various fundamentalist communities. "We traveled up into Canada, down through the western U.S., and across the Midwest," Dan recalls. "As I look back at it now, it was an important trip for me because I got to know my brother for the first time. . . . He's six years older than me. We were never that close as kids. . . . We just didn't have the opportunity."

Day after day, taking turns at the wheel, Ron and Dan rolled across the continent in the old Chevrolet. At times they would drive for hours without speaking, simply gazing up at the massive thunderheads that boiled forty thousand feet into the afternoon sky, transforming the plains into a vast, shifting checkerboard of shadow and sunlight. More often the brothers talked, and when they did it was with passionate intensity. Usually, the topic of conversation was the removal revelation. Ron began to speak, recalls Dan, of "a great slaughter that was to take place."

Sitting in a small cinder-block room deep in the prison's maximum-security unit, Dan tilts his head back and gazes blankly at the ceiling, letting details from that eventful summer bubble back into his consciousness. The road trip stretched into weeks, then months. "I noticed my brother getting more and more agitated," Dan remembers. "It seemed like he was becoming more bloodthirsty. He started saying things like 'It's gonna happen soon.' Eventually, he began to focus on a particular date. After a while he said, 'I think the twenty-fourth of July is when it's going to happen.'

"As I observed Ron going through these changes—and the things he was saying were really freaking me out—all I could do was pray. 'Look,' I told God, 'You know I will do whatever You want me to do. Should I stay with my brother and carry this thing out? Or should I separate from him and have nothing more to do with this?' The answer I got was to stay with Ron."

On July 23, Ron and Dan returned to Provo, accompanied by two drifters in their early twenties, Chip Carnes and Ricky Knapp, who had the very bad luck to accept a lift. The four men spent the afternoon and evening at the Lafferty family home, doing laundry and tuning up the Impala's engine. At some point that afternoon, according to Dan, God spoke to Ron and told him that the next day was "The Day."

Around one-thirty on the afternoon of July 24, Dan eased the Impala into the driveway in front of the brick duplex Allen and Brenda rented on a quiet street in American Fork, twenty minutes up the freeway from Provo. He was accompanied by Ron, Ricky

Knapp, and Chip Carnes. Among the items in the car were a .30-30 Winchester, a .270 deer rifle, and a twenty-gauge shotgun. Ron stepped out and went to the door alone. A ten-inch boning knife, as sharp as a scalpel, was tucked into his left boot.

Ron opened the screen door and "knocked loudly for a long time," says Dan. "I knew he was anticipating taking the lives of Erica and Brenda right then and there. So I was out in the car, praying: 'I hope this is what You intended, God, because if it ain't, You better do something right now!' And nothing happened. No one answered the door. After a few minutes, Ron came back to the car and kind of shrugged his shoulders. I had a happy feeling because I thought the whole thing had just been a test of faith—like when God tested Abraham. . . . I thought, Oh, thank you, God! And then I started the car and drove away.

"Ron was sitting in the passenger's seat looking befuddled. He was the one who always told us where we were going, what to do next. I had driven about a block and a half from the house when I was suddenly overcome by a weird feeling. It was like this thing I once saw on the TV news: A guy was about to get on an airplane, but when he got to the door he turned around and walked away. The plane crashed. They interviewed the guy and asked him why he hadn't gotten on the plane. 'I can't explain it,' he told them. 'I just felt like I shouldn't.' Well, that's what it was like for me. I had this strong feeling that I should turn the car around, so I did."

Dan pulled into Allen's driveway again, walked up the door, and knocked. This time, after two or three knocks, Brenda opened it. Dan asked if Allen was home. She replied that he was at work. Dan asked if he could use the phone. She said no. Dan protested that he wanted to make a very brief call, but Brenda was becoming increasingly suspicious and continued to refuse him entry.

At this point, Dan recalls, "it felt comfortable to push past her and enter the house, so that's what I did." As soon as he was inside, he wrestled her to the ground, pinning her facedown on the floor. Ron heard the struggle and decided he should go in and help. Finding his brother sitting on top of Brenda, Ron asked Dan what he was doing. Dan replied that he was fulfilling the revelation. When Ron asked how he was going to do it, Dan says, "I asked him to give me a minute to pray. And I said, 'What am I supposed to do, Lord?' Then I felt impressed that I was supposed to use a knife. That I was supposed to cut their throats. Ron asked, 'What knife are you going to use?' I had a knife on my belt, and Ron had a butcher knife in his boot. I told him, 'That butcher knife you purchased.' At which time he took the knife out of his boot and set it on the floor where I could reach it. Then he tried to knock Brenda unconscious with his fist.

"He hit her in the face, over and over again, until blood started to splatter on the wall, but he hurt his hand, so he had to quit. By that point, enough blood had splattered that I lost my grip on Brenda, and she stood up. Ron moved around to block her from leaving. Her face looked pretty bad. She was pretty freaked out. She said to me, 'Hold me, please. Just hold me.' I could tell she was doing it in an attempt to get sympathy. Ron told her, 'Yeah, well, I wish I had someone to hold me, too, you fucking bitch. But because of you, I don't have a wife anymore.'

"That shut her up for a minute. Then she said, 'I'll do anything you want.' And Ron said, 'Okay, sit in the corner.' She leaned against the wall and started to slide down into the corner, when Ron turned to me and said, 'Let's get out of here.' I could tell he was frightened. I told him, 'You leave if you need to. I'll take care of what I feel I'm being led to do, then I'll be ready to go.' Brenda must have realized what I was talking about, because she bolted past Ron and tried to leave. He didn't do anything to stop her. I had to jump around him and grab her from behind. She'd made it as far as the kitchen and was trying to reach the sliding glass doors out back.

She'd gotten hold of the drapes. I grabbed her by the hair and pulled her back, popping a number of clips off the top of the drape. When I finally got my hands on her, she fainted, and I just laid her down on the linoleum floor.

"Unlike my older brother," Dan says, "I didn't have bad feelings toward Brenda or Erica. I was just doing God's will. Seeing Brenda lying there in the middle of the floor, I prayed about what to do next. I told Ron, 'Get me something to tie around her neck so she won't regain consciousness.' Because I was feeling now like I was supposed to take the child's life first. Ron cut the cord off the vacuum cleaner and brought it to me."

After tying the cord around Brenda's neck, Dan says, "I went into the front room and picked up the knife. Then I walked down the hall, led by the spirit because I didn't know the layout of the house. The first door I opened was where the baby was. She was standing in the corner of her crib. I walked in. I closed the door behind me. I think the baby thought I was her father, because I had a beard and Allen had a beard at that time. And we have identical voices.

"I spoke to her for a minute. . . . And then I set my hand on her head, put the knife under her chin like this, and . . ." Pausing in his monologue, Lafferty uses his manacled hands to demonstrate how he pulled the razor-sharp butcher knife so forcefully across Erica's neck that he very nearly decapitated her. "I closed my eyes," he continues, "so I didn't see what I was doing. I didn't hear anything. Then I walked down the hall into the bathroom and washed the blood off the knife. I didn't feel anything. At the time, I didn't even know if I had really killed Erica. . . .

"Anyway, when the knife was clean, I walked into the kitchen and stood over Brenda. Straddling her, I untied the cord. I grabbed her by her hair, placed the knife against the side of her neck and drew it across her throat. Again I closed my eyes. But this time I could hear the blade cut through the trachea and feel it hit the bone of her spinal column." Dan shares these details in a preternaturally serene voice, as if he were recounting a trip to a hardware store. "Then I walked back into the bathroom and washed the knife a second time, turned to Ron, and said, 'Okay, we can leave now.'"

The brothers walked out the back door and returned to the car. When Knapp and Carnes saw their blood-soaked clothing, Dan says, "they kind of freaked out."

Frightened by the overpowering smell of blood, Carnes grabbed Dan's shirt and demanded hysterically, "You need to get rid of that smelly thing!"

"When he said that," Dan remembers, "I thought to myself, Hey, it's not even over yet. Why should I change my clothes? We still have two residences to visit." Ron, too, was extremely agitated, but Dan remained calm: "I was completely comfortable that things had happened the way God intended them to happen. Ron was very shaken and very weak. He kept talking about the smell of blood on his hands. I put my hand on his shoulder and tried to comfort him."

As they drove, Ron seemed to regain his composure. Guiding the Impala through the thick July heat, taking care not to exceed the speed limit, he steered toward Highland, where he and Dianna used to live—and where Chloe Low still lived.

The first half of the revelation had been fulfilled. As they drove the short distance to Low's home, Ron and Dan talked about how they would carry out the rest of it. "I'm afraid I don't have the energy if we have to take the life of Chloe Low," Ron confessed.

"You're worrying about things you shouldn't worry about," Dan assured him. "I'll take care of that, just like I've taken care of this. Because it's the Lord's business."

——

In 1985, Ron Lafferty was convicted of first-degree murder and sentenced to die by firing squad for taking the lives of Brenda and Erica

Lafferty. Nineteen years later, thanks to a series of byzantine legal appeals, he is still among the living. But the appeals process has nearly run its course, and it is likely that Ron will finally be executed in 2004 or 2005.

Dan Lafferty was also convicted of first-degree murder in 1985. During the sentencing phase of his trial he earnestly assured the twelve jurors weighing his fate, "If I was in your situation, I would impose the death penalty," and then he promised not to appeal if they arrived at such a sentence. "I was willing to take a life for God," Dan later explained to me, "so it seemed to me that I should also be willing to give my own life for God. If God wanted me executed, I was fine with that." Two women among the jury refused to vote for a death sentence, however, so Dan's life was spared.

Dan thus continues to bide his time within the grim chambers of the Utah State Prison, where he has now spent half of his adult life. He remains utterly convinced that when he slit the throats of Brenda Lafferty and her infant daughter, he was acting according to the will of God. But what if taking these two lives wasn't actually part of the Lord's plan, but was merely a crime of such staggering cruelty that it is beyond forgiveness? When I interviewed Dan in prison shortly after the September 11, 2001 attacks on New York and Washington, I asked him if he had ever considered the possibility that he'd made a horrible mistake. Had it occurred to him that he may in fact be little different from another fundamentalist of fanatical conviction, Osama bin Laden?

"I've asked myself that," Dan conceded. "Is that what I'm like? And the answer is 'no,' because Osama bin Laden is an asshole, a child of the devil. I believe his real motivation isn't a quest for honesty and justice, which maybe were his motivations in his earlier life. Now he's motivated by greed and profit and power."

What about Osama's underlings, the holy warriors who sacrificed their lives for Allah by flying jumbo jets into the World Trade Center?

Surely their faith and conviction were every bit as powerful as Dan's. Did Dan think the sincerity of their belief justified the act? And if not, how could Dan be certain that what he did wasn't every bit as misguided as what bin Laden's followers did on September 11, despite the obvious sincerity of his own faith?

As Dan paused to consider this possibility, there came a moment when a shadow of doubt seemed to flicker across his mien. But only for an instant, and then it was gone. "I have to admit, the terrorists were following their prophet," Dan said. "They were willing . . . to do essentially what I did. I see the parallel. But the difference between those guys and me is, they were following a false prophet, and I'm not.

"I believe I'm a good person," Dan insisted. "I've never done anything intentionally wrong. . . . I've looked back and asked myself, 'What would I have done differently? Did I feel God's hand guiding me on the 24th of July, 1984?' And then I remember very clearly, 'Yes, I was guided by the hand of God.' So I know I did the right thing."

Serene in the knowledge that he has led a virtuous life, Dan Lafferty is confident that he won't be festering behind bars much longer. He is sure that "any day now" he will hear the blare of the trumpet heralding the Last Days, whereupon he will be released from this hell of strip searches and prison food and razor wire to assume his rightful place in the Kingdom of God.

THE OLD MAN AND THE GUN
DAVID GRANN

Just before Forrest Tucker turned seventy-nine, he went to work for the last time. Although he was still a striking-looking man, with intense blue eyes and swept-back white hair, he had a growing list of ailments, including high blood pressure and burning ulcers. He had already had a quadruple bypass, and his wife encouraged him to settle into their home in Pompano Beach, Florida, a peach-colored house on the edge of a golf course which they'd purchased for their retirement. There was a place nearby where they could eat prime rib and dance on Saturday nights with other seniors for $15.50 a person, and even a lake where Tucker could sit by the shore and practice his saxophone.

But on this spring day in 1999, while his neighbors were on the fairway or tending to their grandchildren, he drove to the Republic Security Bank in Jupiter, about fifty miles from his home. Tucker, who took pride in his appearance, was dressed all in white: white pants with a sharp crease, a white sports shirt, white suede shoes, and a shimmering white ascot.

He paused briefly in front of the ATM and pulled the ascot up around his face, bandit style. He then reached into a canvas bag, took out an old U.S. Army Colt .45, and burst into the bank. He went up to the first teller and said, "Put your money on the counter. All of it."

He flashed the gun so that everyone could see it. The teller laid several packets of fives and twenties on the counter, and Tucker inspected them for exploding dye packs. Checking his watch, he turned to the next teller and said, "Get over here. You, too."

Then he gathered up the thick packets—more than five thousand dollars—and hurried to the door. On his way out, he looked back at the two tellers. "Thank you," he said. "Thank you."

He drove to a nearby lot, where he had left a "safe" car, a red Grand Am that couldn't be traced to him. After wiping down the stolen "hot" car with a rag, he threw his belongings inside the Grand Am. They included a .357 Magnum, a sawed-off .30 carbine, two black nylon caps, a holster, a can of Mace, a pair of Smith & Wesson handcuffs, two rolls of black electrical tape, a police badge, five AAA batteries, a police scanner, a glass cutter, gloves, and a fishing cap. There was also a small bottle of medicine for his heart. No one seemed to notice him, and he went home, making what appeared to be a clean getaway.

After a brief stop to count the money, he got back in the car and headed out again. As he approached the golf course, the bills neatly stacked beside him, he noticed an unmarked car on his tail. He turned onto another street, just to make sure. There it was again. Then he spotted a police car pulling out behind him. He hit the gas as hard as he could, trying to outmaneuver them, turning left, then right, right, then left. He went past the North Pompano Baptist Church and the Kraeer Funeral Home, past a row of pink one-story houses with speedboats in the driveways, until he found himself on a dead-end street. As he spun around, he saw that a police car was barricading the road. One of the officers, Captain James Chinn, was reaching for his shotgun. There was a small gap between Chinn's car and a wooden fence, and Tucker, his body pitched forward in his seat, sped toward it. Chinn, who had spent almost two decades as a detective, later said he had never seen anything like it: the white-haired figure barreling toward him seemed to be smiling, as if he were enjoying the showdown. Then, as the car skidded over the embankment, Tucker lost control and hit a palm tree. The air bags inflated, pinning him against the seat.

The police were stunned when they realized that the man they had apprehended was not only seventy-eight years old—he looked, according to Chinn, "as if he had just come from an Early Bird Special"—but one of the most notorious stickup men of the twentieth century. Over a career that spanned more than six decades, he had also become perhaps the greatest escape artist of his generation, a human contortionist who had broken out of nearly every prison he was confined in.

Not long ago, I went to meet Tucker in Fort Worth, Texas, where he was being held in a prison medical center after pleading guilty to one count of robbery and receiving a thirteen-year sentence. The hospital, an old yellow brick building with a red tiled roof, was on top of a hill and set back off the main road, surrounded by armed guards and razor wire. I was handed a notice that said no "weapons," "ammunition," or "metal cutting tools" were allowed, and then escorted through a series of chambers—each door sealing behind us before the next one opened—until I arrived in an empty waiting room.

Before long, a man appeared in a wheelchair pushed by a guard. He wore brown prison fatigues and a green jacket with a turned-up collar. His figure was twisted forward, as if he had tried to contort it one last time and it had frozen in place. As he rose from the wheelchair, he said, "It's a pleasure to meet you. Forrest Tucker."

His voice was gentle, with a soft Southern lilt. After he extended his hand, he made his way slowly over to a wooden table with the help of a walker. "I'm sorry we have to meet here," he said, waiting for me to sit first.

Captain Chinn had told me that he had never met such a gracious criminal: "If you see him, tell him Captain Chinn says hi."

Even a juror who helped convict him once remarked, "You got to hand it to the guy—he's got style."

"So what do you want to know?" Tucker said. "I've been in prison all my life, except for the times I've broken out. I was born in 1920, and I was in jail by the time I was fifteen. I'm eighty-one now and I'm still in jail, but I've broken out eighteen times successfully and twelve times unsuccessfully. There were plenty of other times I planned to escape, but there's no point in me telling you about them."

As we sat in a corner by a window overlooking the prison yard, it was hard to imagine that this man's career had featured wanted posters and midnight escapes. His fingers were knotted like bamboo, and he wore bifocals.

"What I mean by successful escape is to elude custody," he continued, squinting out the window. "Maybe they'd eventually get me, but I got away at least for a few minutes."

He pointed to the places along his arm where he had been shot while trying to flee. "I still have part of a bullet in me," he said. "They all opened up on me and hit me three times—in both shoulders with M16 rifles, and with buckshot in the legs."

His voice sounded dry, and I offered to buy him a drink from the vending machine. He followed me and peered through the glass, without touching it. He chose a Dr Pepper. "That's kind of like cherry soda, isn't it?"

He seemed pleased. When I gave him the drink, he glanced at the candy bars, and I asked him if he wanted anything else. "If it's not too much trouble," he said, "I'd like a Mounds."

After he finished eating, he began to tell me what he called "the true story of Forrest Tucker." He spoke for hours, and when he grew tired he offered to continue the next morning. During our conversations, which went on for several days, we always sat in the corner by the window, and after a while he would cough slightly and I would offer to buy him a drink. Each time, he followed me to the machine, as the guard watched from a distance. It was only during the last trip to the machine when I dropped some money that I noticed his eyes were moving over everything—the walls, the windows, the guard, the fences, the razor wire. It occurred to me that Tucker, escape artist par excellence, had been using our meetings to case the joint.

"The first time I broke out of the can I was only fifteen," Tucker told me. "At fifteen, you're pretty fast."

It was the spring of 1936, and he had been incarcerated for stealing a car in Stuart, Florida, a small town along the St. Lucie River which had been devastated during the Depression. He told the police that he took it "just for a thrill," but as he sat in jail the thrill gave way to panic, and when a jailer removed his chains he darted out. Several days later, a deputy discovered him in an orange grove, eating a piece of fruit. "That was escape number one," Tucker says. "Such as it was."

The sheriff decided to transfer him to reform school. During his brief flight, however, Tucker had slipped a half dozen hacksaw blades through the cell window to a group of boys he had met inside. "They hadn't broken out yet and still had the blades," he says. That night, after sawing a bar, he slithered out, helping two other boys squeeze through the tiny opening.

Unlike the others, Tucker knew the area. As a kid, he had spent a fair amount of time by the river, and it was in the river that the police found him and another boy, about an hour later, hiding with just their noses above water. The next day, the *Stuart Daily News* detailed his exploits under the headline "TRIO ESCAPE BY SAWING BARS OF CELL LAST NIGHT . . . SUPPLIED WITH HACKSAWS, COLD CHISELS AND FILES BY BOY."

"That was escape number two," Tucker says. "A brief one."

Like the outlaws he read about in dime novels who were forced into banditry by some perceived injustice, Tucker says that "the legend of Forrest Tucker" began that morning when he was unfairly sent away for only a minor theft. The story, which he repeated even as a boy, eventually spread throughout the town, and over time the details became more ornate, the theft more minor. Morris Walton, who used to play with Tucker as a child, says, "My sense is he spent his life in jail for stealing a bicycle and simply trying to escape. If he became bad, it was only because the system made him that way."

What Walton knew of Tucker's upbringing reinforced that impression. His father was a heavy-equipment operator who disappeared when Tucker was six. While his mother struggled in menial jobs in Miami, Tucker was sent to live with his grandmother, who was the tender of the bridge in Stuart. There he built canoes and sailboats out of scrap metal and wood, which he gathered along the riverbank, and taught himself to play the saxophone and the clarinet. "It wasn't like I needed a father to order me around," he says.

But as his reputation for cleverness grew, so did his rap sheet. By his sixteenth birthday, it included charges of "breaking and entering" and "simple larceny." After he escaped from reform school and fled to Georgia, he was sentenced to "be placed and confined at labor in the chain gang." Like all new inmates, he was taken to the blacksmith, where a chain was riveted around both of his ankles. The steel gradually ate into the skin, a condition known as shackle poisoning.

"The guards would give you the first three days to let you get your hands broken in with calluses," Tucker recalls. "But after that the walking boss would punish you, hit you with his cane or fist. And if you didn't work hard enough the guards would take you in the bathroom and tie your hands behind your back and put a pressure hose in your face and hold it there until you'd sputter and you couldn't breathe."

Although Tucker was released after only six months, he was soon convicted again, for stealing another car, and sentenced to ten years. By now, "we see a man who has been thoroughly cast out by society," Tucker's lawyer later wrote in a court motion. "Marked as a criminal at seventeen years old and constantly railroaded through judicial proceedings without the benefit of counsel, Forrest Tucker was becoming an angry young man." Tucker himself says, "The die was cast." In photographs taken after he was paroled at the age of twenty-four, his hair is cut short and he has on a white T-shirt; his once slender arms are coiled with muscles. His eyes are piercing. People who knew him say that he was extraordinarily charismatic — that girls flocked around him — but they also noted a growing reservoir of anger. "I think he had this desperate need to show the world that he was *somebody*," one of his relatives says.

At first, Tucker sought work playing the saxophone in big bands around Miami, and he seemed to have harbored ambitions of becoming another Glenn Miller. Nothing came of it, though, and, after a brief failed marriage, he put away his sax and got himself a gun.

The outlaw, in the American imagination, is a subject of romance — a "good" bad man, he is typically a master of escape, a crack shot, a ladies' man. In 1915, when the police asked the train robber Frank Ryan why he did it, he replied, "Bad companions and dime novels. Jesse James was my favorite hero."

When Tucker was growing up, during the Great Depression, the appeal of bank robbers, fueled by widespread anger over defaults and foreclosures, was reaching its zenith. After the FBI gunned down John Dillinger, in 1934, droves descended on the scene, mopping up his blood with their clothes. At least ten Hollywood films were devoted to Dillinger's life; one of them exclaimed, "His Story Is Written in Bullets, Blood and Blondes!"

Because the holdup demands a public performance, it tends to draw a certain personality: bold, vainglorious, reckless. At the same time, most bank robbers know that the society that revels in their exploits will ultimately demand their elimination, by incarceration or death. "They'll get me," Pretty Boy Floyd once said. "Sooner or later, I'll go down full of lead. That's how it will end."

Indeed, by the time Tucker set out to become an outlaw, in the late nineteen-forties, most of the legendary stickup men had already been gunned down. Still, he began to imitate their style, dressing in chalk-striped suits and two-tone shoes, and he would stand in front of a mirror, pointing a gun at his own reflection. Finally, on September 22, 1950, with a handkerchief tied over his face and a gun drawn in the style of Jesse James, he strode into a bank in Miami and made off with $1,278. A few days later, he went back to the same place, this time for the entire safe. He was apprehended as he was trying to crack it open with a blowtorch on the roadside.

His career seemed even more fleeting than that of most bank robbers, but in the county jail Tucker decided he was more than an ordinary stickup man. "It didn't matter to me if they gave me five years, ten years, or life," he says. "I was an escape artist."

He searched the prison for what he called "the weak spot." One day around Christmas, after weeks of looking, he began to moan in pain. The authorities rushed him to the hospital, where doctors removed his appendix. ("A small price to pay," Tucker says.) While convalescing, still chained to his bed, he started to work on the shackles. He had taught himself how to pick a lock using almost anything—a pen, a paper clip, a piece of wire, nail clippers, a watch spring—and after a few minutes he walked out, unnoticed.

He made his way to California, where he went on a spree of robberies, hurtling over counters, pointing his gun, and declaring, "I mean business!" He wore bright checkered suits and sped away in a flamboyant getaway car with tubes along the sides. He even talked like a character in pulp fiction. "This is a stickup, girls," he once said, according to witnesses. "I've got a gun. Be quiet and you won't get hurt."

Hoping to improve his take, Tucker began to cast about for a partner. "I didn't want any nuts or rats," he says, adding, "I'm from the old school." In the end, he found an ex-con named Richard Bellew, a tall, handsome thief with a high IQ and wavy black hair. Like Tucker, Bellew modeled himself on the stickup men of the nineteen-thirties, and he ran with a stage dancer named Jet Blanca. But Tucker chose him for another reason: "He always let me count the dough."

They began to hit one bank after another. After one heist, witnesses said the last thing they saw was a row of suits hanging in the backseat of the getaway car. The heists, which continued for two years, dominated the local headlines, often preempting coverage of the 1952 presidential election and the McCarthy hearings. Tucker and Bellew were depicted as "armed men" who "terrorized" their "victims," but also as "dramatically attired" "holdup artists" who "expertly stripped" the tellers of cash, leaving behind "only an impression of competent banditry . . . and one getaway car."

On March 20, 1953, more than two years after Tucker's escape from the hospital, FBI agents surrounded him as he was retrieving loot from a safe-deposit box in San Francisco. Then they went to search the place Tucker had listed as his residence. There, in a spacious apartment in San Mateo, they found a young blond woman who said she had never heard of Forrest Tucker. She was married to a wealthy songwriter, she said, who commuted daily to the city, and they had just moved into a bigger apartment to make room for their five-month-old son. Her husband's name, she told the police, was Richard Bellew. Yet when the officers showed Shirley Bellew a photograph of the bank robber and longtime prison fugitive Forrest Tucker, she burst into tears. "I can't believe it," she said. "He was such a good man, such a good provider."

She recalled how her husband would come home every night and play with their baby, whom they had named Rick Bellew Jr.

"What's going to become of our little baby?" she asked. "What's his name going to be?"

"Let me tell you about Alcatraz," Tucker said one day as he sat in the corner of the visiting room, his walker resting against his leg. He had spread a napkin out in front of him and was eating a meatball hero I'd brought him and sipping a Dr Pepper. "There were only fifteen hundred and seventy-six people who ever went there. I was number one thousand forty-seven."

Alcatraz, or "the Rock," had been converted from a military prison in 1934 as a way to confine the country's most notorious criminals, including George (Machine Gun) Kelly, Robert Stroud (the Birdman of Alcatraz), and Mickey Cohen. At least half of the inmates had previously attempted to break out of other prisons. Surrounded by the freezing San Francisco Bay and its deadly currents, it was built to be escapeproof. Al Capone, who was sent there in 1934, is said to have told the warden, "It looks like Alcatraz has got me licked."

Tucker arrived on September 3, 1953. He was thirty-three. He had been sentenced to thirty years. In his prison photo, he still has on a jacket and tie; his brown hair is brushed back with a touch of oil; he is slightly unshaved but still striking. Within moments, he was stripped naked, and a medical attendant probed his ears and nose and mouth and rectum, searching for any tools or weapons. He was given a blue chambray shirt with his number stamped on it and a pair of trousers, as well as a cap, a peacoat, a bathrobe, three pairs of socks, two handkerchiefs, a pair of shoes, and a raincoat. His cell was so narrow that he could reach out and touch both sides at the same time. "It was so cold in the cellblock you had to sleep with your coat and hat to stay warm," Tucker says.

As he lay in bed, he says, he thought about his wife and child. He remembered the first time he met Shirley Storz, at an event for singles in Oakland. He remembered how they skied at Lake Tahoe and were married in a small ceremony in September 1951, how she sang in a choral group, and how he'd sit and listen for hours. And he remembered his son being born. "We loved each other," Tucker says of his wife. "I didn't know how to explain to her the truth — that this was my way of life."

Several weeks after he arrived, a guard roused him from his cell and led him into a tiny room that had a small window. Peering through it, he saw his wife sitting on the other side. He picked up the phone. "It was hard to talk," he recalls. "We had to look at each other through a piece of glass. She told me she had to make a life for herself. I said, 'The best thing you can do is make a life for you and our son.' I told her, 'I won't bother you no matter what, no matter how much I want to. I won't ring your phone.'" A few months later, he received notice that their marriage had been annulled.

By now, Tucker had developed several maxims, including "The more security, the more bizarre the method of escape must be." He began to concoct elaborate schemes with a fellow inmate named Teddy Green, an escape artist and bank robber who had once dressed as a priest to elude the police and had broken out of the state penitentiary by shipping himself out in a box of rags.

Along with another inmate, they started smuggling tools from their prison jobs, hiding them in the laundry, and planting pieces of steel wool on other prisoners to set off the metal detectors, so that the guards assumed they were broken. They carved holes in their toilet bowls and tucked the tools inside, putting putty over them. At night, they used the tools to tunnel through the floor, planning to go out by means of the basement.

One day, according to internal prison records, a prisoner in solitary suggested that guards examine the cell toilets; soon a full-scale search was launched. A warden's report summed up the findings:

The result of the shakedown of these toilets was the blow torch as I have mentioned, a bar spreader, a pair of side cutters, a brace and some bits . . . a screwdriver and one or two pieces of wire and a piece of carborundum stone.

All three prisoners were labeled "very dangerous escape risks" and locked in the Treatment Unit, better known as "the hole."

"I remember walking in with no clothes or shoes on," Tucker says. "The steel floor was so cold it hurt to touch it. The only way to stay warm was to keep walking." One night, he heard a haunting sound through the window. He couldn't see anyone outside, but he heard voices from below. They were the guards' children, singing carols. "It was the first children's voices I had heard in years," he says. "It was Christmas Eve."

As the time passed, Tucker began to teach himself the law, and before long he was deluging the court with appeals, which he wrote in a slanting, methodical print. Although a prosecutor later dismissed one of his writs as pure "fantasy," he was granted a hearing in November 1956. According to Tucker, as well as court records, the night before his court appearance, while being held in the county jail, he complained of pains in his kidneys and was rushed to the hospital. Guards were stationed at every door. When no one was looking, Tucker broke a pencil and stabbed his ankle. Because of the wound, the guards removed his leg irons, strapping him to the gurney with his hands cuffed. As he was being wheeled into the X-ray room, Tucker leaped up, overpowered two guards, and ran out the door. For several hours, he enjoyed the fresh air and the sight of ordinary people. He was apprehended, still in his hospital gown and handcuffs, in the middle of a cornfield.

The brief escape, for which he was tried and convicted,

enhanced his reputation as an escape artist. Yet it was not for another twenty-three years, after Tucker had been released and arrested again for armed robbery, that he made his greatest escape. In the summer of 1979, while at San Quentin, a maximum-security facility that jutted out into the ocean and was known among cons as "the gladiator school," Tucker took a job in the prison industries and, with the help of two other inmates, John Waller and William McGirk, secretly gathered together scraps of wood and sheets of Formica, which they cut into strange shapes and hid under tarps. From the electrical shop, they spirited away two six-foot poles and several buckets. Then, in the furniture workshop, they found the final pieces: plastic dustcovers, paint, and tape, which they stored in boxes labeled "Office Supplies."

On August 9, after months of preparation, Tucker exchanged nods with both of his confederates in the yard, signaling that everything was ready. While Waller and McGirk stood watch outside the lumber shop, Tucker drew on his childhood experience and began to fashion the pieces into a fourteen-foot kayak. "A hammer was too loud, so I had to use only tape and bolts," Tucker says. He had just enough paint for one side of the craft, the side that would face the guard towers, and as the others urged him to hurry he stenciled on it "Rub-a-Dub-Dub." Waller, who called the fifty-nine-year-old Tucker "the old man," later told a reporter from the *Los Angeles Times*, "The boat was beautiful; I wish my eyes were as blue as that boat."

They wore sailor hats and sweatshirts that Tucker had painted bright orange, with the logo of the Marin Yacht Club, which he had seen on the boats that sailed by. When the guard wasn't looking, they hurriedly put the kayak into the water. As they set out, the winds were blowing more than twenty miles an hour, and massive swells began to swamp the kayak. "The boat didn't leak a drop," Waller said. "We could have paddled to Australia. It was those damn waves over the side. When we finally reached the edge of the property at Q"—San Quentin—"the son of a bitch sank."

A guard in one of the towers spotted them clinging to the upside-down craft, kicking to shore, and asked if they needed help. They said they were fine, and, as if to prove it, McGirk held up his wrist and yelled, "We just lost a couple of oars, but my Timex is still running!" The guard, unaware that three prisoners were missing, laughed and went back to his lookout.

California soon unleashed a statewide manhunt. Meanwhile, police in Texas and Oklahoma began to report a strange series of holdups. They all had the same MO: three or four men would stroll into a grocery store or a bank, flash a gun, demand the money, and speed away in a stolen car. Witnesses invariably noted that they were all, by the standards of the trade, old men. One even wore what appeared to be a hearing aid. The authorities compared them to the elderly thieves in the film *Going in Style*, and dubbed them "the Over-the-Hill Gang."

"That was when I was really a good robber," Tucker tells me. He is careful not to admit to any particular crime ("I don't know if they still have jurisdiction") or implicate any of his living partners ("Some of them are still out there"), but he says that by the age of sixty he had at last mastered the art of the holdup.

One day, while we were sitting in the prison visiting room, Tucker leaned forward in his chair and began to teach me how to rob a bank. "First of all, you want a place near the highway," he said, putting on his bifocals, his eyes blinking as if he were imagining a particular layout. "Then you need to case it—you can't just storm in. You need to size it up, know it like your own home.

"In the old days, the stickup men were like cowboys," he continued. "They would just go in shooting, yelling for everyone to lie down.

But to me violence is the first sign of an amateur." The best holdup men, in his view, were like stage actors, able to hold a room by the sheer force of their personality. Some even wore makeup and practiced getting into character. "There is an art to robbing a bank if you do it right," Tucker said. Whereas he once cultivated a flamboyant image, he later developed, he said, a subtler, more "natural" style.

"Okay, the tools," he pressed on. Ideally, he said, you need nail polish or superglue to cover your fingertips ("You can wear gloves, but in warmer climates they only draw attention"), a glass cutter, a holster, a canvas bag ("big enough for the dough"), and a gun ("a .38 or semiautomatic, or whatever you can get your hands on"). He said the gun was just "a prop," but essential to any operation.

There was one other thing, he said after a pause. It was the key to the success of the Over-the-Hill Gang and what he still called "the Forrest Tucker trademark": the hearing aid. It was actually a police scanner, he said, which he wired through his shirt; that way, he would know if any silent alarms had been triggered.

He removed a napkin from his pocket and wiped the sweat from his forehead. "Once you've got your cool car parked nearby, you've got your radio, your hands are covered with gloves or superglue, you walk in. Go right up to the manager. Say, 'Sit down.' Never pull the gun—just flash it. Tell him calmly you're here to rob the bank and it better go off without a hitch. Don't run from the bank unless you're being shot at, 'cause it only shows something is going on. Just walk to the hot car, real calm, then drive to the cool car. Rev it up, and you're gone."

After he finished, he seemed satisfied. "I've just given you a manual on how to rob a bank," he said. He reflected on this for a moment, then added, "No one can teach you the craft. You can only learn by doing."

. . .

A forty-year-old sergeant on the Austin police force, John Hunt, was assigned to investigate the mysterious holdups of the Over-the-Hill Gang. "They were the most professional, successful robbers that I ever encountered in all my years on the force," Hunt, who is now retired after a thirty-year career, told me. "They had more experience in robbery than we had catching them."

Then a chain-smoker with a drooping mustache and a slight paunch, Hunt spent long days trying to catch the gang. With the advent of high-tech security, there were fewer and fewer traditional bank robbers; most were desperate drug addicts who made off with only a few thousand dollars before they were caught. The Over-the-Hill Gang seemed to defy not just their age but their era. "They'd get up every day and be on the job," Hunt said. "Just as a welder gets good at welding, or a writer gets good over the years by writing, these guys learned from their mistakes."

In a one-year span, the Over-the-Hill Gang was suspected in at least sixty robberies in Oklahoma and Texas—twenty in the Dallas–Fort Worth area alone. The gang was also believed to be responsible for holdups in New Mexico, Arizona, and Louisiana. "SENIOR CITIZENS STRIKE AGAIN," one headline blared. "MIDDLE-AGED BANDITS PUZZLE DETECTIVES," another read.

In December 1980, Hunt and forty other law-enforcement officers from at least three states held a conference in Dallas to figure out how to stop them. "You can't say how many lives they altered by sticking a gun in someone's face," a former FBI agent told me.

Tucker seemed unable to stop, no matter how much money he accumulated. Although there are no official estimates, Tucker—relying on an array of aliases, including Robert Tuck MacDougall, Bob Stone, Russell Johns, Ralph Pruitt, Forrest Brown, J. C. Tucker, and Ricky Tucker—is believed over his career to have stolen millions of dollars, a fleet of sports cars, a bag of yen, and one Sambo's wooden nickel. In the spring of 1983, he embarked on his most audacious heist yet: robbing a high-security bank in Massachusetts in broad daylight by pretending that he and his men were guards making a routine pickup in an armored car. Tucker believed the plan was "a breakthrough in the art." On March 7, moments before the armored car was scheduled to arrive, they put on makeup and mustaches; Tucker's wig had shrunk in a recent snowstorm, and rather than postpone the operation he decided to do without it.

The teller buzzed them in. Just as they were entering the vault, according to a police report, the manager noticed that "the dark mustache on one man and the white mustache on the other man were not real." One of the "guards" patted his gun and said, "This is a holdup."

Tucker locked the manager and two tellers inside the vault, and escaped with more than four hundred and thirty thousand dollars. But when the police showed the tellers a series of mug shots, they identified, for the first time, the leader of the Over-the-Hill Gang as the same man who had broken out of San Quentin in a homemade kayak three years earlier.

As the FBI, the local police, and the county sheriffs all tried to track him down, Tucker hid in Florida, checking in daily with Teddy Green, his old Alcatraz confidant. One June morning, Tucker pulled into Green's garage and waited while his friend walked toward the car. "I was looking at him," Tucker recalls, "thinking, My, what a sharp suit!"

A man jumped in front of Tucker's car and yelled, "FBI, don't move! You're under arrest."

Agents were everywhere, coming out of cars and bushes. Tucker glowered at Green, convinced that his friend had "ratted me out." Although Tucker insists that he never had a pistol—and none was ever found—several agents said they saw one in his hand. "He's got a gun!" one of them yelled, diving to the ground. The garage filled with the sound of gunfire. Bullets shattered the windshield and the radiator. Tucker, who had been hit in both arms and in the leg, ducked below the dashboard and pressed the accelerator, crashing outside the garage. He opened the car door and stumbled onto the street, his hands and face covered in blood. A woman with two children was driving toward him. "As I got closer," the woman later testified, "he started to look bloodier and bloodier—it was all over him—and I thought, This poor man has been hit by a car."

She offered him a ride, and he climbed into the passenger seat. Then, in her rearview mirror, she saw someone holding a rifle, and her six-year-old son cried out, "Criminal!" When she hesitated, Tucker grabbed the wheel and snapped, "I have a gun—now drive!" Her son began to sob. After a half-mile chase, they veered down a dead-end street. At a muttered "okay" from Tucker, the woman scrambled out of the car and dragged her children to safety. Then Tucker himself stepped from the car and passed out.

A columnist for *The Miami Herald* summed up the capture of the longtime prison fugitive and leader of the Over-the-Hill Gang this way:

> There is something vaguely appealing about Tucker. . . . Old guys are not regularly associated with high crimes. . . . Tucker must also be admired, in a twisted way I admit, for pulling off an incredible escape from San Quentin prison in San Francisco. . . . Tucker might have made a fortune selling the escape yarn to Hollywood and holing up somewhere. Instead he chose to resume the line of work to which he was dedicated. . . . The aging Robin Hood took from the rich, who were probably loaded with insurance.

Tucker's story had, at last, acquired the burnish of outlaw mythology. The battered *Rub-a-Dub-Dub* had been donated to the Marin Yacht Club and was later placed in a prison museum, and the Children's Hospital Medical Center in Oakland requested that Tucker be allowed to serve as grand marshal for its upcoming Bathtub Regatta. Amid the clamor, the FBI showed up at a fancy retirement community in Lauderhill, Florida, where Tucker was believed to have been living. An elegant woman in her fifties answered the door. When they asked her about Forrest Tucker, she said she had never heard of the man. She was married to Bob Callahan, a successful stockbroker whom she had met shortly after her first husband died. When the agents explained that Bob Callahan was really Forrest Tucker, a man who had broken out of jail four years earlier, she looked at them in tears. "I told 'em, 'I don't believe a word you're saying,'" she recalled, nearly two decades later. "But they had him. They shot him three times."

An heiress to a modest moving-company fortune who looked, in her youth, a bit like Marilyn Monroe, she remembers meeting Tucker at the Whale and Porpoise, a private club on Oakland Park Boulevard. She had never encountered anyone so kind and gallant. "He came over and asked me to dance, and that was that," she told me.

She recalled how she went to see him in prison ("still in a daze"), not sure what to say or do. When she saw him lying there, pale and bloodied, she was overcome with love for this man who, she learned, had been in a chain gang at sixteen. As he begged her forgiveness, she told me, "All I wanted to do was hold him."

At first, awaiting trial in Miami, Tucker tried to break out of jail, removing a bar in his cell with a hacksaw and climbing onto the roof with a homemade grappling hook. But after his wife promised—to the consternation of her family and friends—to stay with him if he reformed, Tucker vowed to rehabilitate himself. "I told her that from then on I'd only look at ways to escape," he says, adding, "She is one in a million."

He returned to San Quentin, where he was nicknamed "the captain," and where, for the first time, his seemingly impervious constitution began to show its age. In 1986, he underwent a quadruple bypass. Although guards stood by the door in case he tried to escape, he now considered himself strictly a legal contortionist. Years earlier, at Alcatraz, he had written an appeal that went all the way to the Supreme Court in which he successfully argued that a judge could not, at sentencing, take into account prior convictions received when the defendant lacked counsel. ("It is time we become just a little realistic in the face of a record such as this one," Justice Harry A. Blackmun wrote in an angry dissent.) Now, with his failing health, Tucker unleashed another flurry of appeals, getting his sentence reduced by more than half. "This is to thank you," he wrote one judge. "It's the first break I ever got in my life. I won't ever need another."

He began to pour all his energy into what he saw as the culmination of his life as an outlaw: a Hollywood movie. Tucker had seen all sorts of films that echoed his life, among them *I Am a Fugitive from a Chain Gang*, *Escape from Alcatraz*, and *Bonnie and Clyde*, and he wanted, at last, to see his story enshrined in the American imagination. He began to put his exploits down on paper, five pages at a time. "No one could have written this inside story of the Rock and what really happened there unless they had personally lived it," he wrote. He devoted two hundred and sixty-one pages to *Alcatraz: The True Story*, while working on a second, more ambitious account, which he titled *The Can Opener*. In it, he described himself as a throwback "to the highly intelligent, nonviolent type of criminal in the Willie Sutton mold," and, more grandly, as a kind of heroic underdog, pitted against a vast and oppressive system. "Tucker's obsession with freedom and escape has transformed itself into gamesmanship," he wrote. "This is his way of keeping his sanity in a lifetime of being the hunted. Each new 'joint' is a game, a game to outwit the authorities."

In 1993, he was released, at the age of seventy-three, and settled into the peach-colored house in Pompano Beach, which his wife had bought for them. He polished his manuscript and set up a music room in the den, where he gave saxophone and clarinet lessons for twenty-five dollars an hour. "We had a wonderful life," his wife said. Tucker recalls, "We used to go out dancing. She'd dress up real pretty, and I'd show her off." He composed music for her. "He has all these talents that had been wasted all these years," she told me. From time to time, he played in local jazz clubs. "I got used to being free," he says. But his manuscript failed to captivate people as he had hoped it would—"I called Clint Eastwood's secretary, but she said, 'Unless you have an agent, he won't read it'"— and the author of *The Can Opener* increasingly seemed trapped, an ordinary old man.

Then came the day in 1999 when, at the age of seventy-eight, he painted his fingertips with nail polish, pulled his white ascot over his face, and burst into the Republic Security Bank with his gun. "He didn't do it for the money," his wife said. "We had a new car, nice home paid for, beautiful clothes. He had everything."

"I think he wanted to become a legend, like Bonnie and Clyde," said Captain Chinn, who apprehended him after what was believed to be his fourth recent robbery in the Florida area. A court psychologist who examined Tucker noted, "I have seen many individuals who are self-aggrandizing, and that would like to make their mark in history . . . but none, I must admit, that I heard that would want to, other than in the movies, go out in a blaze in a bank robbery. It is beyond the realm of psychological prediction."

After Tucker's arrest, the police put him in semi-isolation, fearing that even at seventy-eight he might somehow elude them. Despite his lawyer's pleas that his client could die under such conditions, he was denied bail. "Ordinarily, I would not consider a seventy-eight-year-old man a flight risk or a danger to the community," the magistrate said, "but Mr. Tucker has proven himself to be remarkably agile." On October 20, 2000, just before his case was scheduled to go to trial, and with his wife looking on, Tucker pleaded guilty. He was sentenced to thirteen years.

One day, I found a report that the Department of Corrections had compiled, detailing Tucker's life. After pages listing his dramatic holdups and daredevil escapes, it concluded with a different kind of summary:

> The defendant does not know the whereabouts of [his] daughter. He stated he did not have an active part in this child's upbringing. . . . The defendant has no knowledge of his son's whereabouts. The defendant did not partake in the rearing of this child.

"I thought he died in an automobile accident," his son, Rick Bellew, told me over the phone after I tracked him down in Nevada, where he was living and working as a printer. "That's what my mom told me to protect me." He didn't know the truth, he said, until he was in his early twenties, when Tucker was about to be paroled. "My mom was afraid he'd come up to me on the street and freak me out."

He said that after his father was taken away the authorities confiscated all their furniture and possessions, which had been paid for with stolen cash. They had to move in with his grandparents, while his mother worked in a factory to support them. "He left us with nothing," he said. "He turned our world inside out."

After Bellew read about Tucker's last arrest, he wrote him a letter for the first time. "I needed to know why he did it," he said. "Why he sacrificed everything."

Although Tucker could never give him a satisfactory answer, they struck up a correspondence, and in one of his letters Tucker told him something he had never expected: Bellew had an older half sister named Gaile Tucker, a nurse who lived in Florida. "I called her up and said, 'Are you sitting down?' I said, 'This is your long-lost brother.' She said, 'Oh, my God.'" Later, the two met, studying each other's features for similarities, trying to piece together a portrait of a man they barely knew.

"I don't have any ill feelings," his daughter told me. "I just don't have any feelings."

At one point, Bellew read me part of a letter that Tucker had recently sent him: "I'm sorry things turned out the way they did. . . . I never got to take you fishing, or to baseball games or to see you grow up. . . . I don't ask you to forgive me as there is too much lost but just so you know I wish you the best. Always. Your dad, Forrest."

Bellew said he didn't know if he would continue the correspondence, not because of what Tucker had done to him but because of what he had done to his mother. "He blew my mother's world apart," Bellew told me. "She never remarried. There was a song she used to sing to me called 'Me and My Shadow,' all about being alone and blue. And when she had cancer, and wasn't going to live much longer, I broke down and she sang that song, and I realized how bittersweet it was. It was her life."

When I visited Tucker's third wife this spring in Pompano Beach, she seemed to be still trying to cope. A small, delicate woman, now in her seventies, she had had several operations and lived alone in their house. "With Forrest gone, there's no one to fix things up," she said. She paused, scanning the den where he used to keep his musical instruments. "The silence is unbearable." She showed me a picture of the two of them, taken shortly after they met. They are standing side by side, their arms touching. He has on a red shirt and tie, and his wavy hair is neatly combed to one side. "God, he used to be so handsome," she said. "When I met him, he was a *doll*."

She turned the picture of him over several times in her hand. "I waited all those years," she said as she walked me outside, wiping her eyes. "I thought we had the rest of our lives together. What am I supposed to do now?"

One of the last times I met Tucker in prison, he looked alarmingly frail. His facial muscles seemed slack, and his hands trembled. Since his incarceration, he had had several strokes, and a cardiologist concluded that blood clots were gradually cutting off oxygen to his brain. His daughter told me bluntly, "He'll die in prison."

"Everyone says I'm smart," Tucker said to me. "But I'm not smart in the ways of life or I wouldn't have done the things I did." After a brief flurry of attention following his arrest, he had been all but forgotten. "When I die, no one will remember me," he said. His voice was almost a whisper. "I wish I had a real profession, something like the music business. I regret not being able to work steady and support my family. I have other regrets, too, but that's as much as one man can stand. Late at night, you lie in your bunk in prison and you think about what you lost, what you were, what you could've been, and you regret."

He said that his wife was thinking of selling their house and moving into a community where she could see more people. Although he and his wife still spoke regularly, Tucker said, she was too frail to visit.

"What hurts the most . . . is that I know how much I disappointed my wife," he went on. "That hurts more than anything."

As he rose to go, he took a piece of paper from his back pocket. "I made this up for you last night," he said.

On it was a list of all his escapes, neatly printed. At the bottom, there was a number nineteen—one more than he had actually made—left blank. As the guard fetched his wheelchair, he waved him away. "I don't need my chariot," he said. Then slowly, with his back hunched, he steadied himself against the wall and, with the guard standing behind him, inched down the corridor.

━━━

I grew up rarely reading the books I was supposed to: J. D. Salinger or Richard Wright, which were assigned in school and gathered dust on my nightstand, or the pile of sports biographies that all my friends collected. Instead, I read crime stories, the ones that seemed too good to be true but were always hailed on the cover as the real deal. Blood-and-guts stories about Jesse James and Billy the Kid and Pretty Boy Floyd. Stories about gangsters like John Dillinger and the G-men who took him down in a hail of gunfire. Stories, in short, just like that of Forrest Tucker.

Of course, when Tucker initially recounted what he called "the true story of Forrest Tucker"—how he had been put on a chain gang at age sixteen, how he had escaped from San Quentin in a home-made kayak—I found myself slightly dubious, like when I read that Billy the Kid had somehow escaped the fatal bullet of Sheriff Pat Garrett in 1881. When I researched Tucker's past, however, nearly every detail checked out. "I don't need to bullshit," he told me. Indeed, there were so many astonishing elements to his true story that I was unable to detail them all in a single article, including the fact that the police allegedly foiled a plot by the Over-the-Hill Gang to break him out of prison after his 1980 arrest.

There was also one story Tucker told me that I could never prove but that I have little reason to doubt: While at Alcatraz in the summer of 1962, he helped his old friend Frank Morris and two others break out in one of the most heralded escapes of all time. "I would have gone with them," he said, "but I couldn't get moved to a nearby cell." He insisted that he had provided them with crucial tools, and he seemed to resent that he had still not achieved over his own career as an escape artist the fame of his comrades, who were later celebrated in the movie, Escape from Alcatraz, *starring Clint Eastwood. Of course, after some reflection, he noted that the others had in all likelihood drowned in the frigid currents of San Francisco Bay. "It wasn't a perfect plan," he said. Then he got up and asked for a piece of candy.*

STEPHANIE
JAMES ELLROY

Murder files hook you fast and drag you in slow. The crime-scene report wires shock. Read it for facts and milieu. Don't extrapolate. Don't expect clear explication. Big files fill ten boxes. Logic builds and fractures. Chronologies disperse. The act creates the disorder. It leads you to the victim slow.

Summary reports, teletypes, mug shots. FI cards, shredded APBs, canvassing sheets. Wrong-case misfiles, mug-run cards, and rap sheets.

Family photos. The victim's address book. Her scent or your wish fulfillment of it many years old.

Women only. *They* make me read and look. Old paper as perfume. Longing as perceptive tool.

Unsolved files only. Apply your mind male and rude. Reset fractures. Reroute narrative. Make data blips cohere.

I've read a dozen murder files. I started with my mother's file and moved on. I'm not a detective or a cop-wannabe. I come to know the women sometimes.

I study the death pictures. I always do it first. Take me back and show me the horror. Make me feel your loss fresh and new.

Detective Bureau / Homicide Divison / LAPD
DR #65–538–991 [Murder/187 PC]
Victim: Stephanie Lynn Gorman / White Female / Age 16.
DOB: 6-11-49

DOD: 8-5-65

Status: Unsolved / Reopened / LAPD Unsolved Unit at Work

The Crime Scene: West LA/"Beverlywood"/southeast of Beverly Hills. Upper-middle-class Jewish/all-residential/crime stats down around zilch.

A corner house. Hillsboro and Sawyer. Stucco/late-forties/three bedrooms. A rear garage. Side-street access. A cement backyard. A five-foot connecting wall. A street-access wood door set in.

A backyard patio. Sliding-glass doors. A rumpus room. A patio view. A side hallway. Go to the northeast bedroom.

It's by the front door. Windows look out. See the front lawn and street. See the house next door.

A door leads to the master bedroom. A door leads to the hall. Roll thirty-seven years back. Pop the doors and LOOK.

It's a small room. It's the older sister's pad. A west-wall dresser. A north-wall desk by the window. Daybeds lining the south and east walls. They hit perpendicular.

An end table separates them. A lamp and knickknacks sit upright. There's a cold-cream-jar lid in between. There's a match-book on the floor. There's a nightstand in the northeast corner. There's a knocked-over lamp. There's an east-wall portrait. It's the older sister beaming. There's a stuffed-turtle toy on the east bed. Both bedcovers are lime green.

On the floor: Two gray sweat socks. Close by: A lidless jar of cold cream. Gauge in. They're beside the south bed and matchbook.

A chair by the connecting doors. Clothes under it. Panties, denim shorts, one tennis shoe. Gauge in. The matching shoe is on the floor. It's near the west-wall dresser.

There's a cord looped to one south-bed leg. It's mason's cord. The free end is frayed. There's a shell casing on the floor. It's between the wall and the south bed. By the east bed: Three more casings.

Bloodstained carpet. Near the east bed.

The casings are small. The bloodstain is red and bright pink.

There's Stephanie.

She's on the floor. She's on her knees. She's up against the east wall. She's by the east-bed foot.

She's half nude. She's wearing a knit top and bra. They're knife-slashed. The top hangs loose. The bra hangs off her neck and shoulders.

Drag burns on her right hip. Both wrists abraded. Cinched cord on her right wrist: Loose strands pressure frayed.

Gunshot wounds: Two in her chest. One in her neck. One in the head.

Her lower lip and left breast are bruised. Her inner lip is swollen. Her forehead sustained a contusion.

It's a begging pose. She's against that wall. Bullet force bruised her back. The east wall got an indentation.

It happened in broad summer daylight.

Her father and sister found her. 6:00 PM, August 5, '65. Ed and Cheryl Gorman come home. Cheryl's bedroom door is shut. They open it. They enter the room. They see Stephanie.

Ed Gorman goes to her and lifts her. He puts her on the east bed. He covers her with a quilt and some clothing. He calls LAPD. West LA Division responds.

Stephanie's mother came home. Ed Gorman told her. The LAPD arrived.

Lieutenant Grover Armstrong, Sergeants Robert Byron and William Koivu. SID men, latent-print men, photo-lab men, crime-lab men. Ten LAPD men total.

The detectives talked to the family. The family said this: Ed Gorman was a lawyer. He worked downtown. Cheryl worked with him today. Julie Gorman was a housewife. She played tennis today. She came home at 3:00 PM. She saw Cheryl's bedroom door shut. She paid no mind.

She went back out. She went to the beauty shop. She came home to *this*.

The tech men fanned out. The photo men took pictures. Ed Gorman said he disrupted the crime scene. He covered Stephanie. She's up on the east bed. Her head's by the toy turtle.

The cops walked the house. They saw no forced entry. They saw no ransacking. They found a cord strand near the front door. They walked the patio. They found two bloodstained towels.

The detectives rebuilt Stephanie's day.

She went to Hamilton High summer school. She carpooled with two friends: Paul Bernstein and Ilene Jackman. They always left school at 12:30.

The detectives called Ilene Jackman. They told her, and calmed her down. They learned this: They went to school. They drove home. They dropped Paul off first. She dropped Stephanie at 12:45. Stephanie walked through the back gate.

She's in the house now. She's alone.

An ambulance arrived. Attendants took Stephanie to the morgue.

Print men dusted the crime scene. They turned up latent prints. They elimination-printed the Gormans and the cops. The Gormans slept under sedation.

Cops canvassed the neighborhood. The next-door lady said this: She heard screams yesterday. It was 3:30 to 4:30. They came from that northeast bedroom. She thought it was the Gorman girls playing. The lady lived one house north. Her gardener cut the lawn yesterday. He worked 1:30 to 2:30. Neighbors reported a candy-selling crew. They were Negro kids. They were door-to-door knocking. There was a whole slew.

A kid called West LA station. His name was Dave S. He said he parked outside the Gorman pad yesterday. He was looking for this guy Bob G. Bob G. lived there maybe two years ago.

The tip got shined on. The Gorman job made the papers and TV. They had tips up the wazoo.

A neighbor called. She found the Gormans' pet loose. 4:00 PM yesterday. She put the dog in the Gormans' yard. She called to Stephanie. She got no answer.

A neighbor kid called. He was a Hami Hi student. He saw two Negroes cruise the Gorman house. It was yesterday. It was 12:50 PM. They drove a '55 Ford.

A neighbor woman called in. She saw a '53 or '54 Olds parked at Durango and Sawyer. A man got out. He walked to a trash can. He removed a pink blouse.

More neighbors called in. They snitched off the Negro candy crew. They snitched off a Negro church-solicitation crew. A parole officer called in. He snitched off two local rape-o's. A neighbor man called in. He saw two Negroes in a '55 Ford. They were distributing handbills.

Neighbors snitched off Negro workmen. A neighbor woman called in. A male Negro stood on her porch yesterday. It was 11:30 to noon. She lived on Hillsboro. She lived near the Gormans.

The canvassing cops braced local parolees. The geeks ran the gamut: GTA, weapons beefs, burglary, escape. They all checked out alibi-clean.

A bartender called in. He reported weird shit at the Red Rouge Bar. The bartender said this: A guy came in last night. He was white/50/6'/200. He said, "They don't know what's happening. It will be headlines. They'll read about it in the papers tomorrow. It's tough to be a clown."

More canvassers came on. Metro Division supplied them. They house-to-housed. They questioned residents. They worked north to LA Country Club. They worked south to the Santa Monica Freeway.

They worked east to La Cienega. They worked west to Hillcrest Country Club.

Byron and Koivu interviewed the neighbor's gardener. His name was George Iwasaki. He told them this: He worked August 5, '65. He worked 1:00 to 2:00. He saw a man peeping the house. The peeper stood between the house and the neighbor's house. The peeper peeped the northeast bedroom window.

Iwasaki described him:

White male, Latin type, 43 to 45 years old. Five seven, one hundred forty pounds. Sallow cheeks, unshaved, unkempt hair. Attire: Cotton twill shirt and pants. Matching "uniform type." Fresh starched, light blue.

The man gave him a bad look. Iwasaki smelled scuffle. He prepared to *go*. Their eyeball duel ended. Iwasaki did yard work. He did not see the peeper again.

Dr. Harold Kade performed the autopsy: Coroner's file #19597.

Gunshot wound number one perforated her heart and left lung. Result: Massive hemorrhage. Gunshot wound number two perforated her right lung. Result: Massive hemorrhage. Gunshot wound number three penetrated her trachea, esophagus, and vertebral column. Result: Massive hemorrhage. Gunshot wound number four fractured her skull and penetrated her brain. Result: Massive hemorrhage.

Doc Kade checked Stephanie's reproductive system. The uterus, fallopian tubes, and ovaries: "Grossly normal." "No lacerations of the vagina, rectum or perineum."

The Gorman job continued. Homicide Division jumped in. Sergeants J. R. Buckles and W. R. Munkres clocked on.

They found the Negro candy sellers. They cleared them. They questioned the Gorman family. They learned this: Stephanie was a good girl. She did not provoke boys. She got top grades. She held class office. She excelled at Palms Junior High and Hami. She had no enemies. She did not truck with bad kids.

SID kicked back ballistics. The weapon: A small-caliber auto. Right-hand twist/six lands and grooves/Colt-brand autos excluded. In evidence: Four Western brand shell casings, four .25-caliber bullets. In progress: Crime-report cross-checks for the same type gun and MO.

The detectives debunked hysterical tips. They cleared suspicious Negroes. They read recent crime reports. Two nuts-at-large stood out.

Nut number one: "The Shoe-Tree Rapist." At large since February 4, '62. A West Valley habitué. A unique MO. He cruises residential blocks. He spots housewives. He enters their pads through rear doors. He finds neckties or electric cords. He finds vaginal jellies or cold cream.

He wears gloves and masks. He grabs the women and binds them. He stuck a shoe tree in his first victim's vagina. His next five victims fought him off. He never speaks. He may be a mute. He may drive a '48 or '52 Chevy. Witness descriptions vary. He is a white male. He *may* be 19 to 23. He *may* be 30 to 40. *Sometimes* he appears unshaven.

Nut number two: "The Remorseful Rapist."

He's a white male "Latin type." He's about 26. He's 5'11"/185. He hits apartment pads in Wilshire and Central Division. He hits pads near bus lines.

He targets lone women. He cons his way in. He shows a small revolver and subdues them. He tapes their eyes and mouths. He rapes them. He apologizes post-rape. He shows them the gun is a toy.

The detectives worked. They found the Negro church crew. They cleared them. They checked three local meter men. They cleared them. They went to Stephanie's funeral. The crowd ran one thousand strong.

Hillside Memorial Park. Rabbi Michael Albagli presiding. Tears and soliloquy.

The detectives skimmed old crime reports. They read ballistics reports. They read FI cards. They checked out loiterers. They fielded crank calls. A kid called in. He said Stephanie was a hooker. A crank note came in. It snitched off actor Richard Burton. More neighbors called in. They snitched off suspicious Negroes. A Hami girl called in. She said Stephanie dated Paul Bernstein and Steve Spiegelman.

SID retained the slugs and shells. Techs ran comparison tests. The slugs and shells matched no slugs and shells from priors. The print men studied the elimination prints. They found four prints remaining.

A sketch artist worked with George Iwasaki. They created a peeper sketch. The detectives talked to Doc Kade. He offered this opinion: Stephanie Gorman was not a virgin.

The detectives talked to Ed and Julie Gorman. They questioned them per Stephanie and sex. The Gormans deemed her a virgin. She had a checkup on April 3, '65. Talk to Dr. Fred Pobirs.

Buckles and Munkres saw Dr. Pobirs. He confirmed the checkup. He consulted the records. He saw no pelvic-exam notes. He said she was fifteen then. If she wasn't a virgin, I would have told the family.

The detectives questioned Stephanie's friends and classmates. They confirmed Stephanie's good-girl status. They talked to boys she dated. They had August 5 alibis. They denied sex with Stephanie. They were credible. They vouched Stephanie's chastity. The detectives figured this: Doc Kade might be right. Doc Kade might be wrong. Natural function or accidents cause vaginal rupture.

The detectives braced registered sex offenders. They ran RSO mug shots by Iwasaki. He nixed them all.

It was August 11, '65. LA was wicked hot. The Watts riot broke out. LAPD responded. The riot featured arson, sniping, and looting. It was Suspicious-Negro Armageddon. The National Guard arrived. A curfew was imposed. LA stayed indoors. LAPD got swamped. Normal LAPD service got suspended. Hot investigations lost time.

The riot de-conflagrated. South LA got singed to Cinder City. LAPD service resumed *slooooow*.

The Gorman job: Stymied, quicksand, sludge.

Buckles and Munkres wrote a progress report. Lieutenant Pierce Brooks approved it. The report ran hypothetical reconstructions.

12:45. Stephanie gets home. She goes to her bedroom. She drops her schoolbooks and purse. She goes to the kitchen. She has a snack.

Stephanie has dry-skin problems. She goes to the master bathroom. It adjoins Cheryl's room. She creams her rough skin. Maybe the suspect grabs her there. He's already in the house.

The skin-cream bottle—found in the bathtub—not normal there. But:

No forced entry. That cord by the front door. Maybe he knocks. Stephanie answers. Maybe he just barges in.

He hits her. He subdues her. It explains her torn lip. The bruise on her forehead—call it Blow Two. Call it a fall-down bump from Blow One.

He drags Stephanie. Her right-hip brush burns suggest this. Cheryl's bedroom is close. Stephanie is helpless or unconscious. He pulls the south bed out. He throws her on it. He binds her wrists to the east-bed legs. He spread-eagles her. He strips her lower body. He throws her clothes on the floor. He cuts her top and bra up the middle. He goes to the master bedroom. He finds a Jergens jar. He returns to the bedroom. He lubricates Stephanie's rectum and vagina. He tosses the jar and lid. Remember—the jar on the floor/ the lid on the nightstand.

Doc Kade's opinion: Sodomy and rape. Tests for internal residues or foreign fluids: not yet conducted.

The killer assaults Stephanie. Stephanie regains consciousness. Say she struggles then. Say it's like *this*. Say she struggles throughout the whole thing.

Her wrists break free. Remember—the right-wrist cord still on her arm/the cord strands loose on the bed leg.

She gets off the bed. The killer corners her. Stephanie stumbles. She hits the east wall. She kneels—horror/shock/exhaustion. He shoots her four times. His gun's an automatic. The spent shells eject left to right. He's bloody now. He goes to the master bedroom. He grabs two towels. He wipes himself off. He goes out the back door. He hits the patio. He drops the towels. He goes out the back gate. He's on Sawyer Street. He's gone.

And—feature this:

Stephanie dies in Cheryl's bedroom. A sibling resemblance exists. Was Cheryl the intended vic?

The Gorman job faded out newswise. Post-riot shit upstaged it. Stephanie got brief coverage. It played up her good-girl status. She was young, bright, lovely. She got straight As. She was Hami Hi "In" Crowd. She was movie-mad. She got extra gigs in *Pollyanna* and *Bye Bye Birdie*.

The detectives slogged. They issued a bulletin. It featured a crime summary and the peeper sketch. It went out August 24, '65. It went to the Feds and PDs nationwide. LAPD got kickbacks: Similar MOs/divergent MOs/MOs from distant planets. Rape-o killers, bondage rape-o's. Burglar rape-o's, knife rape-o's, gun rape-o's, child rape-o's, girl rape-o's, woman rape-o's, old-lady rape-o's.

Some freaks resembled the sketch. Most freaks didn't. George Iwasaki viewed nationwide mug shots and nixed them. They got no print matches. They got no gun matches. They got more phone tips and more letters. They cleared three hundred suspects. They issued bulletin number two.

They sent slug and shell samples to the FBI and CII. Bulletin number two requested comparison slugs and shells. It begged for kickbacks: All suspects known or in stir.

No matches. Straight kickback zeros.

The Feds had a slug and shell. Ditto CII. LAPD retained two. The bulletin hit Canada and Mexico. Shit: No matches, more zeros.

The detectives slogged. They reinterviewed Stephanie's class-mates. They reconfirmed her good-girl status. They interviewed Cheryl's male friends. They cleared them. They torqued wienie-waggers, glue-sniffers, hopheads, and public-jackoff freaks. They cleared them. They cleared local deliverymen. They cleared Ed Gorman's Negro ex-gardener. They cleared *more* suspicious Negroes. They cleared rape-jacket Negroes citywide.

The Gormans were fine people. Ed was a fine lawyer. Julie's rep gleamed. The "good girl" Gorman sisters were unassailably thus. They did not dick tease. They did not backyard-sunbathe provaca-tively. Stephanie frequented the Standard Club. She wore demure outfits. She never wore ripe bikinis.

"The Shoe-Tree Rapist"—still at large. "The Remorseful Rapist"— likewise. Likewise *très* many sick humps.

The Gorman job slogged on. The Gorman job slogged on full-speed.

They got call-ins. A girl ratted off a local "wino type." Iwasaki saw him and nixed him. The Green Bay, Wisconsin, PD called. Their freak resembled the sketch. Iwasaki nixed a mug shot. Suspect—*adieu*.

Doc Kade called. He had vaginal and rectal semen tests: Incon-clusive. Plus: No other foreign fluids present.

They cleared a Crest Drive wienie-wagger. He flashed his shvantz from his balcony. They cleared a freak nicknamed Wino. He popped goofballs. He pushed Maryjane to kids. They checked out a June 4, 1964 case. A freak kidnapped a Hami girl. It was bold and streetside.

He flashed a knife. He forced her into his car. He made her dis-robe. He kissed her breasts. He let her go.

They checked out a March 12, 1965 gig: A parked-car caper. It featured a Hami girl and boy. The girl was topless. Her name was in Stephanie's address book. They cleared the boy.

"Harvey the Confessor" confessed. Harvey was habitual. He

copped to the Gorman job. The cops heard out his bullshit. The cops cut him loose.

Fall '65 dragged on. They checked out the Standard Club. It was mid-upscale Jewish. The Gormans partied there. Maybe some freak saw Stephanie there. Maybe his hard-on commenced there. Maybe Stephanie flipped his freak switch.

They did 122 interviews. They checked August 5, '65 time cards. They found some freak employees. They found some ex-cons. They looked at them close. They read rap sheets. They charted work histories. They charted work absences on August 5, '65. They leaned on the freaks.

One Negro had two DUIs. Fuck him—he's a lush. One Negro had multiple busts: Burglary/ADW/check-bounce *tsuris*. One Negro had a stat-rape bust.

They leaned on them. They gun-checked them. They print-checked them. They cleared them.

They checked out snack-bar guys, pool guys, lifeguards, tennis pros. They braced a potential rape-o. He picked a girl up at the club. He invited her to a movie. He drove her to the Hollywood Hills. He tried to promote a fuck. She said No Fuck. He drove her home then.

The Standard Club washed out. They ran gun checks, print checks, and show-ups. They got *bupkes*. They punted. They tracked obscene-phone-call reports.

They waded in. They slid through slime. They tracked back four years. It was ugly. Bondage themes and straight-fuck themes ran riot.

"Baby, let's fuck." "I want to eat your pussy." "I heard your sister works at Kentucky Fried Chicken on Pico. Do you and your sister fuck?"

The detectives grilled known phone freaks. They cleared them. Phone freaks were tough to nail. More freaks at large.

They dumped the phone shit—December 29, '65. Cheryl Gorman got a Christmas card. It mentioned a meeting in July '65. The family went to Coronado. Stephanie and Cheryl hit the beach. They met two boys. Cheryl said she was reading *The Collector*. It's about a freak. He kidnaps a woman. She dies in captivity.

The kids played a game. The boys tied up and untied the girls. It was brief chuckles. That was all of it.

That was July. Cut to late December. One boy sends a Christmas card. It mentions the rope trick.

The detectives studied the card. The detectives drove to San Diego. They found the boys. They grilled them. They polygraphed them. They cleared them.

Adios, 1965—1966 struts in.

January 5, '66: The lab tests the south and east bedspreads for semen. The east bed hits positive. There's a blood-type-A reaction.

The result: Inconclusive. The stain is near Stephanie's death pose. The rest of the bedspread tests positive: Blood-type-A reaction. That marks the specific stain inconclusive. That means the semen could match A or O blood. Stephanie was type O. There were no foreign fluid types in her rectum or vagina.

January 7, '66: The lab tests the bloody towels. They get a type-O reaction. It's probably Stephanie's blood. Stephanie might have scratched the killer.

The detectives worked. The lab confiscated *new* crime-scene guns. They examined them. They got nil results.

February 22, '66: SID tests the Gorman hair samples. Most test out to Stephanie and Cheryl. One doesn't. This hair is coarser. It's not a Negro, Mexican, or Oriental hair. It's assuredly Caucasian.

February 22, '66: The lab tests Stephanie's nail clippings. They find no scraped flesh. They find blood traces. They're too small to type. They can't tell if she scratched her assailant.

February 28, '66: LAPD pops "The Remorseful Rapist." It's a traffic stop—2nd and Serrano. He's a male Mexican.

He's packing a toy gun and tape. He stands in a show-up. Thirty-eight victims ID him. The Gorman cops grill him. He's gun-checked, print-checked, poly'd, and cleared.

March 8, '66: A neighbor lady rats off a loiterer. He's standing at Pico and Roxbury. He matches the peeper sketch. Patrolmen haul him in. Detectives grill him.

His name is Julie The K. He's an alien. He came from Bumfuck, Hungary. He's a schizo and a nut-bin habitué. He's got a nation-wide rap sheet: Vag/disorderly conduct/wienie-wagger.

He won't take a poly. They book him for Murder One. George Iwasaki views him. He says maybe, maybe not.

Julie The K. talked. He said he escaped Patton State Hospital. The detectives called Patton. They learned: Julie The K. escaped August 5, '65 — the Gorman snuff date.

But:

Julie The K. split late in the day. The time glitch cleared him. Julie The K. got unbooked. Patton sent a crew down to shag him.

March 24, '66–March 31, '66: Two metro cops hit Georgia Street Juvenile.

They run record checks. They check recent Hami kids. They check the boys for juvie beefs. They check the girls as sex-beef complainants. The girls shoplift clothes. The girls run from titty-pinchers and whip-out men. The boys run the fucking alphabet.

Lots of sex shit. 288PC — forced oral cop. 288 — voluntary. 288 — mutual suck. Voyeur busts, malicious mischief. A kid molests a pre-pubescent girl. Cops pop him. Said kid gets popped at a fruit bar later. Lots of GTA, some grand theft, some sodomy. Wienie-waggers, glue-sniffers, grasshoppers, juiceheads galore. Fruit rollers, fruit teasers, high school fruitettes. Firebugs, chronic runaways. A doozy right after the Gorman job — August 13, '65. Venice Boulevard and Ocean Front Walk.

There's a public rest room. A Mex kid is choking his *chorizo*. The kid states: "I was thinking of a Hami Hi girl."

They went through 5,000–plus names. They turned up 201 rap sheets. They grilled the pure freaks. They print-checked them and gun-checked them. They got diddly-shit.

April 4, '66: The LA Police Commission gets a mailed poem. Said poem reads:

"Did they ever find who snuffed out Stephanie Gorman? Was he of Lago Vista Dr., Beverly Hills? Used to frequent the pool hall in Westwood?

> Poem:
> 'And her name was Stephanie. She came
> from Hills Beverly. A quick roach was he
> around the house.
> I declare, look here, you may find out (An
> idea to a mystery)' "

The detectives worked it. It went nowhere. A cryptographer read the poem. She said it was gobbledygook.

June 20, '66: LAPD gets hip to Dave S. Remember—he called West LA Station. It was August 6, '65. He said he went by the Gorman pad August 5. He looked for Bob G. Bob used to live there.

Dave S. was 21. Dave S. graduated Hami. Dave S. got popped for 288 once. Dave S. had a bad-check warrant: Extant in Orange County.

June 21, '66: Metro cops grill Dave S. He tells his Bob G. story. He parked in the Gormans' driveway. He thought he saw someone peek out a window. No one came out. He split.

The story made no sense. Bob G. didn't live there. Dave S. nixed a polygraph. Dave S. split the interview. Dave S. called back. He said he'd take the poly now.

They set up the test: 7:00 PM, June 21, '66. Dave S. called up and canceled. The detectives talked to Bob G.

Shit, we sold the house. The Gormans bought it in 1961. The Gormans had it in 1965. Shit, Dave S. knew where I lived.

The cops re-braced Dave S. They requested a formal statement. He refused. They arrested him.

They got him a public defender. They booked him for Murder One.

He spent two days in the shitter. He agreed to a poly. He took the test. He came up clean. His prints didn't match. He owned no guns. Iwasaki viewed him. Iwasaki said, "Nix."

They released Dave S. Orange County grabbed him. Bam— bad-check warrant extant.

The Gorman job was eleven months old. It was dead-stalled and fucked.

Rick Jackson told me about Stephanie. My neck hairs stood up.

Rick works LAPD Homicide. He's a superb detective and one of my best friends. We prowl crime-historical LA. We talk CRIME. We dig the horror. We rap logic and moral perspective. We dig crime as social barometer and buffoonish diversion. My wife says we cackle like schoolgirls. Rick synopsized. Details nudged me. A pinprick memory blipped.

It's summer 1965. I'm 17. There's a Hollywood newstand. There's a girl's picture. It straddles a newspaper fold.

Blip—no more, no less.

Rick said the case went active. It was a fluke. It happened like this:

It's 2000 now. The sister's fiftyish. She attends a party. She meets an LAPD man. She mentions her sister's case. She *wonders*. She requests a status update.

The cop checks it out. Phone calls go down. Detective Dave Lamb-kin picks it up. He works the Rape-Special Section. He's a twenty-two-year officer. He doesn't know the Gorman case. Lambkin reads the file. He notes the unknown prints. He sends them to the FBI.

The Feds run them through the AFIS database. They get a single-print match.

The kickback supplies a name. The man was young then and old now. *He's now a suspect.*

That blip. That picture. A slight expansion—her pageboy hairdo. Rick's synopsis. The horror. The Watts-riot bit. My LA '65 summer—stone's throw to *her.*

Show me the file. I need to *see.*

It was December 2000. I booked a room in Beverly Hills. Beverly-wood adjoined it. Stone's throw to Hillsboro and Sawyer.

I drove to Parker Center. Rick introduced me to Dave Lambkin. He was mid-forties, bald and fucking bug-eyed intense. He talked fast and articulate. His thoughts scattergunned and coalesced precisely. He said the file ran fourteen boxes. He gave me a suspect update.

Call him Mr. X. Mr. X is 69. Mr. X was 34 then. He had a minor rap sheet. One receiving stolen goods bounce, à la 1971.

Hence: Prints on file. Hence: The AFIS match. Hence: Major-suspect status.

No Gorman link. That's good. It jukes the random-sex factor. Ed Gorman's dead now. The mother and sister don't know X-Man. They've racked their memories.

So:

We're running background checks. We've placed him in West LA then. We've surveilled him. We've got his prints on a cup. We snatched it at a diner.

We need more facts. They're armament. They'll fuel the search warrant. They'll define the approach.

Show me the file. Show me the pictures first.

We walked to the Rape-Special cubicle. I saw the boxes and binders. I saw taped-on wall tableaux. That memory blip blew out full.

The *LA Times*. The pic on the fold. The pageboy girl.

Lambkin passed me the pictures. They were faded Kodachrome. Shades beamed surreal.

There's the patio. There's the bloody towels. The south bed's askew. There's one shell casing.

I clenched up. I knew she'd be next. I wanted to see it. I trusted my motive. I knew my eyes would violate.

There —

I couldn't peel her beauty back from the horror. I felt immodest *and* clinically focused. Her softness merged with the blood.

I called it quits early. The file boded too big. The pictures held me for now. Dead women own you. Call it blunt and simple. She's Geneva Hilliker Ellroy redux.

I went to the hotel. I time-traveled. I placed myself in context with that blip.

It was "Freedom Summer." I was 17. I was a year and three months older than Stephanie. I lived five miles northeast. I attended Fairfax High School up to mid-March. Fairfax was largely Jewish. I was Gentile and fucked-up. I craved attention, love, and sex. I did nothing constructive to earn it. I lusted for Jewish girls. I bicycle stalked them. I pulled anti-Semitic stunts in school. I got my ass kicked. Fairfax kicked me out.

My dad was old and frail. He let me join the army. I hated the army. It scared me shitless. My dad had a second stroke. I faked a nervous breakdown. An army shrink bought it. My dad died June 4, 1965. The army kicked me loose.

I bopped back to LA. I was 17 and draft-exempt. The army gave me go-home pay. I forged my dad's last three Social Security checks. I had a roll. I got a cheap pad. I got a handbill-passing job. I shoplifted food and booze. I popped pills and smoked weed. I ran 6'3" and 140. Everything frightened me. I read crime books, fantasized, and jacked off. I was a teenage-misanthrope/hybrid-scaredy-cat.

I stalked girls. My mode was the unilateral monogamous crush. My anti-Jewish stance was a shuck. It was kid iconoclasm. It was a love scrounger's yelp for help. Fairfax High was snotty and rigidly stratified. The Fairfax district bordered Hami Hi's. Hami was equally Jewish. Hami was allegedly more snotty and stratified. Hami kids were hip, Hami kids disdained geeks, Hami kids rode the cool zeit-geist.

Proximity.

Stephanie was lovely. I did not doubt her good-girl status. She would have beckoned. I would have stalked her. I would have har-bored tender thoughts. Booze might fuel a real approach—T-Bird chased by Clorets. She might reject me flat. She might reject me gently. She might hear me out. I was tall, I had my own pad, I had a murder-vic mom—sometimes the desperate impress.

Not likely. Desperate boys scare lovely girls. Ed Gorman would nab my shit quicksville. He'd kick my goy ass off his porch.

Yeah, I would have stalked her. No, I'd never harm a hair on her head.

The house was innocuous. The northeast bedroom light was on. Rick and I staked it out.

Daytime crime, nighttime surveillance. Crime locations spoke to us. They inspired time travel. They juked our talk.

We sat in Rick's car. Holiday lights beamed—Christmas sprays and menorahs. I mentioned a book. I read it circa '65. It was a thriller called *Warrant for X.*

Rick said X-Man looked good. He was at the crime scene. They didn't know when. They *did* know he *did not* know the Gormans. He matched the peeper sketch. He was a Latin-type Caucasian.

I speculated. Stephanie fought him. He panicked and shot her. Rick quoted Dave Lambkin. Dave was a sex-crime expert. Dave had this factors-in-place riff.

Would-be killers harbor fantasies. They rarely act. Most would-bes never kill. Sometimes factors converge. The right victim appears. The opportunity hits. Stress factors goose the would-be. Family grief, sex abstinence, booze or dope impairment. His switch flips. He acts.

I said that might apply to my mother's case. It's the victim-killer nexus. Specific men kill specific women and kill no more. They bring fantasies to the act. They juxtapose their rage and lust against a female image. Maybe my mother vibed loose prowess. Maybe Stephanie vibed kindness to plunder. The killer killed my mother. He probably hit her and raped her unconscious. Stephanie screamed and fought. She got off the south bed. She disturbed her killer's fantasy.

He killed her. The act traumatized him. He never killed again.

Rick said maybe, maybe not. It didn't vibe intentional snuff. It vibed rape-panic and rape-escalation. The fuck brought the cord and gun. The gun for threat, the cord for suppression. Most rapes went unreported. Rape as social stigma—1965. Stephanie might be Vic 16 or 60. The nexus, the alchemy—something made him kill her. I said her beauty and softness. Bam—his switch drops. He sees outtakes from his shitty life. His stress context implodes. A happy kid dies.

Women as one-way mirrors. Women as Etch-a-Sketch boards. The killer snags one real image and starts to revise. His revisions tap signals. It's sex semaphore. Details get distorted and magnified. It's a fun-house mirror now. It's all in his head. The woman loses proportion. She gains bizarre shapes. She gets dehumanized.

We shitcanned the analysis. We rapped rude and wrathful. The Gorman job was individual forfeit. The Gorman job was moral default. Nothing justified it. The killer had to pay. His childhood trauma and attendant justifications bought him no mercy. Fuck the cocksucker dead—

I dug into the file. I met Dave Lambkin's partner, Tim Marcia. He was big and athletic. He talked less than Lambkin. He weighed his words and zoomed to the point.

We dug binders out. I read the autopsy and first summary report. I rechecked crime-scene shots. I theorized. I indulged possible wishful thinking.

No vaginal or rectal hurt. No foreign-fluid types. Virgin and non-virgin assessments. No semen or Jergens cream inside her. Vaginal rupture by natural cause.

Doc Kade was dead. Koivu was dead. Ditto Munkres and Buckles. Byron was in a rest home. He was senescent. There was no one to clarify.

My sense: No penetration. The killer didn't rape Stephanie.

Tim Marcia agreed. She was young and tight internally. She struggled. Her legs were unbound. There's no Jergens on bedspreads/no Jergens floor drip. There's the east-bed semen stain. Maybe it's a forced oral cop. Maybe the killer jerked off.

I asked about vault evidence. I mentioned bedspread DNA. Marcia said a cop tossed it. Fucking outrage—some cop on a spring-cleaning kick.

I read reports. I skimmed mug shots. I checked the peeper sketch. Dave Lambkin did a cutout trick. He took a side-view mug shot of Mr. X. He placed it against the side-view sketch. They dovetailed exact.

Mr. X looked good for it. Vengeance beckoned. Knock, knock—come here, motherfucker.

I read the file. I hobnobbed with the "Shoe-Tree" and "Remorseful" rapists. I read the obscene-phone-call log. I found the boy's Christmas card. I read *The Collector* that summer. It turned me on. The captive woman was a redhead. My mother was a redhead. Samantha Eggar was a redhead. She played the captive in the flick. I saw it during the Watts riot. It played in Beverly Hills—stone's throw to Hillsboro and Sawyer.

Tim Marcia and I discussed a wild card. The Gorman job—consensual sex goes blooey.

Pros and cons. Coronado/the rope trick/*The Collector* connection. A secret boyfriend. The gun and rope as props. The boy's shaky psyche. Chaste kicks and Stephanie's imposed limits.

It flew for ten seconds. It flew apart then.

Why use the sister's bedroom? Stephanie's room was out back. Mom and Dad parked in the rear. They're home—oops—let's split. And:

The torn lip/the punch there/the head bump/the drag burns/the cord by the front door.

Dave ran the file by a Fed profiler. He posited a front-door approach. The killer knocks. Stephanie answers. It's her last look at daylight.

I read the Georgia Street juvie reports. I spent a night at Georgia Street. It was August '65. I shoplifted some ice cream. LAPD popped me.

It was scary. Tough kids made fun of me. A friend's dad got me out. He took me to County Probation. I was too old to adopt. Somebody signed a paper. It made me an "Emancipated Juvenile."

The reports detailed a world wild and wimpy. It's all middle-class Jewish freaks. Two names jumped out. I knew one guy at John Burroughs Junior High. I smoked weed with another guy. He knew my pal Craig Minear. Craig crashed his two-seater plane. He died November '70.

I read the file. I became friends with Dave and Tim. We discussed the rape and no-rape angles. We lauded and mourned Stephanie.

Tim and I drove to Hami. We checked old yearbooks and found Stephanie. She's sleek in her Phi Delt sweater. Her pageboy's down and swept by barrettes. Her expression shifts picture to picture. She's a pensive kid.

I told Tim that I loved her to death. He said he did, too.

The investigation built. Dave and Tim built that warrant for X.

They had his CII number, FBI number, LAPD arrest stats. The Auto Track computer system shot them ten prior addresses. They had his wife and ex-wife's stats. The "Family Index" ran one hundred pages. It tallied prior addresses and driving records. Mr. X had a son and a daughter. The son was clean. The daughter had busts: Dope/theft/prostitution.

The case hinged on the print. The case would build off X-Man's denial. No, I wasn't in that house. Bullshit, you *were*.

The print was it. We'll brace him alone. We'll hook him in slow. We'll bring a search warrant.

Dave was writing the warrant now. It was detailed and legalistic. They were looking for this:

Personal records. Vehicle records—late '50s to late '60s. Firearms and ammo. Docs describing X-Man's size on August 5, '65. Mason cord or photos of X-Man with same. Docs establishing X-Man's whereabouts on August 5, '65. Docs establishing connections to the Gorman family. Photos, films, or videos depicting violence against women. Pornography depicting women posed in restraints.

The approach ran tripartite. The print/the warrant search/ X-Man's reaction and/or denial. George Iwasaki was dead. Age would alter X-Man's looks. Eyeball wits were out.

Dave and Tim were swamped. Breaking jobs swarmed their

Gorman commitment. Dave worked the warrant part-time. Other work diverted him. He buzzed through Rape-Special. He passed the wall tableaux. He always said, "Sorry, Stephanie."

I stuck around LA. I cruised the Gorman house AM and PM. I thought about Stephanie. I brought flowers to her grave. I pondered the *Laura* syndrome.

The book and movie define it. Homicide cops dig the gestalt. The title woman is lovely and perplexing. She's a murder vic. A cop works her case. Laura's portrait seduces him. She turns up alive. Laura and the cop fall in love.

It's ridiculous wish fulfillment. It negates the hold of the dead. They inhabit your blank spaces. They work magic there. They freeze time. They render our short time spans boldly precious. They build alternative memory. Their public history becomes your private reserve. They induce a mix of vindictiveness and compassion. They enforce moral resolve. They teach you to love with a softer touch and fear and revere your obsessions.

My obsessions were born in 1958. "Son, your mother's been killed" and the upshot. She was my first untouchable crush. Stephanie was a daughter or a prom date. I don't know her. I can *feel* her. She's twirling. She's showing off her prom gown. I can smell her corsage.

Dave and Tim built the warrant. They planned their questions and signals. They brought some Orange County cops in. A judge signed the warrant. X-Man's ex lived in Riverside County. They planned a dual approach. Dave and Tim would brace X-Man. Two cops would brace the ex. She was with X-Man in '65. She might know some stuff.

The date was set: January 23, 2001.

I went home. My wife and I discussed Stephanie. I reveled in Helen's brilliance and flesh-and-blood life.

We rented *Bye Bye Birdie*. We scanned the crowd scenes. We couldn't spot Stephanie. Rick and I talked. Rick was happy. LAPD was forming a cold case squad. It was all oldies/24/7. Rick, Dave, and Tim were set to start.

Fuck happy. Rick was *thrilled*. Unlimited time-travel.

I rented *Pollyanna*. I saw Stephanie.

She was ten or eleven. She stood stage right. Hayley Mills sang "America the Beautiful." A line of girls flanked her. They all wore the Stars and Stripes.

There's Stephanie—alive and in color. Her eyes dart. The moment flusters her. Her hair was lighter then. She's got hazel-brown eyes like mine.

I hit rewind and fast-forward. I did it X-dozen times. I watched her. I caught every breath. I filled blank spaces up.

The brace went down. It clicked like clockwork.

Two units in place. Bam—X-Man's wife leaves early. Dave and Tim walk up.

They're nervous. They've got badges and IDs out. They knock on the door. X-Man opens up.

He's friendly. They mention an old murder. He doesn't clench up.

He invites them in. They all sit down. He appears befuddled— old murder, huh?

Dave and Tim start to explain. X-Man cuts them off.

That sixteen-year-old girl, right? I remember that. I was across the street. I was at a friend's house.

The sister ran over. My friend was a doctor. He wasn't in then. I ran over to help. I saw the body. The cops came. The cops shooed me out.

Oh, fuck—

He came off credible. He smiled. He betrayed no nerves. The boom didn't drop.

Dave quizzed him. X-Man responded. The doc and wife—alive and well. Yeah, we're still in touch.

There's the boom. It fell on *you*. Oh shit, we're fuck—

They schmoozed up X-Man. His credibility held. They said good-bye.

They found the doctor. They braced him. They braced his wife concurrent. They backed X-Man up.

Heartbreaker/square one again/fluke fingerprint/months trashed and fucked.

Dave called and told me. He described "The worst day of my life." I reran *Pollyanna*. I cued Stephanie up.

——

It's over. It's not over. It's been two years plus. Closure is nonsense. Nothing this bad ever ends. The killer is crucial and irrelevant. He knew Stephanie for ten minutes. He never loved her. His memories are brutal and suspect.

Baby, who were you? How would you grow and who would you love? Did you know you'd touch driven men and teach them?

You've got torchbearers. Three detectives and one chronicler. We want to know you. It's a pursuit. It's a likelier outcome than justice.

We're spinning our wheels. It doesn't matter. We get glimpses. You're twirling in your prom gown. Color us devoted. Color you gone.

TO KILL OR NOT TO KILL
SCOTT TUROW

When Joseph Hartzler, a former colleague of mine in the United States attorney's office in Chicago, was appointed the lead prosecutor in the trial of Timothy McVeigh, the Oklahoma City bomber, he remarked that McVeigh was headed for Hell, no matter what. His job, Hartzler said, was simply to speed up the delivery. That was also the attitude evinced by the prosecutors vying to be first to try the two Beltway sniper suspects. Given the fear and fury the multiple shootings inspired, it wasn't surprising that polls showed that Americans favored imposing what Attorney General Ashcroft referred to as the "ultimate sanction." Yet despite the retributive wrath that the public seems quick to visit on particular crimes, or criminals, there has also been, in recent years, growing skepticism about the death-penalty system in general. A significant number of Americans question both the system's overall fairness and, given the many cases in which DNA evidence has proved that the wrong person was convicted of a crime, its ability to distinguish the innocent from the guilty.

Ambivalence about the death penalty is an American tradition. When the Republic was founded, all the states, following English law, imposed capital punishment. But the humanistic impulses that favored democracy led to questions about whether the state should have the right to kill the citizens upon whose consent government was erected. Jefferson was among the earliest advocates of restricting executions. In 1846, Michigan became the first American state to outlaw capital punishment, except in the case of treason, and public opinion has continued to vacillate on the issue. Following the Second World War and the rise and fall of a number of totalitarian governments, Western European nations began abandoning capital punishment, but their example is of limited relevance to us, since our murder rate is roughly four times the rate in Europe. One need only glance at a TV screen to realize that murder remains an American preoccupation, and the concomitant questions of how to deal with it challenge contending strains in our moral thought, pitting Old Testament against New, retribution against forgiveness.

I was forced to confront my own feelings about the death penalty as one of fourteen members of a commission appointed by Governor George Ryan of Illinois to recommend reforms of the state's capital-punishment system. In the past twenty-five years, thirteen men who spent time on death row in Illinois have been exonerated, three of them in 1999. Governor Ryan declared a moratorium on executions in January 2000, and five weeks later announced the formation of our commission. We were a diverse group: two sitting prosecutors; two sitting public defenders; a former chief judge of the Federal District Court; a former U.S. senator; three women; four members of racial minorities; prominent Democrats and Republicans. Twelve of us were lawyers, nine with experience as defense attorneys and eleven—including William Martin, who won a capital conviction against the mass murderer Richard Speck, in 1967—with prosecutorial backgrounds. Roberto Ramírez, a Mexican-American immigrant who built a successful janitorial business, knew violent death at first hand. His father was murdered, and his grandfather shot and killed the murderer. Governor Ryan gave us only one instruction. We were to determine what reforms, if any, would make application of the death penalty in Illinois fair, just, and accurate. In March 2000, during the press conference at which members of the commission were introduced, we were asked who among us opposed capital punishment. Four people raised their hands. I was not one of them.

For a long time, I referred to myself as a death-penalty agnostic, although in the early seventies, when I was a student, I was reflexively against capital punishment. When I was an assistant U.S. attorney, from 1978 to 1986, there was no federal death penalty. The Supreme Court declared capital-punishment statutes unconstitutional in 1972, and although the Court changed its mind in 1976, the death penalty did not become part of federal law again until 1988. However, Illinois had reinstated capital punishment in the mid-seventies, and occasionally my colleagues became involved in state-court murder prosecutions. In 1984, when my oldest friend in the office, Jeremy Margolis, secured a capital sentence against a two-time murderer named Hector Reuben Sanchez, I congratulated him. I wasn't sure what I might do as a legislator, but I had come to accept that some people are incorrigibly evil and I knew that I could follow the will of the community in dealing with them, just as I routinely accepted the wisdom of the RICO statute and the mail-fraud and extortion laws it was my job to enforce.

My first direct encounter with a capital prosecution came in 1991. I was in private practice by then and had published two successful novels, which allowed me to donate much of my time as a lawyer to pro-bono work. One of the cases I was asked to take on was the appeal of Alejandro (Alex) Hernandez, who had been convicted of a notorious kidnapping, rape, and murder. In February 1983, a ten-year-old girl, Jeanine Nicarico, was abducted from her home in a suburb of Chicago, in DuPage County. Two days later, Jeanine's corpse, clad only in a nightshirt, was found by hikers in a nearby nature preserve. She had been blindfolded, sexually assaulted several times, and then killed by repeated blows to the head. More than forty law-enforcement officers formed a task force to hunt down the killer, but by early 1984 the case had not been solved, and a heated primary campaign was under way for the job of state's attorney in DuPage County. A few days before the election, three men—Alex Hernandez, Rolando Cruz, and Stephen Buckley— were indicted.

The incumbent lost the election anyway, to a local lawyer, Jim Ryan, who took the case to trial in January 1985. (Ryan later became the attorney general of Illinois, a position he is about to relinquish.) The jury deadlocked on Buckley, but both Hernandez and Cruz were convicted and sentenced to death. There was no physical evidence against either of them—no blood, semen, fingerprints, or other forensic proof. The state's case consisted solely of each defendant's statements, a contradictory maze of mutual accusations and demonstrable falsehoods. By the time the case reached me, seven years after the men were arrested, the charges against Buckley had been dropped and the Illinois Supreme Court had reversed the original convictions of Hernandez and Cruz and ordered separate retrials. In 1990, Cruz was condemned to death for a second time. Hernandez's second trial ended with a hung jury, but at a third trial, in 1991, he was convicted and sentenced to eighty years in prison.

Hernandez's attorneys made a straightforward pitch to me: Their client, who has an IQ of about seventy-five, was innocent. I didn't believe it. And, even if it was true, I couldn't envision persuading a court to overturn the conviction a second time. Illinois elects its state-court judges, and this was a celebrated case: "The case that broke Chicago's heart" was how it was sometimes referred to in the press. Nevertheless, I read the brief that Lawrence Marshall, a professor of law at Northwestern University, had filed in behalf of Cruz, and studied the transcripts of Hernandez's trials. After that, there was no question in my mind. Alex Hernandez was innocent.

In June 1985, another little girl, Melissa Ackerman, had been abducted and murdered in northern Illinois. Like Jeanine Nicarico, she was kidnapped in broad daylight, sexually violated, and killed in a wooded area. A man named Brian Dugan was arrested for the Ackerman murder, and, in the course of negotiating for a life sentence, he admitted that he had raped and killed Jeanine Nicarico as well.

The Illinois State Police investigated Dugan's admissions about the Nicarico murder and accumulated a mass of corroborating detail. Dugan was not at work the day the girl disappeared, and a church secretary, working a few blocks from the Nicarico home, recalled a conversation with him. A tire print found where Jeanine's body was deposited matched the tires that had been on Dugan's car. He knew many details about the crime that had never been publicly revealed, including information about the interior of the Nicarico home and the blindfold applied to Jeanine.

Nevertheless, the DuPage County prosecutors refused to accept Dugan's confession. Even after Cruz's and Hernandez's second convictions were overturned in the separate appeals that Larry Marshall and I argued, and notwithstanding a series of DNA tests that excluded Cruz and Hernandez as Jeanine Nicarico's sexual assailant, while pointing directly at Dugan, the prosecutors pursued the cases. It was only after Cruz was acquitted in a third trial, late in 1995, that both men were finally freed.

Capital punishment is supposed to be applied only to the most heinous crimes, but it is precisely those cases which, because of the strong feelings of repugnance they evoke, most thoroughly challenge the detached judgment of all participants in the legal process—police, prosecutors, judges, and juries. The innocent are often particularly at risk. Most defendants charged with capital crimes avoid the death penalty by reaching a plea bargain, a process that someone who is innocent is naturally reluctant to submit to. Innocent people tend to insist on a trial, and when they get it the jury does not include anyone who will refuse on principle to impose a death sentence. Such people are barred from juries in capital cases by a Supreme Court decision, *Witherspoon v. Illinois*, that, some scholars believe, makes the juries more conviction-prone. In Alex Hernandez's third trial, the evidence against him was so scant that the DuPage County state's attorney's office sought an outside legal opinion to determine whether it could get the case over the bare legal threshold required to go to a jury. Hernandez was convicted anyway, although the trial judge refused to impose a death sentence because of the paucity of evidence.

A frightened public demanding results in the aftermath of a ghastly crime also places predictable pressures on prosecutors and police, which can sometimes lead to questionable conduct. Confronted with the evidence of Brian Dugan's guilt, the prosecutors in Hernandez's second trial had tried to suggest that he and Dugan could have committed the crime together, even though there was no proof that the men knew each other. Throughout the state's case, the prosecutors emphasized a pair of shoe prints found behind the Nicarico home, where a would-be burglar—i.e., Hernandez—could have looked through a window. Following testimony that Hernandez's shoe size was about 7, a police expert testified that the shoe prints were "about size 6." Until he was directly cross-examined, the expert did not mention that he was referring to a woman's size 6, or that he had identified the tread on one of the prints as coming from a woman's shoe, a fact he'd shared with the prosecutor, who somehow failed to inform the defense.

This kind of overreaching by the prosecution occurred frequently. A special grand jury was convened after Cruz and Hernandez were freed. Three former prosecutors and four DuPage County police officers were indicted on various counts, including conspiring to obstruct justice. They were tried and—as is often the case when law-enforcement officers are charged with overzealous execution of their duties—acquitted, although the county subsequently reached a multimillion-dollar settlement in a civil suit brought by Hernandez, Cruz, and their onetime codefendant, Stephen Buckley. Despite assertions by DuPage County prosecutors that Jeanine Nicarico's killer deserves to die, Brian Dugan has never been charged with her murder, although Joseph Birkett, the state's attorney for the county, admitted in November that new DNA tests prove Dugan's role with "scientific certainty." In the past, Birkett had celebrated the acquittal of his colleagues on charges of conspiring to obstruct justice and had attacked the special prosecutor who'd brought the charges. He continues to make public statements suggesting that Cruz and Hernandez might be guilty. An ultimately unsuccessful attempt was made to demote the judge who acquitted Cruz, and last year, when the judge resigned from the bench, he had to pay for his own going-away party. In the meantime, the prosecutor who tried to incriminate Alex Hernandez with the print from a woman's shoe is now chief judge in DuPage County.

If these are the perils of the system, why have a death penalty? Many people would answer that executions deter others from committing murder, but I found no evidence that convinced me. For example, Illinois, which has a death penalty, has a higher murder rate than the neighboring state of Michigan, which has no capital punishment but roughly the same racial makeup, income levels, and population distribution between cities and rural areas. In fact, in the last decade the murder rate in states without the death penalty has remained consistently lower than in the states that have had executions. Surveys of criminologists and police chiefs show that substantial majorities of both groups doubt that the death penalty significantly reduces the number of homicides.

Another argument—that the death penalty saves money, because it avoids the expense of lifetime incarceration—doesn't hold up, either, when you factor in the staggering costs of capital litigation. In the United States in 2000, the average period between conviction and execution was eleven and a half years, with lawyers and courts spewing out briefs and decisions all that time.

The case for capital punishment that seemed strongest to me came from the people who claim the most direct benefit from an execution: the families and friends of murder victims. The commission heard from survivors in public hearings and in private sessions, and I learned a great deal in these meetings. Death brought on by a random element like disease or a tornado is easier for survivors to accept than the loss of a loved one through the conscious will of another human being. It was not clear to me at first what survivors hoped to gain from the death of a murderer, but certain themes emerged. Dora Larson has been a victims'-rights advocate for nearly twenty years. In 1979, her ten-year-old daughter was kidnapped, raped, and strangled by a fifteen-year-old boy who then buried her in a grave he had dug three days earlier. "Our biggest fear is that someday our child's or loved one's killer will be released," she told the commission. "We want these people off the streets so that others might be safe." A sentence of life without parole should guarantee that the defendant woud never repeat his crime, but Mrs. Larson pointed out several ways in which a life sentence poses a far greater emotional burden than an execution. Because her daughter's killer was under eighteen, he was ineligible for the death penalty. "When I was told life, I thought it was life," Larson said to us. "Then I get a letter saying our killer has petitioned the governor for release."

Victims' families talk a lot about "closure," an end to the legal process that will allow them to come to final terms with their grief. Mrs. Larson and others told us that families frequently find the execution of their lost loved one's killer a meaningful emotional landmark. A number of family members of the victims of the Oklahoma

City bombing expressed those sentiments after they watched Timothy McVeigh die. The justice the survivors seek is the one embedded in the concept of restitution: The criminal ought not to end up better off than his victim. But the national victims'-rights movement is so powerful that victims have become virtual proprietors of the capital system, leading to troubling inconsistencies. For instance, DuPage County has long supported the Nicarico family's adamant wish for a death sentence for Jeanine's killer, but the virtually identical murder of Melissa Ackerman resulted in a life term with no possibility of parole for Brian Dugan, because Melissa's parents preferred a quick resolution. It makes no more sense to let victims rule the capital process than it would to decide what will be built on the World Trade Center site solely according to the desires of the survivors of those killed on September 11. In a democracy, no minority, even people whose losses scour our hearts, should be entitled to speak for us all.

Governor Ryan's commission didn't spend much time on philosophical debates, but those who favored capital punishment tended to make one argument again and again: Sometimes a crime is so horrible that killing its perpetrator is the only just response. I've always thought death-penalty proponents have a point when they say that it denigrates the profound indignity of murder to punish it in the same fashion as other crimes. These days, you can get life in California for your third felony, even if it's swiping a few videotapes from a Kmart. Does it vindicate our shared values if the most immoral act imaginable, the unjustified killing of another human being, is treated the same way? The issue is not revenge or retribution, exactly, so much as moral order. When everything is said and done, I suspect that this notion of moral proportion—ultimate punishment for ultimate evil—is the reason most Americans continue to support capital punishment.

This places an enormous burden of precision on the justice system, however. If we execute the innocent or the undeserving, then we have undermined, not reinforced, our sense of moral proportion. The prosecution of Alex Hernandez demonstrated to me the risks to the innocent. A case I took on later gave me experience with the problematic nature of who among the guilty gets selected for execution. One afternoon, I had assembled a group of young lawyers in my office to discuss pro-bono death-penalty work when, by pure coincidence, I found a letter in my in-box from a man, Christopher Thomas, who said he'd been convicted of first-degree murder and sentenced to death, even though none of the four eyewitnesses to the crime who testified had identified him. We investigated and found that the letter was accurate—in a sense. None of the eyewitnesses had identified Thomas. However, he had two accomplices, both of whom had turned against him, and Thomas had subsequently confessed three different times, the last occasion on videotape.

According to the various accounts, Chris Thomas—who is black, and was twenty-one at the time of the crime—and his two pals had run out of gas behind a strip mall in Waukegan, Illinois. They were all stoned, and they hatched a plan to roll somebody for money. Rafael Gasgonia, a thirty-nine-year-old Filipino immigrant, was unfortunate enough to step out for a smoke behind the photo shop where he worked as a delivery driver. The three men accosted him. Thomas pointed a gun at his head, and when a struggle broke out Thomas fired once, killing Gasgonia instantly.

I was drawn to Chris Thomas's case because I couldn't understand how a parking-lot stickup gone bad had ended in a death sentence. But after we studied the record, it seemed clear to us that Thomas, like a lot of other defendants, was on death row essentially for the crime of having the wrong lawyers. He had been defended by two attorneys under contract to the Lake County public defender's office. They were each paid thirty thousand dollars a year to defend a hundred and three cases, about three hundred dollars per case. By contract, one assignment had to be a capital case. The fiscal year was nearly over, and neither of the contract lawyers had done his capital work, so they were assigned to Thomas's case together. One of them had no experience of any kind in death-penalty cases; the other had once been standby counsel for a man who was defending himself.

In court, we characterized Thomas's defense as all you would expect for six hundred dollars. His lawyers seemed to regard the case as a clear loser at trial and, given the impulsive nature of the crime, virtually certain to result in a sentence other than death. They did a scanty investigation of Thomas's background for the sentencing hearing, an effort that was hindered by the fact that the chief mitigation witness, Thomas's aunt, who was the closest thing to an enduring parental figure in his life, had herself been prosecuted on a drug charge by one of the lawyers during his years as an assistant state's attorney. As a result, Thomas's aunt distrusted the lawyers, and, under her influence, Chris soon did as well. He felt screwed around already, since he had confessed to the crime and expressed remorse, and had been rewarded by being put on trial for his life. At the sentencing hearing, Thomas took the stand and denied that he was guilty, notwithstanding his many prior confessions. The presiding judge, who had never before sentenced anybody to death, gave Thomas the death penalty.

In Illinois, some of this could not happen now. The Capital Litigation Trust Fund has been established to pay for an adequate defense, and the state supreme court created a Capital Litigation trial bar, which requires lawyers who represent someone facing the death penalty to be experienced in capital cases. Nonetheless, looking over the opinions in the roughly two hundred and seventy capital appeals in Illinois, I was struck again and again by the wide variation in the seriousness of the crimes. There were many monstrous offenses, but also a number of garden-variety murders. And the feeling that the system is an unguided ship is only heightened when one examines the first-degree homicides that have resulted in sentences other than death. Thomas was on death row, but others from Lake County—a man who had knocked a friend unconscious and placed him on the tracks in front of an oncoming train, for instance, and a mother who had fed acid to her baby—had escaped it.

The inevitable disparities between individual cases are often enhanced by social factors, like race, which plays a role that is not always well understood. The commission authorized a study that showed that in Illinois, you are more likely to receive the death penalty if you are white—two and a half times as likely. One possible reason is that in a racially divided society whites tend to associate with, and thus to murder, other whites. And choosing a white victim makes a murderer three and a half times as likely to be punished by a death sentence as if he'd killed someone who was black. (At least in Illinois, blacks and whites who murdered whites were given a death sentence at essentially the same rate, which has not always been true in other places.)

Geography also matters in Illinois. You are five times as likely to get a death sentence for first-degree murder in a rural area as you are in Cook County, which includes Chicago. Gender seems to count, too. Capital punishment for slaying a woman is imposed at three and a half times the rate for murdering a man. When you add in all the uncontrollable variables—who the prosecutor and the defense lawyer are, the nature of the judge and the jury, the characteristics of the victim, the place of the crime—the results reflect anything but a clearly proportionate morality.

And execution, of course, ends any chance that a defendant will acknowledge the claims of the morality we seek to enforce. More than three years after my colleagues and I read Chris Thomas's letter, a court in Lake County resentenced him to a hundred years in prison, meaning that, with good behavior, he could be released when he is seventy-one. He wept in court and apologized to the Gasgonia family for what he had done.

Supporters of capital punishment in Illinois, particularly those in law enforcement, often use Henry Brisbon as their trump card. Get rid of the death penalty, they say, and what do you do about the likes of Henry?

On the night of June 3, 1973, Brisbon and three "rap partners" (his term) forced several cars off I-57, an interstate highway south of Chicago. Brisbon made a woman in one of the cars disrobe, and then he discharged a shotgun in her vagina. He compelled a young couple to lie down in a field together, instructed them to "make this your last kiss," and shot both of them in the back. His role in these crimes was uncovered only years later, when he confessed to an inmate working as a law librarian in the penitentiary where he was serving a stretch for rape and armed robbery. Because the I-57 killings occurred shortly after the Supreme Court declared capital punishment unconstitutional, Brisbon was not eligible for the death penalty. He was given a sentence of one thousand to three thousand years in prison, probably the longest term ever imposed in Illinois.

In October 1978, eleven months after the sentencing, Brisbon murdered again. He placed a homemade knife to the throat of a guard to subdue him, then went with several inmates to the cell of another prisoner and stabbed him repeatedly. By the time Brisbon was tried again, in early 1982, Illinois had restored capital punishment, and he was sentenced to death. The evidence in his sentencing hearings included proof of yet another murder Brisbon had allegedly committed prior to his imprisonment, when he placed a shotgun against the face of a store clerk and blew him away. He had accumulated more than two hundred disciplinary violations while he was incarcerated, and had played a major role in the violent takeover of Stateville prison, in September 1979. Predictably, the death sentence did not markedly improve Brisbon's conduct. In the years since he was first condemned, he has been accused of a number of serious assaults on guards, including a stabbing, and he severely injured another inmate when he threw a thirty-pound weight against his skull.

Brisbon is now held at the Tamms Correctional Center, a "super-max" facility that houses more than two hundred and fifty men culled from an Illinois prison population of almost forty-five thousand. Generally speaking, Tamms inmates are either gang leaders or men with intractable discipline problems. I wanted to visit Tamms, hoping that it would tell me whether it is possible to incapacitate people like Brisbon, who are clearly prone to murder again if given the opportunity.

Tamms is situated near the southernmost point of Illinois, farther south than parts of Kentucky. The Mississippi, a wide body of cloacal brown, floods the nearby lowlands, creating a region of green marshes along orange sandstone bluffs. Tamms stands at the foot of one of those stone outcroppings, on a vast, savannalike grassland. The terms of confinement are grim. Inmates are permitted no physical contact with other human beings. Each prisoner is held twenty-three hours a day inside a seven-by-twelve-foot block of preformed concrete that has a single window to the outside, roughly forty-two by eighteen inches, segmented by a lateral steel bar. The cell contains a stainless-steel fixture housing a toilet bowl and a sink and a concrete pallet over which a foam mattress is laid. The front of the cell has a panel of punch-plate steel pierced by a network of half-inch circles, almost like bullet holes, that permit conversation but prevent the kind of mayhem possible when prisoners can get their hands through the bars. Once a day, an inmate's door is opened by remote control, and he walks down a corridor of cells to an outdoor area, twelve by twenty-eight feet, surrounded by thirteen-foot-high concrete walls, with a roof over half of it for shelter from the elements. For an hour, a prisoner may exercise or just breathe fresh air. Showers are permitted on a similar remote-control basis, for twenty minutes, several times a week.

In part because the facility is not full, incarceration in Tamms costs about two and a half times as much as the approximately twenty thousand dollars a year that is ordinarily spent on an inmate in Illinois, but the facility has a remarkable record of success in reducing disciplinary infractions and assaults. George Welborn, a tall, lean man with a full head of graying hair, a mustache, and dark, thoughtful eyes, was the warden of Tamms when I visited. I talked to him for much of the day, and toward the end asked if he really believed that he could keep Brisbon from killing again. Welborn, who speaks with a southern-Illinois twang, was an assistant warden at Stateville when Brisbon led the inmate uprising there, and he testified against him in the proceedings that resulted in his death sentence. He took his time with my question, but answered, guardedly, "Yes."

I was permitted to meet Brisbon, speaking with him through the punch-plate from the corridor in front of his cell. He is a solidly built African-American man of medium height, somewhat bookish-looking, with heavy glasses. He seemed quick-witted and amiable, and greatly amused by himself. He had read all about the commission, and he displayed a letter in which, many years ago, he had suggested a moratorium on executions. He had some savvy predictions about the political impediments to many potential reforms of the capital system.

"Henry is a special case," Welborn said to me later, when we spoke on the phone. "I would be foolish to say I can guarantee he won't kill anyone again. I can imagine situations, God forbid . . . But the chances are minimized here." Still, Welborn emphasized, with Brisbon there would never be any guarantees.

I had another reason for wanting to visit Tamms. Illinois's execution chamber is now situated there. Unused for more than two years because of Governor Ryan's moratorium, it remains a solemn spot, with the sterile feel of an operating theater in a hospital. The execution gurney, where the lethal injection is administered, is covered by a crisp sheet and might even be mistaken for an examining table except for the arm paddles that extend from it and the crisscrossing leather restraints that strike a particularly odd note in the world of Tamms, where virtually everything else is of steel, concrete, or plastic.

Several years ago, I attended a luncheon where Sister Helen Prejean, the author of *Dead Man Walking*, delivered the keynote address. The daughter of a prominent lawyer, Sister Helen is a powerful orator. Inveighing against the death penalty, she looked at the audience and repeated one of her favorite arguments: "If you really believe in the death penalty, ask yourself if you're willing to inject the fatal poison." I thought of Sister Helen when I stood in the death chamber at Tamms. I felt the horror of the coolly contemplated ending of the life of another human being in the name of the law. But if John Wayne Gacy, the mass murderer who tortured and killed thirty-three young men, had been on that gurney, I could, as Sister Helen would have it, have pushed the button. I don't think the death penalty is the product of an alien morality, and I respect the right of a majority of my fellow citizens to decide that it ought to be imposed on the most horrific crimes.

The members of the commission knew that capital punishment would not be abolished in Illinois anytime soon. Accordingly, our formal recommendations, many of which were made unani-mously, ran to matters of reform. Principal among them was lower-ing the risks of convincing the innocent. Several of the thirteen men who had been on death row and were then exonerated had made dubious confessions, which appeared to have been coerced or even invented. We recommended that all interrogations of sus-pects in capital cases be videotaped. We also proposed altering lineup procedures, since eyewitness testimony has proved to be far less trustworthy than I ever thought while I was a prosecutor. We urged that courts provide pretrial hearings to determine the reliabil-ity of jailhouse snitches, who have surfaced often in Illinois's capital cases, testifying to supposed confessions in exchange for lightened sentences.

To reduce the seeming randomness with which some defen-dants appear to end up on death row, we proposed that the twenty eligibility criteria for capital punishment in Illinois be trimmed to five: multiple murders, murder of a police officer or firefighter, murder in a prison, murder aimed at hindering the justice system, and murder involving torture. Murders committed in the course of another felony, the eligibility factor used in Christopher Thomas's case, would be eliminated. And we urged the creation of a statewide oversight body to attempt to bring more uniformity to the selection of death-penalty cases.

To ensure that the capital system is something other than an endless maze for survivors, we recommended guaranteed sentences of life with no parole when eligible cases don't result in the death penalty. And we also outlined reforms aimed at expediting the post-conviction review and clemency processes.

Yet our proposals sidestepped the ultimate question. One fall day, Paul Simon, the former U.S. senator who was one of the com-mission's chairs and is a longtime foe of the death penalty, forced us to vote on whether Illinois should have a death penalty at all. The vote was an expression of sentiment, not a formal recommendation.

What was our best advice to our fellow citizens, political realities aside? By a narrow majority, we agreed that capital punishment should not be an option.

I admit that I am still attracted to a death penalty that would be applied to horrendous crimes, or that would provide absolute certainty that the likes of Henry Brisbon would never again satisfy their cruel appetites. But if death is available as a punishment, the furious heat of grief and rage that these crimes inspire will inevitably short-circuit any capital system. Now and then, we will execute someone who is innocent, while the fundamental equality of each survivor's loss creates an inevitable emotional momentum to expand the categories for death-penalty eligibility. Like many others who have wrestled with capital punishment, I have changed my mind often, driven back and forth by the errors each position seems to invite. Yet after two years of deliberation, I seem to have finally come to rest. When Paul Simon asked whether Illinois should have a death penalty, I voted no.

———

The Illinois death penalty debate reached a dramatic culmination in 2003. At the time I wrote, the Illinois General Assembly had failed to enact any substantial reforms in the face of the Commission on Capital Punishment's recommendations. In the waning days of Governor George Ryan's administration, Ryan continued to confront a capital system in disrepair that had left 171 men on death row. Despite the controversy George Ryan knew he would invite, the governor decided to commute all Illinois death sentences in his final days in office. Four men, victims of alleged police torture, were pardoned on grounds of innocence. Three others had their sentences reduced to a level commensurate with codefendants. The sentences of the rest—164 persons—were commuted to life in prison without parole.

Despire dire predictions, including mine, about the consequences of emptying death row, polling showed Illinoisans divided evenly about the wisdom of the ex-governor's decision. Given that evidence of substantial public dissatisfaction with the failure to fix the capital system, and Democratic election successes in November 2002 that gave Democrats control of both houses in the Illinois legislature, reform legislation began moving ahead. By the end of 2003, the majority of the commission's recommendations had become law, albeit sometimes in modified form. Videotaping of station house interroga-tions, new lineup procedures, pretrial review of informant and accom-plice testimony, a slight narrowing of felony murder eligibility, and allowing the state supreme court to review the fundamental fairness of any death sentence have now been mandated by Illinois law in capital cases. On the other hand, both a dramatic reduction of eligi-bility factors and the creation of a statewide commission to review prosecutors' decisions to seek the death penalty proved too politically dangerous to gather much support, even from the many Illinois legis-lators in both parties who exhibited great principal in pushing reform ahead. Although I continue to wish for more, I also realize that the Illinois capital system has been dramatically improved.

Ironically, it does not appear that that system is likely to resume operation soon. The new Democratic governor, Rod Blagojevich, has elected to continue Governor Ryan's moratorium on executions, say-ing he remains dissatisfied with social inequities in the application of the death penalty. At the moment, prosecutors around the state may seek capital sentences, but they have done so much more selectively. In 2003, there were no death sentences pronounced in Cook County, which encompasses Chicago and which has been the place where the largest number of death sentences have traditionally been imposed. For the moment, Illlinoisans seem content with a situation in which a small number of murderers are given a sentence of death that may not be carried out.

George Ryan has continued to be venerated by anti–death penalty groups around the country, but closer to home his troubles multiplied. The week before Christmas 2003, the Chicago United States Attorney's Office's long-running investigation of George Ryan's administration of the Secretary of State's office culminated in Ryan's indictment on corruption charges. Ryan has pleaded not guilty and the case is scheduled for trial in 2005.

WATCHING THE DETECTIVES
JAY KIRK

The Texas lawman at the podium is a sullen figure beneath the TV lights, which wash out the projection of a dirt road on the screen behind him and cast the walnut paneling of the Downtown Club in a nervous gloom. Anyone could tell that Chief Deputy David Kinney is out of his element in this old Philadelphia men's club, but no more out of context than the bloody slides we will soon view over lunch, some of us less eagerly than others. Facing him, listening to him with chins pensively resting on knuckles, silk ties tucked, forks paused, are a hundred or so professional and amateur sleuths known collectively as the Vidocq Society. The elegant setting does little to ease the paranoia that comes, for me, from being in a room stuffed cheek by jowl with cops. It is a teeming synod of special agents—FBI, DEA, IRS—explosives and firearms specialists, corporate-fraud investigators, wound-pattern analysts, retired and active police brass, forensic hypnotists, forensic anthropologists, ritual-murder experts, criminal profilers, psychiatrists, and forensic psychologists. Here there are polygraph experts, masters at detecting the slightest galvanic quiver of skin, the anxious culpable heart, the tiny betrayals of the autonomic nervous system—a system upon which I have never much relied, being the sort of person who too easily feels that he is being punished, or should be punished, for some nebulous crime. It doesn't help when one of the detectives tells me that if I leak information he has just voluntarily revealed, he will "hunt me down like a dog."

I am sitting at a table with a private investigator, a forensic odon-tologist (a specialist who can identify human remains by teeth), and a medical examiner, specializing in exhumations, who has the sort of perfect telegenic looks that would destroy her credibility if she were playing the part on TV. The odontologist, over bites of salad, tells me how his expert testimony once caused an uproar when a juror, inexplicably aroused by the dental cast that he'd made of Megan Kanka's teeth (which matched the bite mark on the back of Jesse Timmendequas's hand), began to "cheer" and "pump his fist."

Between the salad and chicken courses I fidget with the plastic novelty "Lie Detector" business card given to me in lieu of a proper interview by Bill Fleisher, Vidocq Society commissioner, expert polygrapher, and former FBI agent with a striped tie and hair whipped back into a severe black meringue. Fleisher started the Vidocq Society ten years ago as a sort of forensic country club for his pals in the field. In a setting devoid of the usual bureaucracy, they could gather to unriddle cold murder cases, keep their games sharp, maybe help some people. Their victories have been as sur-prising as the unorthodox suggestions thrown out during their stately bull sessions. In 1992, for instance, eight years after a Drexel University student had been found barefoot and strangled to death, the Vidocq Society reviewed the case and suggested that investiga-tors look for a faculty member with a foot fetish. When they discov-ered that one suspect, a security guard, had been court-martialed for stealing women's sneakers, he was arrested and convicted. They offer their services pro bono, freely giving whatever insights or clues they come up with, and pay all expenses for their guest presenters. Once enough evidence is found to take a case to trial, Vidocqians frequently travel on the society's nickel to testify as expert witnesses. Today they have a backlog of cases allegedly in the hundreds and have allegedly solved just as many. I use the word "allegedly" because, after being reluctantly invited, uninvited, and then reinvited to last September's meeting, I was eventually cut off entirely by the Vidocq Society. This, as far as I could tell, is because they tend to let in "media" only when they can control the end product. (It may also have something to do with the fact that I went out to lunch with a few members and neglected to invite their communications chaperone.) Regardless, the operation is conducted with style. The members deduce over grilled breast of chicken with sherry rosemary sauce and steamed asparagus.

The only man not dressed in a dark suit and tie, apart from one or two uniformed police officers, is Frank Bender, the Vidocq Society cofounder and token artist. He sits a few tables away from me, wearing a tight-fitting black T-shirt and boots. Now in his early sixties, Frank is a forensic sculptor. He puts faces on skulls. His intuitive powers of granting identity to anonymous bone is so uncanny that last year, with the help of another Society founder, Richard Walter, a criminal profiler and forensic psychologist, Frank re-created a face for a skull found in the woods that had no face left at all. Somehow he was able to summon the features of an identifiable woman, and the killer was convicted last October. Cops speak of Frank with awe. Some even say that he's paranormal. It was Frank who lured Hollywood into buying an option on the Vidocq Society's story (his agent had been floating the idea of a movie about the eccentric crime-fighting artiste for years). This transformation from secretive forensic luncheon club to Hollywood fodder happened in 1997, shortly after the Society, in conjunction with *America's Most Wanted*, resurrected the fifty-year-old case known as "The Boy in the Box," which involved an unidentified dead child found in a J.C. Penney bassinet packing box in the woods of northeast Philadelphia. In a gesture seemingly choreographed for a tabloid newsmagazine, the Vidocq Society erected a black granite marker in the potter's field where the boy was buried, rechristening him "America's Unknown Child." Several studios bid on the Vidocq Society's story, and Danny DeVito's Jersey Films walked away with the life rights of the three founders for a reported seven-figure sum. That option and its renewal have enabled the pro bono society to fly in and put up clients like Chief Deputy Kinney. This afternoon, as I watch a producer weaving between tables with a microphone for Court TV (the cable network currently capitalizing on America's love for all things forensic, with programs like *I, Detective*, an interactive homicide-investigation quiz show), I have to wonder if it was by design or just good timing that this murder-mystery dinner theater became an entertainment commodity as well as a forensic charity.

We have long granted detectives a lofty place in our pantheon, because, like the priests before them, and the oracles before that, detectives are our most reliable curators of life's waning sense of mystery. They sustain us with suspense, and they reaffirm our fables of revelation through death. But since the O. J. Simpson trial turned us into a nation of amateur forensic experts, and shows like *CSI* carried that ball into the pop-cultural end zone, the mechanics of detective work have been laid bare. We all carry a little knowledge about the rate of decomposition or how blood spatter can be geometrically rendered. There seems to be less interest these days in the why than in the how.

With his fierce mustache and mouth of snaggleteeth, Chief Deputy David Kinney looks, at first glance, like the bad guy to be reckoned with in an old Western. He signals to his sidekick, Detective Rick Wooten, a short stub of a man in a tweed coat and flattop, to cue the next slide. An instant later a rusticated-looking man with a shaggy mullet, lopsided mustache, and bright sarcastic eyes leers at us from the screen. This will be the murder victim, Cody Rogers.

It was on a July morning, six years ago, that Chief Deputy Kinney got the call from Cody's father saying that his twenty-one-year-old son was missing. Cody lived with his parents. The last time they'd seen him was the night before, when he and his friend, Lance Barker, had been at the house, eating spaghetti and drinking beer; and then, sometime before midnight, they'd gone off in Lance's pickup. Lance returned the next morning to say that Cody had disappeared along a seldom-traveled dirt road. At first, Kinney didn't think too much of it: just a couple of bubbas out joyriding, and one of them went off with a girl maybe. But the father sounded worried. It being Saturday morning, and the chief deputy not having much on his plate otherwise, he drove out to where he was told the boy had vanished. The father and the missing boy's pal, Lance, a blond, clean-cut kid, were already there, waiting, two diminished figures surrounded by the lurching desolation of the plains.

Lance told the deputy that Cody had disappeared when they'd stopped at this spot to take a leak. Knowing that, as a rule, Cody drank until he passed out, Lance had waited for his friend awhile and yelled his name and gone searching for him up and down the road, turning his headlights out into the rows of cotton that ended abruptly in blackness. His friend was nowhere. He passed the night alternately searching and dozing off in the truck. Come daylight, he said, he knew that his friend had plumb vanished. Kinney smelled something fishy. He tried to get Lance to go over it real slow, step by step.

"Tell me exactly which direction your vehicle was parked," Kinney said. "You got out to take a leak. Where did you leak? Where did he leak? I want to see everything." And once he'd established a vivid enough portrait of Cody at the front of the truck, facing the cotton field, leaking eastbound, and Lance at the back of the truck, facing westbound, leaking into the overgrown cow pasture, he conducted a search. But he didn't find evidence of anyone taking a leak. Kinney then tracked up and down the road looking for footprints. He picked up one set of tracks that he followed into the cotton field.

These he followed east, and then back down another row west, and then he asked to see Lance's boot prints. They matched. Then he asked "old Lance what Cody Rogers was wearing, footwear wise, and he advised me that he thought he was in stocking feet." So he continued tracking until he found what appeared to be sock prints that went down a row of cotton and then came back out and puttered along the sandy orange-pink soil of the ditch. With Lance and Cody's father following behind, he tracked the prints for one hundred yards until they vanished on the southerly farm-to-market road. He couldn't understand why a man would just set off like that in his stocking feet. But the tracks confirmed at least part of the kid's story, so he said, "If he shows back up, call me."

I look around the room to gauge the reaction so far. At the table to my right a SWAT officer stirs sugar into his iced tea. In the back of the room a knot of pathologists pass around autopsy reports: the glossy morgue photos gleam under the chandeliers. A few pick at their plates, looking as bored as judges consigned to hearing traffic offenses. I try to guess which members aren't cops, because in addition to the admirable roster of law enforcers there is a motley assortment of amateurs: an English professor at the local community college, a construction-company owner, a vice president of Estée Lauder, travel agents, a publisher, and entertainment executives with connections to Tri-Star. Steven Seagal, an honorary member, is listed as a martial-arts expert.

Later that evening six years ago, once Chief Deputy Kinney was off duty, after he had eaten supper and checked on his cattle—some of them were calving now—he was watching the news when he got a dispatch about a possible suicide. He didn't know the area, an unpopulated corner of the county with unnamed roads. With only vague directions, he headed for the general vicinity he'd been given until he saw a point of swirling blue in the distant prairie dark, like a light at the end of a dock, and he drifted toward it.

We now view the image of a lonely spavined trailer quarantined by yellow crime-scene tape. A busted window screen dangles from its embrasure. The cop already on the scene, an officer from the little one-man unit up in Anton, told the chief deputy that he was waiting for backup because the owner, a vague retreating figure beside them in the night, had said that several guns were on the premises, and, furthermore, that the door was latched differently than he'd left it, so it was possible armed assailants might be waiting inside. So far this didn't match the initial report of suicide. Kinney turned to the owner, a quiet, young, blond, clean-cut kid standing there with his hands in his pockets. He was surprised to recognize the guy with whom he'd spent the better part of his Saturday morning tracking sock prints. He asked Lance Barker what the hell he was doing there.

"I live here," Barker said. "It's my trailer. My friend is dead."

Still confused, Kinney commenced his building search. The trailer was dark, except for a shaft of light coming from the back bedroom, and as he moved toward it, gun drawn, he passed through a wood-paneled room with a Naugahyde chair in one corner and a television with a little potted cactus sitting on top. On the floor was a steer's skull painted with a bloodred Apache spirit bird. The lit doorway at the end of the dark hall was propped open by a Dallas Cowboys trash can, and just outside the door, on the faded blue-and-white lozenged carpet, lay a spent .30-30 shell. As Kinney moved closer, his senses were overwhelmed by the odor of cheap cologne.

When the chief deputy entered the bedroom, he saw what we also now see: the young man with the bright sarcastic eyes, lying on a bed in blue pajama bottoms, looking like he needs a shave, but much more notable for having been shot in the face. Blood is spattered on the wall behind his head. "He took a round right under that eyeball [which] busted that cheekbone and kind of laid his eye out," Kinney says. Indeed, one blue truant eyeball, its pupil stubbornly dilated in the photoelectric flash, dangles on the powder-stippled cheek.

"Kind of when you're standing in that doorway he's lookin' at you with that eye," Kinney says, wincing. With only one murder or so a year, and sometimes none, the chief deputy can't say he's used to this sort of thing. He joined the marines during Vietnam but was stationed stateside, and when it was all over and his friends had gone off to places like Taos, New Mexico, and Vermont to be hippies, he stayed behind to cowboy on a 40,000-acre ranch, where he could sometimes go for months without seeing another face, where he enjoyed the simple things like branding calves and riding horses at sunset, and the only thing he thought maybe he wanted more was to one day ride as a special ranger with the Cattle Raisers Association, the Texas Rangers' elite cattle-theft unit. In order to do that he had to earn a few stripes as a peace officer first, so he quit being a cowboy to take a job as a deputy until an opening came up, and he's been a deputy ever since. He guesses that the murderer "probably looked at that eyeball looking at him, and he boogered."

Several of the waiters serving coffee and dessert—a white ice-cream truffle—duck their heads to avoid seeing the misery on the screen. Fleisher sits hunched forward, elbows braced on his knees, deeply engrossed by the dish of ice cream between his legs. The next slide shows how surprisingly *liquid* brains really are, especially flushed down the side of a quilt.

Mercifully, the next few slides focus on the victim's shoes and socks: Any fool can tell they didn't walk twenty-three miles—the distance between the spot where Lance Barker said Cody had disappeared and the trailer home. A more vexing technicality is that Lance now says both his guns are missing: the .30-30 determined to be the murder weapon (tool-mark comparisons match the shell retrieved from the bedroom with a shell on the coffee table that Lance admits he'd fired at a coyote) and a .22 rifle. The matter of the unstoppered bottle of Stetson cologne is another mystery altogether.

Given the angle of the gunshot, the medical examiner in Lubbock had said he would have ruled suicide if it weren't for the suspiciously missing .30-30; the same reasoning, more or less, moved Chief Deputy Kinney to arrest Lance Barker on the spot. But the DA made Kinney turn Barker loose for lack of anything beyond circumstantial evidence. Kinney kept digging. He dug four more years. He followed every trace. He interrogated the twelve-year-old boy who had ridden his bike past the trailer on the day of the murder, and who said he'd stopped to latch the front door that Lance, maybe in a boogered rush, had left wide open. The deputy dismissed the likelihood that the boy had pedaled off with the rifles: "I can't imagine a twelve-year-old boy seeing a guy with his brains blown out not freaking out. But that's one of the little stinks in this thing." He was still at a loss when he sent the case back to the DA's office, where it's been for the last two years, awaiting grand jury.

And then, just a couple of months ago, he got the surprise call offering him a free plane ticket to Philadelphia. Cody Rogers's sister had contacted the Society herself after watching a true-crime show in which members had helped to persuade a reluctant prosecutor to convert one missing person and one inexplicably huge swatch of blood-soaked carpet into a plausible homicide. (Coincidentally, the real-life father of the victim whose murder Cody's sister had seen reenacted on TV had also discovered the Vidocq Society while watching a similar show; sadly, he saw it on a motel TV, hunting for his son after the police had given up.) Despite the backlog of cases, the Vidocq Society agreed to review the Rogers case immediately, partly because Cody's father was dying. The next thing Kinney knew he was showing pictures of Cody Rogers with his face shot off to an audience of spiffy-looking ladies and gentlemen eating fancy chicken. Unfortunately for him, the chief deputy does not like chicken.

The volley of questions and observations drifts toward the podium slowly, arising with no particular order. The eclectic wisdom compressed in the room is characteristic of forensics in general, its borrowing from the discordant world of science richly ecumenical: Were the signs of lividity consistent with the positioning of the body when it was found? Were there other people present when the suspect and victim ate spaghetti? Were the stomach contents analyzed? Are the dirty socks still available? Was the air-conditioning on in the trailer? What was the weather like that day? Was the twelve-year-old boy given a polygraph? Do you think that the cologne was used to kill the dead smell? What kind of friends were Cody and Lance? Did you conduct a paraffin test on the suspect's hands? The victim's hands? Were the socks tested for gunpowder? Did the pathologist estimate the distance of the gun from the victim? Did the parents or their co-workers speculate about motive? Were there any women in their lives? Was there any attempt to obtain fingerprints from the shell casing? Was there any possibility that the cotton fields were used to dispose of the weapon?

When a psychologist asks what their co-workers had to say about them—both suspect and victim worked at a Lowe's store—Kinney nods deferentially and says, "Well, the co-workers said that Cody was a pretty good ole boy, but he liked to tease you. And if he ever got anything on you, he'd just drive you crazy with it. Lance Barker, they talked about him as kind of quiet but couldn't take any ribbing. So they was kind of an odd pair."

The next Vidocqian stands waiting for Court TV's microphone bearer to make his way through the chairs. "You mentioned earlier that the victim was full of alcohol. What did you establish with regard to that?"

"Lance Barker drank Coors. Just original Coors. Cody Rogers drank Icehouse beer. And the way they talk, he didn't swap over, that's what he drank."

This jibes with the autopsy report, another pathologist points out, but the victim could not have walked twenty-three miles—despite the inanity of doing so in socks—based on the quantity of alcohol found in his stomach, which empties fluid in less than an hour. "That means Cody Rogers ended up in that trailer in some other way than the one described."

A retired federal agent suggests an explanation for the lack of fingerprints on the cologne bottle by saying that the murderer—if it was his own trailer—may have been counterintuitive enough to wipe everything down, probably from watching too much TV.

"Yes sir?"

"Were the two men involved with each other sexually?"

Deputy Kinney pats his jacket as if to make sure his cigarettes are still there, and he sighs. "We done some checking, asked around, but as far as I know, in our part of the country that's not a very open thing. So we didn't really get a whole lot of detail."

This response, for some reason, elicits a huge gale of laughter.

Making signs that it's time to wrap things up, Fleisher passes around copies of Kinney's report. After two final questions, he presents Kinney with a magnifying glass. The meeting is adjourned.

While the Society members mill about, Court TV's producer drags the Texans around for a few last-minute vanity shots. The final tableau poses Chief Deputy Kinney and the squat and pruned-looking Detective Wooten like two traunt kids with the linguistics expert Donald Weinberg. The underlying principle of Weinberg's work is that humanity has a choice between civilization and barbarism, and that civilization will disappear as it did in the Dark Ages if people like himself, and yourself, and myself, who have chosen civilization over barbarism, allow our fellow humans to get away with too much murder. Wearing a necktie depicting a scene from the Bayeux tapestry—wherein Harold is captured and brought before William the Conqueror—Weinberg prods and parses and deconstructs the statements made by Lance Barker on the morning following his arrest.

"Look at the pattern of pauses," Weinberg says. The gaffer's boom dangles overhead like a dust mop. "Lots of ellipses . . . lots of them . . . this large number of ellipses indicates invention . . . that is, I'm making up this story as I go along." His analysis being that Lance Barker is an unreliable narrator and probably a liar. The Texans nod with a glance at the camera.

"That's your meat and potatoes, there," Kinney says.

It strikes me how possibly depressing it is—and yes, paradoxical—that such a gathering of civilized, reasoning minds is wasted on such a deeply *unreasonable* act as murder—to cleaning up the messes of the barbarians. In a way, the story remains the same. The priests need their steady supply of sinners. The innocent prey on the guilty. But the reason we keep returning to this story, I think, is less because of the connection between the unsolved and the divine than because violence is our most tantalizing sacrament. The sanctimonious ritual of the forensic dissection (as seen on TV) allows us to gaze upon death and sadism not only without guilt but with piety. It is only natural that we have ordained our detectives to the office of celebrityhood.

I am reading my copy of the police report when Frank Bender, the forensic sculptor, pulls me aside and tells me, out of the producer's earshot, that Richard Walter has offered to profile the Texas murder.

Frank has a white goatee and a silver incisor that winks at me from inside his own skull, which is shaped like a centaur's and bristled white. When you speak to Frank you can feel him limning the flesh-obscured contours of your own braincase with his beryllium eyes, as if he's curious how anyone has flesh on their skulls at all.

He asks if I'm wondering why he hadn't made any remarks during the meeting, and before I answer (I'm not), he tells me that he and Walter withheld their insights into the Texans' case in protest of the shameless media circus that certain board members have recently made out of what is supposed to be a cloistered event. It strikes me as funny, since I've spent some quality time with Frank, and I'm under the impression that he enjoys the quasi-celebrity more than the rest. He won't say any more about the inner circle's squabble but tells me that Richard Walter — who is notorious for refusing to write down his profiles — is going to dissect the case, now, out in the lobby by the ballroom. It is a rare opportunity. Walter, he says, is waiting for me.

Frank had already told me about the elusive Richard Walter a week ago, when I sat in his West End studio watching him repair a skull, delivered by the state police in a Rubbermaid cake keeper. The body had been found with its hands and feet and head chopped off, crudely divided between two burn barrels in the Poconos.

A human skull, proof of oblivion, is a surprisingly fragile, almost disappointing artifact: the longer I stared at this one the more incongruous it became to the idea of another human being or anything as interpersonally dynamic as murder. The back was ventilated by a charred hole. The right half of the face was a jagged void, the bone beneath the left socket marred with black like the grease under a quarterback's eye. Frank is comfortable enough with these objects that for an extra $300, if necessary, he would deflesh a head in his studio, but he does not do this much anymore because his wife, Jan, objects to the smell.

He works standing at a plaster-spattered table and wears a headset to field the phone calls that come every few minutes from agents, television producers, cops, or one of the many women eager to play with the bone cobbler come nightfall. Possibly because of the double espresso he downed before getting to work, his hands tremble as he tries to Krazy glue the skullcap back into place; it was removed during the autopsy and is yellower than the rest of the skull, which is bleached from defleshing agents. Dribbling glue around the ridge of the skull, he fumbles and nearly drops the lid. He slips again, catching the pate mid-fall.

When Danny DeVito's partner calls to discuss the third, or maybe it's the fourth, draft of the script, Frank gets the top flush with the rim of the open cranium and flips the skull upside down. The studio has just taken on another scriptwriter—they didn't like what the guy who wrote *Gladiator* had churned out.* Then another agent calls about the book that the author of a bestseller about shark attacks is going to do on the Vidocq Society. I read in the *New York Observer* that he got $800,000 for it, but some think it's a raw deal, since the movie rights were already sold. Frank takes a scorched potsherd of bone the size of a piece of broken toast from the cake tub—a fragment of maxilla—and aligns the upper, toothless jaw-

---

*I only hope that whoever ends up getting the script right for Mr. DeVito thinks to include the story about one of the Vidocq Society's first meetings, in which Frank jumped up and accused the presenter—the owner of a sex shop—of committing the very murder for which he was ostensibly seeking consultation. This is actually one of the reasons that the Vidocq Society now insists that only law enforcement present cases, rather than friends or family, but the story illustrates Frank's sixth sense perfectly. "I felt like he was coming in to find out how smart we were and get information from us so he could stay one step ahead." As usual, Frank turned out to be right, but as a consequence of his dramatic outburst at least one Vidocq member refuses to sit next to him at meetings anymore.

bone with the uncertain angle of the face. He traces Krazy glue along the fracture until it gleams like a milk mustache.

"Beautiful, beautiful," he says.

He walks across his hangar-size studio to a bucket and scoops up a gray clod of clay that he then takes into the kitchen area (a pair of scuffed handcuffs dangles with the woks and soup ladles) to soften it in the microwave. The studio is a renovated meat market (his wife's office is a walk-in meat locker) with taper-spiked gothic chandeliers hanging from iron chains. The place smells faintly of earth, like a city garden in late fall. The frieze of ghostly milch-colored plaster heads crowding the tiered shelves reminds me of gourds rotted white in an abandoned root cellar. Every level space sports a head. There's the bust he did for *People* of the 5,000-year-old man, with a vaguely thawed expression, found in the Italian Alps; there's the age-enhanced Symbionese Liberation Army fugitive he did for the FBI; there's a bald plaster head wearing rose-tinted heart-shaped glasses that looks like a wig mannequin—a facial reconstruction of a skull once tenuously matched to a woman's face on a carton of milk; there's a small cell of dangerous felons he's sculpted for *America's Most Wanted*, such as John List, the man who killed his wife, his three children, and his own mother before going on the lam for eighteen years. Ten days after Frank's bust appeared on the show, List was caught in Virginia. He had remarried, was attending a Lutheran church, and lived more or less under the exact circumstances that Frank and Richard Walter had predicted.

The studio is crammed with buckets, ladders, heads in varying stages of re-creation, maquettes of cop memorials, piles of bricks, postcards of nude Parisiennes, and an endless clutter of erotic and morbid novelties: a hand-carved pistol in the shape of a penis, the .22 rifle with which his father-in-law tried to shoot him in the head.

Once he has the maxilla in shape, his hands steadier now, he gently anchors a piece of lower jaw and sculpts the clay around the missing socket. He adjusts it back and forth like the rudder of a grim toy boat. When he gently shakes off the paper towel lining the cake tub, a thin gritty scree of pulverized bone trickles out. He sorts through the pieces and picks up a chunk of charred face the size of a Scrabble square. He turns it in his hands, rubbing it with his thumb, puzzling over it like a rune. The veins in his hand twitch as he flips and fondles the piece of jaw, oblivious to the fly buzzing around his head. It eventually alights on the rim of the cake keeper.

He sets up a camera on a tripod to look at the skull from different angles. It helps him think, he says, to look through a camera. He steps back, holding one wrist behind his back and kneading a ball of clay in his hidden palm. Using a shutter-cable release, he snaps a few shots, and then pinches off tiny globs of clay, making minute adjustments here and there. Holding the forehead firmly but gently like a father would to remove a speck from his child's eye, he stuffs the hollow until the mouth and throat look gagged with clay. Once the jaw is rebuilt into a discernible—if devastated—mouth, he flips the skull back right side up. The upper lip and chin is a goatee of charred bone. The skull looks as if it has eaten a mouthful of soot.

When he tells me that every face is individual, that each is unique and contains its own sort of divine unpredictable harmony, I believe him. It is Frank's unorthodox, bacchanalian spirit—his appetite for women and self-promotion, if not the eponym's violent misadventures—that makes me think of him as the Vidocqian most like Eugène François Vidocq (1775–1857). A great dissembler, an impostor, a thief, and a murderer, Vidocq spent his entire youth either in prison or on the run. Reading his *Memoirs*, in which the hero is "coupled with villains whose conduct was one tissue of impious blasphemy, atrocious rascality, and unutterable bestiality," I mainly wondered at the incapacity of the eighteenth-century

French penal system to keep a man behind bars for more than a few hours. The number of Vidocq's escapes is staggering. Between slipping out of his fetters under the nose of the bumbling gendarmerie, he joins Napoleon's fleet only to participate in a mutiny, fights duels, is arrested as a pickpocket, escapes, is jailed for brawling. He tricks widows and baronesses out of love and money. He disguises himself as a nun, a hussar, an Austrian butler. He forges a pardon and is sentenced to eight years of hard time, escapes, joins a band of pirates, is initiated into the secret society of the Olympiens. He runs with smugglers, is arrested again, escapes, becomes a mime, is finked out by a jealous clown. During a stint in prison at Toulon, Vidocq makes wooden toys. But after another attempted escape he is deprived of even that minor employment and spends the next six years shackled to his bench. Tired of his celebrity status as the greatest jailbreaker in France—peasants had it that he could turn himself into a bundle of hay to evade pursuit—he becomes a police informer to reduce his sentence. Not until Sammy "the Bull" Gravano will the world see another rat fink of Vidocq's caliber. But once released, he enjoys the work so much that he convinces the police to let him go undercover and to hire other ex-convicts in order to better infiltrate the underworld. "I preferred men whose records had given them a little celebrity," he wrote.

Thus is born the first plainclothes detective bureau in the world, the Brigade de Sûreté. After one raid, in which he led nearly forty men out of a tavern in handcuffs, he announced for all who cared: "I am Vidocq! Remember me!"

Given the scurrilous provenance of the detective, it's no surprise that the profession's reputation suffered for years. They were known deceivers who shared a lineage with the criminals they yoked. One Anglo prototype was the so-called thief-taker, the constable who specialized in regaining stolen goods by tracking down the robber, with whom he then split a portion of the booty before returning the remainder to the owner for a reward, "no questions asked." That detectives with Pinkerton, the first private agency in the United States, rented themselves out as strikebreakers did not help the public trust either.

Despite allegations that he concocted and then solved his own crimes to increase his fame, Vidocq was unquestionably ahead of his time. He made the first plaster casting of a shoe impression. He compared the slug found in a body with a test bullet eighty years before the ballistics pioneer Calvin Goddard. He analyzed bloodstains, dabbled in fingerprinting before Francis Galton, and wrote what may well be the first detective novel, *Les Voleurs*. He was the model for characters in novels by Balzac, Hugo, and the first detective story—or "tale of ratiocination"—by Edgar Allan Poe, "The Murders in the Rue Morgue."

When politics finally turned against Vidocq, costing him his post, he created the first *private* detective agency in the world. His clientele were mostly victims of swindlers and con men who exploited post-Restoration France's newly capitalized economy. The role of the detective in this new urban world—in America as well—was to be a lawful dissembler, a protean eavesdropper. To get at the truth one had to lie a little. Not much has changed, except that it's even easier to fake an identity (or to steal someone else's) and the world is shot through with private investigators. In New York alone the number of licensed private investigators has risen from 672 in 1992 to nearly 3,000 today. Both the increased availability of information on the Internet and the increased affordability of surveillance equipment help to account for the rise. But most PIs I spoke to, in the Vidocq Society and elsewhere, said the popularity of the work could be credited largely to television's glamorous portrayal of the job.

. . .

When Court TV is done with the Texans, we follow Frank out to the lobby, where we are met by a long-faced man in owlish glasses, elegantly slumped in a Louis XV chair, one black shoe crossed at the knee and a lanky arm and cigarette poised haughtily aloft. Looking for all the world like a Sherlock Holmes impersonator, or perhaps a droll public-television host who's been waiting to explain the fine but difficult movie we have just experienced and partly misunderstood, this is Richard Walter, among the four or five most famous criminal profilers in the world.

"I was going to let you just walk out," Walter says as Chief Deputy Kinney takes a chair facing him, and Detective Wooten and I sidle into a Victorian love seat. The detective, who kindly switches places with me so that I can hold my tape recorder under the profiler's nose, is short enough that I have a near-perfect bird's-eye view of his cropped scalp. He holds his fingers laced like one big fist between his knees.

Walter reveals, archly, that he already knows the suspect, Lance Barker, is the murderer. He gleaned this during the chief deputy's presentation by considering a few simple things. The clusters of behavioral *gestalten* . . . the probability factors . . . the subtypes of crimes . . . the constellations of criminal subtypes . . . the subtypes of probabilities: all patterns, to the discerning mind, as traceable as the frilly upholstery upon which the chief deputy is sitting forward uncomfortably, with pink tired eyes, looking as if maybe he's being had by this detective playboy, who finally concludes, with a dramatically circumflexed eyebrow, that this particular case, in his opinion, "is a classic compulsory power-assertive murder."

Deputy Kinney shoots a glance at Detective Wooten, who scratches the side of his scalp, which merges seamlessly downward into five o'clock shadow, and asks, "You said this is a classical what?"

"Power-assertive," Walter says, turning to watch a table the size of a belfry clock go wheeling past us into the ballroom. A second waiter follows pushing a rattling cart of water glasses. "What that generally means, in sex murders for instance, as the sexual emotion, as the sexual dynamic increases, the *percussion* of death increases. Therefore, as I become hotter or more involved, I have to feel the *percussion* of my fist against you. I have to feel the knife going into you. There are a whole constellation of characteristics for power-assertive, m'kay?" A tiny scar on his bottom lip quivers with ratiocinative pleasure. "What *you* have is an atypical."

Detective Wooten grins skeptically, drumming his stubby fingers on the arm of the couch.

Walter jabs a precarious minaret of ash in the detective's direction. "I have over 22,000 felony interviews under my belt, m'kay? I've been around the block, and I have over 30,000 death scenes when I was at the Los Angeles medical examiner's office. So I have some experience with this. I've seen hundreds of these."

The gist of Walter's method—in contrast to Frank's emphasis on the uniqueness of each individual face—is that we are hopelessly predictable. This view is not so different from those held by pioneer criminologists like Cesare Lombroso, the Italian phrenologist, who sought out patterns in the late nineteenth century by studying hundreds of inmates and then compiling a system of identifiable "criminaloid" types based on physical features, such as that "highwaymen have thick hair and odd-shaped heads." He also rejected the notion of free will. Alphonse Bertillon later improved upon anthropometry— the system of identifying criminals by precise measurements of noses, skull widths, arm lengths, height, and other body parts— which was eventually usurped by the more reliable method of fingerprinting devised by Francis Galton. Of course, if you read only the memoirs by retired special agents from the FBI's Behavioral Science Unit, men such as John Douglas and Robert Ressler, who formalized profiling in the 1970s, and consider the way catchy classifications like "organized" and "disorganized" murderer have been injected into the pop lexicon by movies such as *The Silence of the*

Lambs, you might think that they invented the idea.* But the general approach was already in print in 1486 in *The Malleus Maleficarum*, the manual used by Spanish inquisitors to identify witches.

Walter glares at the detective. "Incidentally, I'll also tell you why I know certain things, m'kay? In power-assertive cases, we know that the victim was alive if he was fucked. They will not—a lot of others will, but this particular subtype will not—if you're in the middle of a fuck, and you're strangling her, or whatever else, and she dies accidentally, they'll stop and they won't ejaculate. M'kay? Because it's only a pervert who fucks a dead body. And so I *know* it's a classic PA case. I know that the victim was alive when all that took place. Remember, he's ejaculated and/or masturbated, whether he did it inside him or he pulled his dick out and he groundshot it, then that's why he needed the towels to clean it off the sheets." He regards his watch, two black hands on a black face, without upsetting the still lingering ash of his Kool. He says that he already knows this particular type of murderer is trapped in a macho scenario of his own inflated ego's inadequate making and has killed because he has unforgivably violated his own strict self-image as a good Texan heterosexual. "Rules come into place. Absolute rules come into place. They're deathly afraid of being considered deviant. His style simply will not permit it."

Ressler, also a Vidocq Society member, took credit for coining the term "serial killer," though several other profilers told me that the term was in fact used in the 1950s. As recently as the D.C.-area sniper shootings, when a pageant of profilers came on TV nightly to guess the sniper's identity—most ended up being wrong—it was clear that the world of criminal profiling suffered from the small-pond big-fish syndrome. Since many of Walter's conclusions about criminal patterns were drawn from interviews with prisoners, it's also worth noting that the FBI's own similar research, often known as the "36 Offender Study," for which criminals were interviewed but agents neglected to corroborate the information provided with the case files, was so shoddy that, according to Brent Turvey, editor of The Journal of Behavioral Profiling, no peer-reviewed journal would publish the results.

Deputy Kinney strokes his mustache with a thumbnail, listening. Mouth slightly ajar, scalp damply ashimmer under the chandeliers, Detective Wooten looks hypnotized if not entirely comprehending. Walter's gestures have the tense predatory grace of a stork in a pond full of nervous frogs. I feel hypnotized, too—somewhat uncertain where this rampant speculation is all going. Somewhat like a frog.

"And what it is is, you're two young bucks. You're out. You're talking girls, you're talking this, you're talking that. Girls are not going to get that hepped up over you. So you get a lot of bravado. You get some alcohol in there, m'kay? And then you start playing." He reaches over and thwacks my knee. "And one things leads to the other. I should get a blow job, m'kay? Or sometimes they'll just kind of touchy-feely, whatever. Now you can get various combinations of that, m'kay? Where both parties denying in their mind's eye, because it's not manly to be a homosexual, but lo and behold they find themselves involved in homosexual-type behavior. They're moving toward it, m'kay? All of a sudden, one of them gets a breath of fresh air—*whoa*! Get your goddamn hands off my dick! Or whatever it is, m'kay? And ker-bang!" He lurches forward with the charade of a high-powered rifle in his hands. "It's called homosexual panic, m'kay?"*

---

*Most of the prominent criminal profilers—or at least the ones who sell books—focus on the sexual homicides. Some of the theories, such as Ressler's, smack of Freudian terms like "regressive necrophilia," a term he can legitimately take credit for having coined. "Jack the Ripper's murders, though they did not include coitus, were nonetheless sexual, because the murder weapon was a knife, and the thrusting of the knife into the body was a substitute for thrusting the penis. Most cops and psychiatrists have not understood the psychological significance of the knife or other such foreign objects; I studied the matter extensively, and labeled the practice of using such substitutes for the penis regressive necrophilia." Walter's monograph is on the topic at hand: homosexual panic.

Kinney shakes a Doral from a rumpled pack and balances a crystal ashtray on his knee. Smoke warps through the brush of his mustache.

"It's a situation of circumstance," Walter says. "Let's say the two of you—m'kay?—for whatever reason, are lying on the same bed." A bored, cruel simper lifts the scar on his lower lip. "Say you're drunk, and you're tired, and you're buddies, and you're cops, and you're this and you're that, and it's all cool and you feel machismo. All this kind of stuff. But then you wake up and your mouth is on his dick, m'kay?"

The Texans break out in pained, hysterical laughter, and the chief deputy actually puts his hands on the arms of his chair as if he's standing to leave us, but then he lays his hand across his shoe instead.

"We're not drinking tonight, pal," Detective Wooten says.

Walter leans toward Wooten. "Circumstance incontrovertible! I mean, that's proof. *Whoa!*" Chief Deputy Kinney is now plucking at the piping on the upholstery of his chair. "He knows, m'kay?" Walter makes eyes at the detective. "He's enjoying it. But you feel cheap and tainted."

Wooten queasily shakes his head, and says meekly, "It wouldn't be homicide, it'd be suicide."

"But you're going to shoot him, because he knows," Walter says, twirling a fresh unlit cigarette between his fingers as if he's screwing it into an invisible socket. "Remember this big image of this superman? You've just taken all the air out of that. *You're nothing but a cocksucker.*"

As if to remind Walter that they are talking about somebody else, Kinney slides a photo across the table. The profiler begins to extrapolate about the sissy nature of the victim's underwear, and soon enough the Texans, let off the hypothetical hook, get into the speculative mood, saying that as far as they're concerned the victim's pajamas were pretty sissy, too, not to mention his Mickey Mouse watch and "that mouthy bitch role," as Walter puts it, that the victim liked to play: his obnoxious tendency to get something on you and drive you crazy with it. Once they throw in the funny way the pillows are stacked and the wet sheets—evidence the Texans say made them suspect the relationship between Cody and Lance from the get-go, though they never bothered to test for semen over the course of a four-year investigation—the cops from Levelland and the prestigious criminal profiler have plumbed the suspect's psychological depths in absentia and have concocted a possibly libelous but ultimately probable scenario. The warm petal of Walter's thumb-print flares and then fades next to the dead man's boot.

"It all makes sense to me," Wooten says. "I mean . . ."

Kinney chuckle-snarls. "It shouldn't make sense."

"I was going to let you walk out, but I decided"—Walter lets out a triumphant guffaw that sends cigarette ash down his lapel—"you've got a case! Now, you see, before—you have to think about it a little bit, but I'll just do it for you, m'kay? What we've just done is given you a matrix that accounts for what's not there, what is there, and the staging that occurs after the fact. And behaviorally, now, we're even telling you about his MO. He needs control. He thinks he's being slick. He's taking the time, and he's savoring it in part, but then he has to get ahold of you guys. He thinks you're going to be dumber than dog shit. That you won't figure it out. But he wants you to, on one side. He's exactly in the position that he wants—he's a suspect—because that gives him power and importance."

The lawmen from Hockley County were planning on taking a long detour down to Washington, D.C., tonight to see the Vietnam Memorial and then back up to Baltimore to catch their morning flight home. But Frank and Walter want to show the Texans how the supercops party, though, technically, of course, neither is a cop.

Walter cajoles them into keeping their room at the Comfort Inn. Frank suggests we go to a west-side über-hip bar and restaurant called L2.

Waiting on the sidewalk outside the Downtown Club in the pumpkin light of late afternoon, Detective Wooten, who I now realize comes up only to my chest, asks if it's okay if he waves down our taxi. Frank and Richard have already flagged one and gone ahead. He's never done so before. I insist that he knock himself out, and he steps to the curb, arm lofted timidly.

"Lookit me! I'm wavin' down a cab, man!"

When we get to L2, which the Texans end up thinking is a gay bar, Richard and Frank are in the back, past the velvet curtains, in the cerulean glow of the fish tank, already buzzed. We come in on them venting about colleagues who they felt were playing for the camera at the meeting. Walter, who doesn't have an ounce of flesh on his bones, and in this light reminds me of an Edward Gorey creature, is shivering and complaining about how fucking cold it is in the restaurant. The Texans make shy-polite inquiries about the film Danny DeVito's going to make, to which Walter raises his fourth chardonnay and says, "They're making a movie about us: Frank's the pervert and I'm the guy with the big dick!"

That, Wooten says, wiping away tears of mirth, reminds him of this funny joke his friends like to make at his expense about how what *he's* got looks huge on him but only looks "this big" on another man.

Frank moans when the detective cocks his little finger.

Wooten excuses himself and then comes back a minute later and tells me, under his breath, that the bathroom doors just say "W.C." He's not sure which one to use. I assure him that he can use either.

"It's somewhat ambivalent depending on your mood," Walter says. "You have to sit for both."

The detective looks at me nervously. "Can I really go in there?"

When Chief Deputy Kinney excuses himself for a cigarette, Walter says, "Listen to them. Listen to the way they talk. A-yuk, a-yuk, a-yuk."

Frank orders another Cape Cod.

After the detective returns, Walter leans forward and says, "Listen, we didn't want to tell you, Wooten, but we got a complaint on you. You used the woman's W.C."

"C'mon!"

"You're lucky you didn't fall in," Walter says.

Over the next hour the mood changes as an undercurrent of tension between Walter and the detective, at first invisible, begins to escalate. Walter sees that the detective seems to enjoy being taunted mercilessly, but the nature of the detective's jokes seems to change from being a way of giving us something of himself, to show us that he takes himself lightly, to something more preemptive, akin to tossing chum to a shark. The detective tells me he's used to this kind of harassment, that his friends pick on him like hell for being short. "They say if we didn't love you we wouldn't pick on you." He tells me this with an almost apologetic intimacy. "Well, I wish you wouldn't love me so much."

Chief Deputy Kinney is dead quiet while he eats his meat loaf. When the owner, Nathon, comes over to our table to say hello, casually rubbing my back while he stands there, the deputy looks as if he would like to disappear under his cowboy hat, if only he'd disregarded his wife's advice to leave it at home.

In a lull, I ask Detective Wooten about the police report that I'd read while Court TV was taping Weinberg's deconstruction. I was drawn to several contradictions. At one point the bottle of cologne is described as being in Cody's hand, but then later described as resting at the foot of the bed. Another thing: if Cody was unconscious when he was killed—or while he was having gay ole sex—would he really have been found with a plug of chewing tobacco in his mouth? But the most vexing detail is the one I found in a supplementary report about another alleged suicide, in Lubbock, on the same date—July 19, 1996—just a couple of hours before Cody Rogers was killed. This other body, found shot in the head with a .22, belonged to the live-in boyfriend of a woman named Trwyna Leha Hays, who was Cody Rogers's ex-girlfriend. Trwyna, a topless dancer, had broken up with Cody after he'd punched her in the face a little less than a year earlier. Because the two victims' respective gunshots matched the calibers of Lance Barker's two missing weapons, I'm curious why Chief Deputy Kinney hadn't mentioned this coincidence earlier to the Vidocq Society.

"Whatchyo talkin' about?" Wooten says. "I must've missed that." He says Kinney never mentioned that part of the story. Frank is shocked to hear about it also. Immediately, I begin to fantasize that I've stumbled across a key piece of evidence that will end up providing the missing link and make me, however briefly, a sleuth to be reckoned with.

Frank shrugs, not exactly addressing the deputy. "We can only work with the information that's given to us. Why come to us if you're not going to give it all, you know, especially things like that? We have all these people together for free. Top experts in the country, in the world. I mean, how can we work a case to the max if we don't get the right information? It's like coming in with a half-loaded gun—maybe that's not the example." He twirls the lime in his Cape Cod.

"He committed suicide," Kinney says. "There was a suicide note and the suicide weapon—the .22 pistol—was right there with him. He was a married guy that had been dating this titty dancer in one of them bars."

Wooten slowly comes around. "Oh, yeah. Right. Yeah. It occurred at Ransom Canyon. It was ruled a suicide. Jamie left a note to his child and his parents. Yeah, I remember that now."

"You can't assume anything," Frank says. "You've got to go over the suicide note. You've got to see if it is in fact in his writing. This raises a whole bunch of new questions."

But it was just a weird coincidence, Kinney says. At first, he thought they really had something, too, so they chased down every lead about this woman with two dead boyfriends. "Got my heart beating when we started on that one." But there was nothing to it.

I ask how they know for sure that Lance's .22 was a rifle. There is no gun registry in Texas, after all. Kinney says he knows for a fact Lance owned a .22 rifle because the twelve-year-old neighbor boy who'd stopped by the trailer to latch the door had told him so.

I ask again if it could really just be a coincidence.

"Yeah, I think so," Wooten says. He reiterates what the chief deputy says: the other guy had a pistol.

"And you *know* that it was a .22 rifle Cody was missing?"

"Right." Wooten slaps me on the shoulder. "But that was good thinking, man."

Following Kinney's lead—he has ordered coffee—Detective Wooten orders a Dr Pepper. "Thank you ma'am," he says to the waitress, though he's obviously wishing it were another beer.

The chief deputy has come a long way to get answers, and by now he looks tired as hell. I wonder if he's glad he flew across the country to tell us his story. I wonder how much he regrets having stayed in Philadelphia instead of driving to Baltimore tonight. Cupping his coffee like a man who's leaking protoplasm, he thanks Frank and Richard again for their help today.

"Our job," Walter says, "is to look through bullshit."

Sensing that he's made the Texans uneasy, Walter picks up the tab. Later, standing on the sidewalk, Walter recovers some of his Edwardian dignity. "You're only as good as your current case," he says, shaking Chief Deputy Kinney's hand. "And only a fool rests on his laurels. But you guys had the facts. The guy with the facts drives."

Watching them walk away, Walter says, "I could have talked to them in professional terms, but they wouldn't have known what the fuck I was talking about."*

Frank leaves Walter and me alone in a decrepit bar called Doobie's. There is no reason why we are still out. He buys another round and then I buy him a drink. We seem to be sharing a complicitous, ugly mood. I look at him and I see that he is quite drunk and not at all the same composed mind I first met in the Downtown Club lobby. Slumped on the table in an unbecoming way, I doubt that I much resemble the version of me from nine hours ago either. We are deteriorating in front of each other's eyes. We are in denouement. At least the Texans will go home inspired, their cold case a little warmer, their timid suspicions about love-gone-bad reaffirmed. But they will also go home inspired to think differently, to think more like Vidocqians. They will go over all the evidence again with these new eyes, they will reinterview ex-girlfriends and old high school

*Later, when I told Detective Wooten that I was sorry they had left so early, he told me that Chief Deputy Kinney was afraid the supercops "were gonna get us in trouble." But perhaps they would have been better off if they'd stuck closer to Frank and Walter. "See, we had a little trouble when we left. We were walking around downtown and I was trying to flag a cab down, and the first two turned us down. And this black guy high on dope came up behind us. So we were keepin' an eye on him. And then another black guy, obviously a homosexual, made a crude comment to me. He said, 'Hey man, you want me to suck your dick?' So that ticked me off and I went after him. I was yellin' at him and Dave said, 'Rick, you're gonna get us killed! Let's get out of here!' So he grabbed me and we took off."

teachers and parents and sisters and the boy next door who could have stolen the gun and therefore reinforced the suspicion that Cody's death was a suicide, though it seems to Detective Wooten, the more he thinks about it, that a suicide would not have the prescience to anoint himself with cologne to mask the scent of his own impending decay. And so, with new eyes, the detective will keep returning to the faint yellow stains on the victim's T-shirt that no one else noticed, not even Richard Walter. Taking a chance, he will go out and buy a bottle of Stetson cologne and a hundred-percent cotton white Fruit of the Loom T-shirt. When he sprinkles the cologne over the T-shirt, the same faint yellow stains will appear, identical. He is a real sleuth. Then it will only be a matter of time— so much has passed already it hardly makes any difference—before the lab confirms this insight, and Lance Barker, whose fingerprints have subsequently been found on the cologne, is placed at the scene of the crime, and they will have their long-awaited grand jury. Of course, in this detective story, the identity of the killer was never much in question. Perhaps it is this lack of suspense that gives me the terrible impulse—I have felt it since we came in the bar—to ask the forensic psychologist to profile me. I can see that he sees through me already, like he saw through the detective—like the detective saw through him—but whatever it might mean in this context, I have a self-destructive impulse to reveal my darkest side to a complete stranger, to confess that part of me identifies more with the killer than the victim, because the killer is always a victim of free will. He regards me with sallow features that remind me of pictures of Poe—the dark-circled eyes inverted by the morbid contemplation of the endless sadism of the human soul. For Poe, who said that Vidocq was just a "good guesser," just as some detractors say that profilers are only "glorified mystics," the genius of the detective was not deduction so much as being able to cross into the "spirit" of his *opponent*. It's not so much that I fear Walter will tell me something dreadful as that he won't detect anything at all. But then he tells me that no, he doesn't do that. Not for free. Finally I have the sense to order coffee. Then, having missed the last train, I hail a cab for home.

———

A patient man, Chief Deputy David Kinney is still waiting for the lab results that will tell him whether the faint yellow stain across the front of Cody Rogers's powder-burned T-shirt was in fact Stetson cologne. He remains convinced that this vaguely discernible, fragrant Rorschach will ultimately place Lance Barker—whose fingerprints were found on the cologne bottle—at the scene of the crime. No less comfortable with the possibility that "it might be some gay thing," as he puts it, and as the Vidocq Society so fearlessly insinuated, he is undeterred by the fact that the only DNA found on Cody Rogers's T-shirt belonged to the victim alone.

Another development is that the Vidocq Society movie deal fell apart with the dissolution of Jersey Films. Another studio has yet to pick it up. Detective Rick Wooten rejoined the army as a drill instructor in Chicago, where, one hopes, opportunities to hail a cab remain plentiful.

Frank Bender is now working on the Juárez case in Mexico. Ciudad Juárez, right over the border from El Paso, is the site of one of the most horrific unsolved mysteries in modern history. Over the past ten years, 370 women, many of them young girls working at maquilas, *or assembly plants, have been sexually assaulted, tortured, and murdered. Working independently of the Vidocq Society, Frank is joined by fellow Vidocqian, Bob Ressler, the famous criminal profiler immortalized in* The Silence of the Lambs. *While there recently for a grueling six weeks, working around the clock in his hotel room with five of the unidentified heads, Frank received a death threat in the middle of the night and had to be relocated by the police (police who, as it happens, were later arrested for being tangled up in the local car-tel). His devotion to solving these brutal murders should be inspira-tion for local and federal authorities whose dedication to putting an end to a decade of terror has been shamefully lackluster. Currently, Congresswoman Hilda Solis of California is looking for cosponsors of House Resolution 466, which calls on the U.S. government to take decisive action in Ciudad Juárez.*

A MISCARRIAGE OF JUSTICE
ROBERT F. KENNEDY JR.

The tragedy of Martha Moxley's death, twenty-seven years ago, has been compounded by the conviction of an innocent man.

I know Michael Skakel, my first cousin, as well as one person can know another. He helped me to get sober, in 1983. We attended hundreds of alcoholism-recovery meetings together. In that context and others we have shared our deepest feelings. For fifteen years we skied, fished, hiked, and traveled together, often with my wife and children. During that time I sometimes spent as many as two or three weekends a month in his company. Like nearly everyone else who knows him well, I love Michael. If he were guilty, I would have testified against him. He is not.

Until I recently visited him in prison, the two of us had been estranged for several years. Beginning in 1998, stress from the public focus on Michael as a murder suspect began to affect his personality. He lashed out at the Kennedy family, which he believed was partly responsible for his predicament, and refused to speak to me. On the two days I attended his court proceedings last year, in Norwalk, Connecticut, he was cold and distant. Many people asked me why I would publicly defend him—a cause unlikely to enhance my own credibility. I support him not out of misguided family loyalty but because I am certain he is innocent.

The Skakels rarely discussed the Moxley case among themselves, and mostly didn't read press reports about it—the first because of family culture and legal advice, the second because most of the press coverage was biased, inaccurate, and painful. "We never talked about it," Michael's sister, Julie, recently told me. "Through all the years we never discussed this. We never compared notes." Michael's conviction shocked his six siblings into talking about the case with one another, and with me. For the first time, they shared their memories of the night when Martha Moxley was killed. In preparing this article I spoke to each of them; to other witnesses; to Michael's lawyers; and to investigators. I read police and press reports about the case and put together the story for myself.

MARTHA MOXLEY

Just after noon on Halloween, 1975, Martha Moxley, age fifteen, was found lying facedown on her family property in the Belle Haven section of Greenwich, Connecticut. Her blue jeans and underpants were pulled down. Although strong evidence suggests that the attack was a sexual assault, the police concluded that Martha had not been raped. Her body had been dragged across the grass on a zigzag path from the Moxley driveway to the side of the lawn and hidden below the drooping boughs of a pine tree. She had been struck several times in the head with a Toney Penna golf club—so ferociously that the club had shattered into multiple pieces—and then stabbed in the neck with the broken shaft. The club's handle and part of the shaft had vanished.

Martha was last seen the night before, at the home of the Moxleys' neighbor Rushton Skakel, my mother's brother and the father of six boys and a girl. The Skakel family residence contained many golf clubs, including a set of Toney Pennas that had belonged to Rushton's wife, Anne Reynolds Skakel, who had died of cancer two years before. The Skakels played chip and putt in their yard, and were known for leaving sports equipment scattered around the property. Rushton kept golf clubs at each door, and would carry one on his daily walk in order to ward off the numerous dogs in Belle Haven.

On the evening of Martha's murder Rushton was away on a hunting trip. The family's new live-in tutor, Kenneth Littleton, took the older children—Rush Jr., Thomas, John, Julie, and Michael— to the Belle Haven Club for dinner, along with their cousin Jim Terrien and their friend Andrea Shakespeare. Littleton later told the police that he and the children had had one Heineken each. Tom, seventeen, said they'd had several beers and some hard liquor.

The police established that the Skakel party returned home at 8:45 PM. Martha Moxley and Helen Ix and Geoffrey Byrne, other neighbors, met Michael in the driveway, where they sat in the Skakels' Lincoln listening to music. At 9:15 Tom joined Michael and Martha in the front seat.

Around 9:30 Rush Jr. and John came from the Skakel house and told everyone that they were going to drive Jim back to the Terrien house, twenty minutes away in North Greenwich, where they would watch *Monty Python's Flying Circus*. Tom and Martha got out. Michael climbed into the backseat, as his older brothers ordered, and the four of them set off. Helen and Geoff headed home. They last saw Tom and Martha engaging in romantic horseplay near the driveway.

Eighteen years later Tom would tell investigators that after the other boys left, he'd had a "sexual" encounter with Martha that lasted twenty minutes, ending in mutual masturbation to orgasm. Around 9:50 the two rearranged their clothes, and Martha said good night. Tom last saw her hurrying across the rear lawn toward her house to make her curfew.

Using evidence from the autopsy, the police determined that the murder took place at around 10:00 PM. Several people, including Dorthy Moxley, Martha's mother, Helen Ix, and David Skakel, then aged twelve, heard dogs howling furiously from 9:50 to 10:30

with, Helen said, a "scared violent barking." Michael and his older brothers did not return to Belle Haven until 11:20.

THE FIRST SUSPECTS

The writer Dominick Dunne, a driving force behind Michael Skakel's prosecution, continually accused the Skakel family of using its power and Kennedy connections to intimidate the Greenwich police "to protect one of their own." In 1991 Dunne wrote in *Vanity Fair*, "It is thought in the community and elsewhere that Kennedy influence was brought to bear." In 1996 he told a UPI reporter, "The [Skakel] family is so powerful that since the first night the police have never been able to question family members." In 2000 Dunne said on CNN, "The Skakels were able to hold off the police all these years. . . . If this was a family of lesser stature, that simply would not have happened."

Reporters who conducted serious investigations into Dunne's charges found them to be false. Leonard Levitt, a reporter for *Newsday* who wrote the most thorough journalistic treatment of the Moxley case, concluded that although inept work by a police department that had not investigated a homicide for decades may have let the killer go free, this had nothing to do with intimidation by the Skakels. In an exhaustive 1997 article in *The Hartford Courant*, Joel Lang concluded that Dunne's accusations "probably sprang more from bias than fact." "There was no cover-up," Levitt told Lang. "There was a screwup." John Elvin, who in 1999 wrote a comprehensive investigative piece on the murder for the magazine *Insight on the News*, described the Skakels as "cooperative—somewhat bizarrely . . . even participating in the search for evidence and serving coffee and snacks to the cops." The Greenwich police detective Stephen Carroll, who was one of the first officers to arrive on the scene, told the *New York Daily News* that Rushton Skakel "was so cooperative and there was the feeling that no one there could have done it."

Everyone in the Skakel house spoke to police investigators freely and without counsel. All the Skakels, including Michael, indicated their willingness to take polygraph tests, and at least two family members did take them. In the months after the murder Tom Skakel submitted to multiple interviews and two lie-detector tests; Rushton gave detectives permission to take hair samples from Tom and to obtain his school, medical, and psychological records. With the family's consent the police drained the Skakels' pool and took soil samples from their yard. Rushton allowed the police to use his house as an informal neighborhood headquarters while they investigated the crime. Garbage from the house was searched regularly.

Dunne and, later, his friend and protégé, the former Los Angeles detective Mark Fuhrman (who had become notorious for lying under oath during the O. J. Simpson trial), would complain that the Greenwich police never obtained a search warrant for the Skakel residence, saying they didn't dare. "Someone bowed to influence," Dunne concluded in the 1991 *Vanity Fair* article. But Rushton gave the police a signed consent-to-search form and full access to the house, and allowed them to examine it whenever they wanted. Stephen Carroll and his colleague James Lunney conducted several thorough searches. "It was an open house—he'd never even go with us," Carroll told Fuhrman. Rushton also gave the police keys to his Catskills ski house, in Windham, New York. Carroll explained to *The Hartford Courant*, "People criticize us for not getting search warrants. But [the Skakels'] attitude was, 'Oh, yes, help yourself.'" He explained to Fuhrman, "We never thought there was any reason to get a search warrant, because we had already been through the house. Up one side, down the other."

Contrary to Dunne's assertions, the Skakels never got a break from the police, who immediately began focusing on Tom Skakel and a twenty-six-year-old Moxley neighbor as the primary suspects. Because Tom was the last person known to have seen Martha alive, he was interrogated for nearly six hours at police headquarters as soon as Martha's body was discovered.

This unusual level of cooperation lasted for three months. In late January, as the police intensified their focus on Tom, Rushton Skakel finally hired a criminal lawyer, Emanuel Margolis, to represent Tom. Margolis took the common precaution of shutting down access to his client. Pledging continued cooperation, he asked investigators to submit to him any further questions for family members. Margolis and Thomas Sheridan, Rushton's longtime friend and corporate attorney, met and spoke with the police and the state attorney's office periodically, conveying questions to and answers from family and household members. In the early 1990s the Skakels opened their Belle Haven and Windham houses and allowed police officers to thoroughly search their houses and property with a newly developed metal detector, to gather stain samples from household carpets, and to videotape every room. Tom was willing to testify at Michael's trial; prosecutors called him to Connecticut from Massachusetts, where he now lives, but they canceled his appearance the night before he was scheduled to testify. Michael, too, never hesitated to help police investigators. Last year, when it was reported that the state attorney's office had DNA from scrapings taken from under Martha's fingernails at her autopsy, Michael was perfectly willing to comply with the request for his own DNA for testing. The old evidence could not be linked to anyone other than Martha, however, so the prosecution withdrew its request for Michael's samples.

Sheridan's perception of the Greenwich police contradicts Dunne's. According to Sheridan, "There was a faction within the Greenwich police who were not interested in any evidence that did not point to Tom Skakel." Sheridan believes that police investigators violated Tom's constitutional rights by interrogating him when he was a minor for almost nine hours without counsel, more than five of those with no adult present. The police refused to hand over those interviews to Margolis. The police repeatedly lost or mishandled evidence that might have exculpated Tom, including a piece of the golf-club shaft that was found with the body, a white hair pulled by the roots and found on Martha's body, and vaginal swabs taken by the Connecticut medical examiner. In May 1976 the Greenwich police submitted to the state attorney's office an application for a bench warrant charging Tom with the murder. "The application was based on all kinds of shaky evidence," Harold Pickerstein, the attorney for Jack Solomon, then the chief inspector in the Fairfield County state attorney's office, recently told me. (Solomon, who is now the chief of police in Easton, Connecticut, will not discuss the case.) Solomon and the state's attorney Donald Browne concluded that the application did not meet legal standards for probable cause and refused to sign it. "I read it," Browne recently told me, "and there was nothing in there other than the fact that he was the last to see her alive and that he'd had some mental problems in the past." (Tom had suffered a serious childhood brain injury and related seizures.) Browne also said that he remembers pressure from the police to charge Tom: "There was some suggestion that if you issue a warrant, nobody will accuse you of not doing your job. But I don't do things that way."

In January 1976 Rushton had been hospitalized with chest pain soon after he realized that the police considered Tom a serious suspect. Rather than close ranks to protect a killer, though, as Dunne and Fuhrman claim the family did, Rushton initiated his own investigation to determine whether his children could have had any involvement in the murder. All the children underwent batteries of psychological tests and were hypnotized and injected with sodium pentothal—so-called truth serum, which disinhibits subjects. (Today's justice system regards sodium pentothal and sodium amytal, which also has a disinhibiting effect, with a combination of credence and suspicion similar to that with which it views polygraphs.) Michael, who was not a suspect at the time, took a sodium-pentothal test in 1980 and two more in the early 1990s; after each one, Margolis says, psychiatrists concluded that he had not committed the crime. Tom was examined by prominent doctors and subjected to neurological and psychological testing at Presbyterian Hospital in New York City. In March 1976 the doctors concluded, according to Margolis, that Tom could not have committed the crime. The Skakel family lawyers conveyed the results of these tests to the police.

In the early investigations Michael Skakel was never a serious suspect. Three witnesses said that he was miles away, watching *Monty Python*, when the murder occurred, and John Skakel's testimony was polygraph-certified. To anyone who knew him at the time, the notion that he was the murderer is laughable. (Our families were not then close, and I saw him little.) A scrawny kid who had just turned fifteen, Michael was always the smallest person in his class and at summer camp. He almost certainly lacked both the power to inflict the gruesome damage done to Martha Moxley and the presence of mind to meticulously dispose of the abundant forensic evidence. Don Mallard, a physician who knew Michael and who examined Martha's body, told Mrs. Victor Ziminsky, a Skakel family friend who later told me, that it was "impossible" that Michael could have wielded a golf club with the savagery or strength needed to shatter the shaft and drive it through Martha's body. Mallard, who has since died, said it was equally unlikely that Michael could then drag Martha, who matched him in weight, to the tree, more than a hundred yards from where she was first attacked. The photos used against Michael in court, in which he looks bulky, were taken four years after the murder. Family members told me that at the time of the murder Michael weighed 120 pounds and had a twenty-inch waist.

The case has remained unsolved for so many years not because of Skakel wealth, power, and connections but because it is baffling. There have been more than 600 unsolved murders in Connecticut since Martha's death, several of them in Greenwich. This one was especially difficult because of a parade of more than forty potential suspects. Besides Tom Skakel and the other neighbor these included Franz Wittine, a German gardener who lived in the Skakels' basement and liked to boast of how he had raped and beaten girls as a soldier during World War II. Wittine, who gave four different alibis, liked young blondes and was physically powerful. He was notorious for his lascivious advances toward Julie Skakel and her girlfriends, some of whom were too frightened of him to visit the Skakel house. Back steps leading to his room in the basement allowed him to come and go without notice. Shortly after the murder Wittine disappeared for a short time, quitting his job just a few months shy of the twenty years that would have qualified him for a pension from a Skakel-owned company—a choice that dramatically affected his financial position. He died in 2000.

Also on the list was Ken Littleton, the Skakel family tutor, who in the fall of 1976 emerged as the police's strongest suspect.

KEN LITTLETON

In 1975 Kenneth Wayne Littleton Jr. was a burly twenty-three-year-old graduate of Williams College, where he'd played rugby; he taught science and coached football at the Brunswick School, in Greenwich. Rushton Skakel had hired Littleton as a live-in tutor and companion to care for his motherless children. Littleton had begun work for the Skakels and visited their home the previous week, and moved in on the day of the murder.

Under police questioning the following day Littleton claimed that after arriving home from dinner he had gone to the master bedroom, on the second floor, where he remained until morning. He said he had neither heard nor seen anything suspicious. Two weeks later, on November 14, Littleton admitted that he had not stayed upstairs but had gone downstairs to watch TV and had seen Tom and Michael Skakel outside with Martha Moxley. He would later deny ever having seen Martha. On December 10 Littleton again changed his story, now saying that from 9:15 to 9:30 he had left the house and walked around the property to look for the Skakel boys. Littleton told the police that he saw no one during his search.

On April 2, 1976, Mildred Ix, Helen's mother and a confidante of Rushton's, told the police that "girlie magazines were found in Mr. Littleton's room," and that he was in the habit of visiting the Skakel gazebo in the nude. She urged them to look again at Littleton. When detectives questioned him later that month, he changed his story for the third time, saying that on the evening of October 30 he had come down to the first floor after watching TV upstairs. When he entered the kitchen, the Skakels' elderly nanny, Margaret Sweeney, asked him to check the driveway, where she'd heard "a fracas caused by the kids." Littleton now said that he went to the area and saw no one, but heard rustling noises coming from the bushes. Police records kept by Jack Solomon show that Littleton now recalled leaving the Skakel house at 10:30 PM—an hour later than he'd earlier claimed. Police examiners gave Littleton three lie-detector tests on October 18, 1976. Each test indicated that Littleton was lying when he denied killing Martha Moxley or knowing the location of the missing golf-club pieces. The police confronted Littleton with his test results and asked him to submit to a sodium-pentothal examination. When Littleton refused, the police began looking more closely. They found that his behavior had changed "markedly" since Martha's death.

In April 1976 Rushton Skakel had fired Littleton after the police visited the Skakel home and reported that Littleton had wrapped his car around a tree in a drunken accident and then abandoned it. Littleton moved to Nantucket, where he traded his preppy clothes for a white outfit with a shark's-tooth necklace framed by an unbuttoned shirt. Walking around town, he would look at himself in store windows, fixing his hair and flexing his muscles. People who had known him previously told the police that he was "bizarre and obnoxious" and had changed for the worse. That summer the Nantucket police arrested Littleton on charges of burglarizing several gift shops. In July, Littleton knocked down a woman employee of the Nantucket Police Department after she casually bumped his dancing partner. That month a Nantucket tourist awoke to find Littleton lying naked on top of her. He had broken in through her bedroom window. Littleton was then living with a woman who told police that he sometimes "forced himself on her sexually" and often erupted in fits of violence, smashing things in her apartment.

When the Greenwich police learned of Littleton's arrest, they persuaded Nantucket prosecutors to offer to reduce Littleton's felony charge to a misdemeanor if he would submit to a sodium-amytal interview about the Moxley murder. Littleton refused, and pleaded guilty to the felony—a plea that ended his teaching and coaching career. In May 1977 the Nantucket court gave him a suspended sentence and placed him on probation. In explaining his crime spree to the judge, Littleton said, "When I drink I flip out."

Jack Solomon, of the Fairfield County state attorney's office, and the Greenwich detective Stephen Carroll were convinced that Littleton had murdered Martha Moxley. But they lacked the hard evidence needed for an effective prosecution. The many other plausible suspects would give potential defense attorneys ample opportunity to introduce reasonable doubt, which would prevent a jury from convicting Littleton. The common thinking was that only a confession would result in a conviction. Solomon and Browne resisted the temptation to arrest a suspect in the murder just to appease public demand that they solve it. And so the Moxley murder investigation petered out and became a "cold file."

In 1982 Littleton moved to Florida, where he lived as a street person and was arrested for a variety of crimes, including trespassing, disorderly conduct, drunk driving, public intoxication, and shoplifting. In one incident he climbed a sixteen-story structure and gave President John F. Kennedy's *"Ich bin ein Berliner"* speech. When he was arrested, he told the police that he was "Kenny Kennedy," the black sheep of the Kennedy family.

That year Littleton met Mary Baker, who was also an alcoholic and was in recovery. They moved to Canada and married in Ottawa on April 27, 1983. In a 1991 interview with the Connecticut police conducted in Ottawa—an interview that has never been published—Baker described Littleton as "going nuts" in February 1984 after he started talking about the Moxley murder. He called Martha's father, David Moxley, Baker said, and asked for money to undergo sodium-pentothal testing, offering to give Moxley copies of the tapes. Littleton said he thought the testing would give him peace of mind and perhaps help him to remember things that happened the night of the murder. He told Moxley that Martha's murder was their "mutual tragedy." Despite his offer to David Moxley, Littleton never did submit to a sodium-pentothal test, although, according to his wife, he remained obsessed by the idea.

In Canada, Littleton was unable to work owing to instability and alcoholism. He and Baker played golf and lived off money she had inherited. Baker told the police that Littleton liked pornography and would often visit strip bars. In June 1983 his arm was mangled during a knife fight in Hull, Quebec. That autumn the Canadian police arrested him for disruptive conduct near the Canadian Parliament building. After his release the couple moved to Belmont, near Boston.

By 1984, Baker said in her later statements to the police, Littleton had begun identifying himself again as "Kenneth Kennedy," and believed that he could cause a tornado or a hurricane by flushing the toilet. He ate money, drank toilet water, left golf clubs at synagogues, and collected JFK matchbooks. He was often sick from drinking and occasionally suffered delirium tremens. Baker said that while on a trip through Connecticut in February 1984, Littleton told her he saw pink elephants and believed that he had magical powers. The police took him to a hospital, and he was in and out of psychiatric facilities over the subsequent years. In November 1984 Littleton locked Baker and their new baby out of the house; the Belmont police arrested him and reportedly found a knife collection. Baker explained that Littleton had carried a knife in his sock ever since his stabbing in Canada—which he later described to the grand jury as an attempted hit by the Skakel family.

In April 1985, following another alcohol-induced mental breakdown, Littleton was admitted to Charles River Hospital. In 1986 he became active in an alcoholism-recovery group, but he slipped repeatedly and was plagued by hallucinations and manic depression. In October 1988 he began staying in Williamstown, Massachusetts, where he stalked the Williams rugby team, attended school sporting events, and played golf. According to police reports, Littleton told security officers at Williams that he was a reformed alcoholic and that drinking and drugs had destroyed his life. At one point he cornered the college's dean, William R. Darrow, in his office to request a job advising the rugby team on substance abuse, causing Darrow to "fear for his personal safety" and scaring him "to death." Darrow later described Littleton to the police as "big . . . and extremely angry." Police reports quoted him as saying that Littleton had started talking about the Moxley murder and "became very intense." Darrow told the police that Littleton was "nuts" and that his encounter with Littleton was "one of the most frightening experiences of his life."

According to Baker, Littleton sometimes threatened to kill her. He would become particularly depressed, she told the police, around Halloween, the anniversary of Martha's murder. In October 1989 she threw him out and separated from him. In May 1990 he threw hot coffee on her and tried to force his way into her house. Littleton moved in with a manic-depressive stripper named Kimberly, in

Boston's Combat Zone. He planned to become a male stripper and join Kimberly in her act. He and Baker were divorced on July 12, 1990.

By August 1991, when Connecticut law-enforcement authorities reopened the Moxley case, Littleton, still a prime suspect, had again been institutionalized, for manic depression and paranoid delusions, at McLean Hospital, in Belmont. Jack Solomon; Sergeant Frank Garr, of the Greenwich police; and Detroit homicide detectives, whom the Greenwich police had brought in to help them with their investigation, all believed that Littleton might be responsible for a string of unsolved homicides of young women in Massachusetts, Florida, Maine, New York, and Canada. On September 23, 1991, Garr went to Ottawa to examine the police files on three young women who had disappeared during a twenty-three-day period in 1988. None of the bodies were ever found. In Garr's report he concluded, "All three women were last seen in the same vicinity . . . within close proximity to where Ken Littleton had resided."

That month the Greenwich police interviewed Mary Baker and informed her that they suspected Littleton was a serial killer. She told the police, as described in a previously unpublished 1993 search-warrant application for Littleton's hair and blood samples, that "Littleton had frequently and compulsively" made incriminating statements about the Moxley murder. She said that from the time she met Littleton, in 1982, he had been obsessed and paranoid over the Moxley case and described the incident as "a monkey on his back." She told the police that Littleton had said that "maybe some wickedness took him over for five minutes." She said that Littleton was plagued with "a nagging doubt, because he's not a well man, and [because of] the fact it was not resolved."

On December 4, 1991, according to the search-warrant request, Mary Baker called Garr to say that she'd just had a telephone conversation with Littleton during which he worried that the Connecticut state police might find the missing golf-club handle and trace his fingerprints. "Even if I'm innocent, I could be charged with murder," she said he told her. "Let's say a hunter or someone tripped over them in the woods." She said that he mentioned a pair of pants that he said might have Martha's blood on them. The police knew that Littleton, at his own suggestion, had taken some of the Skakel boys to the family's Catskills cabin the weekend after the killing, and they speculated that he could have disposed of the evidence then. The police report noted that while in Windham, Littleton had borrowed a shotgun from Rushton's friend and attorney Thomas Sheridan, saying he wanted to go hunting in the woods.

With Baker's permission, the police began taping conversations between the estranged couple. In a conversation taped by the police on February 10, 1992, Littleton acknowledged to Baker that he had been in an alcoholic blackout on the night of the murder — a significant admission, because he had previously told the police he'd drunk just a single beer. On the same tape Baker reminded Littleton of a conversation during the previous Thanksgiving when Littleton had "renounced the Martha Moxley secret" to her and admitted he was present when Martha died. She reminded him that he had talked to her about a hunting trip and had said, "I hope they don't find it, I hope they don't find, you know, my pants, I didn't do it, it was an accident." She also reminded him that in September he had described details of the killing. "Oh God," she told Littleton he had said. "She wouldn't die. I had to stab her through the neck." She said to Littleton, "I mean, you convinced me that you did it." Littleton's responses on the tape are noncommittal.

LITTLETON: You think I did it?
BAKER: I, I can't say right this minute. But you convinced me, this is what I've been living with . . .
LITTLETON: Um, um.

When this and several similar tapes, including Littleton's many confused denials of Baker's recollections, were played at the trial, Michael Skakel's prosecutors argued that the police who were recording Littleton's conversations were causing Baker to plant these ideas in his head. Mary Baker herself testified that Littleton "never made any admission as to his complicity in the crime" and that she believed "he didn't commit the murder." But Jack Solomon strongly defended his belief in her earlier statements to the police. At the trial he testified, "Our hope was . . . to corroborate what [Baker] told us about him, all the statements that he made . . . for several months." Solomon said that based on her information his department had devoted enormous resources to searching the wilderness around Windham with officers and dogs for the golf-club handle and pants. "If I put her up to that," he said, "I certainly would not have gone up there and tried to corroborate. The tape speaks for itself."

On December 15, 1992, Littleton took a polygraph exam administered by the nationally recognized polygraph expert Robert Brisentine. The test again indicated that Littleton "was not truthful when he denied causing the death of Miss Moxley." After confirming these results in a second test, Brisentine left the examining room. According to someone close to the conversation, he took Solomon aside and said, "The man who murdered Martha Moxley is sitting in that room. Don't ever let anyone persuade you otherwise." A similar version of the same event is reported in Timothy Dumas's *Greentown* (1998). Brisentine himself recently told me that he doesn't recall having said that, but added that he did ask to interrogate Littleton further at the time, because "even if he didn't commit the crime, he definitely had guilty knowledge of the crime and probably knows who did." By now Littleton had failed five polygraphs about the Moxley murder.

That same month, during a tape-recorded conversation with a

state-retained psychiatrist, Kathleen Morall, Littleton wondered whether he "could have" committed the crime. Earlier that year the forensic scientist Henry Lee had identified two hairs found on or near Martha's body as "microscopically similar" to Littleton's. One of these was later determined to be from someone of Asian descent; the other was destroyed during testing.

In an interview in October 1992, Littleton told the police that he'd heard dogs barking when he wandered the Skakel yard around 9:30 PM. This directly contradicted what he had earlier told the police. In his earlier interviews and during his polygraph tests on October 18, 1976, Littleton had claimed that Margaret Sweeney sent him outside to check on the "fracas" in the driveway area. During those polygraphs, the 1993 search-warrant request explained, "Littleton was specifically asked if he'd heard a dog, to which he answered 'no.' Littleton then volunteered that he did not hear any barking" when he went outside, and that he had heard no barking dogs "throughout the night." Mary Baker later told the police that Littleton had a peculiar hatred of dogs, "specifically when they bark." She did not say when that hatred began.

This is consistent with Solomon's speculation that after Sweeney asked Littleton to check on the fracas, Littleton's hatred of dogs prompted him to grab a golf club stored near the door. Outside he heard the rustling of Tom and Martha in the bushes. Inflamed and in an alcoholic stupor, he followed Martha as she walked toward her house. When she refused his advances, he struck her and dragged her under the evergreen boughs. In Solomon's judgment, the zigzagging path across the yard, first toward a neighbor's house and then back to the pine tree, indicates a perpetrator unfamiliar with the terrain. The tree under which Martha's body was found was adjacent to a path used daily by local children as a shortcut from southern Belle Haven to Walsh Lane, where many of their friends lived. According to Sheridan, the Skakel family lawyer, "Anyone familiar with the neighborhood would have dragged her another ten yards into the tall grass, where she might have remained hidden for days."

Julie Skakel told me that she talked with Littleton as he entered the kitchen from the pantry, at around 10:00 PM. The location is inconsistent with any of his alibis: when he first told of leaving the house, he said he had reentered through the front door. The door to a mudroom off the pantry was the only place one might expect to enter the Skakel home unobserved. Littleton had changed from the plaid shirt he had worn at dinner, Julie said, into a sweatshirt. A part-time security guard, Charles Morganti, had described seeing a 200-pound, six-foot man near the Moxley yard at the time of the murder. A composite portrait based on Morganti's report, withheld by prosecutors during the Skakel trial and released afterward, is a dead ringer for Littleton. The day after the murder the Skakel maid found laundered dungarees and Tretorn sneakers in the laundry room. The pants, for a thirty-six-inch waist, and shoes were too large to fit any member of the Skakel family. The police thought that the clothing had been washed too vigorously for any blood traces to show up, according to Thomas Sheridan. Then the police lost these critical pieces of evidence. Finally, Tom Skakel told me that he and Littleton had watched *The French Connection* after 10:00 on the night of the murder, and that Littleton had kept his body entirely covered with a blanket—something Tom had considered odd, because it was not cold in the room. Julie has no memory of seeing bloody pants. In Littleton's defense, there are inconsistencies and memory gaps among the stories of the dozens of witnesses I interviewed recently. I have no reason to believe that any of them deliberately lied to me.

In February 1993 Littleton told the police that he was no longer willing to cooperate in the investigation. In 1994 Solomon told Sheridan that Boston authorities had impounded Littleton's car after a run-in with a Boston policeman. Sheridan recently told me that Solomon then showed him and Emanuel Margolis, Tom Skakel's lawyer, a black three-ring binder containing photos of the bodies of teenage girls fatally bludgeoned within the vicinity of Littleton's various homes. Littleton was a suspect in the murders, Solomon told him. Solomon said he was trying to assemble an arrest warrant for Littleton in the Moxley murder. For unknown reasons the warrant was never obtained. In the summer of 1998 Connecticut's attorney general granted Littleton lifetime immunity and removed him from the suspect list in exchange for his testimony before a rarely invoked one-man grand jury called to indict Michael Skakel.

In July 1999 Littleton called the *Greenwich Time* from McLean Hospital and said that the Kennedy family was trying to kill him. Shortly after being released he stabbed himself four times in the chest with a kitchen knife. The police who searched his apartment found the charred pages of a diary, torn from the binding and burned. Littleton refused to talk with the police about the stabbing.

DOMINICK DUNNE

I do not know that Ken Littleton killed Martha Moxley. I do know—and as a former prosecutor, I understand the laws of evidence—that the state's case against Littleton was much stronger than any case against Michael Skakel. Many people have wondered why, after years of uncertainty and inaction, Connecticut officials decided to pursue Michael with sudden ferocity. The answer is Dominick Dunne.

Dunne, who has transformed a lifelong fascination with celebrity and wealth into a career as a gossip and a novelist, had personal reasons for his attraction to this case. His own daughter, Dominique, was murdered in 1982, and her killer, a restaurant chef, was released from prison after serving less than three years. "I was so outraged about our justice system," Dunne told a reporter in a 1996 interview, "that everything I've written since has dealt with that system—how people with money and power get different verdicts than other people."

Dunne has built his career on linking notorious murders to powerful people, including John and Patsy Ramsey, Claus von Bulow, and O. J. Simpson. That formula has given Dunne his own measure of celebrity and wealth. His efforts to connect a Kennedy relative to the Mosley murder have been both a decade-long fixation and a profitable venture. "The Kennedys," he has said, "are the greatest soap opera in American history." Michael Skakel would get caught in the crosshairs where Dunne's ambitions intersected with his obsessions.

In the fall of 1991 Dunne, then covering William Kennedy Smith's rape trial in Palm Beach for *Vanity Fair*, repeated a report that the Connecticut state's attorney Donald Browne had requested forensic evidence from Will Smith. Dunne wrote, "Though there have been reports that Willy Smith was a guest of the Skakels [the night of Martha Moxley's murder] no evidence links him to the case." He also wrote that Browne denied the story. What Dunne did not say, and did not know, is that Will Smith had never met a Skakel with the exception of Ethel Kennedy. Not until two years later did Dunne admit that the rumor had been proved false.

Dunne knew almost nothing about the Moxley murder in 1991. Yet in his article about the Smith trial he declared, "Either the [Moxley] investigation was thoroughly botched or someone bowed to influence." Dunne would subsequently enlarge on this theme in a best-selling novel, a TV miniseries, and articles for *Vanity Fair*. In the novel, *A Season in Purgatory* (1993), a thinly veiled John F. Kennedy Jr. murders his young neighbor in Greenwich and gets away with it because of family power. At the time, Dunne was convinced that Tom Skakel had killed Martha, and never lost an opportunity to point out that Tom was still the chief suspect during an extensive national television tour for his novel, which included appearances on programs such as *Hard Copy* and the *CBS Evening News with Connie Chung*, and also interviews with Jay Leno and Joan Rivers.

As Dunne likes to say, his book and the miniseries that followed dramatically raised the public profile of the unsolved murder. Liz Smith reported in a 1993 column that the Greenwich Police Department felt that Dunne had put it on the spot. According to Frank Garr and Donald Browne, it was the publicity generated by the Smith trial, which included a Leonard Levitt article that accused the Greenwich police of having made errors, that led the state to reopen the investigation.

If it didn't turn out that a Kennedy cousin had committed the crime, the story would be worth much less to Dunne. Dunne ignored the strong evidence against Littleton; in his many articles and interviews about the case he never mentioned Littleton's five failed polygraphs, his shifting alibis, his call to David Moxley, his statement to the psychiatrist about whether he could have committed the crime, the physical evidence of hair similarities, his history of sexual misconduct, and his capacity to deliver the blows. Dunne suggested that Littleton's alcoholism and his criminal activity were the result of stress from unfair suspicion. The Skakels never publicly blamed Littleton for the crime. In his *Vanity Fair* article on the murder Dunne offered a purged and abbreviated inventory of Littleton's criminal and mental-health history and then concluded, "But there is one thing I'm sure he didn't do: he did not kill Martha Moxley." No Skakel has ever benefited from the same presumption of innocence in Dunne's writings.

Soon after Will Smith's acquittal, in December 1991, Dunne wrote to Dorthy Moxley, recounting his own daughter's murder and asking to meet her. Their terrible shared tragedies appealed to her trust, and they forged a friendship. Dunne wrote in *Vanity Fair*, "I swore to her that I would help her get justice for her daughter."

Dorthy Moxley, who had previously been as judicious as everyone else, became certain that a Skakel had committed the crime. She has often acknowledged that her theories about Skakel involvement were influenced by Dunne.

In promoting *A Season in Purgatory*, Dunne kept up his needling. "There are only two possible reasons" the murder remained unsolved, he told the *Chicago Tribune*. "Either the police are totally inept. Or somehow power and money have played a part in covering up." Such statements continued to rankle law-enforcement officials. After his book tour Dunne was visited by several members of the Moxley investigation team, including Frank Garr, who brought gifts of a state-police plaque, a T-shirt, and a mug, and asked him to stop criticizing their work. Dunne agreed to a truce. Garr would later lead the efforts to press charges against Michael Skakel. Jack Solomon and Donald Browne retired from the state attorney's office. Garr moved from the Greenwich Police Department to the state attorney's office to take over Solomon's responsibilities.

Although Solomon would not speak to me about the case, a source close to him who wishes to remain unnamed told me in November, "Jack believes that your cousin did not commit the murder. He is absolutely sick and beside himself because he believes an innocent man is in the can. But Jack is a cop through and through, and he will not make any public statement that might embarrass his law-enforcement colleagues."

In May 1996 the miniseries *A Season in Purgatory* aired, and Dunne mounted yet another media blitz. That month he escorted Dorthy Moxley to a press conference to announce that she was raising the reward for information about her daughter's killer from $50,000 to $100,000.

Even though Dunne had said he would stop picking on the Greenwich police, he soon urged his friend Mark Fuhrman to become their Torquemada. He provided Fuhrman with evidence that would be central to Fuhrman's book *Murder in Greenwich* (1998) and, Fuhrman said, the inspiration to write it. The book, with an introduction by Dunne, is a 283-page diatribe against the Greenwich police, who, Fuhrman says in the book, angered him by treating him as a pariah. Fuhrman castigated them as "servants of the rich and powerful." Echoing Dunne, he wrote, "Someone killed Martha Moxley and got away with it. And the reason he got away with it was that the Greenwich Police Department . . . didn't have the courage to go after him."

SUTTON ASSOCIATES

Dunne would later brag that it was his relentless campaign after the publication of his novel that prompted Rushton Skakel to take a step that led to Dunne's bringing Fuhrman into the case—and that eventually doomed Michael. In the spring of 1993 Rushton, who was already suffering from the frontal-lobe dementia and schizophrenia that would later debilitate him, hired at Sheridan's urging Sutton Associates, a private-investigation firm composed of former law-enforcement officials from the FBI and the New York Police Department. The Skakels were convinced that the original police investigation had been bungled, to Tom's detriment, and they were desperate to clear the family name.

Sutton's president, James Murphy, a veteran of fifteen years with the FBI, recently told me, "While Rushton Skakel thoroughly believed his children were innocent, we were told that wherever the chips fall, they, the Skakel family . . . want to know the truth and that the Skakel family recognized Mrs. Moxley's pain and have instructed that any information that develops which contributes to the solution of Martha Moxley's homicide is to be immediately shared with Connecticut authorities." Both Murphy, who is now an ordained Catholic deacon, and Thomas Sheridan, who acted as the liaison between Sutton and the Skakel family, told me that they were certain Rushton would have turned any of his children over to the police if he thought they were guilty.

The Greenwich police cooperated with Sutton, as did most other witnesses. All the members of the Skakel family agreed to talk to Sutton detectives about their memories of that night. It was the first time that most of them had discussed the Moxley murder at any length, publicly or privately, since their original police interviews. Several of them, including John and Julie, underwent hypnosis and sodium-pentothal testing. Sutton interviewed hundreds of people, including Ken Littleton and John Moxley, Martha's brother.

Both Tom and Michael told Sutton detectives details they had not disclosed to the police in 1975. Tom, for example, described his sexual encounter with Martha on the rear lawn of the Skakel property. When I recently asked Tom why he had waited so long to tell the full story, I anticipated his answer—Rushton's severe attitude toward sex. (Rushton, his children told me, considered masturbation "equivalent to the slaughter of millions of potential Christians.") Tom was his father's favored son. "I loved my father and didn't want to lose his respect," he told me. "My father was the most important person in my life. He was a staunch Catholic with strict views about premarital sex. I was frightened of disappointing him."

Michael had equally urgent concerns. The runt of the family, he had always been a target for his father's anger. Rushton Skakel drank alcoholically for four years following his wife's death. (He quit drinking in 1977.) During this period he occasionally hit Michael, and once fired a gun in his direction during a hunting trip. Michael sometimes slept in a closet to escape his father's wrath. When Michael was ten, Rushton had caught him looking at *Playboy* with his friends and knocked him silly. By age thirteen Michael was an alcoholic.

In 1993 he had been sober for eleven years and was a powerful athlete. No longer fearful of his father, Michael, too, told Sutton detectives the full story of what he had done that night. After returning from the Terriens', at around 11:20, high on pot and alcohol, he had gone for a walk to peep through the window of a woman who was known to walk around her house scantily clad. Disappointed that her shades were drawn, he decided to go home. When he passed the Moxley house, Michael saw a light and climbed a tree next to a bedroom he thought was Martha's. He tossed pebbles to get her attention and called, "Martha, Martha," but there was no response. He made a halfhearted attempt to masturbate in the tree before becoming embarrassed and climbing down. On his way home he sensed a presence in the dark bushes near the Moxleys' driveway. He yelled, threw stones in that direction, and dashed back to his house, frightened. The downstairs doors being bolted, he climbed through his bedroom window at 12:30. He had been out for thirty or forty minutes.

Michael told me that when they heard his story, the Sutton investigators burst out laughing. That's when Michael learned, for the first time, that the window he had looked in was John Moxley's, not Martha's. John was out late that night, according to police reports.

Largely owing to Dunne's retelling of the story, it would later become a common assumption that Michael had masturbated in the tree below which Martha's body was discovered. In fact the two trees are on opposite sides of the Moxley house, 300 feet apart.

The Sutton files occupy thousands of pages, filling two file cabinets. At Sheridan's request the company assembled draft "portfolios" that made hypothetical cases against Tom and Michael Skakel and Ken Littleton. These portfolios construct a prosecutor's best case against each one. The one on Michael was titled "Michael Skakel, A Purposefully Prejudicial Analysis of Michael Skakel and His Testimony." Sheridan recently told me why he had asked for scenarios to be constructed against any Skakel who might be considered a suspect: "My old man told me to always ask for the worst case. That way you know you're not being bullshitted." Murphy and Willis Krebs, a retired NYPD detective working for Sutton Associates, told me separately that they believed Michael Skakel was innocent.

In December 1995 Leonard Levitt reported in *Newsday* that anonymous sources had informed him that both Tom and Michael had spoken to private investigators hired by the Skakel family and had elaborated on their whereabouts the night of the murder. The state attorney's office publicly called for a full disclosure of Sutton's findings—to no avail. When pieces of the report began to leak, Tom's lawyer, Emanuel Margolis, who had opposed the Sutton project from the outset and had allowed Tom's participation only reluctantly (Tom was still the only Skakel represented by counsel), demanded that all copies of the report and all underlying evidence be turned over to him. Margolis thought that the report might feed the ambitions of those among the investigators who seemed determined to blame Tom. According to Sheridan and Murphy, Margolis now has the only known full set of the Sutton files, which he keeps under lock and key. No member of the Skakel family has ever seen any part of the Sutton files except those portions of the prejudicial portfolios that subsequently appeared on the Internet.

Before Margolis gained control of the files, however, a twenty-year-old aspiring journalism student named Jamie Bryant, temporarily employed by Sutton to help write the scenarios, reportedly handed them over to Dominick Dunne in November 1996, just as Dunne was leaving to cover the O. J. Simpson civil trial. Murphy told me that Bryant later told him he had stolen the portfolios in an effort to land a job at *Vanity Fair*. After reading them, Dunne passed the portfolios on to both Dorthy Moxley and Frank Garr.

Garr called the Greenwich detective Stephen Carroll and told him that he now considered Michael to be on the suspect list. After debating Michael's alibi, according to Mark Fuhrman, the police officers concluded he could not have committed the crime. Fuhrman, who later befriended Dorthy Moxley by promising to solve the murder, wrote that Garr explained to her at the time that the Sutton files were just speculative "scenarios."

Dunne got in touch with Fuhrman, whom Dunne says he had come to admire during the O. J. trial. Fuhrman was then living in northern Idaho, having left the Los Angeles Police Department in disgrace after the O. J. trial. Dunne later wrote that when he got Fuhrman on the phone, he said, "Hey, Mark, I've got just the one for you, and I have a private detective report that's going to knock you on your ass."

MARK FUHRMAN

Dominick Dunne and Mark Fuhrman discussed the case intensely at a Four Seasons lunch in 1997. Dunne hosted a cocktail party for Fuhrman to introduce him to Connecticut law-enforcement officials. According to Murphy, both men had read the Sutton scenarios on Ken Littleton, Tom Skakel, and Michael, whom the Greenwich police had rejected as a serious suspect. In *Murder in Greenwich*, Fuhrman makes a stronger case against Tom than he does against Michael. Yet he declares Michael the killer.

With breathtaking ease, and without apology to Tom for the years of tormenting innuendo, Dunne turned his sights on Michael. "I firmly believe that Michael Skakel killed Martha Moxley," he declared on *Good Morning America* in March 1999. On the CNN program *Burden of Proof*, when he was asked whether he believed that Michael Skakel did it, he replied, "That is what I absolutely firmly believe." To ease his own shift from Tom to Michael as the designated murderer, Dunne simply made them partners in the cover-up. In January of 2000 Dunne told ABC News, "I firmly believe Michael Skakel killed Martha Moxley and that Tommy Skakel may have helped him move the body."

Fuhrman acknowledges in *Murder in Greenwich* that the Moxley murder attracted him because it reminded him of the Simpson case: "money, power, celebrity, deceit, corruption." On the day he began investigating the crime, he repeated this formulation to Greenwich police officers when they asked him about his interest in the case. Fuhrman had apparently decided before he began his investigation that the killer must be a wealthy, powerful celebrity who had corrupted the police.

In the book Fuhrman exposes the bias in one of his reasons for rejecting Littleton as a suspect, which he says he did "early on": "Littleton had no money, no powerful family behind him, no clout. If Littleton had murdered Martha Moxley, he would not have gotten away with it." Ignoring the fact that Littleton has changed his alibi five times, Fuhrman boldly concludes, "While other suspects have had trouble with their alibis, Littleton has always stuck to the same story." He explains Littleton's failure to pass five lie-detector tests over a period of sixteen years by arguing, "If Littleton is a paranoid, psychotic, bipolar alcoholic, then how could [Greenwich police] expect him to pass any kind of polygraph?"

Garr dismissed Fuhrman's book to the *New York Daily News* as a cut-and-paste rewrite of old newspaper stories and police files, and the Greenwich police said that the book was "riddled with inaccuracies and contains no new information." Nevertheless, the book lit a fire beneath Connecticut law-enforcement officials. On July 10, 1998, one month after its publication, Connecticut authorities convened a one-man grand jury consisting of Judge George Thim. The state's attorney Jonathan Benedict took over the Moxley case and began a multimillion-dollar effort to convict Michael Skakel.

A banner on the paperback of *Murder in Greenwich* advertises it as "the book that spawned the Connecticut grand jury investigation." "I firmly believe," Dunne wrote in the October 2000 issue of *Vanity Fair*, "*Murder in Greenwich*, for which I wrote the introduction, is what caused a grand jury to be called after 25 years."

Right up until the convening of the grand jury, according to Fuhrman, the Greenwich police and state investigators still considered Ken Littleton to be their primary suspect. Why did they give him immunity? The state might have concluded that a prosecution of Littleton—especially if it failed, and any prosecution twenty-three years after the crime stood small chance of success—would not end the public debate over their competence and integrity. Fuhrman and Dunne had already accused the police of giving the Skakels a pass by making Littleton the fall guy. In order to prosecute a Skakel they would need Littleton to testify without taking the Fifth—an action that might suggest to the jury that the witness rather than the defendant was guilty. The only way to compel Littleton to testify was to first grant him immunity. The case against Michael was weak, but by indicting a Skakel investigators could at least quiet Fuhrman's charges that they were "sycophants" and "cowards." Dunne had already sent signals that his objectives would be satisfied short of a conviction, as long as Michael was indicted. "I just want to see this guy with handcuffs—humiliated," he told *Burden of Proof.*

According to Fuhrman, members of Benedict's staff told him that they planned to use *Murder in Greenwich* as the blueprint for the prosecution. In fact, the state followed the book practically line by line. Michael's fuller account was to become the crux of the state's case against him. Adopting Fuhrman's theory, the state argued that Michael fabricated the masturbation story after learning that Henry Lee, the forensic scientist, was about to conduct DNA testing (which was not available in 1975) on evidence from the crime scene. According to Fuhrman, Michael took this precaution to explain the presence of his semen on Martha's body should any be found. In fact, there was no semen found, Michael's or anyone else's.

There are numerous problems with Fuhrman's theory. First, the tree in which Michael said he had attempted to masturbate was a football field's length from where Martha's body was found. The story would therefore not have explained the presence of semen on or near Martha's body had any been found. Second, Michael did not invent the story in the early nineties for his Sutton interview; he has been telling it consistently for at least twenty-three years. Michael told the story to his aunt, Mary Ellen Reynolds, a former nun, in 1979; to his psychiatrists, Stanley Lese and Hyman Weitzen, in 1980; and to many friends before the 1990s. I heard him tell it several times, beginning in 1983. The prosecution's own witness Michael Meredith testified that he heard the story from Michael in 1987 while staying at the Skakel home. Michael's explanation for his failure to tell the story to the police in the first instance—adolescent embarrassment and fear of a wrathful father—is plausible. As Jay Leno suggested, referring to the Skakel trial, many people would rather be found guilty of murder than be suspected of masturbating in a tree. Oddly, Michael's lawyer, Mickey Sherman, never defended Michael against the accusation that Michael had recently invented the story. I told Sherman several times during the trial that I would testify about Michael's pre-Sutton recounting, but I was never called.

Taking their cue from Fuhrman, prosecutors argued that Michael had killed Martha in a drunken, jealous rage after seeing his older brother kiss her. But Michael says, and other Skakels agree, that he was in love at the time with a family friend, Francine Ziminsky. "Martha was cute," he told me when I visited him in prison last September, "but every girl was cute to me." Michael says that he was unaware of any romance between Martha and his brother. "I never knew about Tom and Martha," he told me on the same visit, "until I heard it on TV in 1998."

The next challenge was Michael's alibi. Connecticut law-enforcement officials had in 1975 consulted the nation's pre-eminent forensic pathologist, Joseph Jachimczyk, who established the time of Martha's death as 10:00 PM. He based his conclusion on the condition of Martha's bladder and the contents of her stomach. Martha had eaten a grilled cheese sandwich at around six o'clock, Dorthy Moxley said, and ice cream later; three ounces of undigested food were found during her autopsy. The stomach normally clears most food in two to three hours. That put the time of death between 9:30 and 10:00. The Connecticut police consulted Detroit's medical examiner, Werner Spitz, and two New York City deputy chief medical examiners, Michael Baden and John Devlin. All of them generally concurred with Jachimczyk. The police also relied on nonmedical indicators: barking dogs, Martha's curfew, and Dorthy Moxley's testimony that she heard Martha cry out around 10:00. For twenty-five years the police operated under the assumption that the murder occurred around 10:00 PM. Michael's account for that time had been consistent since 1975. Three witnesses—John Skakel, Jim Terrien, and Rush Skakel Jr.—all maintained from the first time they were questioned that they had left with Michael for the Terriens' house at 9:30, when Martha was still alive, and had returned at 11:20. John passed a polygraph test that the police felt covered all four.

"For Michael's accusers to be correct, the time of death had to be moved up" in order to get around his 10:00 alibi, Michael Baden, who later served as the chief medical examiner for New York City, recently told me. While consulting with the Connecticut police in the Moxley case, Baden had become friendly with the Moxley family. At Dorthy Moxley's request, he acted as a liaison between the Greenwich police and Mark Fuhrman, who despised each other, while Fuhrman was researching *Murder in Greenwich*. In his book Fuhrman solved the problem of Michael's alibi by simply asserting that food can remain in the stomach for as long as six hours, and that the murder might therefore have occurred as late as 1:30 AM.

At the trial Connecticut's former chief medical examiner, Elliot

Gross—who had performed the autopsy and had been called to testify for the prosecution—was never put on the stand. Instead, while the original medical examiner sat idle, Connecticut's current chief medical examiner, Wayne Carver, was called as the expert witness on a case he had never worked on. Based on his reading of Gross's autopsy report, Carver testified that the murder might have occurred as late as 1:30. Sherman's cross-examination was anemic and brief. He asked Carver a single question: Could the murder have occurred at 9:30? Carver answered yes. Sherman sat down. When he read the transcript, Baden told me, "I was very surprised. He never asked Carver the key question: What was the basis of his opinion that the time of death could be both 9:30 and 1:30?"

Prosecutors relied heavily on the Fuhrman-Dunne view of the Skakels as conducting a coordinated cover-up. Both writers assume that all the Skakels concluded from the outset that one of the boys had committed the murder, and immediately circled the wagons. Fuhrman says in his book that the Catskills trip was an "opportunity for the Skakels to confer away from Belle Haven and the Greenwich police." He writes, "If Littleton had committed the murder, I doubt the Skakels would have brought him up to Windham. . . . Since the hunting trip was most probably a legal confab, Littleton was brought along because he knew something— or the Skakels thought he knew something—that was very important." This theory became crucial to the prosecution's case—even though Littleton testified at the trial that it had been his idea to drive the boys to the Catskills for the weekend, to get them away from the ghoulish scene in Greenwich.

The theory of an intricately organized Skakel conspiracy is comical to anyone who knows the family—as neither Fuhrman nor Dunne does. Jim Terrien and Rush Jr. would have been critical to any such conspiracy, as would Tom Skakel. But neither Jim nor Rush was at Windham, though both Fuhrman and the prosecutors implied otherwise. Rush drove to Washington, D.C., on Halloween morning for a Georgetown University homecoming—unaware that Martha, whom he had never met, was dead. The prosecution's theory supposes that Michael killed Martha in a jealous rage toward his "nemesis," brother Tom, who then helped Michael to cover up the murder of the girl with whom he'd had a sexual encounter only hours before. The theory requires that Michael, a drunken teenage murderer, had the clarity to clean himself up, dispose of the murder weapon, and take an active role in maintaining a conspiracy that remained drum-tight for nearly thirty years.

The Skakel clan may be troubled—alcoholism runs in the family, and although they are kind and generous to a fault, some family members can be impulsive, irresponsible, and reckless. They have made a series of disastrous decisions about how to handle this case. But they are not murderers or conspirators. They are deeply religious and lack the moral bankruptcy to carry personal loyalty to the level of depravity—much less the organizational discipline and the cohesiveness to either form or perpetuate such a conspiracy.

I have spoken to all the Skakels about the murder, and they are as confused as various investigators have been over the years about who committed the crime. I have heard different Skakels speculate about the possible guilt of a diverse list of suspects. (Interestingly, most of them told me they have long believed that the strongest evidence points not to Ken Littleton but to Franz Wittine, the former Skakel gardener. After the police and private investigators turned their attention from Wittine to Littleton, early in the case, they never returned intensively to Wittine.) All of the Skakels want to see Martha's killer in jail. None of them ever imagined that Michael would be charged, much less convicted of the crime.

But none of them would lie to protect Michael. Even when during the trial Julie understood Sherman's instructions as a "request to lie" under oath, she refused with the full support of her brothers. At the trial Andrea Shakespeare (now Renna) testified that the night of the murder, before being driven home by Julie Skakel after dinner, she was "under the impression" Michael was still in the Skakel house after the older boys had left for Jim Terrien's—highly ambiguous and uncertain testimony that nonetheless gave jurors reason to doubt Michael's alibi. According to Julie and Stephen Skakel, on the morning that Julie was to testify at Michael's trial, Sherman assembled the two of them; Sherman's legal assistant, Jason Throne; and his son, Mark, who is also a lawyer, at Julie's home. Sherman told Julie, she says, "You have to say that you remember that the boys were still at the house when you took Andrea home." Julie replied, "I can't, that's not true." Sherman admonished her, "You have to—it's the only way." Julie again refused. Stephen later found her weeping outside the courthouse. According to Stephen, she was devastated by the prospect that her refusal to lie might put Michael in jail. Stephen told me that he found Jason Throne and begged him to get Sherman to back off. "I told him, 'You can't do this, she's going to have a nervous breakdown.'"

Sherman denies that he ever told Julie to lie. "We would never have asked her to perjure herself," he told me. "I just asked her to add two and two and come up with four, not five or seven." He explained to me that the Skakels were difficult witnesses, refusing to testify even to obvious facts unless they had clear memories. He cited the example of Rush Jr., who clearly remembered Michael's being at the Terriens' but refused to testify that Michael was in the car that went to the house: twenty-seven years later, he had no clear memory of who was in the car. John Skakel refused to testify about any of the events that night, because he had no independent memories of the details of the evening. John would agree only to testify that he told the truth to the police in 1975; the police report records his saying that Michael was in the car and at the Terriens' house. "They were impossible to deal with," Sherman told me. The children's scrupulousness might have worked against Michael: postverdict interviews quoted jury members as saying they regarded the Skakels' memory gaps not as the product of rigorous honesty but as obfuscation.

Connecticut prosecutors still had the problem of evidence. They had no fingerprints, no DNA, and no witnesses. There was a good deal of physical evidence, but none that could be tied to anyone. Where were the prosecutors to find witnesses to flesh out the Dunne-Fuhrman speculations?

REFORM-SCHOOL WITNESSES

Every Kennedy is painfully familiar with the attention seeker who fashions a chance encounter with a celebrity into a disparaging anecdote. Michael's notoriety made him a magnet for such people—and a February 1996 television program helped prosecutors corral a group of them. In an effort to invigorate the twenty-year-old investigation, Frank Garr arranged for NBC's *Unsolved Mysteries* to film a segment on the Moxley murder and to provide a telephone number for viewers with information on the crime. The phone calls came in—not about Tom or Littleton but, as Leonard Levitt later reported, about Michael. The calls came from former students at the Elan School who were eager to point the finger at him. Following a drunken car accident at age seventeen, Michael had, at his father's behest, been forced into Elan, which practices a controversial behavior-modification program that relies on peer confrontation. It turned out to be a snake pit where Michael was regularly beaten during the two years he was a resident.

Garr was aggressive in recruiting his witnesses, according to Diane Hozman, a therapist in California and a former Elan resident in whom Michael had confided during his time there. Hozman recently told me that she contacted Garr to help clear Michael of the charges when she realized he was investigating the crime. He flew her to Connecticut four times, once with her son and another time with her boyfriend. She said that she thought Garr was bullying and pressuring her into saying that Michael had confessed. "I felt they were desperate to blame Michael," she told me. "Garr took everything I said out of context to make it fit into his puzzle. He definitely didn't want to hear anything good about Michael. I'm sorry I even talked to Garr." The night before she was to testify, Hozman told the prosecution again that she did not believe that Michael had ever confessed. They sent her home without calling her to the stand.

The state called a total of seven Elan witnesses. Of them the two key witnesses were Gregory Coleman and John Higgins. Coleman, who bullied Michael and was assigned to guard him after a foiled escape, told the grand jury in September 1998 that Michael had introduced himself to him by saying, "I'm going to get away with murder and I'm a Kennedy." This highly unlikely statement became tabloid fodder and colored public attitudes toward Michael Skakel.

Coleman told the grand jury that while at Elan he had heard Michael confess to the murder five or six times. At Michael's probable-cause hearing, two years later, Coleman amended that estimate to two times. To explain the discrepancy, Coleman said he had shot heroin an hour before his grand-jury testimony. He admitted to shooting twenty to twenty-five bags a day and said that he was on methadone during the probable-cause hearing. He was incarcerated at the time and had made two requests to Connecticut authorities for cash and a reduced sentence in return for his testimony. Coleman swore that Michael told him he had killed Martha with a driver and had gone to visit her body two days later. In fact the golf club used to murder Martha was an iron, and the police removed her body the next day.

Coleman died of an overdose before the trial. But the trial judge,

John F. Kavanewsky Jr., allowed his earlier testimony to be read to the jury, although there would be no opportunity for Michael's attorneys to cross-examine Coleman at the trial or for the jury to view his ruined demeanor. The confession Coleman described is inconceivable to anyone who knows Michael, beginning with Michael's alleged declaration "I'm a Kennedy"—a phrase no Skakel would be caught dead saying. Coleman's recollection is similar to a *National Enquirer* headline shortly after Michael's arrest, which quoted Michael as allegedly telling Harry Kranick, another Elan character, "I killed that chick . . . it got me excited." Kranick denied that he ever heard Michael Skakel make any of the reported statements; otherwise the police would certainly have made him testify. Judging by his behavior, Coleman himself never expected to testify. He had waited twenty years to tell his story, and did so in an anonymous call to a local NBC affiliate. The station got in touch with the Connecticut police after tracking Coleman through caller ID.

John Higgins was another Elan bully. At the trial Higgins said that he had been on guard duty with Michael when Michael spontaneously began relating his memories of the Moxley murder. According to Higgins, Michael recalled a party that night at the Skakel house, after which he rummaged in the garage for golf clubs; he remembered running through pine trees afterward and waking up at home. That story is obviously contrived. There was no party that evening, and there has never been a garage at the Skakel house. Higgins refused to sign a formal statement, take a polygraph, or allow the police to tape his phone calls to them. They recorded him anyway, and used the tape to force him to testify at the trial. Higgins later admitted to lying to Garr about his knowledge of Michael's confession.

Other Elan witnesses testified that they had never heard Michael confess while at Elan. Higgins "had a reputation for not being truthful," one witness said, and "seemed to really like making Mike Skakel's life miserable." For two years Michael was continually spat upon, slapped, and deprived of sleep. He was serially beaten with hoses and by students wearing boxing gloves, forced to wear a dunce cap and a toilet seat around his neck, and subjected to a long inventory of other tortures. Upon Michael's arrival at the school, its owner, Joseph Ricci, who came from a town neighboring Greenwich and was aware of the Moxley murder, told him he would never leave the facility until he admitted that Tom Skakel had committed the crime. Elan's administration encouraged students to accuse Michael himself of Martha's murder as part of the school's humiliation therapy. Students like Coleman and Higgins had incentives to report such confessions; they would have been rewarded with extra privileges and elevated status and power. Their claims that Michael had confessed while at Elan and that they then kept his secret are, according to other Elan witnesses, incredible. Referring to Coleman's and Higgins's testimony, Joseph Ricci told *Time* magazine that "the notion of Michael's confession is just preposterous." Ricci said, "I was there, and I would know." The facility had only a hundred students, and if Michael had confessed, "two things would have happened," Ricci said. "Everybody in the facility would have known and talked about it. And we would have called our lawyers to figure out our obligations. Neither happened." Unfortunately for Michael, Ricci died immediately before the trial, so the jury never heard his testimony.

Geranne Ridge, not an Elan student but a self-described "part-time model," testified that in the spring of 1997 Michael was at a party she alone remembers, in her apartment—which Michael and a mutual friend of Ridge's and Michael's say Michael never visited. Ridge claims that she overheard Michael saying, "Ask me why I killed my neighbor." That is the exact wording of a chin-to-ankle sign Michael was forced to carry for two months at Elan. The sign was thoroughly discussed in such tabloids as *The Star, The National Enquirer,* and the *Globe.* Ridge admitted on the stand that she had lied when she told a friend in a conversation that he secretly taped that Michael had confessed to the crime. She admitted that her story of Michael's confession was "BS" invented to impress a friend. She acknowledged that she had come forward only because the friend had handed the tape to the police.

Finally, the prosecution produced Matthew Tucciarone, a hairdresser from the Golden Touch Salon, in Greenwich. Tucciarone claimed that Michael, Rush Jr., and Julie came for haircuts in the spring of 1976. As Tucciarone clipped his hair, Michael conversed with his siblings and said, "I'm going to get a gun and kill him." To this, according to Tucciarone, Julie responded, "You can't do that." Michael then said, "Why not? I did it before. I killed before," and Julie reportedly answered, "Shut up, Michael."

Tucciarone described Julie as having a ponytail and showing her navel. At that time Julie had short hair and would never have exposed her navel. "Dad would have grounded her for a year," Stephen Skakel told me. "Absolutely not," Julie said when I asked her if she would ever have dressed that way. Moreover, Julie testified that she, Rush Jr., and Michael would not have gone for haircuts together during that era. The Skakel siblings went to Mike's barbershop as youngsters and later used Subway Barber. No Skakel, the family told me, has ever been to the Golden Touch Salon or met Tucciarone. Coincidentally, according to Tucciarone, Michael's confession occurred on the one day of the week Tucciarone was working alone in the salon—a holiday when the entire Skakel family always left town. Tucciarone waited twenty-six years to tell his tale: he came forward only after casually relating it to one of his customers, a Stamford sheriff, who urged him to report it to the state attorney's office.

These witnesses have so little credence that it's hardly worth describing them. In many cases they had changed or retracted their stories before the trial began, but were called to testify nonetheless. And the jury believed them. In each case the witness did not initially go to the police but bragged about the story to an acquaintance or to the media, who then notified the police. How likely is it that Michael Skakel, who endured years of torture at Elan during which he refused to admit any guilt, would suddenly "confess" to these crackpots but never to any person he knew or trusted?

Prosecutors also relied heavily on another alleged confession—one with which I, as it happens, am familiar. Many years ago Michael told me a story with his customary honesty and humor. At age sixteen he had once draped himself in a dress of his late mother's and fallen asleep in his room. His father discovered him and went wild. Michael called a family handyman who sometimes drove the children and asked to go to his psychiatrist's office, in New York City, although he did not have an appointment. The driver testified that during the ride Michael said "he had done something very bad and he either had to kill himself or get out of the country." On the way back to Belle Haven, the driver continued, Michael tried to jump off the Triborough Bridge. The prosecution offered that statement as a confession to the Moxley murder. In fact, despite widespread press reports to the contrary, Michael never said he was the murderer—to the driver or to anyone else. The handyman never intended to come forward with the story, but not long before the trial he offhandedly told his bank manager, who reported it to the authorities.

MICKEY SHERMAN

Michael's problems were aggravated by an overconfident and less than zealous defense lawyer who seemed more interested in courting the press and ingratiating himself with Dominick Dunne than in getting his client acquitted. To defend Michael the Skakels had hired Mickey Sherman, a high-profile partner in a small Stamford law firm, at the recommendation of Emanuel Margolis, Tom's lawyer—a recommendation Margolis now deeply regrets. Sherman promoted himself as a public-relations expert who could undo the damage to the family's reputation caused by nearly a decade of Dunne's accusations. His appetite for the limelight turned out to be as voracious as Dunne's—but he was a much less effective spokesman.

Soon before the trial began, the *Greenwich Time* quoted Sherman as saying that his relations with Court TV had turned him into a "television lawyer." "We make fools of ourselves," he was quoted as saying, "in return for limo rides and cheap doughnuts in greenrooms." (Sherman now says he "disavows" that report.) The family was distressed by Sherman's seeming lack of attention to the trial, what they saw as his failure to prepare them adequately before their testimony, and his undisguised friendship with Dominick Dunne. On at least one occasion Sherman arrived at court in a limousine with Dunne; he spent at least one evening at Dunne's house, at a party. The day after the conviction Sherman told me that he was going to a Court TV party for Dunne. When I questioned the propriety of his attending, he said, "We're friends. What can I say, I'm a kiss-ass." (He now claims not to remember making this remark, but he recently said, "I make no apology for being cordial to Dunne. I got valuable information from him over the years.")

Following Michael's conviction Sherman startled CNN staffers with an unscheduled greenroom appearance to visit Dominick Dunne and Dorthy Moxley as the three awaited separate *Larry King Live* interviews. He told Moxley that he was "happy" for her. Dunne instantly reported the remark. At Michael's sentencing Sherman, quoting a probation report, said that Michael was "an entirely different person today than he was at fifteen." Both statements left public doubt that Sherman believed in his client's innocence— although Sherman protests that this was not his intent and told me he is certain that Michael is innocent.

Perhaps in recognition of Dunne's solicitude toward Ken Littleton, Sherman refused, Julie said, to allow her or the other Skakels to testify about the strong evidence against Littleton. When I asked Sherman during the trial why he was not aggressively questioning Littleton, he said, "He's a pathetic creature. I don't want to look like I'm beating up on him." When Sherman called Jack Solomon to the stand, Solomon appeared with a three-ring binder containing nearly three decades' worth of police information about Littleton and a summary of the state's case against him. That information might have proved critically valuable to Michael's defense. Sherman did not have the binder marked as an exhibit or placed in evidence.

Even before the trial began, Sherman failed to make an interlocutory appeal based on Michael's strongest legal argument—that the court no longer had jurisdiction to hear a case against anyone who was accused of a murder that took place in 1975, because at the time the statute of limitations for murder was five years. Sherman says that he thought the right time for such an appeal was "after the final judgment." (A state supreme court decision on the statute of limitations is now pending.) "The whole point of an interlocutory appeal," however, as Hope Seeley, the lawyer in charge of Michael's appeal, recently explained, "is not to have to wait for a final judgment—or endure the expense and emotion of a lengthy trial." An early victory in such an appeal would have deprived Sherman of the nationally publicized trial he expected would boost his career.

By the time Sherman's behavior became worrisome to the Skakels, it was too late to change lawyers, Julie told me: "We'd already paid Mickey a million dollars, and at that point it was too much." The family had originally been persuaded, they said, by Sherman's charm and confidence, and especially by his frequent assurances before the trial that he was in control and there was no chance Michael would be convicted.

Sherman allowed the seating on the jury of a policeman

(unheard of in the world of criminal defense) and of someone who admitted to sharing a friend with the Moxleys. At the time, trial watchers were amazed at the speed of the jury selection and called it "unprecedented" for this type of case. Most disturbing, Sherman, as noted above, proved inept in countering Andrea Shakespeare Renna's ambiguous testimony that she was "under the impression" that Michael was in the Skakel house when she left. A more skillful cross-examination of Renna would have clearly revealed the weakness of her claim, since she could never give any explanation of her belief that Michael did not go to the Terriens'. Sherman should have objected to Renna's testimony because it was speculation not based on personal knowledge.

During the trial Sherman seemed more interested in trying to convince the members of the jury that he was affable and the press that he was television-ready. Judging by their subsequent remarks, he instead disgusted them. And despite the $150,000 the family says Sherman billed them for time he spent with the media, the public's impression of Michael Skakel couldn't have been more negative. Given the gift that every great defense lawyer yearns for, a genuinely innocent paying client, Sherman squandered a fortune and sacrificed Michael on the altar of his ego.

MICHAEL SKAKEL

The person who murdered Martha Moxley was a demon—mean and vicious. Dunne and Fuhrman's portrayal therefore required that Michael be demonized. Dunne depicted Michael as a spoiled rich kid with unlimited money and a lavish lifestyle, and claimed that his father had feigned mental illness to avoid testifying in court. In fact Rushton Skakel suffers from debilitating and progressive dementia, diagnosed in 1992. Except on rare occasions he is unable to recognize his children. His attorneys and his children are now selling Rushton's house, liquidating trusts, and pooling family funds to pay Michael's legal bills. Since the conviction the family has come together, taking an active interest in the quality of Michael's legal representation and becoming thoroughly familiar with the details of his case. They hired the firm of Santos and Seeley to represent him in his appeal, which most likely will be heard in September.

Rather than being someone who "wallowed in" self-pity, as Dunne suggests, or is overwhelmed by his troubles, Michael remains highly motivated. He got sober in 1982, at age twenty-one, and has given his life to service ever since. Dunne portrays a man riding on his relationship with the Kennedys. But Michael never identified himself as a "Kennedy cousin." On the contrary, the Kennedy and Skakel families were never close. The Skakels were Republicans who took steps against my father that my mother considered hurtful, and the families' relationship was distant for many years. I rarely saw the Skakel boys growing up, and would not have been able to identify Michael or his brothers in 1975. The Skakels have a rightful pride in their own family.

When I finally did get to know Michael, he was struggling with addiction. For twenty years I have watched him overcome, with notable personal strength, his genetic and cultural burdens and make himself a productive member of society. After getting sober he went back to school, fought an uphill battle against dyslexia, and graduated from Curry College. Despite his bulk, he is a superb athlete, and his hard work and brutal training regimen earned him a place on the U.S. national speed-skiing team in 1993. In October he celebrated twenty years of sobriety without any slips. His primary passion is helping other alcoholics in recovery.

Almost nothing the press wrote about Michael was true. Dominick Dunne made himself the arbiter in virtually every public discussion about the Moxley case: He promoted his agenda in *Vanity Fair* and on practically every talk show on the air. He branded Michael with a new first name, "Kennedy cousin," and drove the national press into a *Lord of the Flies* frenzy to lynch the fat kid. Unfortunately, the national press corps, seduced by a celebrity trial, rarely questioned Dunne's mischaracterizations. And the Skakels were hampered in defending both Tom and Michael by their principled unwillingness to point the finger at another suspect.

As someone who grew up revering the American justice system as nearly infallible, I share Dominick Dunne's indignation that a skillful defense lawyer, in the service of a wealthy client, can get a guilty defendant acquitted. However, it is even more dismaying that, as every district attorney knows, a skillful prosecutor can persuade a jury to convict an innocent man—a fact attested to by the numerous DNA exonerations of death-row inmates in recent years. As Dunne and Fuhrman know, juries make mistakes. The law acknowledges the power of a prosecutor's office in the doctrine of "prosecutorial discretion," which allows prosecutors to refuse a winnable case if they believe that injustice might result. A prosecutor has a duty to exercise independent judgment and not cave in to public opinion or the goading of a celebrity journalist. But sometimes political heat leads a prosecutor to proceed with a case when his better judgment tells him to take a pass.

In the Moxley case, after resisting the temptation to prosecute for twenty-three years, Connecticut gave Littleton full immunity and then spent millions to convict Michael. The prosecution had so little faith in its underlying case that during the trial Dorthy Moxley had to make a public plea for more witnesses to come forward, and Jonathan Benedict made a last-minute attempt to add to the original charges a manslaughter count, which carried the possibility of no jail time. But that was before Benedict's brilliant summation. During the last ten minutes Benedict unveiled a dramatic and sophisticated multimedia display that some legal analysts have since criticized as deceptive and prejudicial. The display superimposed Michael's statements, out of context, on gruesome pictures of Martha's slain body. In a 1998 taped interview with a ghostwriter for what was to be an autobiography, Michael had described his reaction when he was awakened in a daze on Halloween morning by Dorthy Moxley. "Michael, have you seen Martha?" she asked. Michael did not then know that Martha was dead; he said on the tape that he was panicked that Mrs. Moxley might have witnessed his masturbating—a context never explained by the prosecution when they played the tape for the jury. "And I was like, 'Oh my God, did they see me last night?' And I'm like I don't know and I remember just having a feeling of panic, like, oh shit you know like my worry of what I went to bed with, I don't know. You know what I mean, I had a feeling of panic."

As the prosecution played the audiotape, Michael's words appeared on a giant screen, turning red and exploding in size. Each time Michael said the word "panic," the display flashed a crime-scene photo of Martha's body. Observers, including Dominick Dunne, credited Michael's conviction to this dramatic summation.

There were at least four other suspects against whom the state could have marshaled enough circumstantial evidence to indict. With Benedict's brilliant techniques and a jury eager to give the Moxleys justice, any of those suspects might have been convicted. The desire for closure apparently trumped the critical principle that guilt must be established beyond a reasonable doubt. It was Mickey Sherman who pointed out that the case was like musical chairs, and that Michael Skakel got caught standing when the music stopped.

"Notorious crimes have to be very carefully prosecuted," Michael Baden, New York's former chief medical examiner, recently told me, "because it is so easy to get a conviction without physical evidence. This is the very time to be more cautious, not less cautious, so that a bad decision isn't made because of an inflamed public.

Look at the five kids in the Central Park jogger case. There was no trace evidence—but with notorious cases, jurors can find you guilty anyway."

Dunne continues to make an industry out of the Moxley murder. Most recently he parlayed his role in the case into a new Court TV series he hosts—*Dominick Dunne's Power, Privilege and Justice*. Mark Fuhrman has also done well: The USA Network last fall aired a highly fictionalized docudrama based on Fuhrman's *Murder in Greenwich*, lionizing Fuhrman for his role in solving the Moxley murder. According to press reports, Fuhrman's newest book is a far-fetched effort to link the death by alcoholic overdose of a man named Christopher O'Connor, last seen being beaten by bouncers outside a Queens nightclub, to the Kennedy family.

Dunne's objective since 1991 has been to link the crime to a "Kennedy cousin," whether it was Will Smith, John Kennedy, Tom Skakel, or Michael Skakel. Describing the day of Michael's guilty verdict, Dunne crowed in *Vanity Fair*, "The whole courtroom stared at [Michael], transfixed by his humiliation. This trial has ruined a once proud family. Their besmirched name will outlive them all." In *Vanity Fair's* December issue Dunne makes the wild claim (which he repeated on *Larry King Live*) that he has information from a mysterious source that four others were involved in cleaning up the crime scene with Michael.

Dunne says he has "contempt for the behavior of the Skakel family" because they came from privilege and abused it. Fuhrman echoes him: "[The Skakels] lived a privileged existence" and they "frequently abused that privilege." But the capacity to write, to publish, and to hold public attention are privileges that Dunne and Fuhrman have abused. The media have duties too.

At its best, every profession—law, science, medicine, journalism—is a search for the truth. But personal bias can distort and pervert that mission. As one who has experienced the murder of family members, I sympathize with Dunne's anguish over his daughter's murder. But the worst dishonor to her memory is that her death has inspired not a search for justice but a campaign of revenge, with an innocent man its victim.

———

My Atlantic Monthly *article prompted a letter from Crawford Mills, a former Brunswick School classmate of Michael Skakel who told me that another classmate, Tony Bryant, had information about the crime that had not emerged during trial. As the Skakel case proceeded to trial, Crawford Mills passed this information to Michael Skakel's prosecutor Jonathan Benedict and his attorney, Mickey Sherman. Neither of them followed up.*

Tony Bryant knew two men who he believed had murdered Martha Moxley. He had kept the secret for thirty years. Initially he and his mother, with whom he had shared the information, were fearful that Tony, who was black, might become an easy scapegoat for the crime if he came forward. He maintained his silence during the trial because he never believed that Michael Skakel would be convicted. Following Michael's guilty verdict he felt conscience-bound to speak up. When I called Bryant, a Florida businessman, he told me, "I've been waiting for this call for thirty years." Bryant had previously told his story to only one person—his old classmate Crawford Mills.

Bryant told me that he had brought two boys to Greenwich on the night of Martha Moxley's murder; he described the boys as New York City street toughs named Adolph and Burr. Adolph had a crush on Moxley based on several earlier visits to Greenwich with Tony. The two boys were drinking and taking drugs. They obtained golf clubs from the Skakel yard and declared that they intended to "get a girl caveman style" by knocking her over the head and dragging her into the bushes. Following the murder, both boys made statements to Tony Bryant to the effect that they had "accomplished their mission." I later spoke to both Adolph and Burr who admitted to having been in Belle Haven on Halloween Eve 1975 and on prior occasions. While both men denied having committed the crime, Adolph said that he would probably fail a lie-detector test on the subject. The hair of an African American had been discovered on Martha's body by the Connecticut coroner's office. Its presence has never been explained. Adolph is African American. There is other compelling new evidence of Michael's innocence as well.

The Skakel case is currently on direct appeal to the Connecticut supreme court. Michael's new attorney, Hope Seeley of Santos & Seeley, filed a brief in the Connecticut supreme court in November 2003; the State will be filing its brief in April 2004. Seeley will then file her reply brief in May 2004. The matter will be set down for oral argument by the supreme court once the reply brief has been filed.

A petition for new trial, which will raise a number of issues based upon newly discovered evidence, will be filed once Seeley's investigation into these matters has been completed. Some of this new evidence supports Seeley's argument that the prosecution deliberately suppressed exculpatory information.

NOT GUILTY BY REASON
OF AFGHANISTAN

JOHN H. RICHARDSON

This much is certain: On the night of October 3 of the year 2001, a man named Nathan Powell brutally killed a man named Jawed Wassel. The causes of death noted by the coroner included two stab wounds in Jawed's back and signs of "blunt force trauma" that included broken facial bones and an "eggshell type" fracture of his skull.

The coroner's job was complicated because he was working from fragments. As he stated in his report, speaking in the eternal present tense of dictation, "body parts are received separately and these consist of a torso, a severed head, and dismembered upper and lower extremities."

The pieces of Jawed Wassel arrived in various bags and boxes. The torso was in Box 1, Bag A. In Box 2, Bag B, the coroner found "a dismembered lower extremity including upper leg, lower leg, and foot." In Bag D of the same box, he found bloodstained bath towels and socks and a V-neck pullover shirt of the Club Monaco brand, along with a segment of blue hacksaw blade with bone tissue still adhering to the teeth. In this box he also found sponges, paper towels, a Brillo pad, and one bloodstained hand towel "with a Christmas holiday pattern."

Jawed's head arrived in a refrigerator drawer. "The bony portion of the neck is transected through the body of the fourth cervical vertebra. The right arm is dismembered by incision of the skin and soft tissues including muscle, tendon, nerve, and blood vessels. . . . Sectioning of the brain reveals typical distribution of gray and white matter and deep cortical structures."

These things are true. They are solid. The ventricles of Jawed's brain were not dilated. His cerebellum, pons, medulla, and brain stem were all "unremarkable," which is the word scientists like to use because *normal* is too vague and easy to dispute. His paratracheal soft tissues were unremarkable. The endocardium of his heart was unremarkable. His aorta was unremarkable and his vena cava was unremarkable and his pulmonary vasculature was also unremarkable.

And that is all I can tell you that is certain and solid.

This is a story for our time, dark and violent and complicated almost beyond understanding. In one version of the story, the Twin Towers fall and raise a cloud of madness and paranoia that sends Nathan Powell, a man with a young daughter and no criminal record, off on his own personal war on terrorism. He commits an act of senseless murder that makes sense to him, which has both narrow legal implications in terms of his motive and also larger implications in terms of the horror all around us. In the second version, there's little sense and no point in puzzling over it. There's nothing but greed and cunning and a monstrous attempt to use the falling towers to blame the victim, and Jawed Wassel is the first casualty of a phony war. Either way, Nathan Powell has pleaded not guilty by reason of temporary insanity, and the difficult truth behind his terrible crime becomes a warning sign of the world we entered on September 11, 2001.

First, Nathan Powell's version of the story. This is how he has told it to me, to the police, to his lawyer, to several psychologists, and to a polygraph examiner. He's also written it out numerous times. Although some versions are more detailed than others, the essential story has varied little.

In 1996, after a troubled childhood, a couple of failed relationships, and a few stints at studying film at Columbia and Hunter College, Nathan was thirty-three and living in New York when he started working with an Afghan immigrant named Jawed Wassel on a film called *FireDancer*. He was the producer and Jawed was the writer and director and they split their deal down the middle, fifty-fifty. In 1997, Jawed went to Afghanistan and came back with stories of fighting against the Taliban with the Northern Alliance. Nathan says he saw pictures of Jawed with an AK-47 and also heard Jawed making anti-American declarations—that the United States was responsible for the suffering in Afghanistan because Ronald Reagan supported the Afghan rebels against the Soviet Union but then abandoned them, or that the United States didn't care about Afghans so much as an oil pipeline through Uzbekistan. But Nathan didn't give it much thought because that kind of talk was typical in artsy circles, and anyway he'd heard the same kind of thing many times from his father, a banjo-playing socialist who worshiped Pete Seeger and Woody Guthrie.

In 1999, Nathan and Jawed went to Washington, D.C., to start shooting their film and immediately ran into many troubles, such as a huge squabble over a line in the script that suggested that one of the characters in the movie might not be a virgin. This led to physical threats and a lot of talk about honor killing, the tribal custom of avenging stains on a family's name with blood. Around that time, the lead actor was replaced with Baktash Zaher, who had trained to be a pilot at a flight school in Florida. And members of a Taliban delegation to Washington stayed at the house of one of the Afghans supporting the production, sharing quarters with a couple of crew members.

In November 2000, Jawed mentioned that his contacts in northern Afghanistan had offered to arrange an interview with Osama bin Laden. When Nathan told another friend about this, the man offered to pose as a journalist and kill bin Laden, so Nathan tried to contact the CIA through an acquaintance named Marc Palmer, who brushed him off.

In June 2001, Nathan and Jawed attended a meeting with another *FireDancer* producer named Kate Wood, and Jawed told them that he was going to Afghanistan to make a documentary and please not to tell anyone where he was going. When he came back six weeks later, he was limping and wouldn't answer any questions.

Then the planes hit the Twin Towers. Nathan had a clear view of the whole thing from the window of his loft just across the East River, sitting there with his wife and their four-year-old daughter. At one point he used binoculars and saw a person jump. Then he talked to Jawed on the phone and Jawed said America was finally getting a taste of its own medicine.

On TV, Nathan saw pictures of Arabs in Jersey City celebrating the attacks. The next day, he says, he saw some Arabs on his own street pumping their fists and cheering. A few days later, he went to Jawed's house and found Jawed watching the news with Baktash and his sister, Vida Zaher-Khadem, who was Jawed's associate director. When they started glancing at the screen and "whispering among themselves in Farsi," it made him suspicious. What were they hiding? Then Jawed said the CIA must have organized the attacks to provoke a war and bail out the floundering Bush administration.

Later there was a disturbing meeting with Jawed and a man named Eric Rayman, who argued that the movie should say "something positive" about the Taliban. Nathan couldn't believe it. What was going on here? Jawed had always said he opposed the Taliban, but maybe it had all been a horrible lie. And what about Baktash training at that flight school in Florida? *Why didn't Baktash ever actually become a pilot?*

Over the next few weeks, Nathan couldn't sleep, or fell into vivid nightmares. He stopped taking cabs because he thought the cab-drivers might be terrorists. He made plans to leave the city, but he didn't tell people because he was afraid they'd think he was crazy.

All through this, Jawed was pushing him to use the attacks to promote *FireDancer.* At first he thought it was a horrible idea, but an investor named Tom Fox encouraged him, and he was still so emotionally invested in the movie himself that he sent faxes to *60 Minutes, 20/20,* and the *New York Daily News.* When the *Daily News* asked to interview Jawed, Nathan issued an ultimatum: Denounce the Taliban or else I'll tell the investors the kinds of things you've been saying about America and the CIA. Jawed said he didn't want to say anything "political." They must have argued for forty minutes.

And freaky things kept happening. One day six agents from the Drug Enforcement Administration appeared at Nathan's door and asked to search the files of the moving company that shared his loft. (Nathan worked there answering phones.) Another day, four police officers showed up to poke around, saying they had gotten a 911 call. At night Nathan dreamed of poisonous fogs and burning people who screamed without making a sound.

On September 30, saying he was afraid for their safety, he put his wife and daughter on a plane to Seattle.

On the morning of October 3, Jawed called to say the *Daily News* article had come out. Still hoping for the best, Nathan ran downstairs and bought a stack of copies. But there was just one line about the Taliban "holding 18 million to 20 million people hostage" and another saying that *FireDancer* "couldn't have been made anywhere else but in America" before Jawed ruined it all by saying that the Afghans were "pawns . . . for the Americans."

At around six that night, Nathan met Jawed at the subway station, and out of the blue Jawed mentioned an idea for a movie about an honor killing. Then Jawed asked what Osama bin Laden would do to Nathan if he knew about the plot to kill him by posing as a journalist—and suddenly Nathan realized that al Qaeda had killed the famous Northern Alliance leader Ahmed Shah Massoud exactly the same way. Jawed must have given them the idea! So it was true—*Jawed was in league with the Taliban!*

By the time they got to Nathan's loft and Jawed pulled a contract out of his backpack, telling him that since they'd been disagreeing so much, it was time for him to take over the film, Nathan was already on the brink of losing control. He said he'd never sign, that he'd tie the movie up in court and it would never see the light of day, and Jawed retaliated with the fatal threat that pushed Nathan over the edge: "With one phone call or one letter, you will have no family!"

And Nathan did what he felt he had to do—what any good husband and father and patriot would have done if he had walked in his shoes for the last month through the dust of all those vaporized buildings and people.

Of course, Jawed Wassel's friends and relatives and defenders view this version of events as vile, repugnant, and offensive. What a preposterous story! What a pack of lies! With one voice, they insist that Jawed was a kind and peaceful man who spoke four or five languages, who loved poetry and European films, who dedicated himself to telling the story of Afghanistan through movies. He used to say that art was the best way to "thread the needle of human understanding," one friend remembered. At least three of his American friends said he was a great patriot who especially appreciated the freedom of expression that gave him a chance to tell his story. His brother, Khaled, told me that when he thought about Jawed, he remembered his brother as a man who always tried to do the right thing. The suggestion that he would bad-mouth the United States or support the Taliban is beyond insulting—it's another violation.

"If Nathan's claiming that Jawed was some sort of Taliban or terrorist," a cinematographer named Bud Gardner told me, "that's the ultimate misnomer and a complete piece of crap."

If you want to know Jawed, his friends say, look at his movie. And certainly *FireDancer* shows that Jawed's essential attitude was humane. The lead character is a solitary artist haunted by images of Russians killing his parents in Afghanistan, the woman he pursues an aspiring fashion designer who is being pushed into an arranged marriage with a thuggish Afghan man. In one scene, she cuts the face out of a burqa and gazes through the hole. In another, the artist makes a plea to stop the violence that could have come right out of a Spike Lee film.

"There was something in Jawed that made all of us believe in him," said Vida Zaher-Khadem. After Jawed's death, Vida took over the job of finishing *FireDancer*. "I should have been working on my own film, but I wanted to finish his because I believed in him. And Nathan robbed him from us—a person who would have done so much."

Backing Jawed's family and friends are the police and prosecutor and the media, who have all lined up behind the second version of this story—that Nathan was a weirdo and loser who latched on to Jawed early in the making of *FireDancer* but couldn't cut it as a producer and made people feel so uncomfortable that he slowly got squeezed out of the movie. This made him jealous and angry and he retaliated in petty ways, such as refusing to give Vida points or credit although she had done most of his job. He was also greedy. From the beginning, one of his coproducers said, Nathan seemed to have an unrealistic sense of how much money *FireDancer* could make. So he must have seen 9/11 as a great marketing opportunity that would give him a perfect way to satisfy both his lust for money and his lust for revenge—doubly so because his contract with Jawed specified that if one of them died, the other would get complete control of the film. So Nathan began to plot his heinous crime, sending his family out of town not to protect them but to clear the way. He built a trail of "evidence" by mooning over 9/11 to his friends and ranting about the Taliban, and he cut up the body not in some kind of "fugue state" (as his attorney now claims) but in a spirit of cold calculation that shocks the soul—as evidenced by his storing Jawed's head in his freezer so he could dispose of it separately and reduce the chances of getting caught. And finally, he concocted his ridiculous tale of trauma in the most monstrous imaginable exploitation of the 9/11 attacks, literally to get away with murder. In some ways, this is the most shocking thing of all. As prosecutor Fred Klein said in various media interviews: "To use that awful tragedy to somehow justify a brutal murder is insulting." Nathan "never mentioned any trauma of the World Trade Center or the Pentagon. This was a business dispute with the victim." In another news report, Klein repeated this quite definitely: "His statement to police clearly shows the motive was money, not politics."

Nathan Powell invited this skepticism and hatred, and it's likely that there's nothing that anyone can say that will keep him from being convicted of a ghastly murder. Especially given what he did afterward.

First he went to a friend's house and watched *The West Wing*. On his way home, he stopped to buy plastic bags and paper towels. Then he cut up Jawed's body with a hacksaw and wrapped the pieces in plastic before packing them in boxes. At one point he stopped to make a phone call to a friend in California. The next day he went to work and, in the evening, put on a suit to attend a viewing of *FireDancer* at a DuArt screening room—where he came face-to-face with Jawed's brother and mother but somehow managed to act as if nothing was wrong. He even went with Jawed's brother to the police station to report him missing. Then he went home and loaded the boxes into a van and drove out to Long Island to dispose of the body, stopping at Home Depot to pick up a shovel, pick, charcoal, and lighter fluid. He stopped at the first dark spot he saw and went into the woods and started to dig, then stopped and went back to the van and started to drive, forgetting to turn on his headlights. A few minutes later, a police officer named Peter McGinn pulled him over.

And then Nathan started telling lies. Testifying at a preliminary hearing, McGinn said that when he approached the van, Nathan was panting "very heavily" and his "whole face, hair, neck, and shirt" were soaked with sweat. When McGinn asked his name, Nathan simply didn't respond. Asked who owned the van, he still didn't answer. Asked what he was doing, he said he was delivering a couch. Asked where he was delivering the couch, he said he didn't remember. Asked who he was delivering it to, he said a friend. Asked the friend's name, he said he didn't remember. Asked what he was doing in the woods, he said first that he stopped "to take a leak" and then, when the officer asked about the shovel and the dirt and the sweat on his face, answered, "All right, I'll level with you. I was just looking for $10,000 that I buried three years ago."

"Well, whose boxes are those?" McGinn asked.

"What boxes?"

"Those boxes."

"What boxes?"

"Those two boxes right there."

Nathan said he hadn't noticed the boxes. Maybe they were there when he rented the van. And when McGinn pointed out that he had just said that he worked for a moving company, Nathan offered to throw the boxes into the woods.

And so it continued, until at last Nathan opened the door to look for his wallet and the officer saw blood on the boxes. When he drew his gun and told Nathan to lie on the ground, Nathan started to cry. (When Nathan's lawyer took him back to this moment, McGinn couldn't hold back his contempt: "He started to cry and then he laid on the ground and he cried some more.")

There were more lies to come. While Nathan was handcuffed in the backseat of a police car, a detective named James Cereghino asked his name and address. Nathan said he lived at 317 East Seventy-third Street in Manhattan and that his roommate was a man named Ed Greissle. He repeated this again an hour later when Cereghino and a detective named John McHugh began the formal interrogation at the police station, adding that he had been living there for about a year and paid "between $1,500 and $1,800 a month." It was only after about three hours in custody that Nathan finally told them where he really lived.

By the time they got around to asking about the murder, the cops were clearly fed up. You can hear it in Cereghino's account of what happened when they discovered Jawed's head wasn't in any of the boxes. "The first question we asked him, 'Where's the head?' He stated, 'It's in the freezer in my apartment.' I asked him, 'Why didn't it go in the box?' He said that it wouldn't fit. I asked him, 'What do you mean it didn't fit?' And he just stated it wouldn't fit."

Nathan has told other lies. On the bio he released with an early *FireDancer* press kit, he claims to have been an associate producer of a Beverly D'Angelo movie called *Pterodactyl Women from Beverly Hills*. The director and producer of that movie is a man named Philippe Mora, and he told me he'd never heard of Nathan. Nathan said that he met several times with Jay Leno's wife, Mavis, and officials of an organization called the Feminist Majority Foundation about investing in the film, but a spokesman for Mavis Leno denied it and no one at the Feminist Majority remembered him either. And Kate Wood says *she's* the one who met with the Feminist Majority. "If Nathan was having three or four meetings with Mavis Leno, Jawed and I and Vida would have heard all about that."

And *lie* may be too strong a word, but it's safe to say that Nathan's memories of his skills as a producer are much different from what others remember. He tends to talk in a rather grandiose way about his "contacts" and his film experience, but Kate Wood says that she and Jawed would give him an assignment and weeks would go by and they wouldn't hear from him. Cinematographer Renato Tonelli says that Nathan was out of his league, seemingly clueless about simple things like arranging locations in advance and bringing in food for the crew. One day he got arrested for driving an equipment truck without a license, and even though it carried at least $200,000 worth of rented equipment, he just kept on driving. "Now it makes sense," Tonelli says. "There's a problem here, an underlying problem. But at that point we just chalked it up to being incompetent."

But this is where it gets complicated. Because at least part of Nathan's story is true, and he did tell the whole strange tale to police after his arrest. Technically, prosecutor Klein doesn't seem to have been lying when he said that Nathan didn't specifically mention the World Trade Center or the Pentagon. And the statement Nathan signed the next morning does narrow the dispute exclusively to business: "Our relationship had deteriorated but I had to stay around him or I wouldn't get my money." Nor is there anything in the statement about the Taliban or honor killing or 9/11. Nor did any of these details appear in the supplementary document prepared by detectives called "Oral Statements of Nathan Powell." Nor do they appear in notes Cereghino made during the interrogation.

But Nathan didn't actually write his official statement. It was prepared for his signature by Detective McHugh, and the notes McHugh made that evening show that he left a lot out: "Italian project—Afghan marries outsider. Family sends killers. Summer 2000—Afghanistan. Jawed—interview Bin Laden. WTC—increased problems Jawed—CIA responsible. Jawed—2 faced, thought nice—Taliban supporter."

During Cereghino's testimony at the preliminary hearing, more inconvenient details surfaced. Yes, Nathan told them that Jawed was a Taliban sympathizer. Yes, he said that he and Jawed had discussed a plot to kill Osama bin Laden. Yes, he said that Jawed had "made some very unpatriotic statements." Yes, Nathan told them that Jawed had made a trip to Afghanistan just before the 9/11 attacks.

And some of it checks out. Jawed did go to Afghanistan that fateful summer. Baktash did train at a flight school in Florida. And there seems to be some truth to the Osama bin Laden story too. Several of Nathan's friends remember him talking about it at the time. So does Marc Palmer, a lawyer and building inspector who is not his friend. Reluctant to talk at first, Palmer eventually said that yes, his retired father-in-law did once work for the CIA and there was a day about a year before the murder when Nathan came over to his house to show him a trailer of *FireDancer* and told some complicated story about someone the government or the mob was after. "There were some weird machinations that he wanted me to get involved in. I don't recall much because it got very convoluted so I sort of blanked it out."

This is the problem: Nathan faces a charge of second-degree murder, which in New York is applied in cases of deliberate intentional killing or killing with depraved indifference. To defend against this charge, Nathan's attorney—a rumpled admirer of William Kunstler named Tom Liotti—would have to prove that Nathan acted "under the influence of extreme emotional disturbance for which there was an explanation or excuse, the reasonableness of which is to be determined from the viewpoint of a person in the defendant's situation under the circumstances as the defendant believed them to be."

This means that Nathan's case really hangs on one thing: Was he really and truly afraid of Jawed in the moment that he killed him?

Liotti argues logic: If Nathan had planned to kill Jawed, why did he do it in his loft instead of some back alley? Why did he assault him with a pool cue, a weapon of convenience, instead of a gun? Only fear explains it, and only fear explains why Nathan went through with the horror of cutting up the body—because he was sure that if they knew what he had done, Jawed's family would be bound by the rules of honor killing to come after his wife and daughter.

Because no one believed his story, Nathan asked for a lie-detector test and wrote up a list of hundreds of questions he wanted to be asked. In the first round, the polygraph expert asked him three questions:

1. In November 2000, did Jawed say he could set up a meeting with Osama bin Laden?

2. Did Jawed tell you that he would have supported the terrorist action publicly if it were not for the loss of life?

3. Did Jawed tell you, on 9/11, that the United States was getting a little of its own medicine?

Nathan answered yes to all the questions, and the polygraph expert says he was telling the truth.

But Nathan wanted to answer more questions, so his mother paid for another test. This time the most important questions were:

1. Did Jawed Wassel threaten the lives of your family that night on October 3, 2001?

2. Did you strike Jawed Wassel over the head with a pool cue in order to stop him from killing you?

Nathan answered yes to both questions. And the polygraph expert says that he did not lie.

· · ·

So who is Nathan Powell and what was going on in his mind the night he killed Jawed Wassel? Nathan's mother, Gail, is a short, plump woman with bowl-cut gray hair. She attends a Baptist church. In 1959, she was a waitress in an ice-cream parlor in New Hampshire when Ralph Powell came in and swept her off her feet, talking about folk music and socialism. After scuffling around a bit, they ended up living in Ithaca, New York, where Ralph worked at a typewriter factory and a Boy Scout summer camp before landing a job as a librarian. They called themselves husband and wife though they never did get married, and Ralph collected thousands of books and always talked about the big important book he was going to write that would explain everything.

In 1963, Nathan was born, and Ralph taught him to read and how to play chess. When Nathan was three, Ralph chased Pete Seeger up a hill so the boy could shake his hand. But later he starting wanting Nathan to be perfect, which meant learning Russian and wearing a suit and tie to school and stopping all that silly talk about becoming an astronaut because that would mean working for the government.

When the couple broke up in the late sixties, Ralph went off to live in a tent and blamed his failures on the FBI. Then one day Nathan went out to play basketball and never came back—it turned out that Ralph had left a plane ticket for Nathan at the airport.

Three years later, Ralph called Gail up and said she had to take Nathan back right away—this day, this hour, this minute. Gail was mystified. But it's only six weeks before the end of the school year, she said. Why now?

"He's an enemy in my own house," Ralph said.

The only explanation she could get out of him was that Nathan had let ice cream melt in his dresser drawer. In a voice that scared her, Ralph made a threat: "Either you take him now or I'll put him in a reform school or I'll bury him in the backyard."

When he got back to Ithaca, Nathan went up and lay on his bed. "You know," he said, "my dad really wants me, but he thinks I can get a better education here."

Gail cried then and cried again telling me the story. That's the thing about Nathan, she said: Because his father was so intolerant, he always wanted to be the total opposite. He wanted to be good.

Before going to college, Nathan went all the way to Russia to check out the workers' paradise and came back to tell his father he was "totally wrong." After that they didn't speak for a long time, which is one reason Nathan was so obsessed with Osama bin Laden. "Because of my father and how I grew up," he told me, "I've always kept track of enemies of the United States."

In April 2001, six months before the murder, Nathan's father died.

By that time, Nathan was living in an illegal loft with bedsheets for walls with his wife and their four-year-old daughter. Around that time his wife changed her name from Jenny to Maia because she wanted a new name to go with a new life, maybe somewhere out west.

The daughter of a Hawaiian blues musician, Maia's thirty and has Nathan's initial tattooed on her leg. When she talks about Nathan in the weeks leading up to the murder, she paints a picture of a man who was steadily coming unhinged. She doesn't mind that. She just wants you to understand *why*. She met him in Manhattan in 1996, found him too short and an "appallingly bad dresser," but loved talking to him because he was so thoughtful and idealistic. His favorite movies were *Robin Hood* and *Tombstone* and *Braveheart*, his favorite book was *The Lord of the Rings*. When he started working on *FireDancer* with Jawed, the three of them would sit on the floor at Barnes & Noble and tear the script apart. The way she remembers it, she was the first to get suspicious of Jawed, in part because she's got Hawaiian blood and Jawed took that as license to criticize America when Nathan wasn't around. "It was like my country had also been raped by America so I could understand him the way Americans couldn't," she says. She insists she isn't shading things just to defend Nathan. "He'd always talk like that. He would say Americans are just fat idiots, and if he had his way he'd live in France."

When they started to shoot *FireDancer*, Jawed would tell her every day never to trust an Afghan, that they'd been lying to one another and backstabbing one another for thousands of years. "He'd go, 'Shh shh shh,' and I'd say, 'What?' and he'd say, 'That person is Taliban' or 'That person is Northern Alliance.'" She also remembers the threats over the virginity issue, and "all this honor stuff."

And yes, she heard Nathan and Jawed talking about the offer to meet Osama bin Laden. And yes, definitely, Nathan freaked out after September 11. Right away he started saying he wanted to get out of the city, that it wasn't a safe place anymore. She was there when Nathan saw the Arabs pumping their fists in victory. She remembers him getting so quiet and not sleeping, and she remembers the day he came back from that investors' meeting talking about this idiot named Eric who suggested they say something good about the Taliban. And the day he came home all upset because Jawed said something about the CIA bombing the Trade Center — and the day the DEA showed up at the loft, asking questions about Arabs, and the day she left town with a sprained ankle and Nathan wouldn't let her take a cab because he had this thing about terrorist cabbies. "It was ridiculous, it was nuts. . . . It got to the point where I was crying. He'd never acted like that before."

And she also remembers Nathan saying that maybe they shouldn't release the damn movie at all. "He would say he didn't want anyone who felt like that to make money off of it, and he felt very strongly about that. And it was hard for him, because he had worked a long time on the film."

When Maia came to say good-bye, she brought their daughter. Standing on a street corner in a red Supergirl T-shirt, her loopy grin shining through a mass of tangled black hair, she said, "I wrote a story for my daddy."

"What is it about?"

"It's about a wizard and a mommy and a daddy who go to the beach."

"And what did the wizard do?"

And Nathan's daughter flashed her grin, eyes narrowing with the delicious secret on the tip of her tongue:

"He turned the sand blue!"

Steve D'Ambrose is the guy Nathan called after he cut up Jawed's body. These days Steve is working on a master's degree in screen-writing at UCLA. He seems gentle and idealistic and spoke to me after some hesitation because, he said, it was the right thing to do. He said that Nathan was a good and loyal friend who loved heroic movies and stories about knights in armor, a man who dreamed of using movies to do good.

When he met Nathan in the late eighties, Nathan was jolly, good-natured, likable. He knew a lot about Christianity and the religions of the early American tribal peoples. Steve's not surprised that Nathan was a failure as an on-set producer because that was never Nathan's thing. "What he always told me in film school is that he wanted to be the background guy—the invisible producer motivating the artist. That was something I always found kind of fascinating, because most other people in film school wanted to be famous."

He also knew Jawed slightly but didn't really have much of a take on him. There was one strange incident. When Nathan and Jawed were raising financing for *FireDancer*, Jawed asked Nathan to ask Steve to go visit an uncle of Jawed's who lived in Beverly Hills. But when Steve mentioned Jawed's name the man started screaming at him. He apologized and got back in his car and started to drive away. "And this is where it gets really weird. He got in his Mercedes, chased me, cut me off, and then got out of his car and ran to my car yelling and screaming. I mean this guy literally chased me down."

So Steve understands why Nathan might have been freaked out by some of these Afghans. He also remembers Nathan talking about the offer to interview Osama bin Laden.

But mostly he remembers that haunting call at midnight on October 3. "It was a weird phone call, to say the least. One of the key points that stuck in my head was that Nathan apologized to me. He said, 'I'm sorry for not calling you earlier about 9/11.' Which I thought was odd, because I was in LA and he was in New York, and if anybody should have called it should have been me."

They talked about September 11 and the likelihood of future attacks. Nathan asked if Steve's family was okay. "And he said something else that really stuck in my head. He said that all the Afghans who were here should be put in jail."

Steve was shocked. That was not the Nathan he knew. "So I told him, 'You know, Nathan, that's wrong. That would be the equivalent of interning the Japanese Americans during World War II.'"

Nathan went silent.

Of all the people who loved Jawed, the one who spoke most openly was Kate Wood, a dignified older woman who was drawn to *FireDancer*'s idealism after a long career in educational TV. The first thing she told me was that she never felt comfortable around Nathan, even avoiding simple things like riding in a car with him.

"I was scared," she told me. "There was no basis for it, but I knew that I did not want to be riding home with Nathan."

But there were good things about him, she said. She liked the way he talked about his daughter—"I would think, He's got to be okay, he's just so wrapped up in his child"—and she always believed in his love for *FireDancer*. "I heard him say to investors, 'I read this script and it made me cry.' I didn't doubt that. I still don't doubt that."

Alone among Jawed's friends, Kate was willing to say—after a certain amount of verbal squirming—that there was truth in Nathan's stories about Jawed defending the Taliban. "There were a lot of people who said the Taliban were good for some women in Afghanistan because the Russians had done such terrible things to women. The Taliban were protecting the women. I did hear him say things like that. But at the same time he said, 'Now they've gone too far.' It was always in context."

It's also true that Jawed was secretive about going to Afghanistan in the summer of 2001, she said. Her impression was that Jawed felt that the various factions in the Afghan-American community might not understand what he was doing over there. "He just thought it was better if people didn't know."

People in this story are afraid of reprisals. Maia doesn't want anyone to know where she lives. Vida Zaher-Khadem doesn't want anyone to know where she lives. It's as if the distinction between paranoia and justified fear has blurred for all of them.

During a break at Nathan's preliminary hearing, Vida approached him and hissed in a low voice. A few minutes later, Liotti described the scene to the judge. "She said to Nathan, 'We're going to kill you.' And those are her exact words."

Liotti milked the moment for all it was worth, offering to swear to the quote under oath "as an officer of the court" and demanding an investigation and extra metal detectors. The judge asked if anyone else had heard it. A court officer named Dan Robinson said he had. "Your Honor, as you left the bench she approached the rail here, leaned over, became abusive, started using foul language." But Robinson said he didn't hear the specific words.

Later, describing the moment to me, Liotti got worked up all over again. "A woman comes over and says, 'We're going to kill you.' And after I bring it to the court's attention and the court bars her from the courthouse for the duration of the case, she doesn't say, 'I didn't mean that, I didn't mean that.' To me she looked like she was very resolved and very mean and knew exactly what she was saying, and the part that's also very disturbing—I don't know who the 'we' is. I have an ongoing concern about these folks, I really do."

One night, I sat down at a Starbucks with Vida, Khaled, Jawed's friend John Roche, and Eric Rayman. Rayman, who once worked as an attorney for *The New Yorker*, had already told me he didn't want to talk about the case. "I want to see him convicted," he said. "And I don't want to do anything that might undermine that." Instead they wanted to know what I thought of Jawed's movie. I said that while it seemed very humane, the Afghan-American culture seemed depressing and crazy—the forced marriage, the obsession with virginity. Rayman immediately started lecturing me on the difficulties of "culture clash," insisting that in context, back in Afghanistan, the Afghan culture was just fine. Roche joined him, arguing that some women actually like wearing burqas. And I know that they were just worried I might not understand the cultural complexities and take away a negative impression of Afghans, but at the same time I couldn't help thinking that in the wrong circumstances, in a very dark time, if you were kind of crazed already, it might sound like they were defending the Taliban.

But the reason they met me was to talk about Jawed. He was a father figure, they said. He liked the novels of Robert Musil and the philosophy of Frederich Nietzsche. "He used to say that through cinema we can do a lot for Afghanistan," Vida said. "Everybody thinks of us as beards and guns. Nobody knows us."

Did he fight for the Northern Alliance? Did he think the CIA bombed the World Trade Center? Did Eric say they should say something good about the Taliban? All that was off-limits, and they clearly thought it despicable of me even to ask.

At one point I asked what went wrong that first week of filming.

"Nathan lied and cheated," Vida said.

"Don't talk about that," Eric said.

"Why can't we say that Nathan lied and cheated?" John asked.

Later, the incident in the courtroom came up. I asked Vida to tell me what happened. But again Eric shook his head, and she fell silent.

When I met Nathan at the Nassau County jail, he was waiting for me in a bare room with one glass wall. The fluorescent lights on his orange jumpsuit made everything seem vaguely clinical. "I have one request before we start," he said. "Please don't mention where Maia is living in your article."

Prison had improved his looks. He'd burned off his fat, shaved his goatee, cut his hair. In some of his old pictures, he looked soft and lost. He didn't look that way anymore. He answered all my questions in a quiet and somber voice, looking me right in the eye. And it was a bit odd the way he told his story almost exactly the way he told it to the cops, to the psychologists, to his lawyer. I kept wondering if that was just because he'd repeated it so many times, or if he was holding on to the narrative so tight because it was the only thing left for him to hold—or if he really was a fiendish evildoer mustering all his powers to keep his load of crap from shifting.

Two things surprised me. One was a certain sophistication; he referred to a Woody Allen movie and quoted John Lennon, mentioned that he'd volunteered for John McCain but said he believed in spiritual solutions more than political ones. The other was his anger. I expected him to be more contrite, but when he talked about Arabs celebrating 9/11 and said that "all foreign-born" Muslims should be expelled from the country, there was an icy bitterness in his voice that was almost shocking. "It bothered me that everybody was being so damn politically correct right away," he continued. "I don't know which journalist it was, Brokaw or Peter Jennings, who said they were worried about the impact on Arabs. What about the impact on *us*?"

Nathan's anger reminded me of the way he attacked the prosecutor in one of his written statements. "Fred Klein should be ashamed that he feels the need to conceal evidence that Jawed was anti-American. . . . Fred Klein is trying to drape an American flag over an Afghan who at best sympathized with terrorists and who at worst actually aided the attackers by providing planning, expertise, information, and money. . . . My life is no man's game, Mr. Klein, and you may take my life away from me but you will never take my honor."

Before I left, I told him that I had met his child. "You have such a beautiful daughter," I said.

"Thank you," he whispered.

"It seems crazy, that you would do this thing."

"Does to me, too."

In two and a half hours, he didn't once express regret that Jawed Wassel was dead.

FireDancer, the film Nathan Powell made with Jawed Wassel, is Afghanistan's official nominee for Academy Award consideration in foreign-language film. In April, in Nassau County, New York, Powell will stand trial for the murder of Wassel.

What first struck me about this story—this tragedy—was that the initial press accounts seemed to bend over backward to insist that it had nothing to do with the events of September 11th, even though it happened in New York just a month after the attack and the murderer insisted he thought the victim was some kind of Taliban supporter. I could understand why the prosecutor wanted to portray it as "just a business deal gone bad." I could understand why nobody would want to listen to anything that tried to excuse such a horrible crime. But there was a tone of mockery in those initial reports that disturbed me. Maybe Nathan Powell expressed the murder in all our hearts a little too well.

It turned out to be the most depressing bit of reporting I have ever done. When I met Nathan, he seemed so much like someone I would know, only something had gone terribly bad inside. To cope with what he'd done, he seemed to be taking refuge in hatred. Then I met the family and friends of the victim, and most of them seemed to be taking refuge in hatred too. And when I met Nathan's kind mother and sweet wife and adorable child, the whole thing just made me so sick and sad. That's why I wrote such a clinical lead, taking my own kind of refuge in precision and detail. I wish I could say it made it better.

Nathan ended up getting twenty years, which seems about right.

UNFORTUNATE CON
MARK SCHONE

When he was fifty yards from his target, Bruce Gabbard dropped to his knees and began to crawl through the high grass until he reached the tree line at the edge of the field. It was nearly twelve on a hot July night. Rising to a crouch, he peered through binoculars across a chain-link fence and a lawn and into the window of a wood-and-brick house. In a square of light stood his friend Jim's wife and a few other women. Between Gabbard and the light, at the edge of the lawn, lay a hot tub and a gray shed that held the metal safe he intended to steal.

That afternoon, J. H. "Jim" Hatfield had been found dead in a hotel room, an apparent suicide. Just seven weeks earlier, Hatfield had told Gabbard, "If anything ever happens to me, I want you to make the safe in my backyard office disappear. It holds my secrets. I don't want them to fall into the wrong hands." Hatfield had hinted that those secrets might have something to do with the CIA and President Bush. So ten years after his military service in the Gulf War, forty-year-old Bruce Gabbard found himself on a stealth mission behind a ranch home in Bentonville, Arkansas.

He scaled the fence and crept behind the shed. The latch of the little building's rear window had been left open. Gabbard climbed through.

The office was tidy, as it had always been. Paperback thrillers and file folders, the orderly rubble of Hatfield's controversial career as a writer, lined the shelves. Gabbard jerked the hundred-pound safe from its hiding place beneath a custom-built desk and lifted it through the window.

He humped the weight a sweaty half mile through pastures and woods. It was a heavier load than he'd ever carried in the military, and it took him almost an hour to reach the field where he had parked his Jeep.

For hours Gabbard listened to his police scanner and drove the silent streets, the metal box in the back. He was afraid. Hatfield had intimated that powerful forces wanted to silence him, and now Hatfield was dead. Gabbard's own wife waited at home with the light on and a pistol nearby. He was reluctant to call her because he didn't know who'd be listening.

Finally, right before the sun came up, when he was certain he wasn't being followed, Gabbard drove home. Later that morning, he met with his attorney, then drove to a storage complex and moved the safe into a locker. Jim Hatfield's secrets were secure.

Two years before, on the afternoon of Tuesday, October 19, 1999, Jim Hatfield was sitting in his editor's office at St. Martin's Press eating sushi. Though he longed to be home in Arkansas with his six-day-old daughter, he was excited to be in New York instead, in a corner office on the seventeenth floor of the Flatiron Building, waiting for reporters to call. It was the official release date of the book that was going to make him famous.

The editors and publicists of St. Martin's, meanwhile, were happy to finally meet their new star. Until a few days earlier, Hatfield had been no more than an upbeat drawl on the phone. In person, he turned out to be a balding, high-strung forty-one-year-old with a nervous yen for other people's cigarettes and a striking likeness to Billy Bob Thornton.

When Hatfield signed a contract for a biography of George W.

Bush in September 1998, he was a mid-list author of science fiction trivia guides. He told St. Martin's that he had freelanced for alternative papers in Texas and had won the Isaac Asimov Foundation Literary Award for his biography of *Star Trek* actor Patrick Stewart. He hardly seemed the best choice to profile the leading GOP presidential contender, but editor Barry Neville, who'd hired him for a quickie bio of Ewan McGregor for the Berkley Publishing Group (part of Penguin), had moved to St. Martin's, and when Hatfield sent him a proposal, Neville vouched for his professionalism. St. Martin's, a reputable but second-tier publishing house, was only paying a $25,000 advance anyway and didn't expect much more than a repackaging of previously published material. Hatfield's editors were pleasantly surprised in June when he handed in a polished manuscript that listed more than one hundred people as interview subjects. They were floored when he called them on September 2 and told them that he urgently needed to add an afterword to the book, because he now had a scoop that would make *Fortunate Son* a bestseller. "We contracted for a bland, nice clip job," said one of the editors, "not a bombshell."

According to Hatfield, three unnamed sources from the Bush camp had informed him that in 1972 Bush had been arrested for cocaine possession, and that the arrest had been covered up with the help of a Houston judge. One of the sources had noted that the judge was a Republican. In the now infamous afterword, Hatfield explained that he'd read an article on Salon.com about a rumor that Bush had been sent to work at the Martin Luther King Jr. Community Center in Houston as part of a deal to hide a coke bust. The Salon reporter had quoted the director of the center denying that Bush had spent any time there. Since, at the elder Bush's request, George W. had logged several months at a different Houston community center called P.U.L.L., Hatfield had decided to investigate whether P.U.L.L. might hold the key to the coke rumor instead:

To confirm my suspicions regarding Bush's community service, I chose three confidential sources who had been extremely helpful with other sections of the book. . . . If I was going to get any one of them to talk . . . a poker game was certainly in order. With each of them I would have to claim that I had numerous sources who were confirming the allegations "on the record." . . . Basically, I would tell them I was holding a royal flush, when in reality I would be sitting at the table with nothing at all.

Hatfield said his first source, a Yale classmate of W.'s and longtime friend of the Bush clan, yielded to the faux flush with surprising ease. "I was wondering when someone was going to get around to uncovering the truth," Hatfield quoted him as saying. Hatfield said that the second source, an "unofficial political advisor," also confirmed the rumor.

The last of Hatfield's alleged confidantes, a man who had supposedly described himself as a "close associate" of Bush's, was the most important. The man had called him out of the blue months earlier, Hatfield said, to see how his book was coming along, and to make sure he was getting his facts straight. Hatfield reported that he told the man he'd already turned in a manuscript, but the source suggested they meet anyway because Hatfield could always revise the galleys. According to Hatfield, the pair decided to rendezvous at an enormous man-made lake south of Tulsa called Eufaula. The purported meeting made Hatfield's wife, Nancy, so nervous that she begged him to take a gun.

For three days in late June, claimed Hatfield, he and his mystery date fished and talked, after which Hatfield was told not to contact him again unless it was an emergency. A few months later on September 2, Hatfield said he phoned his Lake Eufaula connection again. Hatfield reported that his man said "I wish you hadn't called me," then cursed him for using a cordless phone. He did, however, agree to call Hatfield back. Hatfield asserted that thirty minutes later the Lake Eufaula connection confirmed the P.U.L.L. story and closed with a warning—"watch your back"—and a slap at his boss: "You know what makes me sick about all this shit?" said the source. "It's Bush's hypocrisy. . . . I've known George for several years and he has never accepted youth and irresponsibility as legitimate excuses for illegal behavior—except when it comes to himself."

Hatfield declined to tell anyone at St. Martin's the name of the Lake Eufaula man. When publicist John Murphy challenged Hatfield to tell him how someone with no national reporting experience could beat the media elite to the story of the year, Hatfield explained that he had access through his Texas-bred wife to Bush pals in Houston. "I'm a good old boy," he said, "I know how to talk to these people."

With the biggest scoop of the 2000 race in the bag, St. Martin's gave *Fortunate Son* a code name: M.J., as in Michael Jordan, as in the Franchise. They raised the print run from 20,000 to 100,000 and pushed the publication date up to October 19.

Murphy sent more than two hundred advance copies to newspapers, magazines, and television stations and awaited a barrage of phone calls.

By M.J. Day, though, it was apparent that something was amiss. After a day of investigating Hatfield's claims, *The New York Times* declined to run a piece about the book. "They couldn't get confirmation," says Murphy. "They had three different reporters working on it." All the networks ignored the Hatfield story as well, and the *CBS Evening News* shelved a pretaped interview because of concerns about Hatfield's credibility. A reporter from the *New York Post* challenged Hatfield on his facts: A GOP judge couldn't have buried Bush's cocaine charges, because there were no GOP judges in Harris County, Texas, in 1972.

. . .

By the time Hatfield ordered sushi on October 19, John Murphy was worried, but he was still thinking bestseller. That's when the publicity department fielded a call from a *Dallas Morning News* reporter named Pete Slover. Slover said that someone named James Howard Hatfield had been convicted of soliciting murder in Dallas in 1988. "I got a mug shot of this guy," Slover said, "and I think it's your guy."

Hatfield looked Murphy in the eye and swore the charge wasn't true. Then Hatfield got on the phone with Slover and tried to turn suspicion onto the Bush campaign. "Doesn't it seem a little bit weird to you," he said, "that all of a sudden, the guy that's accusing potentially the next president of the United States of having a criminal record expunged, all of a sudden miraculously has a record himself in the state of Texas? . . . If I've got a secret past, I'm damn sure not going to be going all over the country plastering myself all over the newspapers or TV."

He repeated his denials to the whole St. Martin's team. He threatened Pete Slover with a lawsuit. Then he left the building and went back to the InterContinental Hotel. "We were trying to get him the next morning at his room," says Murphy, "and he had disappeared."

Hatfield *was* the guy in the picture. On October 20, *The Dallas Morning News* ran a prominent story revealing Hatfield's criminal record. When Hatfield was exposed as a felon, the mainstream press interpreted this revelation as evidence that he was lying about the coke tale, too. On the 22nd, St. Martin's pulled *Fortunate Son* out of circulation; a company spokeswoman described it as "furnace fodder." Before it became a collector's item, however, the controversy pushed *Son* to number thirty on *The New York Times* bestseller list.

In the weeks that followed, the media ripped the book apart. Hatfield claimed in his source notes to have interviewed hundreds of people. Reporters at *Texas Monthly* and *Brill's Content* contacted twenty-seven of Hatfield's purported interview subjects and not one recalled speaking to him.

As for the sensational afterword, most observers rejected it outright. Texas reporters had been hearing stories about W.'s party-boy days since his first gubernatorial run in 1994. In a half dozen years of digging, they'd never found anything but smoke. Then some hick burst out of Arkansas with three unnamed sources and a fish story. The mainstream press took Hatfield's felonious past and feeble cover-up of same as proof he was P.U.L.L.ing their legs about the coke tale, too. The media wolf pack scattered without investigating Hatfield's scoop and without asking why: True or not, why would a closeted ex-con tell such a radioactive yarn?

Bentonville, Arkansas, had no stoplights when Hatfield was a boy. Today it's a boomtown famous for being the world headquarters of Wal-Mart. There are few people still around who remember that "Tammy Stewart" was ever married to Jim Hatfield. Actually, even Stewart's teenage kids from a later marriage don't know, and she prefers to keep it that way. She won't meet a reporter in person or let her real name be used, but she agrees to chat on the phone about her first marriage and Hatfield's first trip to New York to meet with a publisher.

In 1976, Stewart, a pale, insecure majorette at tiny Bentonville High, fell in love with Hatfield, who drove her school bus. She was a sixteen-year-old sophomore; he was an eighteen-year-old Bentonville grad who had dropped out of college and come home to work. They exchanged vows as soon as the school year ended. "I was young and dumb," says Stewart, who was married to Hatfield for about a year and a half, "and no man had really paid attention to me before."

Stewart says Hatfield seemed to have been overindulged by his mother, Pearl. His only sibling, Ray, was fifteen years older, and his father, Ralph, a county worker, was distant. Pearl, however, still packed her younger son's lunch every day—with detailed instructions on which items to eat first. Stewart would later learn that Hatfield's mother had told his father, "You ruined the first one. This one's mine."

But Hatfield captivated Stewart with his bright blue eyes and his compliments. Most of all, he enchanted her with his ambition to be a famous writer, a goal he'd had since childhood, when Ian Fleming, author of the James Bond novels, became his hero. For his twelfth birthday Hatfield had requested an electric typewriter. At Bentonville High, Hatfield was vice president of the Library Club. He was so single-minded about writing that at sixteen he arranged a meeting with a local author of horror novels named Ruby Jean Jensen.

Hatfield's new bride helped him edit his first novel, a thriller called *Year of the Snake*, about giant mutant serpents gone berserk. In lieu of a honeymoon, the couple flew to New York to pitch his book to publishers. Stewart waited nervously in a hotel room while Hatfield hit the pavement, manuscript in briefcase. He'd vowed to knock on every door in Manhattan till he found a publisher. Recalls Stewart, "He came back just a few hours later and said. 'They bought it! I got an advance!'" When they returned to Bentonville, Hatfield wrote a check for a new Ford LTD and put a $50,000 down payment on a suburban mansion.

Though Hatfield wanted to be a famous writer, the patience needed to earn success the plodding, orthodox, workaday way was, apparently, beyond him.

The checks bounced. Hatfield had printed them up on a copier. There was no $100,000 advance. There hadn't even been any meetings with publishers. "He flat chickened out," says Stewart. "I think he went to one place, and he realized how hard it was going to be."

Hatfield was arrested. But his behavior was so delusional that instead of sending him to prison, the judge shipped him to the state mental hospital in Little Rock for a month of observation.

Fewer than six months later, in April 1978, Hatfield was in trouble again. After his release from the hospital, he had continued to tell people that he'd sold *Year of the Snake* for a fortune. He began breaking into houses and snatching art and potted plants. The things he stole were props for his fantasy of success. Arrested on five counts of burglary and three counts of theft, he was sentenced to five years in prison. "He had some great dreams," says Stewart. "I just didn't think he had the guts to achieve them by legal means." After less than a year, Hatfield was paroled.

By 1981, Hatfield was in Dallas. Larry Burk, president of a real-estate firm there called Credit Finance Corporation, instructed Kay Burrow, his vice president, to hire a thin, well-dressed twenty-three-year-old transplant from Arkansas as her personal assistant. Two years earlier, Hatfield had rented an apartment at the Leigh Ann, one of Burk's federally subsidized housing complexes in the south Dallas suburbs. The manager of the low-income low-rise had noticed the bright, friendly country boy and given him a job. Burk was ordering Burrow to promote him to the main office in the Cotton Exchange building downtown.

Though Burrow and Burk have since moved to a different Dallas skyscraper, they still work together, as they have for thirty-five years. Side by side at a long oak table in a conference room, they bicker good-naturedly about Burrow's former assistant.

"The first time I met Hatfield, the hair stood up on my neck," says Burrow. She gives her boss an accusing smile. "But Larry was so naive about him. He was charmed."

Burk concedes the point. "He seemed like a decent young kid from Arkansas who was interested in literature."

"He was good with the baloney," Burrow says.

Most of the women working at CFC's headquarters liked Hatfield's ready smile, his curly brown hair, and his flirtatious manner. And they were impressed when he told them that he wrote books in his spare time, including a thin volume of love poetry called *New Beginnings*. They learned that the height of Hatfield's ambition was to write a James Bond book.

Several years into his tenure at CFC, Hatfield announced that he'd won a license to continue the Bond series in a contest sponsored by the estate of the late Ian Fleming. Hatfield said that his first 007 book would be titled *The Killing Zone*, and would feature a curvy blond killer named Lotta Head and a gay Nazi drug lord. "Bond's narrow eyes squinted with a hint of anger," read one passage. "'Who is this bastard Klaus Doberman?'"

Hatfield shared the most intimate details of his ambitions with his best friend, Norma Rodriguez, a receptionist at CFC. Rodriguez was a stocky, brassy Mexican-American a dozen years his senior. She and Hatfield became so close they vacationed together. Much like Hatfield's first wife, Rodriguez tells a story of waiting in a Manhattan hotel room while Hatfield pretended to take a morning meeting with his "publisher." At the CFC offices, he would often tell Rodriguez that he was expecting to hear from his other publisher in London about the Bond book. "Every time I went to the bathroom," says Rodriguez, "this guy would call. Jim would say, 'You *just* missed it!'"

Rodriguez glimpsed a side of Hatfield that he hid from everyone else at CFC. "He always said he wanted to be rich," she says. "He always said he would make a lot of money before he reached the age of thirty-five." The only obstacle, as Hatfield saw it, was his immediate superior, Kay Burrow. Says Rodriguez, "He wanted her gone so he could be Mr. Burk's right-hand man."

In 1986, after five years at CFC, Hatfield invited both Rodriguez and Burrow for a weekend in Mexico. On a pleasure boat in Puerto Vallarta's harbor, Hatfield asked Rodriguez to lure Burrow to the front of the boat, where he could push her over the side. "He showed me how the propellers would rip her apart," says Rodriguez, still amazed. "He was very serious."

Rodriguez didn't fetch Burrow, but she didn't tell her to fly home either. By that evening, the unlikely threesome was drinking margaritas together at the bar of a cavernous nightclub, watching Mexicans dance to salsa. Hatfield was getting drunk and morose. "C'mon, Jimmy," Burrow said. "Get out there and dance." He refused. She kept insisting, until finally Hatfield exploded and kicked a chair across the room.

"I said I didn't want to!" he shouted, then stormed out of the bar. Burrow and Rodriguez returned to the hotel suite, rifled through Hatfield's bags until they found their airline tickets, and flew home.

After the Puerto Vallarta trip, Rodriguez tried to keep her distance from Hatfield. He'd begun to lapse into unprovoked table-pounding temper tantrums about Burrow. Rodriguez finally decided to warn her. Recalls Burrow, "That's when Norma said, 'He's not your friend. Don't ever believe he is.'"

Realizing that her initial distrust of Hatfield had been justified, Burrow contacted the Ian Fleming estate in England and learned that the executor had never heard of Hatfield. Burrow didn't confront Hatfield with her discovery, but she let others in the office know. When Hatfield presented his office mates with self-published copies of *The Killing Zone*, Burrow probably wasn't the only one who snickered at the hand-drawn bullet holes on the front cover and the typo on the back: "Bond has his hands full as he battles a lucious [sic] lady assassin."

Then, in January 1987, Burrow figured out how Hatfield could afford to have *The Killing Zone* printed. A year before, Larry Burk had made Hatfield responsible for paying vendors who worked on CFC's two dozen HUD-subsidized properties. By inspecting Hatfield's checks for irregularities, Burrow noticed that a vendor's name had been slightly altered. When she flipped the check over, she saw that the firm's account number had changed too. As ATF agents would later discover, Hatfield had talked an elderly female teller into letting him open several accounts without proper identification. Each phony business had a name very similar to a CFC vendor. Before Burrow caught him, he'd funneled $100,000 into these lookalike accounts. On advice of counsel, Burk says he decided to forgo prosecution and simply have Hatfield fired.

A few weeks later, at 9:45 AM on February 9, 1987, Burrow slid into the driver's seat of her blue Buick in the Cotton Exchange parking garage. Her new assistant, Gordon Jennings—Hatfield's replacement—got in beside her. Burrow turned the key in the ignition and put the car in reverse. An explosion lifted the front of the big sedan about a foot in the air. Flames billowed from under the crumpled hood, but other than shaken nerves and bruised knees, Burrow and Jennings were not injured. "Call the fire department. The battery blew up," said Jennings. "No," shot back Burrow, "call the police."

The bomb was ineptly constructed. The Buick had been parked over a mound of black powder primed with a blasting cap. Black powder is an unreliable explosive, and not all of it detonated. "That device could've killed fifteen people," says veteran ATF agent Gary Clifton, who handled the case. "But the net effect was about as powerful as if you ran over a culvert and hit the bottom of your car."

"I knew right away. I knew it was him," Burrow says. A week before the bombing, on his last day of work, Hatfield had walked Burrow out to her parking space and hugged her good-bye. "He said how much he loved me and how much he liked to work for me," Burrow marvels, "when he already knew he was going to try to kill me."

Though Hatfield had established an alibi by flying to Mexico before the bombing, Clifton agreed with Burrow about the prime suspect, especially after his first face-to-face encounter with Hatfield. Clifton's assessment is direct. "A shit-bag sociopath," he snaps. "A spineless, backstabbing son of a bitch. Everything is always somebody else's fault. He was incapable of making a complete statement without part of it being untrue."

Eventually, Clifton squeezed a confession out of another suspect, a CFC maintenance man named Charles Crawford. Both Rodriguez and Hatfield knew him. Crawford said that Hatfield had hired him to kill Burrow. But it was Norma Rodriguez who became the prosecution's star witness. In front of a grand jury, she said that the night before the bombing Crawford had come to her apartment and admitted that Hatfield had paid him $5,000 to kill Burrow. He wanted her murdered with a knife or a gun, something "up-close and personal," as Rodriguez testified, but Crawford didn't have the guts. Instead, he'd checked a book on bombs out of the public library.

Hatfield copped a plea and got fifteen years in state prison. With good behavior, he would have been free in five. But not long after entering the Beto II penal facility in Palestine, Texas, Hatfield devised a scam that led to his third confinement. As FBI agent Larry Guerin puts it, "He was just intelligent enough to get himself into trouble, but not intelligent enough to stay out of trouble."

In 1990, while at Beto II, Hatfield wrote a letter to the inspector general of HUD alleging that his old mentor, Larry Burk, was a crook. In secret meetings, claimed Hatfield, Burk had taught him how to bill the government for repairs to private property. HUD took Hatfield seriously enough to launch an audit of CFC.

Guerin and a HUD investigator visited Hatfield. The agents found him to be an arrogant grifter who talked fast and repeated himself. He bragged about the famous people he'd met, the books he'd written, the great things he'd done. He insisted he'd been an important vice president at CFC. Recalls a HUD agent, who wishes to remain anonymous: "He had delusions of grandeur."

But he also had what sounded like credible evidence against Burk—until, to establish believability, he confessed to some wrongdoing of his own. He admitted to the investigators that he'd embezzled money and that he'd tried to kill Burrow because she caught him cooking the books. Hatfield had somehow convinced himself that he couldn't be charged for embezzlement if he was already doing time for the attempted murder.

The informant turned into a suspect. When Larry Burk's lawyer called HUD and told them that Hatfield had offered to withdraw his accusations if Burk paid him $25,000 upon his release from prison, the agents realized that Hatfield's real aim had been to use them in an extortion scheme. The investigation of Burk ended; Hatfield was charged with one count of embezzlement and one count of making false statements. He cut a deal and pleaded guilty to the latter. When he was paroled from Beto II in April 1993, he was sent immediately to a federal facility in Oklahoma to serve time for his latest conviction.

When Hatfield finally got out of prison for good in December 1994, on federal probation and state parole, he had nowhere to go but home. He returned to Bentonville. His mother had died while he was in jail, and his brother had moved to Tulsa long before, but his seventy-two-year-old father was still there, scraping by on a meager pension. Hatfield moved in with him.

For eight months, Hatfield did things the hard way. He hefted boxes at a Wal-Mart warehouse, walking to his grunt-level job till he'd saved enough money to buy a used pickup. He hadn't listed his prison record on the application. "We tell them not to lie," shrugs his parole officer, Eddie Cobb. "But we also tell them they have to work. What are they going to do?" Hatfield began dating a co-worker, and eventually told her about his years in prison. When their relationship fell apart, the woman retaliated by calling his boss at Wal-Mart and blowing the whistle. Hatfield was fired.

At that point many ex-cons would've packed it in. They would've closed the deal by doing crimes till they got locked up again for good. Instead, at the lowest point of his life, middle-aged, unemployed, and living with his dad, Hatfield began making his childhood dreams come true.

At age sixty-two, George Burt is an ex-con success story. There are three limited-edition sports cars in the air-conditioned garage of his mansion on a golf course in the Dallas suburb of Plano. He's proud of what he's achieved since leaving Beto II. He's built a multimillion-dollar computer-consulting business with big-name clients. Seven years ago, he decided to share some of that success with his best friend from prison, Jim Hatfield. Burt, who was doing time for attempted murder, had bonded with Hatfield over a mutual interest in science fiction.

In August 1995, after Wal-Mart fired him, Hatfield called Burt and proposed a partnership. Hatfield would write science-fiction books and Burt would handle the marketing and finances. When Burt's research convinced him there were 30,000 hard-core fans who'd buy anything associated with the *Star Trek* franchise, he agreed to give the plan a shot. "But I didn't do it for money," insists Burt. "I did it to help a friend realize a lifetime dream."

According to their agreement, Burt would pay Hatfield a monthly stipend of $2,500 plus $500 a month to lease a car. The men would share royalties and writing credit for any book they sold. They began with a couple of self-published quickies. Using the pen names Jake Dakota (Hatfield) and Scott Steele (Burt), they slapped together a trivia guide called *The Quotable X-Files* and a book of aphorisms called *The Teachings and Sayings of the Vulcan Surah* and sold both books over the Internet. Hatfield then renewed the only real publishing contact he'd ever had, Ruby Jean Jensen, the same local author he'd schmoozed as a sixteen-year-old. She vouched for him with her publisher in New York, Kensington Books.

In 1996, Hatfield, who had written many books, held in his hands a copy of the first book he hadn't paid to have printed, *The Ultimate Star Trek Trivia Challenge*, published by Kensington. Within six months, Kensington released two more titles by Burt and Hatfield, including a biography of Patrick Stewart, Captain Picard of *Star Trek*.

With his career in motion, Hatfield turned to improving his personal life. He proposed to a twenty-seven-year-old transplant from Houston named Nancy Bledsoe. Like Tammy Stewart, Bledsoe is reluctant to talk about her marriage to Hatfield. She'll only answer, via e-mail, the most general questions about their relationship. "He was extremely outgoing and fun-loving," she explains. "He enjoyed life to the fullest, which made people want to be around him."

Hatfield captivated Bledsoe with his love for writing, as he'd done with Stewart, but he also claimed to have other, more earthbound yearnings. He told her that he'd found big-city life in Dallas unsatisfying, and that he'd come home to Bentonville to settle down. Says Bledsoe, "He wanted a nice, quiet life with a house, children, friends, a wife, and a dog."

Through his wife's circle, and his own magnetism, Hatfield quickly made friends, including computer technician Bruce Gabbard and an emergency-room doctor named Mark Rubertus. Hatfield was unafraid to talk about religion and politics, and soon he was the center of attention among his new acquaintances.

His job gave him the freedom to sit in his backyard hot tub drinking beer at three in the morning. "I think one of the reasons we liked him so much," says Kitty Rubertus, Mark's wife, "is that we lived vicariously through him."

Kitty asserts that Hatfield was more than just a con artist. "You really couldn't say anything bad about him," she says. "The Jim who did that stuff in the past is not the Jim we knew." Mark agrees, and he understands why Hatfield could never bring himself to tell his new friends, or his own wife, the truth about his past. "He wanted himself to begin [in 1996]."

Hatfield soon had a happy, comfortable life. Bledsoe got pregnant; they had a BMW and a Durango and plans to buy a ranch-style house. And in a city without much of a literary scene, even a paperback writer enjoyed limited celebrity. "Everywhere you went he knew somebody," says George Burt.

Hatfield told publishers he'd been a freelance writer in Texas. The day-to-day deceit was harder work. Embittered by the betrayal of his Wal-Mart girlfriend, Hatfield never admitted to his wife or his new friends that he'd ever been in prison. When they asked about his past, he would change the subject. Recalls Kitty, "He'd say, 'Oh, it's a long story.' We'd say, 'We've got time.' But he wouldn't tell us anything."

Burt realized Bledsoe was in the dark the first time he met her. "She made some comment about me and Jim being in the military together, the Special Forces." Hatfield also never told her about Burt's stipend.

Gradually, though, for the benefit of Bledsoe and his friends, Hatfield had to fill in the blanks. He suggested that while in Dallas, along with writing for newspapers, he'd worked for the CIA as an undercover profiler. Bledsoe got the liveliest version of this fable. For example, the man who'd stopped by the house and introduced himself to Bledsoe as a "parole officer," Eddie Cobb, was, according to Hatfield, a CIA operative.

No matter how absurd his ruse seems in retrospect, it worked. His friends say there was nothing in Hatfield's demeanor that suggested he had anything sinister to conceal. There were none of the angry outbursts that had frightened Norma Rodriguez back in Dallas. And though he lied about his past, he was supporting his new life with honest labor. The delusional scammer had become a workaholic who pounded out a book every few months—real books, printed by a real publisher.

The hard facts of Hatfield's life and the long-nurtured fantasy of it were beginning to dovetail. By early 1999, he even had a baby daughter on the way. Then, as always, he overreached.

First, he wrote a biography for Penguin on the actor Ewan McGregor without telling his nominal co-author, George Burt; the sole byline meant an increase in status, but Burt, miffed, stopped sending the monthly paychecks.

Then he took on the Bush biography, which was inspired by the same phone conversation with his literary agent, Richard Curtis, that had produced the McGregor book. Explains Curtis, "I said, 'Who do you think is going to become famous?' He said, 'The guy in *Star Wars* and George W. Bush.' I said, 'Write a campaign biography. Be the first one out of the gate.'"

Hatfield saw the Bush biography as a chance to leave the world of pulp paperbacks behind. *Fortunate Son* would be a hardbound tome on a serious subject, and for the first time he'd be doing real journalism. "That book was his lifeline," states his friend Mark Rubertus. "He really thought he'd hit the big time."

As much as he wanted fame, Hatfield recognized that the book meant an increased risk of exposure as an ex-felon. When he got the contract at St. Martin's, he asked if he could use a pen name, saying he didn't want to be mocked as a sci-fi hack who was out of his depth. But the publisher balked, and Hatfield dropped the issue. Still, he might have escaped detection if he hadn't received an e-mail from St. Martin's editor Barry Neville on August 31 telling him the book was postponed.

By then, it had been nine months since Hatfield had received a check from George Burt. A month's delay in the publication of *Son* would only exacerbate his financial problems. It also meant that Hatfield's chance of fulfilling his dream would be lost, since four other books on Bush were on the verge of publication. He began to search for something that would make St. Martin's reconsider. Two days later, on September 2, he found it, and he wrote the infamous afterword.

On October 19, as the reporter from Dallas prepared to fax a mug shot to St. Martin's, Hatfield realized he'd lost his bet. But once home in Arkansas, he began to fight back. He told people that Bush's father had forced St. Martin's to kill the book, and that the Bush camp had threatened reporters with total loss of access if they discussed the coke story. He complained to friends and associates of death threats on his answering machine and armed men in his yard. Richard Curtis recalls Hatfield warning him to check his telephone line for taps. "I really f—ing freaked." Curtis says. "He got me very creeped out about Bush Jr. and Bush Sr."

In reality, Hatfield had launched his own operation to suppress the truth. A month before the release of *Fortunate Son*, he'd mailed George Burt a multistep plan on what to do in case of emergency. If his past was revealed as a result of the bio, or if "something tragic" happened, Hatfield had instructed Nancy to call Burt immediately. "If you have received that call," he wrote Burt, "I need you to do the following: Call [my father] . . . and advise him that Nancy never knew the truth about me . . . I don't want Nancy or my child to think of me as an ex-con that lied to them repeatedly. If it is publicized that I have a criminal record . . . please explain to her that it is all planted . . . records can be created, etc., [as] part of a smear campaign."

As it happened, Hatfield was able to handle steps one and two himself. And two years later, when "something tragic" did happen, it was Bruce Gabbard who carried out step three, which begins, "Go to my office and the safe is in the far corner. . . ."

. . .

By late 1999, the *Son* storm had blown apart Hatfield's carefully fabricated life. "There's not a day goes by," he lamented to filmmakers
Michael Galinsky and Suki Hawley, who began shooting a documentary about him in November 1999, "that I don't regret [*Fortunate Son*]. I wish I'd never, ever, ever f—ing sent in a proposal."

He lost his country-club friends. One couple turned on their
heels when they saw the Hatfields in a restaurant. Two other cou-
ples canceled a planned camping trip. "It was like a death in the
family," observes Bruce Gabbard. "What had died was Jim's reputation, and by extension Nancy's."

More important, he lost his career, modest as it may have been.
Penguin Books and St. Martin's paid him $15,000 for two books they
had contracted him to write, but told him not to bother turning in
the manuscripts. He completed a children's book—*The Zoocairitas*—
but even in the realm of children's literature he was a pariah. "I
couldn't sell *Zoocairitas* under his real name," concedes Richard
Curtis, "and it was too dangerous to sell it under a pseudonym."

To anyone else, this might have been a sign. But not to Hatfield.
He could have disavowed *Fortunate Son*, moved to a new town, and
taken a job flipping burgers. Instead, he tried to sustain the persona
of an important writer, the Hatfield he'd created after leaving
prison. With his wife and friends, Hatfield started boasting that he'd
rebounded from the scandal with a six-figure contract from a major
Hollywood studio for multiple screenplays. In fact, the only venue
that ever published any new work by Hatfield after October 1999
was the lefty Web zine *Online Journal*, which ran his increasingly
vitriolic anti-Bush screeds. The only sure source of cash and glory,
meanwhile, was a reissue of the book that caused all the problems
in the first place.

When *Fortunate Son* was killed, Hatfield's eager embrace of martyrdom had found a public. Unaware of the length of Hatfield's rap sheet, unimpressed by the corporate media's quibbles, a conspiracy-minded slice of the left decided he'd been gagged for speaking truth to power. The very speed with which he was discredited and dispatched only strengthened that conviction. To Hatfield's defenders, *Fortunate Son* was an instant classic of suppressed literature.

A month after St. Martin's dumped the book, Hatfield had an offer from tiny Soft Skull Press to republish it. Run out of a basement on Manhattan's Lower East Side, Soft Skull specialized in offbeat, left-wing titles. It operated on a tiny budget, but founder and CEO Sander Hicks had scraped together $15,000 to entice Hatfield to let Soft Skull release *Fortunate Son*.

Hatfield accepted the offer. Hicks then urged him to write a new foreword and come clean about his past. But Hatfield couldn't. He still hadn't admitted to anyone in Bentonville that he was guilty of anything. When the media had revealed his stint in prison, he'd been able to persuade Bledsoe and some of his more gullible friends that he'd done the time as an undercover CIA assignment.

So instead of fessing up, Hatfield's brainstorm was to lie some more. He invented a new version of the Cotton Exchange bombing. In the first Soft Skull edition of *Fortunate Son*, 46,000 of which were printed, he wrote that Kay Burrow had been blackmailing Larry Burk, and Burk wanted her dead. Hatfield claimed he was a mere middleman who had hired a hit man because Burk put his arm around his shoulder and said, "Look, Jim. I need your help on this. You're like a son to me."

Now, in addition to the still-questionable afterword, *Son* had a libelous foreword. Larry Burk sued. Many months and many thousands of dollars in legal fees later, Hatfield signed an apology to both Burk and Burrow, and Hicks agreed to pull the foreword. By then, *Fortunate Son* had nearly killed Soft Skull. The company was $60,000 in debt and had lost its distribution deal.

Hatfield, meanwhile, owed a lawyer more than $100,000. Desperate for cash, unwilling to tell Nancy the truth about his dwindling bank account, on July 16, 2000, he resorted to blackmailing his best friend. It was his first financial crime in a decade.

A man calling himself R. J. Hendrickson and claiming to be an AP reporter FedExed George Burt a letter warning him that he was writing a 48,000-word feature article that would run in papers nationwide. The story, to be called "Fortunate Felon," would expose Burt, the millionaire computer consultant, as an ex-con. For $18,000, however, Hendrickson would sell Burt the rights to the article. "Tomorrow is the deadline," wrote Hendrickson. "I hope you are overnighting the signed contract and fee . . . or life as you know it will change dramatically."

Burt hired a private detective, who quickly learned that the Oklahoma mailbox to which Burt was supposed to send cash had been rented with a check signed by Jim Hatfield. Burt did not respond to any of Hendrickson's subsequent e-mails. He stashed printouts of the e-mails and the original FedEx next to the rare coins and Krugerrands in his bank safety-deposit box, just in case. And he changed his mind about his former best friend. "I decided that basically, mentally, this man is really a criminal."

In the spring of 2001, Hatfield got one last shot. With the Larry Burk libel suit settled, Soft Skull found a new distributor for its titles. Amazingly, Hicks wanted to release yet another edition of *Son*.

Tall, muscular, and striking, the thirty-two-year-old Hicks started Soft Skull while working at a Manhattan Kinko's. Between running the press, writing plays, singing for a punk band, and working as a building superintendent, he decided to rescue *Fortunate Son*.

Explains Hicks, "I wanted to do my part as an American and as an independent media person to support freedom of the press, and to get the truth out about the Bushes." Counters Jim Fitzgerald, a former St. Martin's editor who helped Hicks prepare the book for reprinting: "[Hicks] hated Bush and he saw it as a political statement. Nothing else to it."

As Hicks now admits, he never bothered to look into Hatfield's past or investigate *Son's* afterword because he was certain that St. Martin's had quashed the book for political reasons.

In January 2000, the month Soft Skull released its first edition of *Fortunate Son*, Hatfield and Hicks had been walking down Ludlow Street on the Lower East Side with two friends when Hatfield told Hicks that they needed to have a private chat. The two friends were waved on. "Jim was looking like Jack Nicholson in his navy peacoat," remembers Hicks. "It was me and him on that street corner." Hatfield leaned toward Hicks and divulged what he hadn't told anyone at St. Martin's, the name of the Lake Eufaula connection.

"My understanding," says Hicks, "was that I would take this information to my grave."

Because he believed in Hatfield, Hicks had stuck with him through the failure of the first Soft Skull edition of *Son* and the disastrous lawsuit. He kept the relationship going even though Hatfield, under stress, had reverted to the worst of his Dallas-era behavior. Hicks didn't know about Hatfield's attempt to blackmail George Burt, but he did have to weather tantrums. "Hatfield is a jerk," groused Hicks to the documentarians Galinsky and Hawley. "I'm coming to the conclusion he's a crisis magnet with a temper."

Hatfield had been especially prickly after Hicks informed him in April 2001 that he wanted to promote Soft Skull's second edition of *Son* by telling the world the secret they'd shared on a New York street corner. They argued, but in the end Hatfield agreed to allow Hicks to write a publisher's foreword that revealed the names of his three confidential sources. He also agreed to accompany Hicks to BookExpo America in Chicago, where on June 1 they would relaunch the book and drop their bomb on the media.

Before setting off for BookExpo, Hatfield began to hint that something bad was about to happen to him, that he might be arrested or die or disappear. On Thursday, May 31, 2001, the day before he flew to Chicago, Hatfield asked Bruce Gabbard to meet him at a bar in Fayetteville, thirty minutes south of Bentonville. When Gabbard arrived, Hatfield was already many beers ahead of him.

Hatfield told Gabbard that the threat of a Writers Guild strike had put his multipicture screenplay deal on hold. To make money, he had to do two things, both of which threatened his personal safety. First, he had to return to his old job at the CIA. He'd already been to Little Rock, he informed Gabbard, for a security check and a psychiatric evaluation.

Then, says Gabbard, Hatfield's mood shifted from resigned to cryptic. "He started talking in puzzles," recalls Gabbard. He mentioned James Bond and his birth date and the safe in his backyard office. Hatfield told Gabbard that he'd once had an agreement with George Burt to dispose of his safe in case of an emergency, but that the CIA had told Burt to keep his distance. Now it was up to Gabbard. "If something happens," Hatfield said, "I know from your history you know how to make it disappear."

On the first day of June 2001, Hatfield met Hicks at BookExpo. Hicks had decorated Soft Skull's booth with airbrushed paintings so that it resembled a New York subway car covered with graffiti. He passed out wooden nickels stamped with W.'s face and fliers touting a Soft Skull press conference the next afternoon. Hatfield gamely signed books and shook hands.

At 4:00 PM on June 2, Hicks and Hatfield stood behind a podium in Room A of the McCormick Center, facing reporters from Reuters, *The Washington Post*, *USA Today*, and a half dozen other major media outlets. Hicks read off two of the names of Hatfield's sources: Clay Johnson, a lifelong Bush friend and campaign aide, and, sensationally, the Eufaula connection: Karl Rove, Bush's chief political advisor. (The other reputed source, Jim Mayfield, the president's pastor, was not mentioned at the press conference.)

"We allege that this was a deliberate media disinformation campaign," concluded Hicks, and then handed the mike to Hatfield so he could take questions.

The reporters were stunned. Hatfield was claiming that his Deep Throat was the man so identified with W.'s rise that he's been called "Bush's Brain." Bob Minzesheimer of *USA Today* wanted to hear it from Hatfield's mouth. "Are you saying Karl Rove was your source on the cocaine arrest?"

"Yes, Karl Rove was one of my major sources," replied Hatfield. He said that Rove had given the scoop to him, a felon, so that no one would believe it.

For any reporters who were interested, Hicks had brought copies of a hotel bill that showed Hatfield had spent two nights on Lake Eufaula in June 1999, and phone records from September 2, 1999, that proved he'd dialed the numbers of all three men. An attached "phone chronology" explained each entry.

After the press conference, Hicks and Hatfield, with the documentarians Hawley and Galinsky in tow, rushed out of the convention hall and piled into a rental car, laughing and breathlessly congratulating each other. "We had a huge euphoric adrenaline rush," remembers Hicks. "Jim said, 'Can you imagine the White House press office right now? Their phones are probably ringing. Their fax machines are probably going. How are they going to spin this?'"

In fact, they didn't have to do any spinning. Only the *New York Post*, *The National Enquirer*, and Inside.com ever ran items on Hatfield's revelations, and Inside's piece trashed him as "rambling and at times incoherent." They didn't believe his tale about Rove. They didn't think his hotel bill and "phone chronology" were even worth investigating.

. . .

Hatfield's writing career was finally over, and he knew it. When the high from the press conference abated, he dropped his happy sales-man's mask. On the night of June 2, Hawley and Galinsky filmed him as he smoked a cigarette on a Chicago street.

In the footage, his eyes are tired, his face red and puffy, and there's brown Just for Men hair dye daubed into his goatee to hide the spreading gray. Backlit by the floodlights of a gas station, he looks into the camera and all but tells Hawley and Galinsky he's going to die, though he's ambiguous about who to blame.

First, he fingers the president. "The thing that scares me is now what the hell's going to happen? The first time we just pissed off the Bush campaign, and we saw what they did. This time it's the White House. . . . They could say we searched your home and found weed, and that's all it takes."

Then, finally, he begins to look at himself. "I used to bitch and moan to [my wife] about those trivia books. . . . I've known guys in prison and the thing they always told me was that greed will get you every time. And maybe that's what got me on this. I wanted to make that big leap. I wanted to get off that mid-list.

"If anything happens to me, you guys get this [documentary] sold, okay? Get it out in the press. Can you do that much?"

Seven weeks later, just after checkout time on July 18, 2001, the staff of the Days Inn in Springdale, Arkansas, found Hatfield in room 312, dead. The police ruled it a suicide. Within hours, an outpouring of conspiracy theories appeared on the Web. "Karl Rove killed the book," squawked one Web site. "God only knows who killed the author." His friends wondered too.

"They got him," says Gabbard. "That's what went through my mind."

On behalf of all the true believers, Sander Hicks took a road trip to Arkansas to investigate Hatfield's death. In a back room of the Bentonville police department, Chief James Allen shoved a file across a table at Hicks and waited, hands clasped, as Hicks read.

The file showed that on a single day in April, Hatfield had applied for five credit cards. He'd done it again on June 21. Several of the cards were taken out in George Burt's name. They were supposed to be shipped to a Mailboxes Etc. in Bentonville. Hatfield had been caught when MBNA, a major credit card company, made a routine verification call to Burt in Texas. At 9:00 AM on July 17, Bentonville police officers arrived at Hatfield's house to arrest him. Hatfield let them in without protest, and sat calmly in the living room waiting for his lawyer. At 11:00 AM, with his lawyer present, Hatfield struck a deal with Detective Don Batchelder. He needed a few hours to settle his affairs, but he'd turn himself in at the station at 3:00 PM. Batchelder agreed, and he and his partner left.

At fifteen minutes past noon, Hatfield filled prescriptions for Clonazepam (often prescribed for panic attacks) and Celexa (depression) at a Wal-Mart in Bentonville. He drove his BMW south to nearby Springdale. At 12:34, he purchased grapefruit juice and 1.75 liters of Gordon's Vodka at Last Chance Liquors. Paying $75.22 in cash, he checked into the local Days Inn. He parked his car behind the building, took the elevator up to his suite, and locked himself in.

The housekeeper and the manager found him just after noon the next day, his head propped up on three pillows. He was partly on top of the covers, his legs crossed, a watch on his right wrist. Underneath the body was a picture of Hatfield with his daughter, Haley, in his arms and his wife next to them, beaming. The booze was on the nightstand, three-quarters gone. Empty pill bottles had been shoved beneath the mattress. There was no sign of trauma.

Detective Batchelder's business card lay on a dark wood desk to the right of the TV. On the back, Hatfield had scrawled: "Don— Thanks for giving me some time. You were only doing your job."

There were multiple notes to Bledsoe. One told her where to hold the funeral and who to have as pallbearers: Gabbard, Rubertus, and a few others. Another, scratched on a hotel notepad, said, "Forgive me for screwing everything up."

The longest note was as close to a confession as Hatfield could get:

> I just tried to keep us afloat, at least until Zooks sold or FS made some $$. You'll be okay, my love. I wanted to grow old with you and walk my daughter down the aisle, but it's not going to happen. . . . I'd rather her grow up with no father than one she's afraid of, ashamed. . . . [T]here is no other way. Now, you can finally raise your head in this town and blame it all on me.
>
> I'm not going to complain or whine. I brought this all on myself. It's been all downhill since Oct. '99 and this day was my destiny. . . . I am complex, deceitful, and just remember, no matter what anyone tells you, I was a good man who got caught up in bad circumstances. But I'll meet my maker with the knowledge that I loved 2 great ladies . . . and tried my best to the very end.

Nowhere did Hatfield blame Karl Rove or the Bush team or the media or anyone else for his predicament. There was no reference to the truth or falsity of the big scoop of fall 1999. The truth Hatfield wanted to establish was one he left on a Fisher-Price Magna Doodle pad that he had borrowed from Haley. Above his lavish, swooping signature, he'd written in block letters: "I LOVE MY FAMILY."

When Hicks finished reading the file, he ventured a mild protest: "There's still a small inkling of a chance that there might be some sort of involvement by people that are bigger than all of us."

Chief Allen disagreed. "Every single thread leads to Hatfield."

. . .

Sander Hicks wrote a "Suicide Diary" about his pilgrimage to Arkansas, and posted it on the Web. "Reading the suicide note is like colliding with a building," he wrote. "These days, I'm between my stubborn initial defensive posture about Jim and realizing that he was a scam artist, and not a good one. . . . I need to revisit all assumptions."

Hicks was convinced, however, that Hatfield told *one* truth in his life. "As a writer, as a researcher, I accept that he was not perfect," admitted Hicks, "but did he lie about the afterword? I don't think so."

It's a measure of the tenacity of Hicks's faith that he never fact-checked Hatfield's phone chronology or tried to account for Karl Rove's whereabouts in June and September 1999. He drove from New York to Arkansas to look at a police file, but he never spoke to any of Hatfield's supposed sources.

If he had, he'd have been very disappointed. He'd have learned that the "evidence" that Hatfield used to support the most dramatic scoop of campaign 2000 was fiction. Setting aside the fact that Mayfield, Johnson, and Rove all denied they'd ever spoken with Hatfield—such denials mean nothing to conspiracy theorists—every entry in the phone chronology raises questions about Hatfield's competence and honesty.

At 12:49 PM on September 2, Hatfield called Democratic party headquarters in El Paso, Texas. The phone chronology claims that he spoke to his "frequent source, Robert Grijalva . . . to question him about the possibility that Bush had been arrested in 1972 for cocaine possession and had performed community service at Project P.U.L.L. in Houston." Grijalva, a party volunteer who happened to be manning the phones that day, remembers the conversation. It was actually the first time he'd ever spoken to Hatfield, and Hatfield didn't ask him any questions about P.U.L.L. Instead he went on and on about a timeworn rumor that George W. had impregnated his Mexican maid and hidden their offspring in a border town: "He said he'd come up with credible evidence . . . and that the bastard son was living over in Ojinaga. He needed a little extra information to confirm it."

It was an anecdote with a particular appeal to Hatfield. Twenty years earlier in Dallas, he was sitting at the Leigh Ann pool with his best friend Norma when he began talking about writing a bio of Lyndon Johnson. He had a surefire way to sell it. Explains Rodriguez, "He said, 'Everybody knows he liked Mexican women. I want you to go out to the media and we're going to spread this about how you were one of his mistresses. . . . They'll pay you for interviews! We'll go halves!'"

Twenty years later, faced with a delay in the printing of *Fortunate Son*, Hatfield reached for a similar fable about Bush as a fast way of getting St. Martin's attention. That's why his supposed investigation of a Houston coke bust started 750 miles west in El Paso. Says Grijalva, "He told me he really wanted to make sure the book came out before the primaries."

Grijalva knew nothing about any Mexican baby. The chat devolved into an all-purpose gossip session about the GOP frontrunner. Grijalva happened to mention that Bush had changed his driver's license number when he became governor. Hatfield, who'd missed that nugget when it appeared on MSNBC.com, got excited. He wondered whether Bush had changed the number to hide a past arrest. Says Grijalva, "He started talking about this cocaine rumor. He was the one telling me about P.U.L.L., not the other way around."

After he got off the phone with Grijalva, Hatfield finally shifted his attention east. He did call Karl Rove. His cellular bill shows a two-minute call at 5:10 PM to Rove's residence west of Austin. Hatfield's story that he spoke to Rove, however, and that Rove phoned him back thirty minutes later, seems implausible. On the afternoon of September 2, Rove was in Los Angeles, sitting on a dais, watching Bush deliver a speech to the Latin Business Association. "I was sitting behind [Rove]," attests Ken Herman, reporter for the *Austin American-Statesman.* "I was staring at the back of his head." At best, Hatfield left a two-minute message on Rove's answering machine or spoke to whoever happened to pick up the phone.

The supposed evidence of the three-day Lake Eufaula meeting with Rove is no stronger. The LaDonna Inn registry shows that Jim Hatfield checked in at 2:15 PM on Saturday, June 26, and stayed two nights, checking out Monday. Bush had officially launched his presidential candidacy just two weeks before in Iowa, and Rove was constantly at his side. On Friday, June 25, Rove accompanied Bush on his first fund-raising trip to Florida, flying back to Austin late that night after a cocktail party in Miami. On Monday, Bush held a reception in Austin, then flew to San Diego to start his first fund-raising swing through California, with Rove in tow.

Rove must have been very tired (and sunburned) if, as Hatfield claims, he drove five hundred miles from Austin to Lake Eufaula, went fishing, then drove the five hundred miles back—all in time for the reception.

The registry at the LaDonna Inn says that Hatfield was alone.

Throughout his life, when reality wasn't good enough, Jim Hatfield invented fantastic encounters to fill in the missing pieces of a dream. He'd gotten Bledsoe and the St. Martin's editors to believe in a secret meeting with a secret source the same way he'd fooled his first wife, Tammy Stewart, and his best friend, Norma Rodriguez, into thinking he had appointments with publishers.

By writing George W. Bush into his private drama it was Hatfield, not Rove, who immunized the presidential candidate against drug rumors. The public lost interest in W.'s past and became suspicious of all accusations about it, legitimate or not. It can be argued that without *Fortunate Son*'s discredited afterword, the last-minute revelations of W.'s drunk-driving arrests might have swung the election to Gore.

Fortunate Son is now in its third edition with Soft Skull Press, and continues to sell reasonably well. The conspiracy theorists and the dead con man fill each other's needs — one to believe, the other to be believed. Hatfield's death means they can pursue their romance forever, free from the inconvenience of fact. They can close their eyes and see Hatfield and Rove adrift on Lake Eufaula. They can hear Rove groaning, when Hatfield confronts him with the P.U.L.L. scoop, "Ooh, you got me." If you can't prove Rove didn't answer his home phone on September 2, they reason, then he did — maybe he had it forwarded to his cell phone in LA. If you can't prove he never called Hatfield back, then he did. If you can't prove Rove wasn't Hatfield's Deep Throat, then he was.

After Hatfield's death, Bruce Gabbard gradually accepted that he'd been tricked into committing a burglary. Chastened, Gabbard returned the safe to Hatfield's widow. Together, they decided to open it.

Gabbard and Bledsoe walked the brick path past the hot tub to Hatfield's backyard office. There, on the left, on the shelf above his desk, right where he'd said it would be, was *The James Bond Trivia Quiz Book*. It was a guide to the spy novels Hatfield had loved since he was a child, and a model for the trivia books he himself had written in the days before *Fortunate Son*. As directed, Gabbard opened to page fifty-eight, the year of Hatfield's birth, and in the margin found a four-digit combination.

While Haley played in the yard, Gabbard opened the safe. Inside there were no CIA files, no audiotapes of Karl Rove, no contracts for screenplays. Instead there were only secrets he'd been keeping from Bledsoe, legal papers documenting that he had done time in Arkansas for burglary, in Texas for attempted murder, and in Oklahoma for making false statements. One file revealed that he would have been finished with parole in April 2003. Two more years and his wife and daughter would never have known. The reinvention of Jim Hatfield would have been complete.

———

During the first week of September 2001, an editor at Rolling Stone *called and asked me to look into the strange case of James H. Hatfield. For one brief moment this obscure writer from Arkansas had been the biggest news of the last presidential campaign. In his 1999 biography of George W. Bush,* Fortunate Son, *he claimed that three secret sources had confirmed that Bush had been arrested for cocaine possession as a young man and the bust had been covered up with the help of a judge. Soon, however, reporters discovered that Hatfield himself was hiding a criminal past. His scoop was dismissed, his book was pulled from the shelves, and two years later Hatfield was found dead in a hotel room.*

Because I'd written a book about a pair of con artists, the editor thought I'd be a good choice to determine whether Jim Hatfield was just a grifter who'd committed suicide or a lonely tribune speaking truth whose death bore further investigation. Was there anything to his accusations about Bush's party-boy past?

After some digging, I was able to inform the editor that the writer, not the president, was the real story. Why Hatfield decided to tell tales about George Bush was far more interesting than the increasingly remote possibility that the tales were true. Then the planes hit the World Trade Center, and the president's youthful indiscretions, real or imagined, seemed like news from another era. I kept digging, nevertheless, and delivered the article in early 2002. But no matter how compelling, the sad, intricate, and very long saga of a self-invented striver couldn't find a home in the pages of Rolling Stone post September 11. It looked like the story would remain untold, until a Southern literary magazine called The Oxford American agreed to publish it in 2003.

My intended audience didn't seem to notice. When Hatfield died, the flakiest fringe of the left suspected that he'd been murdered by the Bushes. A much larger and more lucid contingent continued to insist that his claims about secret sources and a coke bust were valid. I didn't expect the revelations of "Unfortunate Con" to make any impression on the first group, but I did hope to get the attention of the second. It hasn't happened. Hatfield's book is back in print and continues to outsell most other Bush biographies. Its durability is a testimony to the power of faith. People believe in, and spend years investigating, conspiracies and cover-ups. In reality, politicians do the bulk of their bad deeds right out in the open, in plain view of an easily distracted—and easily conned—public.

MEGAN'S LAW AND ME
BRENDAN RILEY

I'm a sex offender. I'm not a child molester or a pervert, and I don't consider myself a rapist, because I never forced anyone to do anything. The victim in my case consented. But during my trial, a few slick prosecutors, with the help of some greedy psychiatrists and a biased press, managed to convince a jury that she couldn't legally consent, and I spent a few years in prison. I was eventually released, but I wasn't set free. Because in twenty-first-century America, a branded sex offender is never truly free. Not only am I restricted by the policies of parole, but I'm forced to accept some special conditions known collectively as Megan's Law.

I was tried and convicted in New Jersey, where Megan's Law originated. It was named after Megan Kanka, a seven-year-old from Hamilton Township who was raped and murdered by Jesse Timmendequas, a convicted child molester living across the street. No one in the neighborhood was aware of Timmendequas's criminal record, which is what New Jersey lawmakers wanted to change when they passed the Registry and Community Notification Law in 1994.

While I was in prison, I knew the stories about mug shots flapping from telephone poles and houses burned to the ground; I pictured schoolchildren chanting my name in class and avoiding my house when they walked home. But at first, no one really explained how the law would affect the rest of my life. I'd still be in my twenties when I was released. That's why I almost died on September 19, 1999—or at least thought about dying.

I was sitting in a locked jail cell staring out a barred window when someone slipped a newspaper article about Megan's Law under my door. I didn't know who it was, and that alone was troubling, because it meant someone knew my secret. A known sex offender in prison is like a slow antelope on the savannah: In order to survive, he's got to know where the lions are. My only fight in prison was a result of jailhouse justice; apparently, a few misinformed gang members thought I was a "rape-o," so they jumped me. I wasn't really hurt, but I had to do time in the hole, and that wasn't a pleasant experience.

But my worries about another unprovoked attack seemed inconsequential after I read the article. The headline boldly stated: AFTER PRISON, SEX OFFENDERS DO LIFE SENTENCE. Life sentence? Those two words petrified me. I went on to read that a provision in New Jersey's Megan's Law required judges to impose "community supervision for life" on people convicted of sex crimes. Because other states didn't provide this supervision, released offenders had to remain in New Jersey—for life.

I dropped the paper and lay back on my bunk, my jaw slack, my breath shallow. I'd never been so down. I could take a guilty verdict. I could take prison. I could not take staying in New Jersey forever, forever, forever. My family had left New Jersey; most of my friends didn't live in New Jersey; I barely knew anyone in New Jersey. How could I be forced to remain in this godforsaken state for the rest of my life? For a single mistake when I was a teenager?

Eventually, my friends, family, and the prison chaplain convinced me the article had dramatically distorted the truth. And they were right. Because, as I later learned, New Jersey's law divides sex offenders into three tiers. Only the most violent, repetitive, and compulsive—those in Tier Three—are typically subjected to community supervision for life, which means that local schools and neighbors are informed of their presence. They probably deserve it, too. But Tier One offenders like me—those at low risk of committing another offense—are granted more freedom, so they have a better chance to salvage what's left of their lives.

My own life after prison has turned out to be nothing like I'd expected. After petitioning two parole boards in two states, after submitting letters of recommendation from employers and teachers and priests, after signing extradition agreements and parole papers and Megan's Law provisions, I was able to move far away from New Jersey. Because my new state categorizes me as a simple sexual offender rather than a sexually violent predator, I'm not subjected to community notification. So in my neighborhood, mug shots don't flap, houses don't burn, and children don't chant my name. Of course, law-enforcement officials know who I am and where I live, and so do concerned citizens who access the sex-offender registry. But apparently these are reasonable, responsible people, because they let me live in peace.

I work in a small restaurant with people my age. Almost everyone knows my history, but it doesn't bother them. Actually, it seems to make me more intriguing: The guys love to hear stories about jailhouse brawls, and the girls love to confide in me. I think they're confident I won't be judgmental. Consequently, I have an inordinate amount of information about friends with DUIs, husbands on parole, and boyfriends busted for drugs. Sometimes I feel like a priest. On Monday and Friday nights, I play soccer at the YMCA. I learned to play soccer in prison, so during a typical game, I get at least one yellow card for yelling "*Shit!*" when I miss a shot. You're not allowed to curse at the Y. I suppose I could tell my teammates why it's so hard for me to stop talking that way, but I hate discussing it; I'm trying to leave the past behind. And that's hard enough with the Megan's Law restrictions.

Most of them are simply inconveniences. Every year, I have to sign and date a letter verifying my name, address, and telephone number, then send it by certified mail to the local police. Further-more, every time I move I must inform them of my new address ten days in advance. Then my parole officer must be notified, the address verified, and the sex-offender registry updated. It's a rather complicated process, and if the correct forms aren't filed with the correct people on the correct date, I could be charged with a Class F felony. I'm not exactly sure what that is, and I don't want to find out.

Another Megan's Law provision stipulates I attend psychiatric counseling. I hated this at first, because I thought it wasted time and money. I didn't see how some psychiatrist could cure my sexu-ally deviant behavior when there was no sexual deviant behavior to cure. But I was just being obstinate, being proud. Gradually I real-ized my psychiatrist is more concerned about my future than about my past. And because I'm also interested in my future, I now find the sessions helpful.

I'm also required to provide blood samples, if requested to, for DNA testing, but this doesn't bother me. It seemed like they took my blood in prison every time some new DNA evidence was unearthed, so I now have a junkie's regard for needles.

Finally, I must allow the state to publish my name, address, and photograph on the Internet sex-offender registry. This is the most difficult aspect of Megan's Law for me, because it virtually guaran-tees I'll never escape the stigma of being a rapist. I realized this on my second day of freedom, when I reported to the local detention center for registration. I walked in smiling, wearing my old, familiar civilian clothes instead of uncomfortable prison attire, clothes that gave me the feeling of slipping on running sneakers after wearing wing tips all day. But after I told the supervising sergeant the reason for my visit, I didn't smile anymore. He was professional; he didn't say anything derogatory or demeaning, but as he recorded my infor-mation, he stared at me as if I had somehow let him down. I felt like I had dropped his perfect touchdown pass and lost the Super Bowl. Of course, he wasn't familiar with my case; he knew nothing about my offense or how I had accounted for it. But it didn't matter. His silent, judging stare made me feel tentative, unsure, guilty; I know, because he caught all those feelings in a photograph. It's now posted on the Internet, a permanent visual reminder of the shame I feel when someone thinks I'm a rapist. Sometimes I just stare at it and wonder if anyone else is staring at it too. What do they think? How do they feel? What would they say if they met me?

Still, these restrictions aren't as harsh as I'd feared. Not only do they provide released sex offenders enough freedom, but they also provide communities enough information to keep neighbors and children safe. That's why I support Megan's Law. After all, I might be a father one day.

———

Writing about Megan's Law was a difficult task for me. After prison, most sex offenders hope to live their lives in anonymity. But the provisions in Megan's Law, and the existence of the Internet, make that hope a dream. Even if they never break the law again, they'll still be different; they'll be like choirboys wearing normal clothes instead of issued cassocks. But that's reality for a sex offender. We know it, we accept it, and we struggle to make the best of it by trying to avoid attention. So at first, I was justifiably hesitant about writing a Megan's Law article for a popular magazine. I was afraid the notoriety would induce a backlash from the community, or a crackdown by parole. But when a senior editor at Details *agreed to publish the article under a pseudonym, I reconsidered. I thought that by using a pen name, I could write candidly about Megan's Law while maintaining anonymity. And I was right. Since the magazine's release, I've encountered no derogatory treatment nor increased restrictions due to the article's publication. However, there have been other developments.*

Recently, new directives in my state restructured the Megan's Law statute. I was unaware of these revisions until my last visit with parole. That's when my officer said, "As of February seventh, it's a

whole new ballgame." Apparently, in less than a week, all sex offend-
ers in my state will be subjected to an intensive supervision program
that bans interstate travel, limits personal contacts, and increases
scheduled parole visits to up to three times a week. Of course, this
news demoralized me. After eight years of bail, after four years of jail,
after nearly three years of parole without any serious trouble, the free-
dom I'd struggled so long to attain was now being rescinded. And I
had done nothing to deserve it; it happened because of circumstances
completely beyond my control. I have no recourse; there's nothing I
can do. Unfortunately, I am, and forever will be, lumped into a group
of psychotics that's the modern equivalent of a leper colony: We're dis-
dained by the public. But that's life for a sex offender, whether I like it
or not.

CODE OF DISHONOR
CLARA BINGHAM

Four young women dressed in civilian clothes entered an office conference room in Colorado Springs on July 10, 2003. They sat down and one by one told their stories of how, while attending the nearby United States Air Force Academy, they had been raped by fellow cadets and subsequently punished by the academy's administrators. The women were not addressing a judge or a jury. They spoke instead to seven people: a former congresswoman, two retired generals, a retired colonel, a military sociologist, a rape-victim advocate, and a psychiatrist, all of whom had been handpicked by Secretary of Defense Donald Rumsfeld to investigate the burgeoning scandal at the academy.

By the end of the private two-hour testimony, every member of the audience had tears in his or her eyes. "It was just devastating," retired lieutenant general Josiah Bunting III said later. "I couldn't get over it. Listening to their stories was harrowing. It was a moment of cataclysm for me."

Bunting knows military academies. As the former superintendent of the Virginia Military Institute, Bunting opposed allowing women to attend that school, which had been a Southern male bastion since 1839. But in 1996, when the Supreme Court ordered the publicly funded military academy to admit women, it was up to Bunting to find a way to peacefully and safely matriculate female cadets. Recently retired from VMI with his mission accomplished, Bunting was a particularly astute choice to serve on Rumsfeld's

panel, which was headed by former Republican congresswoman
Tillie Fowler. But even the reports Bunting had read on the academy
scandal in the newspapers, and his own experience with the macho
rigors of VMI's infamous "rat line," a hazing ritual, did not prepare
him for what he heard in Colorado Springs on July 10. "It was
much worse than what I had ever expected to find," he confessed.

Women make up roughly 16 percent of the Air Force Academy's
cadet wing (as the student body is referred to). Bunting's realization
that life for them was nearly intolerable came six months after the
first news of trouble exploded onto the nation's airwaves and front
pages. It all started in January when a handful of female cadets
broke the code of silence and began telling their stories to the
media and a few members of Congress. In the following months,
even as women were flying strike sorties in F-16s and B-2s in the
skies over Iraq, more and more victims came out of the woodwork.
Many had never made rape allegations to academy authorities,
often out of fear that their claims would not be taken seriously, or
that they themselves might end up being punished for minor trans-
gressions of academy rules. Indeed, officials seemed to be dragging
their feet, or worse, when an investigation led by an air-force general counsel concluded in June that there was "no systemic acceptance of sexual assault at the Academy [or] institutional avoidance of
responsibility." But by September, sixty-one academy women had
told Colorado senator Wayne Allard's office they had been raped or
assaulted, four top academy administrators had been replaced,
dozens of rules and regulations had been changed, and the Pentagon had launched three investigations, which in turn were being
closely scrutinized by Congress. As revelations mushroomed, the
Air Force Academy's problems began to make Tailhook—the 1991
navy pilots' and marine corps aviators' convention in Las Vegas
where eighty-three women were groped—look like a case of mere
high jinks.

The numbers are staggering. Over the past ten years there have been 142 formal allegations of sexual assault at the academy. (Three of the victims were men.) But as high as this figure may seem, it reflects only a fraction of the truth. A recent Defense Department inspector general's draft survey revealed that 80 percent of all sexual assaults at the academy go unreported, meaning that the true ten-year casualty list could be as high as 700. The same survey indicated that 7.4 percent of last year's female student body at the academy were victims of rape or attempted rape, and 18.8 percent were victims of sexual assault. (By way of comparison, a 2000 Department of Justice study reported that nationwide 1.7 percent of female college students claimed to have been raped.) To this day, no cadet has been incarcerated for raping another cadet.

While the academy struggles to change its culture, the looming question is: Who will be held accountable? Members of the Senate Armed Services Committee, which has been holding hearings on the subject, are pointing fingers at air-force secretary James Roche for mishandling the scandal; his nomination to become secretary of the army is for the time being on hold. Meanwhile, the Fowler panel has singled out one current administrator, Brigadier General David Wagie, and two former academy officials, Brigadier General Taco Gilbert and Colonel Laurie Sue Slavec, for review by the Defense Department inspector general—a move that likely ensures the end of their military careers. Major General John Dallager, the academy's former superintendent—the school's equivalent of president—was reprimanded in July, and later forced to retire with two instead of three stars.

But the problems at the Air Force Academy go deeper than just an administration that has been ineffective at best: interviews with current and former cadets paint a portrait of an institutional culture steeped in hostility toward women, a hostility made even more dangerous by the school's sometimes brutal hazing of new cadets. And as students in the academy's newly entered class of 2007 finish their first semester of courses amid shifting rules and with their behavior being observed in microscopic detail, another question hangs over their heads: Will the military ever fully integrate women?

When Beth Davis joined the ranks of the United States Air Force Academy's cadets in 1999 with the class of 2003, it was high summer, and she thought the campus setting was awe-inspiring. At that time of year, the wind blows down from the Rockies, sweeping across the vast green acreage known as the Terrazzo, which, marbled by white, sunlit pathways, forms the heart of the 18,000-acre wooded campus, built in 1958. Its 7,258-foot altitude—"far, far above that of West Point or Annapolis," goes the academy boast— yields wind that can make a newcomer feel airborne. It whistles through the spires of the Cadet Chapel, a gigantic, white modernist structure whose seventeen A-shaped peaks look like the teeth of a colossal government-issue paper shredder. The wind wafts past Fairchild Hall, a hive of 250 classrooms, forty-five science labs, and thirteen lecture halls. It chases cadet units—the wing is divided into thirty-six squadrons—off the Terrazzo and into Mitchell Hall, the three-story, 1.5-acre dining area, one of the largest mass-dining facilities in the world, where the entire cadet wing of 4,000 men and women assembles to consume meals in twenty minutes flat. The wind swirls over the gym and field house, the library, and the quarter-mile-long dorm, Vandenberg Hall—white, monolithic shapes in the academy's gargantuan geometry, the scale designed to make the individual feel subordinate to the institution at all hours, from reveille to taps.

As if the place itself weren't formidable enough, the rules and regulations that were still in place when Beth Davis arrived in Colorado

Springs could make life nearly unbearable for a new cadet, or "four-degree." These procedures have been eased somewhat this year as the academy has sought to reform itself, but up until this summer all four-degrees, also known as "doolies," lived under the complete domination of upperclassmen, especially sophomores, called "three-degrees," whose job it was to train the newcomers. Juniors ("two-degrees") and seniors ("first-degrees," or "firsties") ran the squadrons, meted out punishments, and controlled everyone beneath them. The four-degrees, male and female, spent their first nine months in a state of constant hazing. The resulting terror, humiliation, and powerlessness were made all the harder for standout cadets of both sexes and especially for pretty young women such as Beth Davis—a tall brunette with long hair, big blue eyes, a soft voice, and the clear, honest innocence of a girl from a nice rural family who had grown up on a small, quiet farm.

At 6:30 every morning, with boots shined and rooms spotless, doolies were subject to draconian inspections, the worst coming on Saturdays. Before meals they stood at attention in their dorm hallway and, in a carefully synchronized chant called "minutes," shouted out the schedule: "There are eight minutes until the first call for the breakfast meal formation! Menu for the meal includes scrambled eggs and sausages! Cereal! And orange juice! Uniform is blues!"

From Monday to Thursday, all cadets wore "blues." Originally created in 1956, the uniforms were designed by Cecil B. DeMille Studios in Hollywood. The lines of the blue suit were drawn with barrel chests and stiff, straight backs in mind. Expertly pressed and worn with pride, a cadet's uniform received special scrutiny throughout the doolie cycle. Even at mealtime in the galactic din of vast Mitchell Hall the four-degrees were subject to a strict code. Doolies had to eat at attention, "squaring" their forks by using the utensil to cut a perfect right angle in the air as they took food from the plate and brought it to their mouths. They were permitted to chew no more than seven times before swallowing. Doolies also had to memorize the preferred beverages of their superiors and serve them accordingly.

Rules followed doolies day and night. They were not allowed to walk into a dorm area other than their own. On the Terrazzo, they had to run, not walk. They could never initiate a conversation with an upperclassman, much less strike up a friendship; if they tried, both would be accused of "fraternization," or "frat." The worst of all frat offenses was sex between a four-degree and an upperclassman. Despite coed dorms and the natural urges of 4,000 college-age, hormonally charged students, consensual sex was officially prohibited on campus, though the rule was often disregarded. "Falcon love," or "doing blue"—sex between two cadets—was accomplished by "creeping," sneaking into each other's rooms.

Doolies, however, rarely had time for that. Twenty-four hours a day they were at the beck and call of their superiors. On a whim, doolies could be summoned to an upperclassman's dorm room or, more common in recent years, to their computer screens to answer an instant-messaging (IM) request, no matter how trivial. If they displeased an upperclassman, doolies, also called "smacks," could be made to submit to physical punishment, called "beat-downs," during which, in cycles lasting up to an hour, a three-degree would scream "up-down" orders in their ears: push-ups one minute, jumping jacks the next. Even the word "doolie"—taken from the Greek word *doulos*, for slave—institutionalized their servility.

The hell had an end to it. In March, just before spring break, the doolies were "recognized" and finally allowed to become equal members of the cadet wing. There is, of course, a method to all this. In order to achieve its mission of transforming outstanding individuals (the average SAT score for the class of 2007 is 1290, the high-school grade-point average 3.9, and 84 percent had been varsity athletes) into a team of highly motivated career officers dedicated no longer to personal desires but to a lifetime of duty to the air force, the academy believes it has to break its trainees down and then build them back up by inculcating a value system designed to instill one quality above all others: trust.

According to this covenant, Beth Davis, in order to do what was expected of her, in order to endure the severe physical and emotional toll of her initiation, would have to trust her superiors. She would have to trust that the upperclassmen putting her through these nine months of hell would be guided by the academy's vaunted honor oath and a strong moral sense.

At first, Beth liked the structure of the academy because the discipline was not unlike that required to run the family farm on Maryland's Eastern Shore; she was used to waking up every morning at five to feed the animals before going off to school. Even as a girl she had wanted to fly fighter planes. Her uncle had flown P-3s for the navy for twenty years, and Beth had set her sights on the Naval Academy, in nearby Annapolis. She wanted the challenge of landing jets on aircraft carriers. Due to the high number of students applying from her area, Beth's application to Annapolis was also forwarded to Colorado Springs, and while the Naval Academy accepted her only for its one-year prep school, which some students attend to prepare for the academic rigors of Annapolis, she was admitted to the Air Force Academy in full. She decided to go, sight unseen.

In June, new cadets start basic training. During "in-processing," Beth's long brown hair was chopped into a bob just like all the other women's, but owing to her bright-blue eyes and delicate features she still stood out, and she was apparently picked on more than other female doolies. Tan lines where her rings had been, along with the highlights still in her hair, compelled the three-degree cadets to nickname her Prom Queen and Daddy's Little Girl. But Beth didn't let the hazing get the better of her. She held her own on the long rifle runs and grueling obstacle courses, and, though 5 percent of her fellow four-degrees washed out by August, Beth survived basic training and was placed in a dorm with the Number Thirteen squadron, "Bulldawgs."

She was severely restricted in her personal possessions. Doolies were allowed no more than two items (typically a framed family photograph and a personal memento) in their rooms. E-mail and letters were unrestricted, but telephone use was confined to Sundays and cell phones forbidden. Except on the very rare "blue weekend," when doolies could venture off campus, the outside world was forbidden. Television, music, movies, and civilian clothes were considered contraband.

According to Beth's account of her doolie year, contraband was what first introduced her to a three-degree named Chris (not his real name). Soon after Beth moved into his squadron, Chris sent out an e-mail to all doolies in the squadron offering to hide their contraband in his room, where he said it would go undetected. On Parents' Weekend, in early September, when Beth's mother and father realized the extent of her privation, they tried to spoil her with several CDs, DVDs, and a pair of blue jeans. Beth hid the banned items in her laundry bag and decided to take Chris up on his offer.

She had never met him before. He was sitting at his desk when she entered with her laundry bag, but he didn't look up. Curiously, he kept his gaze averted from her throughout their first exchange. Beth said, "What would you like me to do with this, sir?" Chris said, "Don't call me 'sir' again. Put it in the cabinet above the door." Beth tried several times but could not reach the cabinet, and the bag kept falling down. Chris never got up to help her; he told her to leave the laundry bag on his bed.

Soon after that Chris e-mailed Beth on her computer to ask if she had instant messaging. He wanted her screen name. She felt reluctant to share this information, but at the same time she had been taught that the consequences of refusing such a request from a superior would be an hour of murderous calisthenics. She replied with her screen name, and Chris started IMing her.

At first he seemed to want to get to know her, but as Beth kept up her part in the exchange, she dutifully observed protocol, addressing Chris as "sir," which infuriated him. Then, even more dismaying to Beth, he started asking about her sexual experience, and, though she would later say that there wasn't much to tell, she avoided Chris's questions. The instant messaging became constant. "I felt like every time I walked into my room—even if the hallways were empty—he would know I was there and a message would pop up," she later said. Adding to the eerie feeling of being watched and controlled was the fact that she rarely saw Chris in person.

By early fall, he was attaching pornographic images to his e-mails, cataloging sex acts he wanted Beth to perform. In particular, she recalls, "he wanted me to 'suck him off'—those were his words." Disgusted, Beth nevertheless did not feel free to turn off her computer and pull the plug on Chris. To alienate him in any way was to risk angering a superior. "That is your job as a subordinate," she remembers thinking. "You're supposed to make your superiors happy."

One night in October, Beth says, Chris snapped. It was two in the morning, and he had kept Beth on a string in her dorm room, peppering her with instant messages. Trying once more to coax her to describe past sexual experiences, he suddenly lashed out at her when she refused. He told Beth he would turn in her classmates for drinking alcohol, and when they got into trouble she would be to blame. He said he would use the well-oiled machinery of the cadet rumor mill to tell her superiors that she was not the innocent farm girl everyone thought she was. He would blacken her reputation all over the academy. The smear would follow her throughout her air-force career. Even the long blue line of academy grads, or "ring knockers," would be talking about Beth Davis. Beth looked on, stunned, sickened, as a long line of crude names filled her screen: "Cocksucker . . . Dickface . . ."

The garish glow from the computer was the only light in the room. Beth stared at the screen in tears, unable to move, unable to understand how she had gotten herself into this situation. She says her roommate, who had been trying to sleep, heard her crying and told her to get off the computer. Suddenly, another message came through: Chris would be downstairs, outside the dorm, if she wanted to talk. Then he disconnected.

Thinking that she would reason with Chris and come to some kind of understanding, Beth sneaked downstairs and out into the chilly mountain air. She saw him standing in the dark outside Vandenberg Hall. Without a word, he started walking toward some trees. Beth called to him. Where was he going? What was he doing? He wouldn't answer. She trailed after him, but as soon as she came to the edge of a nearby grassy area she stopped. She decided she did not want to go any farther. Chris turned around and came back. As he approached, he ordered her to drop to her knees.

She just stood there, frozen. Facing her, Chris put his hands on Beth's shoulders and shoved her down to her knees. He lowered his pants. Later, she wished that at that moment she had jumped up and run away. He took her head in his hand and pulled it forward. She was now weeping, and as soon as he forced himself into her mouth she choked. "I had my hands on him, trying to push away. . . . I was gagging and really a mess," she later said. After he was finished, he pulled away quickly and left Beth where she was kneeling. But before he disappeared, he warned her to wait until he was inside the dorm before she returned to her room.

Like Beth Davis, Sharon Fullilove entered the academy with the class of 2003 and was singled out by upperclassmen because of her looks—large gray-green eyes, a button nose, full lips, blond hair. Like Beth, Sharon toughed it out through the hazing, not minding the loss of personal control. She had set her heart on becoming a cadet at the Air Force Academy and hadn't applied to any other colleges. While many cadets talked about "five and dive," leaving the service after performing the five years of active duty required to pay the air force back for a $300,000 education, Sharon wanted to make the air force her career. "That was part of the appeal. I knew where I was going for the next twenty to thirty years," she says.

Her mother, Michaela "Micki" Shafer, is an air-force colonel who met her second husband, an air-evacuation medic, Gary Shafer, in flight school. The air force had been her mother's and stepfather's lives. Micki, a Ph.D. in biomedical research, worked in air-force hospitals for most of her twenty-year career. From January 2000, six months after her daughter entered the academy, through mid-August 2003, she served as the director of inpatient services at the academy hospital. When Sharon was admitted to the class of 2003, her mother was overjoyed. "It was very prestigious," says Micki. "We were proud as peacocks."

Sharon was in many ways the ideal cadet for the twenty-first-century air force. As a second-generation air-force woman who had set her sights on a career in the service, Sharon personified the mission that the academy had taken on since Congress, in 1975, giddy from the recent passage of the Equal Rights Amendment, forced all of the military academies—despite loud protest from military brass—to accept women. With the draft having ended in 1973, and the military now relying on an all-volunteer force, recruiters focused on a new generation of young women to fill more and more of its jobs. And as the composition of the military changed, so did the academies. Traditionally, they specialized in training officers to lead in combat. Now, in order to include the "weaker sex," who were not permitted to serve in frontline positions, Congress required the academies to alter their mission. As of June 1976, when the first class that included women began basic training, the academies would train not just combat officers but also *career* officers, who perform all of the other functions required of military leaders.

At the time, the air force limited the fields women could participate in. They could fly, but only on noncombat planes such as refueling tankers and personnel carriers. Colonel Debra Gray, the Air Force Academy's new vice commandant of cadets, was a member of that first class of women. "We were often confronted with the question: Women can't go into combat, so why are you here?" she says. "Our answer was okay, maybe we can't fly [fighter planes], but we can go into other career fields, and when they do open things up, we'll be able to compete."

Fighter pilots run the air force and the academy. They are the commanders, the generals, the men who have stars on their epaulets. It was not until thirteen years after Gray had graduated that the Pentagon changed combat restrictions and allowed women inside the cockpits of fighter jets. Today, 99.7 percent of all air-force jobs are open to women—a higher percentage than in the army (67.2 percent) or the navy (94 percent). By 2001, according to the Pentagon, there were 114 female active-duty fighter and bomber pilots in the U.S.

That was Sharon Fullilove's goal, to become a fighter pilot. At Parents' Weekend, she told her mother and stepfather about the

McDonnell Douglas F-15E, a tactical fighter plane bristling with laser-guided munitions and cluster bombs used on deep interdiction missions. "That," she announced, "is the plane I'm going to fly." In the meantime, she thrived in basic training and endured the hazing, understanding as if it were her birthright the compact she had made with the Air Force Academy. She was in exceptional shape, so the physical rigor didn't faze her. She could knock off one hundred push-ups with one hand. She made such good friends during the ordeal that she proudly told her parents, "I have fifty new brothers."

Everything changed the Sunday before Thanksgiving. Sharon called her mother during phone privileges. She was in hysterics. She begged her mother for permission to withdraw from the academy. Sharon would not say more, but Micki had an immediate and instinctive sense that Sharon had been raped.

This was not long after Beth Davis claims she was assaulted. To her immense relief, Chris's instant messages and e-mails stopped completely after the incident outside the dorm. Then, a week later, Chris sent a message telling Beth that she was lousy at oral sex, but that, for her own good, he would do her the favor of taking the time to teach her how to improve her technique.

Over the next five months, a pattern established itself. Chris, in a towering rage, would e-mail Beth and summon her to a study room in the dorm. "Being my superior, it meant all the diamonds in the world that he was mad at me," she later recalled. As soon as she had reported to him in the study room, he would step between Beth and the door and lock them in. Then, pulling up a chair, he would sit down and say, "You know what you have to do." Each time, Beth would say that she did not want to do it and could they please work this out. Chris would reply with silence or verbal coercion. "I was always in a position where I knew what was happening but couldn't do anything about it," says Beth. "It was always him getting infuriated and me trying to appease him, trying to make things better."

After each meeting the e-mails would stop for about two weeks and then start up again. Each time he summoned her, she would use any excuse she could think of to avoid going to the study room, but each time fear that he would turn in her classmates for drinking and spread rumors that she was a slut overwhelmed her. "I was so afraid of him," Beth said later. "It's a fear that you cannot describe to anyone who hasn't been [a student at the academy]." Supported by the cadet system of superiors and subordinates, "he could do whatever he wanted. . . . He had told me that he could get away with anything at the academy. That he knew how to work the system."

Finally, in March, just days before recognition, when she would no longer have to bow and scrape as a doolie, Chris forced her to a mattress that had somehow appeared in a study room, and penetrated her and sodomized her.

During that period, in which Beth Davis says she was sexually assaulted four times and finally raped, she kept her silence. She did not tell her roommates or her parents, and she did not report the incidents to any authorities.

At the beginning of her second year at the academy, she went running one night with a fellow cadet from her civil-engineering class. Their route took them away from the main part of campus. It was around ten, and as Beth and the young man kept running, the lights of the academy grew more and more distant. Beth felt an attack of pure panic overcome her. She dropped back and told her friend she didn't want to run anymore.

Incredibly, he guessed her secret. Sobbing, she told him the whole story. He encouraged her to report it and volunteered to help her find justice. "This is something," he said, "that needs to be reported."

Beth told her friend that she didn't want to lose her career over it. She also didn't want to be an example of why women shouldn't be in the air force. She felt that although women had been at the academy for two and a half decades she was still a pioneer in this world, and she wanted to make it, she wanted to finish, and she wanted to succeed, even if her success was on terms other than her own. She knew that rape charges would ground her permanently, and like so many others, as it would turn out, she believed that she was alone in her torment. "I thought," she says now, "I was the only one."

Many female cadets say that the academy's aggressive, hypermasculine military culture, combined with the fact that women are such a small minority, makes for an inevitably alien environment for them. "They resent us being there, for taking away their pilot slots, for going on rifle runs and wearing their uniforms," one former female cadet says of certain male cadets. "Slowly but surely, like a storm, it starts to brew and it's just saturating. . . . There's a lot of pressure to do your best and be your best and be able to fit in."

Some female cadets react to the pressure by developing eating disorders. Women who gain weight are teased by the male cadets for having "Colorado hip disease" or "Terrazzo ass." Beth Davis remembers numerous women who suffered from anorexia, bulimia, or diet-pill addictions. She herself took diet pills when she was a cadet. Beth knew women who tried not to eat in front of the men in the dining hall for fear of being mocked. "In the middle of the night, you can see girls in the hallway picking food out of trash cans because they have these phobias against eating in front of guys in the lunchroom."

In 1999, the class of 1979—the last class before women were

admitted to the academy—celebrated its twentieth reunion. Known by their self-assigned initials, L.C.W.B., for Last Class With Balls or Last Class Without Bitches, the '79 graduates walked around campus with the letters printed on their hats. At the football game that weekend, L.C.W.B. was triumphantly flashed on the scoreboard for all 54,000 spectators to see. The graduates even spelled out L.C.W.B. in huge letters on a hillside visible from the Terrazzo. At first, Sharon Fullilove, who was a freshman that fall, didn't know what L.C.W.B. meant. "You'd ask people and finally they'd tell you. It was so ridiculous that they were proud of that. Unfortunately, it seems like the rest of the military is progressing and the Air Force Academy is stuck in 1965."

Sharon also noticed that the male cadets frequently accused the women of being products of affirmative action. "Guys would always say, 'A perfectly good male candidate didn't get in because of you.'" The fact that female cadets usually outpaced their male counterparts in both academic and military rankings never seemed to make a difference. In the spring of 1999, for example, 60.3 percent of the female seniors made the dean's list, whereas only 47.6 percent of the male seniors did. A higher percentage of women—39 versus 31—also made the commandant's list, which scores military performance.

Jeanette LeBlanc, an army veteran with a Ph.D. in management and administration, worked at the academy's Center for Character Development, serving for more than a year in the late nineties as the chief of human-relations-program evaluation. After conducting a series of "climate surveys" of the campus social environment, she came away with the strong impression that many of the male cadets believed the female cadets were receiving preferential treatment and benefiting from quotas. "A vast majority of the guys think these women are on their turf and are not as deserving."

Every year, without fail, the climate surveys would show a startlingly high rate of resentment and harassment of women cadets. In 2002, 63 percent of women respondents said they were the subject of derogatory comments or jokes by other cadets based on their gender. Thirty-four percent said they were avoided or shunned by other cadets because of their gender, and 57 percent felt generally discriminated against. When LeBlanc had tabulated the results of her 1998 survey (similar to those in 2002), she says she was shocked by the extent of the negative gender climate. But when she briefed the academy's superintendent and commandant on the survey, they seemed unfazed.

The Fowler panel has analyzed the climate surveys and concluded that on average one in five male cadets believes women do not belong at the academy. On the 2002 survey one cadet wrote, "Even with women in the Armed Forces, they should not be at the military academies." Another noted, "Women are worthless and should be taken away from the USAFA." As Tillie Fowler pointed out at a hearing, the cadets surveyed in 2002 hadn't even been born when the first class of women graduated from the academy. "These young men have no memory of an Air Force Academy without women, yet somehow they believe it should be that way," she said. "The warning signs were there but went unnoticed or were ignored." Indeed, the previous academy administration had dismissed the surveys because they were deemed statistically inaccurate.

The irony is that the air force is considered the most women-friendly of the military branches. "The air force has the highest percentage of women, and virtually all of its positions are open to women, including fighter pilots—the most prestigious," says Dr. Laura Miller, a military sociologist at the Rand Corporation. Miller, who studies the integration of women into the military, also served on the Fowler panel. "The air force," she says, "offers the nicest living conditions for its members, is more family-friendly than the navy, which sends sailors to sea for extended periods of time, and its jobs tend to contrast sharply with the heavy-labor grunt positions in the army and marines." The incidence of rape at the academy, Miller believes, has nothing to do with the more corporate culture of the air force versus that of the navy, army, or marines. "The real issue here is that the institution failed to respond to legitimate complaints. Inaction or, even worse, blaming the victim creates a climate in which rape, harassment, and general denigration of all women can flourish."

But the greater opportunities for women in the air force could be the very reason for the backlash female cadets feel at the academy. Women are a clear threat to the hidebound, male-dominated world of airmen. "The beau ideal at the Air Force Academy is to be a fighter pilot," observes General Bunting. "That person is deeply resentful of women who fly fighter aircraft." Says Lory Manning, a retired navy captain who studies issues involving women in the military, "The more accessible the jobs, the fiercer the protection."

By January 2000, Sharon Fullilove was at her parents' air-force-issued house on the academy grounds—a basket case. She slept all day, fell into random fits of tears, and quickly gained thirty pounds. It wasn't until March that Sharon finally confirmed her mother's suspicion. She told her that a two-degree in her squadron whom Sharon knew and trusted had taken her for a drive, pulled off a remote road, locked the car, and raped her.

Sharon explained that she didn't want to report the rape at the time, because she thought she would be forced to leave the academy. During basic training, at a sexual-assault-awareness briefing, some academy graduates had taken Sharon and a group of her classmates aside and told them, "If you get raped, don't tell anyone, because they'll find a way to get you kicked out." Sharon took the advice seriously. "I decided I would stay and not tell anybody," she said later. "The only thing I ever wanted to do was fly planes and so I tried to forget about it." But two days after she was attacked, when her rapist came to her room in an attempt to smooth things over, she realized that she would not be able to bury her fear.

Now that Sharon had left the academy, her mother argued that she didn't have anything to lose by reporting the rape. Moreover, by identifying her rapist, she might prevent him from assaulting other cadets. Micki took Sharon to the academy's Office of Special Investigations (OSI), the equivalent of an in-house FBI, where Sharon was questioned for several hours by two investigators. "I had to type out my statement, and after I was done, they told me I had made the whole thing up," Sharon recalls. "Then they went into the hall and told my mother I was a liar because my story didn't match my stepfather's statement." What on earth did that mean?

It turned out that earlier that week, when Micki had called Gary at Wright-Patterson Air Force Base, in Ohio, where he was stationed as a reservist, to tell him that Sharon had been raped, she had not passed on the details. Enraged by the news, Gary went straight to Wright-Patterson's OSI office. "I need some leadership here. I've got a big problem," Gary said. He was initially encouraged by the investigators' response. "We want to get this creep," they told him. "Now please write a statement telling us what happened." Gary said that he could not do that, because he didn't know any of the details. The agents talked him into writing a statement that Gary described as "pure speculation." He refused to sign the piece of paper.

When Sharon's story didn't check out with her stepfather's sketchy version of events, an OSI agent told Micki he suspected Sharon was making the story up so that she could get back into the academy. "He asked why we couldn't afford to send her to a civilian college," recalls Micki. "It became apparent right off the bat that they were after her." A few weeks later, the investigation ended, and the Shafers never saw the report.

Micki—officially, Colonel Shafer—went on a mission. "I tried to talk to the superintendent, General Oelstrom, but he wouldn't see me. So I met with Brigadier General Mark Welsh, who was the commandant"—the academy's second-in-command. "My kids went to the same school as his kids. I spent two and a half hours in his office explaining what had happened to Sharon, and he never acknowledged that it was a problem on campus beyond Sharon. He was sympathetic, but at one point he told me that I should get help," meaning psychiatric counseling. Micki became more and more frustrated and angry. "I would tell anybody who would listen what happened to Sharon. I was so sick of the cover-up. People in the military just would not believe that I would talk. They just bury their heads."

Beth Davis was having no better luck getting her story heard. Urged on by the friend to whom she had first unburdened herself, who assured her that it was the right thing to do, and motivated by the desire to protect other female cadets from Chris, Beth finally decided to report what had happened to her. In September 2000 she found herself crying once again as she recounted every sordid detail of the assaults to the agents at the Office of Special Investigations. The academy's victims' advocate, Alma Guzman, was also in tears, as was the OSI commander who grabbed a tissue box and declared, "I'm not supposed to get emotionally involved in these things, but this SOB is going to court. He's going to die."

"He kept preaching this," Beth says, recalling how the commander had announced that he was going to take the case himself because he felt it had to be done right. In fact, the commander did take the case, according to Beth. He interviewed almost fifty people, and computer forensic experts managed to retrieve many of the e-mails Chris had sent Beth. OSI's probe encouraged her; everything was moving forward. "I felt really good about it," she recalls.

Then, all of a sudden, about six months into the investigation, things started to change. "They brought me in one day and said, 'Chris passed the polygraph test.' I was floored. There were two or three of these agents sitting around a table." Beth noticed that the commander, who had begun the investigation and been so moved by her story, was not there. When they asked her to explain why Chris had passed the test, she theorized he must have convinced himself that the assaults hadn't happened. "They said they wanted me to run through the nature of our relationship prior to the first incident. I felt so odd about it. I felt like I had told them fifty thousand times before. They had it in writing. They had my account."

Soon after that meeting, Beth was called in to the OSI once again and given the news: The investigation was being shut down. Despite the e-mails the legal office at the academy had, Beth was told it had deemed the evidence in the case insufficient to prosecute Chris. Beth suspected she wasn't getting the whole story, so she checked with the legal office herself. A lawyer there told her that the office knew nothing about her case. Beth soon learned that the training-group commander, Colonel Alfred "Marty" Coffman, a top academy official who was known around campus for being a tough disciplinarian, had intervened and shut down the case.

"I went to Colonel Coffman," Beth recalls, "and he said that there was insufficient evidence and he thought I would end up looking just as bad as Chris." Beth had made friends with a couple of Chris's classmates in her squadron. One of them had seen some of Chris's e-mails and was so infuriated he offered to go and beat

Chris up. Beth had mentioned these friendships to the OSI agent, and now Colonel Coffman informed her that her actions amounted to fraternization. Beth knew that fraternization was not as grave an offense as rape, and that the academy had an amnesty policy dating back to 1993, when thirteen female cadets had come forward to say they had been sexually assaulted. The amnesty was intended to protect victims from being punished for rules they may have broken at the time of their rapes. But now she could see that the amnesty policy did not seem to apply in her case.

Coffman punished Beth with three class-D "hits"—the most severe of four levels of offense. The first hit was for alcohol; Beth had known that Chris was buying alcohol for her classmates but had failed to report him. The second hit was for fraternization with an upperclassman. The third was the most unbelievable of all: sex in the dorms. The fact, as Colonel Coffman assured her, that Chris was getting more hits than Beth was cold comfort. Beth left his office in tears and disbelief, dejection quickly turning to rage. If she didn't appeal the punishment, she would be walking "tours"— marching back and forth underneath Vandenberg Hall, rifle on her shoulder, with all the other cadets who had gotten into trouble— every weekend until graduation day.

Nearly a year had passed since Beth made her rape allegation. Her grades had begun to suffer and so too her stamina. When her third year of classes started on August 8, 2001, she didn't go. She realized that she needed some time off, so she applied for an administrative "turnback," a form of leave that would allow her to remain on active duty and wouldn't be a blemish on her record. But when Beth handed in her papers, her AOC (air-officer commander, the officer directly in charge of her squadron) told her that Colonel Coffman objected to her request. Instead of an administrative turnback, he wanted Beth to take a medical turnback. Beth knew that medical turnbacks, unlike administrative ones, gave the academy the opportunity to evaluate the cadet's status and find grounds for a discharge. "Colonel Coffman was almost belligerent about putting me on medical turnback," she says, "and he told me to report immediately to a psychologist on base. The psychologist was on the phone with Colonel Coffman when I walked into his office."

The psychologist casually went down a list of post-traumatic-stress-disorder symptoms and promptly diagnosed Beth with a chronic case as well as with anxiety and depression. "He showed the diagnosis to me, and I said I still didn't understand what was behind a medical turnback. So I went into another room and called an officer friend of mine, who said, 'Beth, he just took your pilot status and probably your commission away from you,'" the reason being that the air force doesn't look kindly on pilots or officers who supposedly suffer from crippling emotional disorders. Beth was furious. "I walked back into the psychologist's office and challenged him. He crumbled, saying, 'Please don't hold it against me—I was just following Colonel Coffman's orders.'" Nevertheless, she was forced to take a medical turnback. (The Pentagon would not make Colonel Coffman or any other officer available to discuss specific cases.)

That September, Beth enrolled at the University of Tennessee, in Knoxville, for one semester, purposefully far away from home as well as the academy. Most of her family still did not know what had happened to her, and she didn't want to go home to face them. Meanwhile, a few weeks into the new semester at the academy, the school's medical board convened to evaluate her case under the terms of the medical-turnback protocol, and, finding Beth unfit for cadet status, recommended her for discharge. Beth appealed to the superintendent, and her discharge was repealed, but the damage was done. She knew her hopes of ever sitting in the cockpit of a fighter jet were gone forever.

. . .

When change finally came, it came in a relative torrent. In September 2002, Lisa Ballas and Jessica Brakey, two seniors in what had been Sharon and Beth's class, met for the first time at a support group for rape victims set up by the academy's counseling center. "We went around the room and told our stories. All of the cadets were in despair and so frustrated," says Jessica Brakey. "Lisa and I were the only two who were pissed off."

"Aren't you angry he got away?" they asked the other women at the meeting. Jessica was amazed by the sense of defeat in the room, how listless and hopeless the women were. "They had given up on themselves," she recalls. Two years earlier, Jessica says, she had been raped by an upperclassman during field training exercises in a wilderness area. She kept the rape to herself. "I wanted to pretend like it never happened," she said later. It would take two years before she finally reported the rape. By that time, her attacker had already graduated.

After the meeting, Jessica and Lisa—each relieved to have met the other, a woman like herself with enough anger and guts to buck the system—banded together and decided that they would try to find out how many young women at the academy had been raped. Very soon, their list grew to fifteen current cadets.

"I had so many people come talk to me and tell me their stories of how they were raped and were afraid to come forward," says Lisa Ballas. "I got tired of hearing them say, 'This happened to me, but I would never report it. You are so strong because you reported it.' They were afraid of getting punished for the rules they had broken at the time of the rape, like drinking—which made me so mad, because rape is a felony."

. . .

One of the few cadets who did report a rape during this period was Kira Mountjoy-Pepka. She claimed to have been assaulted the year before by DonCosta Seawell, the star of the academy's boxing team, but had kept the rape a secret for months, until she learned that Seawell had been charged with raping a civilian woman—this, she says, gave her the courage to come forward. But a few days after going to authorities, she was given a class-D hit for being too affectionate with her boyfriend. Her rape case was dropped due to the lack of physical evidence—she had not had a rape examination performed directly after the assault. Later, after she asked the academy to enforce a no-contact order against Seawell (who, she claims, threatened her), she was called into the office of Colonel John "Lucky" Rivers, the vice commandant of cadets. "He told me I was a 'promiscuous little slut' and inferred [sic] that I deserved what had happened to me," she recalls. (In October 2002, Seawell pleaded guilty to one charge of "forcible sodomy" in the case involving the civilian woman and was sentenced to two years in a military jail.)

Lisa Ballas, meanwhile, had taken her rape case much further than most. When she was allegedly raped by a cadet named Max Rodriguez at an off-campus party in October 2001, during her junior year, she went to the hospital the next morning, had a rape examination, and reported the incident to academy authorities. Her case got as far as an Article 32 hearing, the military equivalent of a grand-jury proceeding, but the case was later dropped.

Lisa had lobbied the new commandant of cadets, Brigadier General Taco Gilbert, a '78 academy graduate, to take her case further and convene a court-martial. Gilbert agreed to meet with her, but instead of letting her state her case, he took the opportunity to berate Lisa. He told her that her behavior on the night of the alleged rape, when she had been drinking and playing strip poker, was "wrong and won't be tolerated." According to Lisa, he told her, "If I had my way, you'd be marching tours right next to Cadet

Rodriguez." The officer said Lisa was responsible for her own actions that night: "You didn't have to go to the party, didn't have to drink that night, didn't have to play the card game, and didn't have to follow him into the bathroom." Lisa responded with "You know what, sir? He didn't have to rape me."

After the meeting with Gilbert, Lisa, who had grown up on an air-force base, and whose father was a '71 academy graduate, became deeply disillusioned with the system. "My whole world turned upside down. There was a huge paradigm shift in the wrong direction. I didn't know what was right anymore, what was real anymore." After exhausting all channels up and down the chain of command and not seeing any hope that changes would be made, Lisa and Jessica took a leap of faith and went public.

On October 29, 2002, Jessica clicked Send on an e-mail aimed at 150 media and government addresses. The e-mail read:

> Dear Sir or Ma'am:
>
> I am a senior at the air force academy . . . and since I have been here I know of many females who have been sexually assaulted (including myself) . . . and the academy has done close to nothing to provide recourse, assistance or aid to the victims. . . . The program they do have is inadequate, and fact is most girls who are raped end up leaving on their own after being "pushed out" by the system, or if they choose to stay endure so much political garbage that most of the time it deters them from reporting at all. The office of special investigations here has been known to purposely and negligently foil necessary evidence for rape victims . . . all in the name of protecting the academy's reputation. Is there anything that can be done? Can your office help somehow?
>
> Thank you for your time.

. . .

The following Sunday morning, November 3, Jeff Harris and Kurt Silver, investigative producers for KMGH-TV, in Denver, drove south for an hour and a half to Colorado Springs. Though they were skeptical of Jessica's e-mail, the producers were curious to see if her story had legs. They sat down for breakfast at Mimi's Café with Jessica and Lisa. The two young women were noticeably nervous. Going to the press, Jessica told Harris, was "career suicide." Harris felt instantly that they had both been victimized. "You just knew it," he says. "There were things at the surface that were very painful to both of them." The two cadets told the producers that they were not the only ones; the other rape victims were just too scared to talk.

Together with the station's investigative reporter John Ferrugia, Harris and Silver dedicated the next three months to tracking down current and former female cadets all over the country. Their goal was to find as many rape victims as possible to show that Lisa's and Jessica's were not isolated cases. "We thought that the story was not just about sexual assault at the academy," says Ferrugia. "The issue was: What does this mean systemically?" Ferrugia remembers making cold calls to women who had left the academy, introducing himself, explaining the project, "and before I could finish I would hear sobs on the other end of the line, and the women saying, 'I thought I was the only one. I never thought anyone would believe me.'" In three months, Ferrugia, Harris, and Silver got similar accounts from eleven alleged victims of sexual assault. "What amazed me," recalls Ferrugia, "was that their stories were exactly the same."

When he finished his investigation in late January, Ferrugia contacted Colorado Republican senator Wayne Allard for comment. Allard, who serves on the Senate Armed Services Committee as well as the academy's Board of Visitors—the equivalent of a board of trustees—had been watching the academy closely; indeed, his staff had spoken to Beth Davis just a few days before Ferrugia's call. The problem, Ferrugia explained to Allard, was much bigger than just one or two isolated cases. On February 12, KMGH-TV aired the first in a series of three long pieces on the Air Force Academy. The first story, featuring Beth Davis, Jessica Brakey, and Lisa Ballas, ran fourteen minutes—an eternity in television news. The piece closed with Allard and Senate Armed Services Committee chairman John Warner, an unlikely pair of conservative champions for women's issues, pledging to launch a major Pentagon inquiry into the allegations.

That same week, by coincidence, Allard hired Victoria Broerman to help with health-care issues at his Colorado Springs office. Broerman, thirty-eight, a former emergency-room nurse, had spent much of her career counseling rape victims. Her arrival in Allard's office could not have been more perfectly timed, for just as Broerman had finished learning to operate the photocopier and placed a picture of her four daughters on her desk, the senator's phone started ringing off the hook. Ignited by Ferrugia's story, Air Force Academy cadets and alumnae were calling from all over the country, wanting to tell their stories.

The first calls came from graduates who had kept their secret for years. "When those women cadets went public, it was amazing to me that they had the courage to do it," says an '87 academy graduate who says she called Allard's office to report the rape she had experienced as a freshman. "There was such a code of silence for so many years, and they really blew it open." This particular graduate, who does not want to reveal her name, had endured the code of silence for two decades. When she returned to the academy in the 1990s as a faculty member, she found herself consoling several of her students who had also been raped.

Soon, word got out that Broerman had experience with rape victims and was a trained, sympathetic ear. Current cadets began to call, sometimes as many as six a day. Overnight, Allard's office became an ad hoc clearinghouse for information about academy rape victims. Other senators and representatives who had been working on isolated cases involving cadets who lived in their state sought help from the powerful Armed Services Committee member. Broerman and Andrew Merritt, Allard's state director, met with cadets and their families and began collecting drawerfuls of investigation reports and interview transcripts.

At an official event in Colorado Springs, just the sight of Senator Allard's name printed on the tag on Broerman's chest sparked a startling conversation. "A man introduced himself to me and told me that he was an academy grad, and his daughter also went there and was raped," Broerman recalls. "His daughter is an air-force pilot now, and her father confessed to me that he had advised her not to report the rape, because he knew how much she wanted to fly. Tears were falling down his face as he told me, 'I've lived with this burden for too many years.'" By September 2003, Allard's office had been contacted by thirty-eight former cadets, twenty-three current cadets, and one civilian, all of whom said they had been raped by Air Force Academy men.

Any benefit from this outpouring would come too late for Jessica Brakey, who by the time she sent her October e-mail was already on her way out of the academy. Stress from the rape, she says, had caused her to unravel emotionally, exacerbating problems that dated back to a turbulent childhood. An air-force psychiatrist had diagnosed her with a personality disorder, she was on academic probation, and she had been arrested by police for fighting with her boyfriend. Three days after she sent her e-mail, Jessica was forced to leave the academy with an honorable discharge. Lisa Ballas, who was in her final semester before graduation when the first news reports hit, turned out to be one of the victims who benefited from the publicity. "I got the looks and a lot of people were not talking to me," says Lisa. "But as far as overt retaliation, nothing happened. A lot of people said I did the most protective thing I could have done by talking to the press."

In March 2003, the top four academy commanders were "reassigned," and a new team moved in, charged with cleansing and changing the culture of the academy. When Brigadier General Johnny Weida, a decorated Thunderbird pilot, took over as acting superintendent, this past April, he began implementing a nine-page manifesto handed down by the secretary of the air force called the "Agenda for Change."

Weida's first step was altering the four-class system. The class of 2007, which started basic training in June, will have doolie status only until Thanksgiving, no longer through March. Doolies will not be trained exclusively by the three-degrees. Now seniors, trusted for their maturity and experience, will be in charge of the newcomers. "We have to teach them from day one what's a lawful order and what's an unlawful order. What's a professional relationship and what's an unprofessional relationship," Weida said last spring in an interview in his office, with its picture window overlooking snowcapped mountains and its walls festooned with photographs, paintings, and drawings of F-16s. "We have to do everything we can to prevent the coercive use of power. If there is anything in the environment that is subtly telling female cadets that they are not an equal part of the wing, it creates a culture that allows for sexual predators. . . . I say fix it, ruthlessly enforce our standards, and don't tolerate anything."

Weida and his number two, Colonel Debra Gray, the vice commandant of cadets, adopted the standards for handling rape cases that are used in the active-duty air force and at the other two military academies, which require rape victims to report to the chain of command. After the 1993 sexual-assault scandal, the Air Force Academy changed its policy by giving rape victims the choice of whether or not to report the crime. While this exception to the military guide-lines had benefits in that it gave power back to the victim and allowed her to preserve her anonymity, in the end it also allowed for rapes to go underreported and underinvestigated. "This is a crime, not an infraction," says Colonel Gray, who heads a new response team that meets every week to go over sexual-assault cases. "The old system handled the information in such a closed environment that no one knew who needed help," she says. "My goal is to take the shroud off this process." A compromise proposed by the Fowler panel that would allow for victim-therapist confidentiality is being adopted.

Colonel Bill "Trapper" Carpenter, the director of admissions for the past three years, acknowledges that the culture of the academy may not change until more women join the cadet ranks. "Service academies are tough, masculine environments," Carpenter, a '73 graduate, said in May. It's hardly a surprise that the Air Force Acad-emy has had a hard time keeping its female cadets: Through the 1990s women dropped out at a rate of 33 percent, versus 28 percent for men, despite the fact that the women routinely performed better academically.

"I'd like to bring the percentage of women at the academy up to 25 percent," says Carpenter. That would equal the percentage of new female recruits for the air force at large; 25 percent of today's air-force ROTC candidates are also women. "I'm no expert in inte-gration, but the more women we have the better," says Carpenter. "There is a cadet squadron right now with only two female doolies. What kind of environment is that? And how many [of the thirty-six total] AOCs are female right now? None. We need to have more role models out there."

Another of the Agenda for Change items that General Weida began enforcing requires air-officer commanders to get a master's degree in counseling. The AOCs are usually fighter pilots, and as the saying goes, "In the air force we man equipment—in the army we equip men." What that means is that, unlike in the army and the navy, where young officers lead troops or sailors, most air-force officers are in charge of manning planes, which doesn't necessarily equip them with the human skills they need for handling the problems of college-age students. (This is not to say that West Point and Annapolis do not have their share of problems with sexual harassment and sexual assault. A 1995 survey of the three academies by the General Accounting Office indicated that 80 percent of the women students at West Point and 70 percent at Annapolis had experienced sexual harassment on a recurring basis. The Defense Department inspector general is investigating the way all three military academies handle rape cases.)

Meanwhile, the Air Force Academy has stepped up its prosecution of current rape cases, and three are now pending. But the air force has recently admitted that sixteen graduates who were accused of sexual assaults are currently serving as officers in the military. For current male cadets, the new scrutiny is disorienting. "There have been so many changes," cadet Ian Holt said with a sigh in early May during an interview in the academy library, "that I'm almost numb to them." Holt and many of his fellow cadets have reacted angrily to the bad press that has besmirched the name of their school and the reputations of its male cadets. Morale on campus appears to be at an all-time low. "A lot of us feel like we are getting picked on by the press," said Holt. Adds Cadet David Vincent, "I feel like we've all been labeled as rapists. Maybe one percent are rapists, but unfortunately they are the ones who get represented by the media." Other cadets have reacted to the scandal with shock and disgust. "I find it weak and pathetic to have to coerce sex," says Ryan Roper. "You are not a man if you have to do that."

. . .

In July, with the Agenda for Change largely in place, acting super-intendent General Weida stepped down and the school's new leader, Lieutenant General John W. Rosa Jr., also a decorated fighter pilot, was sworn in. In September, the Fowler panel issued a blistering report to Donald Rumsfeld and to the Senate and House Armed Services Committees. After ninety days of research, the panel concluded that a serious failure of leadership "helped create an environment in which sexual assault became a part of life at the Academy." The panel also accused the earlier air-force general-counsel investigation of failing to hold anyone accountable and attempting to "shield Air Force Headquarters from public criticism." Blame was laid for the first time squarely on the heads of the former top four members of the academy administration.

While Congress decides whether or not to hold Secretary Roche ultimately responsible, and the Pentagon decides whether or not to discipline the academy's previous leadership, a group of seven alleged rape victims are considering filing a lawsuit against the insti-tution. The former cadets have hired Jim Cox, a litigator in the Atlanta office of Greenberg Traurig, a firm that represented victims of sexual abuse in cases involving the Catholic Church, and Joseph J. Madonia, an entertainment lawyer and litigator from Chicago. "Our clients have lost their education and their military careers," says Cox. "They don't have jobs, they don't have counseling, their lives have been shattered." Adds Madonia, "It's time for them to get help putting their lives back together, and if it takes a lawsuit, then we'll do it."

Beth Davis, who is now engaged to be married to a civilian pilot and is living with her parents in Maryland, found that she was spending so much time fighting for her cause that she could no longer keep up with the classes she was taking at a local community college. She has yet to reenroll.

Sharon Fullilove was at the University of Arizona studying to become an orthodontist, but could not afford the out-of-state tuition this fall and had to leave. The betrayal by her beloved academy is still hard to stomach. "It's a terrible feeling when someone does this to you and gets away with it, and then you report it and the system punishes you. It's almost worse than the actual act, that the system failed you."

"As a female officer," says her mother, Colonel Shafer, "I feel responsible to these girls who will get hurt. I can't get through to their mothers to tell them not to send their daughters to the academy." As for her daughter, who after three years of emotional instability has made a good recovery, "you're so happy to have your kid back, but you know they'll never be the same."

Jessica Brakey currently lives with a cousin in Denver and is working as a telemarketer. She sees herself as a sacrificial lamb. Reporting her rape and going public hurt her career, she believes, but she hopes she has helped other victims.

Lisa Ballas has remained in the air force. She graduated from the academy last May and is now attending an air-force flight school in Pensacola, Florida. She wants to fly an F-15E. "I would be honored to die for my country," she says. "That's my job. As far as I'm concerned, it's an occupational hazard."

———

In February 2003, as the nation prepared to invade Iraq, thousands of soldiers deployed overseas. Many were women leaving young families to serve in newly minted combat positions. I spent that month researching a book about how well the military had succeeded in integrating women into its ranks. I had written books about women working as legislators on Capitol Hill and as miners in the Iron Range of

Minnesota and was fascinated by the subject of women breaking gender barriers in untraditional jobs. But on March 26, 2003, when news of a rape scandal at the United States Air Force Academy in Colorado Springs made national headlines, the Pentagon abruptly announced a plan to reassign the Air Force Academy's top four commanders. Maybe the integration wasn't going as well as my sources had claimed.

Vanity Fair sent me to Colorado Springs, and after several months of reporting from both Washington, D.C., and Colorado, I began to write the story. All told, I interviewed nine cadets who had been raped by fellow cadets at the Air Force Academy. They had gone to the academy at different times and come from a variety of social backgrounds and races. One was a cadet in the 1980s and returned as a professor in the 1990s only to find herself counseling her students who had also been raped. As I listened to each of their stories in lengthy phone and in-person interviews, the pattern of their rapes and subsequent ostracization by academy officials became clear. Each had a horrific tale to tell, yet eerily each story was the same.

One of the challenges I faced in writing the piece was how to tell all nine stories. In the end, I realized that if I tried to tell each woman's story the final result would be repetitive and, in effect, shallow. Instead, I decided to chronicle one woman's ordeal in a detailed narrative, while revealing the others in brief but striking vignettes. Beth Davis's rape ultimately came to represent all of the other victims' rapes. I also struggled over the question of how much graphic detail to use, not wanting the piece to be prurient and sensational. In the end, I decided that I had to write the full, horrifying account of one woman's rape so that the reader could understand the enormity—universal to all victims—of this woman's trauma.

In the end I realized that the rape scandal is really about a culture of rape that existed for years at the Air Force Academy. That culture is rooted in the belief held by a majority of the men on campus that women do not belong at the elite academy, much less inside the cockpits of expensive, high-tech fighter jets. Meanwhile, as the Pentagon brass and a handful of senators on the Armed Services Committee tried to get to the bottom of the scandal, women flew those very same expensive, high-tech fighter jets in sorties over Iraq.

CSC: CRIME SCENE CLEANUP

PAT JORDAN

A woman sits on the edge of the sofa in the living room of her ranch-style house in Romeoville, Illinois, fingering her First American Casualty Insurance policy and crying softly. She watches her husband lead two men down a narrow hallway to their teenage daughter's bedroom. He points through an open door and says, without emotion, "It was a shotgun." Then he goes back to his wife as one of the men begins taking photographs of the room.

There are posters of rock stars on the walls. Eminem. Korn. Limp Bizkit. There is a big television, a VCR, stereo, stacks of videos (*Titanic*), piles of CDs (Britney Spears, Wynonna Judd), and a glass bookcase filled with limited-edition Barbie dolls in wedding and evening gowns, swimsuits, and jogging outfits. On top of the bookcase are softball trophies and a photograph of the girl: a pretty strawberry blonde, hugging her boyfriend, a slim, unsmiling kid in glasses. On her unmade bed lies a piece of lined paper with neatly printed letters that read CARRIE 'N' KYLE. There is no body in sight, but on the rug next to the bed a teddy bear sits about two feet from a pool of coagulating blood that, after six hours, has turned from red to burgundy. White bits of skull and gray brain matter are evident in the blood, which is also splattered across the TV, the CDs, the walls, the door, and the bedsheets.

"The halo effect," says Kevin Reifsteck, twenty-nine, a short man with a crew cut and bodybuilder's bulk.

"Her boyfriend probably broke up with her," whispers Greg

Banach, thirty-three. "That's the main cause of teen suicides." Greg looks like a thin, young Buddy Hackett in a black T-shirt that reads OUR DAY BEGINS WHEN YOUR DAY ENDS.

Kevin goes to the kitchen to show the parents the contract he wants them to sign. He explains that he and Greg will have to throw out a lot of bloodstained items but that their homeowners' insurance policy will cover the cost of cleaning up the room. "We can probably save the mattress," Kevin says.

"No. Throw it out," the father says.

"She barely even knew him," says the mother. Kevin raises an eyebrow quizzically. She explains that her seventeen-year-old daughter had been stalked by a nineteen-year-old boy who once worked with her. The boy phoned the house that morning to say he was coming to kill himself in front of the daughter. When he arrived, he broke through a living room window while the mother and daughter fled out the back door to a neighbor's house. The boy went to the daughter's room, knelt on the rug, tilted his head back, put the shotgun in his mouth, and blew half his head off.

Greg, listening in the doorway, says, "There are a lot of whack jobs out there. Unfortunately you met one. Thank God he only killed himself."

After the police came and took the mother's statement and carted off the body, she waited for them to clean up the room. That wasn't their job, they explained. Then one of the officers gave her a name, Aftermath, Inc., and a telephone number: 877-TRAGEDY.

Aftermath, Inc. of Plainfield, Illinois, is a biohazard recovery company licensed by the Environmental Protection Agency and certified by the Occupational Safety and Health Association to clean up and dispose of hazardous waste. Or, in the words of the company's brochure, Aftermath specializes in "easing emotional trauma at a time when it matters most. We provide specially trained technicians who remove your burden during the untimely death of a loved one." In short, Aftermath crews—including the two-man team of Greg Banach and Kevin Reifsteck—clean up the body parts and blood police leave behind. Registered in nineteen states, Aftermath is one of the largest and most respected companies of its kind, which until recently were of the mom-and-pop variety—husbands and wives working part-time to clean up various crime scenes while holding down full-time jobs. Aftermath has been described by Illinois police as "providing an irreplaceable service" and as "extremely professional and reliable."

Say hello to America's newest growth industry. Look at any tabloid or local newspaper: Death is mentioned on every page. As the culture becomes simultaneously more sanitized and more violent, death cleanup has become a specialty market. And when the misfortune of suicide or murder or unattended death intrudes on our TV time, who are we going to call? Aftermath is one of many companies that have sprouted to fill a contemporary need. They even have a lobbying group, the American Bio-Recovery Association (founded in 1996), which puts the annual revenue for the fledgling industry at $20 million to $25 million, showing growth every year.

Aftermath employs twenty technicians, who receive twelve hours of cleanup training and many more hours of sensitivity training. They are also required to get three vaccinations for hepatitis B, which is their biggest health hazard. (Some pathogens, like tuberculosis, can be killed on contact with decontaminating sprays. Others, including HIV, can live for days outside a body, and hepatitis B can live much longer than that and reanimate itself.) Most of Aftermath's technicians have backgrounds in law enforcement or medicine and are accustomed to gruesome crime scenes. They are paid between $25 and $40 per hour, with some earning $70,000 per year.

The average cost of an Aftermath job is $2,500, though price will vary widely, depending on the time required (a few hours to as long as a month). Typical fees are $100 per hour, per technician, $500 for supplies, and $200 for the disposal of hazardous waste. Most body fluids seep into walls and floors, so technicians spend less time wiping away such things than they do cutting out and disposing of parts of a room. Aftermath has a construction crew, Force Construction, that will completely rebuild a room or rooms so they look exactly as they did before the incident.

In 1995, Chris Wilson and longtime friend Tim Reifsteck (Kevin's brother) worked selling newspaper subscriptions. They always talked about becoming entrepreneurs but hadn't yet come up with their big idea. Then a neighbor's son committed suicide with a rifle. The parents were horrified when the police didn't clean up the area after the body was removed from their home. Chris and Tim offered to do it. They spent two and a half hours scraping off bits of brain and skull from walls and sopping up blood from carpets. Halfway through the process, it occurred to them: They had discovered their niche business. The next day they called funeral parlors and coroners' offices to ask who provided such a service. They were told, "We wish someone did."

Before they opened for business, Chris and Tim spent six months researching crime scene cleanups. They learned about OSHA certification, vaccinations, and medical waste disposal licenses. Most important, they discovered there were no books or courses on such cleanups; they would have to figure it out on the job. Then they opened for business in a small office in an industrial strip mall in Plainfield.

During the next two years they would learn many things: the proper technique for cleaning up blood, the equipment and disinfectants that kill germs and odors, the difference between a fresh death and an unattended death, the various stages of corpse decay, the reasons people die, the ways people die, the legacy of death for the families left behind. In time, they would learn more about death than they ever wanted to know.

The technicians at Aftermath are intimately familiar with the smell of decay—a sickly combination of vomit and flowery perfume. They can judge the time of death by how blood clumps and coagulates; they can instantly distinguish fluids of a fresh corpse from those of an aged one. They have dealt with the consequences of someone who has expired in the night with a whisper of death on his lips, and they have seen the destruction and butchery of murderers. They know, odd as it seems, that the scene left by a quiet, lonely demise can often be more gruesome than the most violent death. They are janitors of the human condition.

A typical Aftermath workweek has Wilson and Reifsteck monitoring the activities of teams operating in various states. Theirs is a cell phone–driven business. I join them on a Tuesday, with the expectation that I will be sent on a job as soon as one comes in. We're getting acquainted over lunch in a Mexican restaurant when Chris, a handsome thirty-year-old with slicked-back hair, gets a call about a suicide in Michigan. "Shotgun or handgun?" he asks. He's told a shotgun, which means the cleanup will take much longer. He starts arranging a team.

"About 30 percent of our deaths are suicides," Tim explains, pointing out that most happen during the holidays, in January (after people receive their Christmas credit card bills and tax forms) and in summer (when heat tends to bring out people's hostilities).

"Only 10 percent are homicides, which usually occur outside of homes," he says. Chicago had 645 homicides last year; more than 500 of those occurred outdoors—no-man's-land. "The cops just hose down the street," Tim says. "About 10 percent of our deaths are accidents. The rest are natural causes, with almost 50 percent being unattended deaths"—an industry term for a body that is discovered after as long as two years.

"Most suicides we see are influenced by divorce, child custody problems, or depression," Chris says.

"We had one guy who hung himself," says Tim, "but he wasn't dying fast enough, so he shot himself too. There was also a kid who shot himself twice in the head and lived. He called his father and said, 'Dad, I can't do anything right.'"

The waitress brings our food and we begin to eat. Chris says, "Remember the guy who failed his paramedic's exam? He put a stick of dynamite in his mouth and blew his teeth through a wall." My companions dig into their burritos without hesitation.

"Another guy," Tim adds, "a disc jockey, put in earplugs and taped his eyes shut so they wouldn't blow out. Before that he put down plastic so that the blood would go down the bathroom drain, then stuck the gun in a pillow."

"I remember that one," says Chris. "It made for a quick cleanup."

Grim as these deaths are, the worst involve children. Aftermath's youngest suicide was a nine-year-old boy who shot himself in the head because he was being tormented in school. The youngest body the team has dealt with was eight months old—a distraught ex-boyfriend shot and killed the baby, his two siblings, the mother, and then himself.

"How could anyone kill a baby?" says Tim, the father of two small children. He's boyish-looking in jeans and T-shirt, with a crew cut. "I mean, there was a Winnie the Pooh toy in the crib. Soon after that my little niece got the same toy for Christmas, and I was devastated."

Chris and Tim have mopped up after people who have died in every conceivable way and for every conceivable reason. They freely discuss their experiences, as if they've compartmentalized them in order to cope.

They say the most vicious death they have seen was a murder-suicide. In late August 1998, Daniel Jones of Lynwood, Illinois, got tired of being kidded about the affair he believed his estranged wife, Tammy, was having with his co-worker James Castronovo. Jones put on a suit of body armor, gathered two handguns, a shotgun, and a semiautomatic AR-15 rifle, and set his trailer home on fire. He then went to his wife's Schereville, Indiana, apartment, where he pumped more than 300 bullets into Castronovo and used the AR-15 to sever the man's arms and legs. When Castronovo pleaded with Jones to kill him, Jones set his testicles on fire, and finally finished Castronovo off by shooting him in the head. Then Jones killed himself. When Tim and Chris arrived on the scene, they say, they were stunned by the palpable hatred of the act.

"It took six technicians two days to clean up that place," says Tim. "The neighbors sat outside on deck chairs and watched us work. They brought coolers of beer as if it were entertainment."

Later in the week, I am teamed with the two-man crew of Kevin Reifsteck and Greg Banach, just back from a suicide job in Detroit. "We haven't seen our wives in two days," says Greg. "We just spent fifteen hours cleaning up a self-inflicted death. But we once worked for nine days straight. We lived on Slim Jims and Mountain Dew."

From Detroit, they went directly to a gruesome unattended death in Crystal Lake, Illinois, where they were confronted with a situation that has caused more than one Aftermath technician to quit on the spot. The body was at least a month old—what is known as a "filth job."

"Most can't deal with this type of situation," says Greg. "Especially the maggots. We've walked into rooms that have a wall of flies. They eat off the body first, then lay their larvae, which become maggots. The maggots feast on the corpse, then hide in the walls until they become flies. Sometimes it takes three weeks to get rid of them. Rats and mice just run away when we come. Even worse than maggots are roaches. They get into your clothes."

"I remember one cleanup where the scalp of the corpse had been separated from the head," says Kevin. "The maggots were inside the scalp, and it appeared to be actually crawling across the floor."

"I'm immune to it," Greg says. "There is no scene I can't handle, but I'll take a blood job over a filth job any day. It's different every time. It's interesting to learn the inside story of a crime."

Unattended deaths are a preoccupation for those working at Aftermath: Paradoxically, they are often the saddest deaths, the most unsettling scenes, the most challenging to clean. Chris Wilson delves into the subject. "A lot of unattended natural deaths happen on the toilet," he says. "Defecating slows the heart rate, which can cause a heart attack. If a corpse is unattended for more than two days, it begins to bloat. By the third day, gas and fluids explode through the navel and mouth. They drain out and seep into every-thing: floorboards, cracks in tile, the walls. The stench is so bad even the things the fluids don't touch have to be thrown out. After three to four weeks the body begins to liquefy. I remember a guy who was dead for more than two years. His daughter kept him in a room she had sealed off, and she'd put 150 air fresheners around to mask the stench. She didn't want anyone to know he'd died, so she could collect his Social Security checks. By the time we got there, there was nothing left but the sweet smell of death and a filmy sub-stance on the floor. That muck was once his body."

In the worst unattended deaths, not only does a room stink of rot-ten meat and spoiled body fluids, but it also stinks of the filth that the person lived in when he was alive. Such was the case of a 450-pound man who lived in a room that reeked of dirty clothes, decaying food, and cigarette butts. He drank himself to death and lay unat-tended for a week. When his body was finally removed it fell off the

stretcher and literally exploded in the hallway. Aftermath technicians cleaned up the hall, then went into the bedroom where the
corpse had been. It was crawling with maggots.

"That's the worst part of our job," says Tim, "dealing with those
little buggers after they've been hosting on a body. They're hard to
kill. When you disturb them they scatter everywhere, into the walls,
and we have to track them for weeks. A lot of our guys don't have
the stomach for it. Maggots bother them because they're alive."

It takes a certain kind of person to be an Aftermath technician,
say Chris and Tim. Obviously, he or she must develop an insensitiv-
ity to blood and gore. Most of Aftermath's technicians are men; of
the three women at one time employed by Aftermath, one, college
student Stephanie Hayes, went on to work for the New York City
Medical Examiner's office, taking photographs and writing up
reports at death scenes. Another, Cassandra Seaburg, worked as a
technician until she hurt her back. She became a secretary for the
company and will soon open a branch of Aftermath in Hawaii. The
third female tech quit because of trauma, referred to in the trade as
critical incident stress syndrome. It is not uncommon for Aftermath
technicians to be haunted by what they see. Some have terrible
nightmares; others form an aversion to eating red jelly or rice.

"We get them counseling," says Chris. "A lot of them quit because
they can't believe what people are capable of."

"They burn out," says Tim. "They can't deal with families pleading with them to 'bring back my son.'"

Aftermath makes a point of not hiring people who, Chris says,
"are intrigued by crime scenes. We avoid those guys who just want
to go under the yellow tape."

"Crime scenes get those types of people overly excited," says Tim.
"They scare the hell out of us. The best guys can handle blood, but
more important, they can communicate with distraught people. They
have to be meticulous, serious, no kidding around. Just focus on the

mechanics of the scene. If the family sees you're distraught too, it makes them worse. You have to see this job as part of a healing process."

"After we do a job," says Chris, "most families hug us. 'Who would we have turned to?' they say. We can't bring back their loved ones, but we can help them move on with their lives. I remember one scene in which the coroner was removing a kid's body and he hit the kid's head against a wall and laughed. The mother went ballistic until we calmed her down. It can be hard to deal with the emotional trauma of cleaning up one room while the family is crying in another room because a husband of thirty-two years committed suicide."

Often, Aftermath gets letters of thanks. One man wrote that his family "was deeply touched and appreciative. Your kindness has helped restore our faith that good people do exist." Another woman wrote, "Thank you so much for all your help cleaning up my father's apartment. This has been a very difficult time and your assistance has made it a bit easier. Also, thank you for working with me on the price. Things have been tight, not to mention unexpected."

Tim takes me into a garage behind his office to explain the company's techniques. When they started in the business, Aftermath techs would appear on a job with a shop vac, mop, broom, scrapers, rags, buckets, and a variety of decontaminate chemicals. They soon learned that a simple wipe-down of some scenes was insufficient. "Before we came along," Tim says, "the cops used to just throw coffee grounds around to kill the smell."

The company has since developed a process to completely clean a death scene. First, they use a pump spray with Microband-X disinfectant to sanitize a room and kill bloodborne pathogens that could cause HIV, TB, and hepatitis B and C. Then they wipe down the room with lemon-scented TR-32, which deodorizes and sanitizes, and properly dispose of anything that can't be salvaged. For any lingering odor they use a UV fogger that sprays a mist to counter airborne particles.

Tim points out equipment lined up against the walls. A fan. A pressure sprayer—"for jumpers," he says. A generator. A portable heater. Air filters. Fifty-gallon drums for fecal matter. Shop vacs. "We go through forty a year," Tim says. He points to a pile of black garbage bags. "The bags have to be three millimeters thick." He looks down at the floor and smiles. "Watch where you step," he says. A maggot.

The second floor of the garage is where they keep the towels. "We spend at least $60,000 a year on towels," Tim says. On shelves are chemicals such as Cavicide, muriatic acid, Unsmoke, and UN-Duz-It to kill germs, and protective equipment such as Code Blue gloves, Knot-a-Boots, and Tyvek suits with hoods and masks. They also use respirators, like the kind in the movie *Outbreak*.

"We spend over $300,000 a year just on supplies," Tim says. Aftermath's total expenses run around $1 million. The company, which Reifsteck and Wilson co-own, grosses about $1.75 million annually and has made both partners relatively well-off. Chris drives a two-seater Mercedes-Benz; Tim drives a Hummer.

The phone rings in my hotel room. "We have a shotgun suicide for you in Romeoville," Chris says. "One body." It's a bloody scene, he says, but a fresh one, so it won't be too gory. I should have eaten earlier, I think. Then I drive to the scene, where I will meet the distraught mother and angry father before walking into the bedroom of their daughter, ruined by the suicide of her stalker.

It's a beautiful late spring day. The sun is shining on the neat ranch homes that line the street. A young girl is jumping rope in her front yard and young boys are riding their bicycles. A man is walking his dog. There is a red-white-and-blue GOD BLESS AMERICA

sign on a fence. A woman is standing in her yard, smoking a cigarette, talking on a cell phone, and staring across the street at the
white Aftermath van in the driveway of her neighbors' home.

After Kevin and Greg talk to the parents and make their initial
inspection of the bedroom, they go back outside. Kevin spreads a
large blue plastic sheet on the front lawn. He puts cardboard boxes
labeled HAZARDOUS WASTE on the sheets, then ties orange biohazard
crime scene tape to one end of the house, and around the front lawn.
He and Greg go into the van to change. They strip down to underwear and put on Tyvek suits, plastic booties, Code Blue gloves, protective eyewear, and respirators.

In their extraterrestrial gear, they step out of the van, adrenaline
pumping, ready for action. The parents have left the house, the way
the men prefer it. Greg shuts off the heat in the living room; the Tyvek
suits are hot. He walks down the hallway to the girl's room.

"This is a clean scene," he says. "No smell, no decay. We should
clean it up in a few hours."

Greg kneels on the rug near the large puddle of blood and begins
cutting a large swath with a razor.

"You have to be careful with rugs," Greg says over his shoulder.
"Carpet tacks can cut you just like drug needles." Kevin examines
the girl's open closet to see if any blood has hit her clothes. He picks
up her phone, sprays a lemon cleanser on it, and wipes it off. When
he examines the girl's bed, he finds blood splattered on the sheets
and pulls them off. He takes the sheets outside and drops them into
an empty box on the blue plastic.

Greg rolls up the large piece of bloody carpet and puts it into a
black plastic bag. The wood floor underneath is saturated. "We'll
have to cut out the floor," he says, "but first I have to sop up the
blood so it doesn't splatter." He puts towels soaked in disinfectant
on the bloody floorboards and throws them into the plastic bag.

Kevin carts out the mattress, passing Greg in the hallway. Greg points down at his foot. "Watch your step," he says. He's found a skull fragment. "I've got an eye for body parts," he says to me. "At one suicide, the cops told us the guy had shot himself in the room where the body was discovered. But I found part of his lips in another room. I told the cops he shot himself once there, and then a second time in the room where he died." Often, Aftermath technicians find things the police have missed—a knife, bullet casings, a gun, even a suicide note.

Kevin kneels on the floor to inspect the girl's CD boxes, which are splattered with blood. He takes the discs out of the jewel boxes and throws them into a dresser drawer. The boxes are then tossed into the garbage bag. He stops, pulls the girl's hair dryer out of the drawer, wipes off a tiny spot of blood, and puts it back.

Behind him, Greg says, "You can't hurry on this job or you'll miss things." That's why Greg and Kevin always "blue light" (use an ultraviolet light to illuminate any remaining traces of blood) a room. "Actually we call it a black light," Greg says.

After working for a few hours, Greg and Kevin go outside for a break. They discard their booties and gloves. Before they reenter the house they will put on new ones.

Before working for Aftermath, Greg had a job with the Illinois Department of Public Health, disposing of hazardous materials. When he read about Aftermath in a newspaper article three years ago, he applied for a job and hasn't looked back. "I always liked horror movies," he says.

Kevin liked horror movies, too. He also raised snakes and fed them live mice. His ambition was to become a doctor, but at twenty he joined the army to be a medic. He left the service as a sergeant five years later and began to work for his brother at Aftermath. His first job was a two-day "bleed out" (suicide by razor blade). "It didn't bother me," he says. What does bother him are some of the people he comes into contact with at death scenes.

"People will walk over their dead grandmother to get her Social Security check," he says.

"I won't let my wife go into a highway rest stop without me," says Greg, "ever since I cleaned up a rest stop where some scumbag had beaten a woman to a bloody pulp, then raped her."

"You become suspicious," says Kevin. "Most people never see what we see, like a guy who's excited he found $2,000 in his grandma's room, where she's bleeding out on the floor, or two guys fighting over a dead relative's TV."

"Even some of the families we clean up for are unpleasant to us," says Greg. "There's no tipping in our job. It's not like delivering pizzas. We take away loved ones, and sometimes people want to lash out. I once found a clean skull fragment from an eighteen-year-old boy, and when his mother saw that it had her son's hair on it, she wanted to keep it. She went nuts on me."

When we go back into the home, I ask Greg and Kevin if this is one of their better scenes. Greg says, "There's no such thing as a good death." As proof, he goes to the van and returns with photographs of bodies he has cleaned up: a man whose arm was caught in a printing press and whose entire body was then sucked into the machine; another man who had been dead a week and whose skin had turned black; a man lying in the road whose head had been crushed by a truck. "People were just driving around him," Greg says. Then he describes the most difficult scene he has cleaned: a man who had fallen forty-six floors down an elevator shaft.

"I had to clean up body parts and blood on every floor in the shaft," he says. "I rappelled down the shaft, picked up parts on each floor, and handed them to my workers. The guy's arms weighed as much as a dog. It took us six days to complete the job."

Greg and Kevin finish the cleanup around midnight. The last

thing they do is run a fogger to remove any lingering odor in the room. Then they talk to the girl's parents, who have returned home. The mother is still upset. Greg tries to reassure her. "This is a happy ending," he says. "That guy won't harass your daughter anymore."

The following morning I'm back at the Aftermath office. Cassandra is making calls. Chris is on his cell phone. Tim is sitting beside me at a card table piled high with Aftermath brochures.

"So, how did you like your first suicide?" he asks with an impish grin.

"Not as bad as I expected," I say. "I went out to dinner afterward."

"Really?" Tim reaches down and brushes something off my shoe. "Just a maggot." I shake my foot quickly.

He grins. "Just kidding."

Chris gets off his cell phone. "You didn't throw up?" he asks me. I shake my head. Chris looks crestfallen. Then he brightens. "Your photographer almost did." It seems to make him feel better. Despite their protestations, they all feel a certain macho pride in their ability to do a job most people can't stomach. It requires a special temperament, like that of soldiers in battle who devise various mind-sets to get through the horrors they must face. Chris jokes about the things he sees. Tim is coolly detached from them. Kevin focuses on the mechanics of "tidying up." Greg reduces his job to a contest, like a puzzle, finding the clues that others miss.

What these guys have in common is the tendency to see in life's cruelties the natural order of man. They don't see the murder and suicide and inhumanity through a moral prism. That would be psychologically debilitating. Instead, they see the scenes of destruction as the facts of man's existence. Kevin once said, "We human beings like to separate ourselves from animals, but we're just like them — only they're better."

"Someone has to do it," Tim says of the job. He adds that this is not exactly the kind of career he aspired to when he was eight years old. But it's a job he has the perfect temperament for. "I'm able to separate myself from my work and my life. Some people say we're sick, but they don't see what we do for families. I'm very happy in my job. I'll retire doing this and pass it on to my kids—if they want to do it." I ask him what he has learned over the years. He says, "If a person wants to kill himself, you can't stop him."

"Exactly," says Chris. "Suicide is such a selfish act. Most suicides are attempts to get back at someone."

Before I leave, I ask Chris one more question: "Are you religious?" He smiles, then shrugs. I look at Tim.

"No," he says. "This job makes you not believe in much."

———

I am a squeamish person. I can handle pain, up to a point, but the sight of blood makes me dizzy and weak. When I was getting married in 1961, my soon-to-be wife and I went to her doctor, a tiny, wizened old man, for our blood test, which he took in his office in his old Victorian house. I watched him stick the needle in my soon-to-be wife's arm and saw the blood being drawn into it. I grew faint. When the doctor plunged the needle in my arm and I saw the blood being drawn into it, I fainted. The next thing I remember was my limp but upright body being held up by my tiny doctor and my tiny wife-to-be, my arms draped over both their shoulders as they dragged me to the front door and then outside where the fresh air revived me.

Needless to say, I don't go to slasher movies where heads explode and blood spurts out of bodies and arms are sliced off. In fact, just writing this is making me sick to my stomach. Yet, a few weeks before my sixty-second birthday, my editor at Playboy, *Chris Napolitano, called me with an assignment I ordinarily would have turned down: crime scene cleanup crews. "Double homicides and shotgun suicides," he said. "We want you to describe it all." I was getting sick just listening to him. But I got even sicker realizing that my mortgage was due and I was short of cash, so I took the assignment.*

I flew to a little town southwest of Chicago to interview the owners of Aftermath, Inc. They were nice guys who talked casually about all the bloody messes they'd cleaned up while we ate lunch at a Mexican restaurant. "No salsa for me," I told the waitress. Then I went back to my hotel room and waited for them to call me with a fresh cleanup, which I was dreading. After two days, they still hadn't called. I became hopeful no poor soul in Illinois would blow his brains out before I left in two more days. But it was not to be. On my next-to-last day there, they called me with a fresh shotgun suicide. I went out to the house, where their technicians were already suited up. I followed them into the house and the bedroom where a lovesick boy had blown his brains out in the bedroom of a girl who had rejected his affections. I stared at the pool of blood and brains on the floor, the splatters on the wall and on her bed, closet, and dresser, and waited to get sick.

"Watch it," one of the technicians said to me. He pointed at my feet. "Some brain."

I watched them for more than two hours, and then, blessedly, I left. I went to a bar for a drink. I had two, three, and then I ordered a hamburger with fries. I poured the ketchup on my fries and wolfed the whole thing down. The barmaid came over to me and asked if I wanted another drink. "Sure," I said. "I'm celebrating tonight. It's my birthday."

"Congratulations!" she said. "And what did you do on your birthday?" I told her.

THE PROFESSOR AND THE PORN
ELISABETH FRANCK

On the evening of August 15, 2002, just days before new students were to arrive for the fall semester, an e-mail titled "Distressing News" went out to the community of New York Law School, in lower Manhattan. Because of the alarming heading, many professors clicked the e-mail open thinking it might announce the death of one of the faculty.

"I'm saddened to report to you that I learned this afternoon that our colleague, Professor Edward Samuels, was arrested on charges relating to possession of child pornographic images," the dean of the school, Richard Matasar, had written. "The Law School has placed Professor Samuels on paid administrative leave so that he may attend to his defense. . . . Our hearts go out to Ed and his family as they face the difficult time ahead."

Several faculty members promptly called each other to report that a hoax had been perpetrated, and at least one called the dean to warn him that a hacker had infiltrated the system. The following morning, however, the story was splashed across the pages of several newspapers, including the *New York Post*, which proffered the irresistible tabloid headline: PROF PORN STUNNER — STAFF FINDS XXX KID PIX ON HIS OFFICE COMPUTER.

Indeed, computer technicians at the school had happened upon pornographic pictures of young girls while trying to fix Samuels's computer, the papers reported, and a police search of his apartment on the Upper West Side had yielded 159 disks of illegal images. Later reports would detail the gruesome and disturbingly cruel nature of some of the photographs—young girls being raped by adults or dogs; babies being sexually assaulted; young children bound and whipped. Samuels had more than 100,000 pictures, the largest stash ever seen by the Manhattan DA's office.

Colleagues were staggered. The balding, diminutive Samuels had been, for twenty-six years, a highly respected member of the faculty and a dedicated copyright scholar and professor. He was described as quiet and thoughtful by peers and was popular with students. As one longtime faculty member put it, "You always hear 'the last person in the world,' and I'm not saying I can think of someone else who would have done this, but this totally blew you away."

By the following Monday, when staff and faculty were back at school, no one could talk of anything else. "We were all looking at each other and going, 'Can you believe it?'" one professor said. Staff members who were friendly with the technicians who'd discovered the porn confirmed the information for incredulous professors.

"It made me sick," recalled Joan Argento, who had been Samuels's assistant for five years. "There were times when I had my daughter at work and he said, 'Hi, honey, how are you?' It just made me sick."

But if staff members were appalled, for Samuels's faculty colleagues and friends the discovery posed a much more complex dilemma. Even after he pleaded guilty to possessing one hundred images, many of them remained torn. And when the two computer technicians who had discovered the pictures were later fired, there was a conspicuous lack of interest in rallying to their defense.

New York Law School is not the only academic institution that has recently been linked to child pornography. In the past few years, professors at Yale and Penn have been enmeshed in similar scandals.

Antonio Lasaga, a Yale professor and housemaster, was charged with possession of 150,000 images of child porn, including two video-tapes of him raping an eleven-year-old boy. He received fifteen years for possession and twenty for rape—sentences he is currently appeal-ing. Paul Mosher, the head of libraries at Penn and a vice provost, resigned in April when he was caught downloading thousands of images and paying for them with his credit card. The crimes, well covered by the media, seemed all the more shocking for involving figures of authority entrusted with the welfare of young people.

While New York Law School is hardly an Ivy—professors there describe it as a middle-of-the-pack law school—to the community, the case was deeply unsettling. But not entirely in the ways outsiders might imagine. Of course, there was the fact that the fifty-four-year-old Samuels had clearly been assembling his vast trove of images for years, while professionally he remained beyond reproach. It occurred to many of his colleagues that he had deliberately invited techni-cians to examine a computer on which he must have known they might find incriminating evidence—causing some to wonder if he had wanted to get caught. And then, to quote a 2003 graduate of the school, there was the ultimate truism that, after all, "you expect a law professor to be a law-abiding citizen."

Unlike Lasaga and Mosher, Samuels did not resign immediately. Protected by tenure, he stayed on paid administrative leave for months, deepening the fault lines that began to appear within the school community. To the staff, from clerical workers to security guards, it was obvious that Samuels should give up his post. The faculty and senior administration, however, were much more conflicted. To expect that they would shun an alleged child-pornography addict would be to underestimate the propensity to agonize in academia. Especially legal academia. And especially when you factor in the deep ambivalence among legal scholars about pornography. Some criticized the staff for rushing to judgment before the investigation was over. Others criticized the dean for turning the images over to the DA without warning Samuels.

"The school had a duty, which they failed to do, to talk to Ed and say what's your explanation for this," says Randolph Jonakait, a fellow professor. "The notion of going to the police and not talking to Ed seems to me incorrect; it was wrong from a workplace point of view and wrong from an academic-freedom point of view. Anyone who's concerned with issues of academic freedom should be concerned about this."

And several challenged the validity of the law Samuels was accused of breaking.

"This is close to a victimless crime," says Jonakait, who later solicited letters on Samuels's behalf for the judge who'll be sentencing him June 23. "There is no allegation or proof that Samuels did anything other than view this stuff. You take him out of the market, and you're not even removing someone who has put money into the pornographic commerce."

Even the dean who made the decision to alert the district attorney in the first place, Matasar, admits wrestling with the subject. "When there's no purchase or sale of these materials, I don't know," he says. "As a lawyer, I am ambivalent on these issues."

It was more than a matter of colleagues circling the wagons. If the staff responded viscerally to the content of the material at issue, some professors reacted almost as viscerally to the constitutional issues it provoked—the First Amendment's guarantee of free speech and the Fourth Amendment's guarantee of privacy rights.

"I'm in disagreement with some colleagues who are my best friends," said one professor who supports the child-porn laws. "They are utterly hostile to the idea of a law regulating something done in the privacy of your own home that's not harmful to others. But I think that society can make laws to protect children from any risk, even if it's not a direct risk. Our views differ rather dramatically."

As one professor put it, what the New York Law School response demonstrated was "just how abstracted faculty can be from the real world."

Often overlooked in the ongoing debate about possession of pornography—one of the more inflammatory contemporary legal issues—are the crucial differences between adult and child pornography. Possession of child porn is both a federal and, in New York, a state crime. The images lack First Amendment protection because their creation requires a criminal act, the abuse of a child.

"Possession is where you see very clearly the difference between obscenity laws and child-pornography laws," explains Amy Adler, a professor at NYU School of Law and a specialist on child-porn laws. "In obscenity laws, the rationale for banning possession of images is thought control, and that's a First Amendment violation. In child-pornography law, the thinking is that it has nothing to do with First Amendment thought control and everything to do with the fact that child pornography is created through violating a child. We have to ban the pictures themselves because they result from a crime. Someone, somewhere, has to have committed a crime."

The first thing the FBI's Crimes Against Children Unit will tell you is that child porn is not *Lolita*. Or Sally Mann. "It's not just little children playing naked or little girls in their underwear," says Belisa Vranich, a clinical psychologist who has worked with FBI child-porn experts. "A lot of it is extremely violent, and the images show children obviously in a terrific amount of pain. Because it involves children, the sexual acts recorded are always rape. Some of the victims appear to be unconscious; a lot of them are drugged and bound. It's not so much sexual as it is extremely violent."

The FBI's Austin Berglas adds: "People think this is *American Beauty*–type stuff. It's not. It's violent crime."

Child porn, unlike adult porn, is rarely for sale on the Internet. In its 1984 Child Protection Act, Congress recognized that since much of the material isn't produced for commercial purposes, its distribution and production should be illegal regardless of no intent to sell. Nowadays, putting up your credit-card information on the Internet for child porn would be the equivalent—as the Who's Pete Townshend learned in January and Penn's Paul Mosher realized in April—of holding out your hands to be cuffed. But to law enforcement, the fact that these images are disseminated for free, by the disturbed cottage industry of fathers, stepfathers, uncles, and boyfriends who produce most of them in their bedrooms, living rooms, or garages, is no excuse to leave them up. According to Vranich, the sheer volume of porn out there creates online communities where "you think what you're doing is completely normal."

Law enforcement targets the end user—even though no money is changing hands—in order to discourage production of the images. "The idea is that this is an underground industry and we have to go after the end users because it's so difficult to find the original perpetrators," explains Adler. "If we punish enough end users, and enough people are scared to go to jail, the argument is, no one will create the images."

Law enforcement's commitment is a response to the increased accessibility of child porn on the Internet. And, experts say, the sheer quantity of child porn available on the Internet has raised viewers' thresholds. Marianna Novielli, a Secret Service agent with the National Center for Missing and Exploited Children, explains that cases involving infants have become more and more frequent in the past six years. "The belief is that it's just not exciting enough to have a child victim; it's even more stimulating to have a younger victim, an infant, even more taboo."

According to Berglas, most active viewers of child porn hoard and trade images like baseball cards. With his 100,000 images, Samuels was certainly an obsessive, but he's by no means alone. "A lot of the computers we find and seize have pictures cataloged under headings like 'Girls 12 and Under' or 'Under 10 Boys,'" Berglas says. "Often the series are labeled by name and collectors can ask each other, 'Hey, does anybody have the Linda series? Does anybody have the Peg series?'"

On the afternoon of Sunday, June 2, 2002, Dorothea Perry arrived at New York Law School without the slightest inkling that she was about to trigger a chain of events that would lead to Samuels's arrest and, she contends, her own eventual firing. A thirty-six-year-old computer technician who worked on the school's IT help desk, Perry had received a message the previous Friday that Samuels thought his computer had a virus. Around 2:30 PM, she entered the professor's neat, orderly office on Worth Street, with its odd screen of stacked Coca-Cola cans Samuels had erected against his window—which she later concluded had been put up to prevent people across the street from seeing in—and sat down to reinstall an antivirus program. She restarted the computer, but the machine kept dumping memory and giving her what she called "the blue screen of death." After about two hours, she left a note saying she had worked on the machine unsuccessfully, and that someone would come in to make another attempt the following morning. Then she left a message on the voice mail of her colleague Rob Gross, asking him to see if he could solve the problem.

The following day, Gross tried and failed. Following the guidelines of their company, Collegis, a subcontractor to the law school for all IT-related matters, Perry and Gross decided to give the professor a new machine while they worked on his. This meant they had to back up his files on the school's network in order to later transfer them to the new machine, something Gross had done hundreds of times in similar cases. Noticing a folder labeled "My Music," Rob thought, *This is something he might want.* He clicked on an imbedded folder labeled "Nime2" and photographs popped up on the screen. There were two dozen of them, and they showed girls, maybe eight or nine years old, who seemed to be "trying to look sexy." Not, Rob thought, your average family photographs.

"Oh, my God, Dorothea," he called across the office. "Come take a look at this."

Perry walked over to his cubicle and peered over his shoulder. She noticed the girls had no pubic hair. They were flat-chested. She had never seen images of child porn, but as a single mother with an eight-year-old boy, who had also helped raised her younger sisters, she felt certain that these were pornographic images of children. She reported them to Collegis's executive director, Margaret Perley, who agreed to alert the associate dean for finance and administration, Fred DeJohn, her liaison at the school.

The following day, June 4, was Richard Matasar's birthday. He went out for drinks and snacks with members of his staff—his assistant Harry Althaus, DeJohn, and associate dean Joan Fishman. DeJohn took the opportunity to broach the subject of what they had found. "Let's talk about it tomorrow," Matasar told him, realizing the situation could be sensitive. "But don't tell me who it is yet." On June 5, Matasar and DeJohn sat down together to discuss the issues. Were the pictures on the computer of a professor who did research in the area? Matasar wanted to know. Was there a possible explanation? Alas, there was not, and later that day, Matasar and DeJohn took a look at three of the images. One of them could have been a family photograph taken on a beach, Matasar said. But the other two he described as being "on the other side of that line . . . whatever that line is."

As Perry would later explain, the images were very sexually provocative. *We have a* real *problem here*, thought Matasar.

After stories detailing the violent content of some of the photos appeared in the tabloids, Samuels phoned several of his colleagues to assure them that the rape images the authorities had found at his home were not the images he intended to amass; he was only interested in the ones of naked children. As Jonakait speculated, it's possible he inadvertently received harder-core porn than he wanted while downloading a whole magazine about children. Law-enforcement sources confirm the nature and amount of the images they saw, but some colleagues remained doubtful. "I was skeptical about the accuracy of press reports, and I continue to be somewhat skeptical about what the DA said," Matasar says. "Professor Samuels said, 'Regardless of what you heard, don't believe what you read, that wasn't what I collected or what I was interested in.' He wanted me to know and wanted people in our community to know that the worst of what was reported was not what he was doing.

"He wasn't trying to say 'I'm a good guy,'" adds Matasar. "He was trying to say 'I'm not that guy.'"

Exactly which guy Samuels is became a puzzling issue. One of the school's longest-serving professors, he had grown up in Paragould, Arkansas, and come east to Yale and then Columbia before arriving at New York Law School, his first and only academic posting. "He always rolled up his sleeves to chair committees," said James Simon, the Martin Professor of Law, on the faculty since 1973 and a former dean. "He was very conscientious and dedicated."

In the past few years, Samuels had also started doing his bit to help raise the school's profile. He was finally building a reputation as a significant scholar. Part of the explanation for his newfound energy, some said, was that Samuels's two children—Richard, a

Tufts graduate who now works with a tech firm in Massachusetts, and Claire, a student at Brandeis—were gone, leaving him more time to work. His wife of more than twenty years, Marcia, an editor at John Wiley & Sons, was also spending more time at work.

In 2002, Samuels filed an amicus brief on an important copyright case before the U.S. Supreme Court that established him as one of the top authorities in his field. He also kept up with the technological advances that have affected copyright law over the past few years, and his 2000 *Illustrated Story of Copyright*, a user-friendly overview that included drawings, caricatures, and photographs, devoted two chapters to computers and the Internet. Curiously, it even featured a photograph of Samuels's home computer setup, the place where police presumably found his stash of porn, a Power Mac outfitted with a miniature video camera, a scanner, and two printers.

If Samuels's colleagues were shocked by the charges, so too were students, some of whom said he had a winning teaching style. He "tried to make things fun," one said, by bringing props related to the cases under discussion, like Mickey Mouse figurines or pictures he had taken of the Grand Canyon, and actively helped students find internships and jobs.

With the staff, however, he seemed to have been more aloof. Argento, Samuels's former assistant, said that in the five years she worked for him, Samuels never once walked into her office, located about twenty feet away from his, to say good morning. She estimated that they had four or five conversations in five years. Her work for him was limited to faxing and copying. Though she had the password to every other professor's computer, she never had Samuels's password, and she never did anything that would have meant using his computer. She was baffled to find herself thanked in his book. "We chalked it up to 'He's a weird guy,'" she said.

. . .

During the first lengthy faculty meeting after Samuels's arrest, a number of issues surfaced, among them how the technicians had found the images. "There was a lot of 'You mean anything that's on my computer, anyone at school can see?'" one professor remembered. "People tried to divert it to 'What are our privacy rights?' and the dean was put on the defensive, not because the majority of the faculty felt this way but because they were the most vocal."

Samuels remained on leave until the investigation was complete. But some staff and faculty members complained that he appeared to be unrepentant, using his "leave" to update his Web site and advance his research. Though he often showed up after-hours in the office, he also popped in on regular workdays. And shortly after his arrest, he'd arrived in the IT department to work on a computer, only yards away from the technicians who had discovered his secret.

"It was very uncomfortable," one longtime faculty member said. "He came to a meeting where hiring of faculty was discussed, and people would say, 'We may have an opening in copyright, depending on what happens with Ed,' and Ed was sitting right there."

In an open meeting held soon after with faculty, Matasar asked for a show of hands on who was uncomfortable with having Samuels around. Not a single hand went up. Yet several faculty members said that a silent majority of professors were appalled and uncomfortable with the situation.

"Most professors were being very professional with him, looking at it from a legal standpoint," said Argento, who left the school in February. "I told them, 'I'm not asking you from a legal standpoint, I'm asking you from a personal standpoint: Did that turn your stomach?'"

If the staff had felt uncomfortable with Samuels's presence, what came next ensured they would feel downright queasy. On Tuesday, October 22, Dorothea Perry and Rob Gross were fired. Neither had been in trouble before the Samuels job. Perry, who had worked at the school for twelve years, had received her evaluation from Collegis the previous November, and her work had been rated "excellent." Gross, who had been there since 2001, had received an evaluation three months before the Samuels discovery that read "fully competent plus." "I knew I had been punished for Samuels," Perry says. "When I was fired, I told them, 'I know you have children. I know all of you have children. How could you do this?'"

The time line leading to their dismissal was suspicious. Both employees were put on probation after the discovery and were fired shortly before Collegis renewed its multimillion-dollar contract with the school. In addition, Perry had said on a number of occasions that she felt Samuels had committed a grave offense. Four days after her discovery, for instance, she e-mailed Perley, her Collegis supervisor at the school, to tell her that she had looked into the matter of child porn and now knew it to be a serious crime. The e-mail was sent before the school contacted the DA.

Their story is not, however, a classic example of whistle-blowers being punished. In this case, the institution alerted the authorities as soon as it had gotten advice from counsel, and cooperated fully. Matasar strictly followed the DA's directive not to alert Samuels, which would later earn him the wrath of some professors.

But there are a number of reasons why Collegis might have wanted Perry and Gross gone. A former Collegis director said that these kinds of cases bring negative publicity to the company, putting it at risk of losing IT contracts with other universities. "The last thing you want to do is piss off a client," the former director said. "If you piss off a client, you're history."

Outraged, Perry and Gross have since filed a $15 million civil suit against both New York Law School and Collegis. After receiving his first probation letter, Gross e-mailed Margaret Perley: "I feel as if I am being martyrized for my finding," he wrote in July. "After complying with your request for a written statement and a personal interview with . . . a member of the District Attorney's office, I thought this matter was over and felt I would not be penalized for protecting the rights of children."

Matasar says he had specifically asked Collegis to reform the help desk, where Gross and Perry worked, and that their dismissal was probably the result of his demands. The computer labs were in terrible condition, Matasar says, and he got countless complaints from students about them. Professors were also complaining that their machines were not getting fixed fast enough. Although Nadine Strossen, the head of the ACLU and a faculty member, gave Perry a letter of recommendation when she left the school, a number of professors seemed to think there might have been a good reason to fire the employees. One mentioned that Perry "came and went as she wanted" and added she was "sort of brassy."

"We did absolutely nothing wrong," Matasar said heatedly during an interview. "We were the whistle-blowers. We. I. And this law school. I, as dean of the law school under advice from our counsel, made the decision to turn this information over to the DA's office. We, the law school, placed Edward Samuels on leave. We, the law school, have had to deal with the consequences of losing a twenty-five-year member of the faculty. . . . If we are to be held captive by bad employees by the mere circumstance that they were involved in discovering criminal activity, we couldn't get our work done!"

Collegis denies the firings had anything to do with Samuels and says the timing was a coincidence. Professor Jonakait agrees: "I don't think the firing looked particularly good, but I did not come to the conclusion that there was a connection."

On April 14, Samuels pleaded guilty to one hundred counts of possessing child pornography, and most of the professors wanted him out. But again, he didn't resign immediately; instead, he haggled over how much he believed he should be paid to leave. A faculty inquiry was commissioned. Samuels's salary was probably over $150,000 a year, and according to Matasar, he was demanding "a lot of money." It wasn't until ten days later that the two sides reached an agreement, and Samuels resigned. "I want to have sympathy for him," one longtime member of the faculty said. "But I find it hard because he didn't do the right thing as soon as he was capable. If anything, he seemed to be pushing in the other direction."

Despite his guilty plea, some professors feel that the public scrutiny his case has received, and the destruction of his career, have been punishment enough.

Martin Levin, a former student and current adjunct faculty, said Samuels was more to be pitied than censured. "This may be a class-E felony, but it's a psychiatric problem," he said. "If he were an alcoholic or a drug addict, wouldn't he be sent to counseling?"

Jonakait has received about twenty testimonials, which have been presented to the sentencing judge. The letters, he said, express a great deal of respect for Samuels's integrity as a professor, and many writers, he added, mentioned that knowing the facts of the Samuels case didn't affect their regard for his professionalism.

Since his arrest, friends claim, Samuels has been in therapy, and his family has stood resolutely by him. In a brief exchange in the lobby of his apartment building, Samuels declined to be interviewed for this piece.

No one has organized a letter-writing campaign for Perry or Gross. Since they were fired, they have sent out countless résumés, but both are still unemployed.

As Samuels now waits in sentencing limbo, some of his former colleagues still hope he won't end up in jail. "There can't be a happy ending, but there ought to be some kind of soft landing," says Levin. "I don't like to see somebody who's creative and been so useful ending up in this kind of situation."

CHIEF BRATTON TAKES ON LA
HEATHER MAC DONALD

The Los Angeles Police Department desperately wants to reclaim its sullied reputation; its new chief, former New York Police Commissioner William Bratton, would like to clinch his shining one. Their union could be historic. If Bratton can repeat his crime-busting success in this radically different city, he will destroy the criminologists' destructive myth that policing can't cut crime. In addition, he will show how to overcome the corrosive, racially charged anti-cop politics that dominated policing nationwide for the last decade and that brought the once-proud LAPD so low that it forgot its very reason for being.

Today, a dozen years after the 1991 Rodney King beating that—wrongly—made the department a byword for violent, racist policing, the LAPD operates under federal control, subject to rigid management constraints that check a strong chief like Bratton at every turn. Given these restrictions and the department's deep demoralization, no one should underestimate the magnitude of the new chief's task. He himself certainly doesn't. After a particularly murder-soaked week early in his tenure, he asked himself, "'What am I doing here? What the hell is going on here?' The department was messed up, worse than I thought."

Ironically, the LAPD was expressly crafted to prevent its getting messed up in just this way. In the 1950s, when corruption in big-city forces was still the norm, legendary chief William Parker labored to mold a department that the politicians couldn't touch. The result was a corps that for decades commanded respect as the pinnacle of efficient, incorruptible policing. And so it viewed itself. Recalls gang detective Jack Cota: "Our department was based on, 'We're the best; we have integrity.'"

The core challenge of LA policing has not changed since Parker's reforms: to cover a huge area with a woefully small force. Angelenos have always balked at funding a police department big enough for its responsibilities, perhaps because most of the tax revenue comes from neighborhoods with little crime: gangbangers don't do drive-by shootings in Bel Air. Today, 9,000 Los Angeles cops police 467 square miles, which works out to 19 cops per square mile. New York's 37,000 officers, by contrast, oversee 321 square miles—115 cops per square mile. So while New York's commanders, with one officer for every 216 residents, can throw manpower at problems, their Los Angeles counterparts, with only one officer for every 417 residents, must engage in constant triage.

Chief Parker's no-nonsense solution was to insist that officer quality would trump quantity. He gave cops up-to-the-minute technology and rewarded rapid response time to radio calls. Once on the scene, LA officers took control, got the information they needed, and returned to the road as fast as possible, wasting no time schmoozing with the citizenry. The attitude, recalls Hollywood officer Mike Shea, was: "I'm the police; I'll tell you what needs to be done to stop crime in your area; we're the experts; now shut up."

In an era when police authority was far less contested than today, Parker's cops asserted their power more aggressively than most. James Ellroy, author of the novel *L.A. Confidential*, remembers the LAPD of his youth as "buffed and turned out. If you ran, they

would beat you up. If you mouthed off, you would get beat up."
Even into the eighties, officers would "hijack" murder witnesses
and take them to the station house to ensure their testimony, says a
longtime LAPD vet.

This command-and-control manner alienated many black residents. And the LAPD, a creature of its time, was no model of racial
sensitivity. George Beck, a retired deputy chief who wrote the
nation's first police manual for Los Angeles, worked in Watts during
the fifties and sixties. "Some cops were really racial," he says; "a lot
were not, and some were in the middle." The LAPD was one of the
first departments to try to stop crime before it happened by inter-
vening in suspicious behavior; in practice, this meant that "in certain neighborhoods, if you were a black man with another black
man, you would automatically be pulled over," recalls Ed Turley, a
gang-intervention worker. And cops' behavior during a stop could
be egregious: James Ellroy saw two white officers give a black driver
a sobriety test in 1971 by making him scratch himself like an ape.

Even so, for years the LAPD rode high in national opinion, promoted tirelessly by its chief as the big blue machine, steely and
untouchable. But Parker's public-relations success came back to
haunt his beloved agency. A growing army of anti-cop advocates
converted his carefully crafted image of the department into an
insult, and used it to bludgeon the LAPD into submission, long after
the department had ceased in any way to resemble the Parker corps.

Beginning in the late 1970s, cop-hostile politics began to reshape
the LAPD. Typically, a politics-induced change would produce
unintended negative consequences, which led to an even greater
anti-LAPD backlash, in an ever-downward spiral. For instance, in
1981, in response to the emerging politics of "diversity," the department settled a lawsuit by agreeing to hiring quotas for women,

blacks, and Hispanics. The result: lower standards of competence, character, and physique—even though the less physical strength an officer has, the more he (or she) will have to rely on weapons to sub-due resisting suspects, provoking more excessive-force complaints.

In the same spirit, politics determined tactics. An outcry over civilian deaths from the improper application of the choke hold, used to incapacitate violent offenders, understandably forced its ban. But without the choke hold (which police professionals endorse, when used properly), officers had little alternative to the baton when suspects resisted. And use of the baton would provoke an even greater crisis in the Rodney King affair.

Politics shaped the LAPD budget, too. Mayor Tom Bradley loathed Chief Daryl Gates and expressed it by slashing police funding—just as violence between black and Hispanic gangs was exploding in East and South Central LA. With the crime rate soaring 26 percent from 1984 to 1989, law-abiding citizens demanded a decisive police response.

The logic behind Chief Gates's answer was unimpeachable, though the result was not. Operation Hammer, launched in 1988, would compensate for the chronic manpower shortage by tem-porarily flooding high-crime areas with officers, and would use all available laws, including quality-of-life statutes, to get gangsters off the streets—much like 1990s New York policing. But inadequate supervision resulted in hundreds of indiscriminate stops of young black males, generating ill will that cop haters nourish to this day.

For sheer devastating destruction of reputation and morale, however, nothing had ever approached the video of three LA cops beating the struggling Rodney King in March 1991. Officers speak of the pre-King and post-King eras. After King, a "culture of cowardice," as one sergeant puts it, descended on the top brass, and criminals showed open contempt for a psychologically defeated force.

The common understanding of the King beating as racially driven brutality is wholly wrong, as Lou Cannon has demonstrated in his magisterial LAPD history, *Official Negligence*. When officers finally stopped the drug-addled King after a 115-mile-an-hour car chase, they tried to take him into custody without hurting him, using commands, a gang-tackle and handcuffs, and a Taser. Only after the powerfully built King charged at them did they resort to their batons. That charge was edited out of the videotape that was shown worldwide for months afterward, leaving sixty-eight seconds of seemingly unprovoked baton blows. Officer Laurence Powell's frenzied counterattack did not grow out of a culture of official racism or violence in the LAPD, but out of his terror, his weakness compared with King (the result of lowered hiring standards), and his ineffectiveness with the baton. Had it been a white driver behaving similarly, his fate would have been the same.

But international public opinion instantaneously deemed the episode pure racial animus. And the influential commission charged with investigating both the event and the LAPD, headed by LA establishment lawyer and future U.S. secretary of state Warren Christopher, did little to dispel the widespread public misconception. The commission seized on a handful of radio messages to condemn the department for tolerating bigotry, even though many of those messages had nothing to do with race. The solution to this alleged bias problem, according to the commission: more racial and gender quotas. The commission also charged the department with tolerating excessive force and impeding civilian complaints about police conduct.

A year later, it became stunningly clear how thoroughly the anti-cop publicity machine had emasculated the LAPD, when the department failed completely to quell the riots that raged after the acquittal of the Rodney King officers. As the jury debated the assault charges, signs that violence was in the wings abounded, but, because of fears that riot preparation would provoke the "community," as Mayor Tom Bradley put it, the department did nothing. Once the violence started after the acquittals, management remained paralyzed, and, as rioters pulled drivers from their cars and beat them mercilessly, officers stood by passively. Unwilling to use the necessary force, the commander of the 77th Division, ground zero of the increasingly savage violence, ordered his officers to retreat, knowing full well that unsuspecting white, Asian, and Hispanic motorists, arriving at the intersection of Florence and Normandie, faced certain brutal attack. Trucker Reginald Denny, whose skull Damian Williams gleefully crushed with a brick, was a casualty of this shameful retreat. Even as the death toll mounted, police brass at the ill-equipped riot-command post, fearful of another brutality accusation, told officers not to engage or arrest the rioters.

With the violence spiraling out of control, Chief Daryl Gates went AWOL, attending a tony political fund-raiser miles from the mayhem. When he returned, he still issued no orders. Other commanders, dutifully obeying the political mandate for outreach, went to a unity rally at the First African-American Methodist Episcopal Church, as if nothing were happening. The final toll: 54 lost lives, 2,328 hospitalizations, and nearly $1 billion in property damage.

Nothing—not even the King media circus—so destroyed rank-and-file morale as the department's abdication during the riots. Having to stand by as public order crumbled represented a galling betrayal of officers' oath to protect and serve. The message cops took from the episode was that, for their bosses, fear of criticism trumped public safety.

After the smoke cleared and Mayor Bradley forced Chief Gates out of office, the troops yearned for strong leadership to give them their pride back. They didn't get it. The key political consideration in selecting a new chief was that he be black, and Willie Williams, the corpulent and unkempt chief of the lackluster Philadelphia police, got the job. Added to his endemic inability to pass the mandatory police qualifying exam, the revelation that he had accepted gifts from Las Vegas casinos sealed his doom as a one-term chief.

Alas, his successor, LAPD insider Bernard Parks, was worse still. A tall, dashing African American with a square jaw and arrow glance, his tenure is a textbook example of the power of leadership to make or break an organization. Parks took office in 1997 surrounded by high hopes, since he had worked his way up the command ladder and knew virtually everything about the department. But, says Mike Downing, commander of the Hollywood division, he lacked "wisdom"—wisdom to delegate, to learn from subordinates, to change course.

Though Parks's initial moves were promising—above all, he implemented a version of Compstat, the NYPD's computer-assisted crime-analysis program that had driven New York's unparalleled crime drop in the 1990s—he also disastrously implemented the Christopher Commission's demand that the department thoroughly investigate every civilian complaint it received. Hitherto, field supervisors could dispose of patently unfounded complaints after preliminary investigation. Now, a charge that a cop had stolen the *Apollo* lunar lander from the moon would have to be investigated all the way up to the top of the department, with reports from supervisors and commanders at every step. Within a year, complaints processed jumped 400 percent. Every station house had to dedicate three or four supervisors to complaint duty, leaving far fewer to oversee officers. Sergeants were crisscrossing Southern California, tracking down witnesses to interview for clearly bogus complaints.

Officers shut down in fury. The no-discretion complaint system penalized good police work, since criminals routinely file complaints as payback for an arrest. Gang detective Jack Cota says: "Gangs knew that the easiest way to keep officers off the streets was to complain." The result: officers avoided low-enforcement actions with a high likelihood of retaliatory complaints.

Perhaps Parks, despite his martinet inclinations, would have made the complaint process more rational over time, but once the Rampart scandal broke, any chance that supervisors would be given more leeway evaporated. The Rampart area, a 7.4-square-mile district of small, closely clustered bungalows and bodegas just west of downtown skyscrapers, is mecca for about 30 Central American gangs, with some 8,000 members. Frequent contact with the gangs' violent indifference to human life develops in officers a politically incorrect loathing of gang culture, which most cops learn to live with, however uneasily. But a very few start fudging the law to ensure punishment for such depravity. The Rampart scandal grew in part out of this vigilante impulse, but the participants' own evil soon overwhelmed any pretensions they may have had as defenders of the good.

Ringleader Rafael Perez and his cronies in the Rampart division of CRASH—the LAPD's undercover gang unit—planted evidence on gangbangers to get them off the streets. They beat them up to get them to talk or to keep them from filing complaints. They also sold stolen drugs and shot people, usually gangsters.

The crimes of Perez and his colleagues would never have gone so far without a total breakdown in oversight. "Once an officer puts on dirtbag clothes, you need good supervisors," says retired commander George Beck, and supervision is precisely what Rampart CRASH lacked. The division's two feuding top commanders were not talking to each other. At all hours, Perez and his partners had unmonitored access to their remote office, where they could beat up gangsters and uncooperative witnesses. They became a rogue gang within the LAPD.

Rampart CRASH's corruption didn't make the whole LAPD corrupt, but the media storm after the scandal broke in 1998 took just that line—one more body blow to the rank and file. "We felt helpless; we wanted to tear that guy's face apart," remembers Robert Duke, a downtown officer. "Being called a dirty cop—and you put up with *so much* on this job! Everyone had their secret desire to leave."

True to form, the LAPD just rolled over and played dead. It disbanded CRASH citywide, leaving no gang cops on the street. Chief Bratton marvels at this overreaction. "When we had the Dirty 30 in New York," he says, "we didn't dismantle all 75 precincts." When the department reconstituted an anti-gang detail, it made sure it was neutered, according to Bratton: "No plainclothes, no unmarked cars, no informants, no narcotics enforcement—it's like asking a carpenter to build a house without nails or a hammer." Cops across LA got the message: We don't trust you.

And now the LAPD's troubles really began. The U.S. Justice Department moved to put the department under federal control, invoking an ill-conceived 1994 law allowing Justice to sue local police forces for engaging in a "pattern or practice" of denying individuals their constitutional rights. The threat of terrifyingly costly federal litigation almost always leads local governments to give up local control and accept a federally appointed police monitor without a fight.

The Rampart scandal, however egregious, had revealed no pattern or practice in the LAPD of encouraging or tolerating such behavior—especially not after all the post–Rodney King discipline, diversity, and community-outreach measures. But the Clinton Justice Department's campaign against the LAPD was all about power, not reform—as witness DOJ's nonnegotiable insistence that the department begin racial data collection to show if cops were "racially profiling," a Clinton Justice buzzword. The Rampart scandal, however, had nothing to do with alleged racial profiling, and Rodney King, even if the episode were a relevant marker of LAPD practices seven years and two chiefs afterward, was stopped for his speeding, not his race.

Chief Bernard Parks's greatest moment was fighting the Justice Department, something no other top cop has done as publicly. The LAPD, he said, was correcting the Rampart scandal. A consent decree's busywork would only drain resources away from his effort to tighten management controls. What do federal civil rights lawyers know about running a police department, anyway? he asked. They couldn't even keep track of ten boxes of sensitive records they had demanded from the LAPD—and lost. Moreover, not only did his cops base their enforcement actions on suspicious behavior, not race, he said, but DOJ had no valid methodology for analyzing the racial data it wanted him to collect.

The chief's resistance earned him the contempt of the *Los Angeles Times* and the city's political elites. City attorney James Hahn—now the mayor—the city council, and the Police Commission finally forced Parks to accept a five-year consent decree in 2000—without ever making Justice defend its baseless charge of a "pattern or practice" of civil rights violations at the LAPD.

Since the settlement, it gets clearer day by day how right Parks was. After eight years of decline, possibly due to changes in the city's demography, serious felonies rose for the first time in 2000, by 6.7 percent, and they went up alarmingly for the next two years. But the decree has hamstrung the department's ability to respond, by draining money and manpower away from crime busting—some $40 million the first year, and upward of $50 million every year thereafter, according to city estimates, in addition to 350 officers pulled from crime fighting to decree-tending so far. Meanwhile, current chief Bratton has been vainly begging the city council for 320 new officers.

Justice attorneys, the consent decree makes clear, view policing not primarily as crime fighting but as report writing, with reports written upon reports upon reports. Some of those reports, such as audits of the accuracy of arrest data, represent good management practices. But the decree unwisely locks the department into a draconian and wholly inflexible schedule for completing them. Failure to reach full compliance with all 190 provisions by 2004 means that the decree can continue indefinitely beyond its scheduled expiration in 2006.

Full compliance may well be impossible, judging from the August report of the federal monitor, Michael Cherkasky, who heads the Kroll Associates security firm. A control freak with the most unforgiving interpretation of deadlines, Cherkasky seems unaware that the department sometimes has to tear itself away from report-generation to fight crime. For example, though captains managed to complete required reports on instances of nondeadly force, such as twisting someone's arm to cuff him, within the mandated fourteen days 94.3 percent of the time, Cherkasky judged the department out of compliance—a remorseless standard of bureaucratic fidelity that few modern organizations could meet.

More troublingly, the consent decree rests on a highly dubious managerial philosophy. It presumes that brutality and racism are so ingrained that only oversight systems with zero managerial discretion can stem constant civil rights abuses.

Its rules for investigating deadly force, for instance, presume collusion in lawlessness right up the chain of command. This July, three cops happened to witness a gang shooting in a supermarket parking lot. They jumped out of their car, drew their weapons, and shouted, "Drop your guns." One gangster wheeled and shot; two cops shot back. Everybody missed.

For the rest of the night, each officer was guarded in a separate area of the parking lot, so the three couldn't talk to one another, while investigators canvassed the scene. Three sergeants taken off patrol duty for the rest of the night accompanied their every bathroom visit. At dawn, a separate car transported each officer to the station house. Deputy Chief Earl Paysinger, a rising departmental star, judges: "If you can't trust an unbiased supervisor to put two cops in his car and tell them not to talk to each other, we need to find other supervisors." Such obsessional regulation, he says, "compromises the fabric of that very elusive thing we call trust."

The department's mandated investigations of officer-involved shootings also suggest a perverse set of priorities. That night, twice as many detectives investigated the officers' self-defense shootings for possible civil rights or criminal violations as investigated the gangsters' attempted murder of the officers.

Reports will cascade forth, as is de rigueur. Say a cop struggles with a robbery suspect while arresting him. Even if the suspect admits he wasn't injured, the officer's sergeant still has to write a use-of-force report, interviewing the officer, the suspect, and all potential witnesses, and taking photos. "A two-page arrest report generates a twenty-page use-of-force report," a frustrated sergeant grouses. "It may take you four to five hours to document. Then you get an investigation supervisor to study your report; it takes him four hours. Someone else reviews it. By the time everyone's finished, that's a $2,000 report." The racial data-report mandate has a similar effect. "You wouldn't believe what it does to slow my progress down," says a downtown officer, working on a tall stack of them after a night patrolling Skid Row.

. . .

By the time Bratton arrived on the job last November, the LAPD was a shadow of its former self. "We were going through the motions, as if running in mud," says Deputy Chief Paysinger. "We weren't doing police work," sums up a downtown cop.

What's more, the ugly battle to oust Chief Parks in 2002 had left a bitter racial aftertaste. While the city's left wing, including new mayor James Hahn, criticized the chief for not making enough progress on the consent decree and on "racial profiling," the black establishment stoutly defended him, showing that race politics is even stronger than anti-police and even anti–racial profiling politics. After his ouster, Parks promptly got elected to the council from a black district, where he lies in wait to ambush either the new police chief or mayor. Bratton understands the tension. As he told a group of community representatives in June: "Believe me, I had concerns as a white coming in after two black chiefs, and after the controversy of the last removal."

But in choosing Bratton, the Police Commission showed how desperately the city wants to reclaim policing from race politics. The commission—and the mayor—wanted someone who would put modern management techniques into the relentless service of cutting crime. Bratton had jump-started New York's historic crime drop—bringing homicides down 44 percent and serious crime down 25 percent in twenty-seven months—by holding managers accountable for measurable results: fewer shootings, homicides, and armed robberies, better quality of life across all neighborhoods.

Bratton is fashioning a powerful blueprint for repeating that success, and from the very start he set out to build support for his vision of policing. "In the first few days I don't think he slept at all," recalls police union president Bob Baker. "He was at every community meeting in the city." His message: The LAPD is getting back into the crime-fighting business, and it's going to win. "For the past five years, this department has been on the bench; it hasn't even been on the field," he tells audiences.

He has broken some prevailing taboos to speak the truth. At one community meeting, when activists started complaining about the big, bad LAPD and demanding that Bratton control his cops, Bratton shot back: "Control your kids!" He has stressed that crime-ridden communities cannot expect the police to solve all their problems—that parents and neighbors must take responsibility for stopping gang violence, too. At other events, he called criminals "mental nitwits" and gangs "domestic terrorists." He suggested that an appropriate response to a suspect who had fled from the police would be to "hang 'em high."

Such rhetoric was a shot of adrenaline to patrol officers, but the black elite, still nursing its wounds from the Parks ouster, blew up. Its members declared themselves deeply troubled by Bratton's language, and the entire left-wing commentariat piled on. Journalist Mike Davis, the Marxist fabulist of LA history, complained about Bratton's plans to attack graffiti, and anti-cop attorney Connie Rice penned an uproarious *Los Angeles Times* op-ed that reverentially quoted a member of the murderous Grape Street Crip gang who argued that—in essence—fighting graffiti was no different from drive-by shootings: "How they 'spect us to respect them when they act like us?" whined this sensitive Crip.

But then something remarkable happened. In a scathing editorial, the ultimate arbiter of fashionable opinion—the *Los Angeles Times*—broke ranks, mocking the black establishment's "selective war on words." It pointed out that Bratton's critics had failed miserably to quell street violence, and it said Bratton was right to call that violence domestic terrorism. In a hopeful augury for the future, the new chief's lock on the pinnacle of elite opinion has held firm. Not only has the *Times*'s editorial page consistently backed his calls for more cops to fight crime, but Hollywood moguls Steven Spielberg and David Geffen have donated cash to help update the department's technology.

Following his New York playbook, Bratton searched for the talent among the command staff. His promotions of Jim McDonnell and Mike Hillman to assistant and deputy chief thrilled the rank and file, for they are tough crime-fighters whom the Parks regime had shunned—both marks of honor in the eyes of the street cop. Such personnel choices have convinced officers that their new chief will back them up for smart, assertive policing. Equally crucial to restoring morale has been Bratton's decision to return reasonable discretion to the complaint process. "Bratton is tough on discipline," union chief Baker observes. "But the only thing cops want to know is: 'Does he care?'"

Next, Bratton set priorities, with quelling gang violence at the top of the list. To do that, he put drug and gang enforcement under one command, since gangs dominate the LA drug trade. Gang czar Hillman has reenergized the gang units and ordered them to respond aggressively to shootings. "Do it right, do it legally, but don't wait three days for approval before acting," he tells them. Once-moribund multiagency task forces—drawn from, for example, the city attorney, probation officers, and the LAPD—are finally cooperating effectively.

But these policy changes cannot be fully effective unless the beaten-down detective corps recovers its zeal and its mandate for crime-fighting. "In the old days," says LAPD chronicler James Ellroy, "when you had a murder, the detectives would roll on it till they dropped. They'd work through the night." Today, thanks to bureaucratic constraints, detectives spend most of their days filing reports on arrests that patrol officers have already made, not on solving crimes. And thanks to the politics of gender, they spend too much of their remaining time on domestic-violence cases, to meet politically correct state mandates.

Bratton's inner circle is trying to turn them back into detectives. The morning after a prostitute had been killed this August, Deputy Chief Paysinger asked the detective on the case what the vice officers had said about her. The vice officers don't get in until 2:00 PM, the detective replied, so he hadn't spoken to them yet. "They have phones, don't they?" Paysinger responded caustically. "For Christ's sake, someone's dead." The department is also requiring detectives to go to every shooting, even if no one was killed, instead of showing up only at homicides or near-homicides, as before. As Paysinger explains, "If we don't have a greater awareness of the most violent of crimes, as purveyors of the peace we're done."

The LAPD reengineers are hammering home to detectives how valuable search warrants are as a tool for preventing crime before it happens. "Even if you find nothing, as you search, you may see a parolee at large, or someone who wants to be a witness, or other weapons in plain sight," says Paysinger. "You're telling the crook: 'I will always be there watching.'" But until recently, few detectives even remembered how to write a search-warrant request to a judge.

Bratton is using Compstat, the crime analysis and command accountability sessions he pioneered in New York, to reinforce these lessons in proactive policing. A sign in the large Compstat room reads: WHO ARE THEY? WHERE ARE THEY? HAVE THEY BEEN ARRESTED? — the conceptual framework for the weekly Compstat meetings. During those meetings, top brass grill area commanders on their knowledge of crime patterns in their jurisdictions and their plans for solving them. Jim McDonnell, who heads the sessions, reminds commanders about some basic crime-fighting tools imported from New York, such as questioning all suspects about other unsolved crimes. After a gang shooting, he tells them, don't let your officers mill around guarding the perimeter of the scene; get them quickly into the shooter's home turf, in anticipation of a retaliatory drive-by.

Besides Compstat, Bratton's biggest New York policing innovation was to demonstrate the power of order-maintenance enforcement. When he headed the New York Transit Police, his troops began arresting turnstile jumpers and subway panhandlers—until then, viewed as harmless victims of poverty—and caught serious criminals. As NYPD commissioner, he cracked down on public drinkers and graffiti vandals, and by so doing moved once chaotic neighborhoods toward greater civility and safety.

Bratton is showcasing order-maintenance (or "broken-windows") policing in three Los Angeles neighborhoods—downtown's Skid Row, the sadly deteriorated MacArthur Park in Rampart, and Hollywood, with its hookers and hustlers. Skid Row (also known as the "Nickel" for the cheap flophouses that vagrants once used) is the greatest challenge.

The most amazing discovery a first-time visitor to the Nickel will make is that its few legitimate residents think it looks *good*—compared with before Bratton arrived. Until you've stood on Fifth and Wall, you haven't really seen a vagrancy problem. Nothing in New York's most chaotic days in the 1980s comes close to the squalor and madness that have taken over block upon block of the warehouse district. Addicted men and women fill entire streetscapes, some sitting in lawn chairs outside their tents, others sprawled out facedown on the sidewalk. Pushers peddle drugs hidden inside cigarette boxes spread out on the sidewalk. Outside the women's missions, teenagers strut threateningly, while their newest illegitimate siblings are parked in baby carriages on the sidewalk. Transvestites in bikinis gesture defiantly at the occasional passing squad car.

A few hardy toy and fish wholesalers remain. Holly Sea Food has sold fish downtown since 1923, but over the last few years, one-third of its neighbors have left. "You can't sell your business or hire help," laments owner Rick Merry, in his air-conditioned wood-laminate office. "We've had an ad in the *Times* for a bookkeeper. Candidates will just drive by without stopping. They later call: 'I'm sorry, but I won't work there.' The female postman put in for a transfer. Ladies were leaning up against her truck, defecating. The bad part is: My wife works here. Guys will walk right up to the gutter and whip it out, and there she is, staring at someone's privates."

Four months ago, a vagrant's tent across the street from Holly's warehouse exploded in flames as the occupant slept inside, pay-back for a bad drug deal. The target would have died had the surrounding bums not pulled him from his tent.

Downtown LA's "homeless" problem may be unparalleled in scale and concentration, but its causes are the same as everywhere else: politics and misguided "compassion." The lawless bum lifestyle depends on the subsidy of self-proclaimed do-gooders, who provide everything legal that a street person could desire. At 6:00 AM one day this summer, a tangle of garments and half-eaten plates of food, which volunteers had doled out the night before, strewed an entire sidewalk block. The "homeless" left the city's sanitation service to clean up what they didn't want.

The brightly colored tents that fill the sidewalks were another gift of the homeless advocates—a gift intended to foil law enforcement, on the theory that, if the vagrants could claim ownership of their street domicile, rather than scrounging it from dumpsters every night, the police would not be able to remove encampments from the streets. The success of this strategy waxes and wanes with the politics of the moment.

Even before Bratton arrived, the former commander of downtown's Central Division, Charles Beck, had tried to stem the anarchy. "I was abhorred by it," he says. "It drove me nuts. My dream was to clean up downtown LA. You need the collective will to say that this conduct is not allowed any longer."

But Beck made little progress: Advocates had the city council under their thumb. The shrillest activist, Alice Callahan, could call the council and say: "Do you know that an officer just told a homeless person to wake up?" and the police would get an incensed phone call in ten minutes, recalls officer Daniel Gomez. Business owners, by contrast, could tell the council: "We have a serious problem," and the response would be, "Yeah, *whatever*."

Now, though, some newly elected council members recognize the truth: Conditions on the Nickel are unacceptable in a civilized society. Their election to the council could not be more timely. Chief Bratton needs all the political backing he can get to battle the advocates.

Every Bratton initiative to civilize Skid Row has sparked a lawsuit. The radical National Lawyers Guild sued to prevent arrests of parole and probation violators, while the ACLU asserts that enforcing a law against blocking sidewalks constitutes "cruel and unusual punishment." Undeterred, the LAPD continues to target drug dealing, violence, and other illegal behavior, without exempting people who choose to live on the streets. A team of officers patrols Skid Row every morning, referring people to housing and services, yes — but also making arrests for lawless conduct.

Bratton's attack on street disorder has dramatically improved public space downtown, according to local businesses. "Eight months ago, there were fifty tents across the street," says fish merchant Rick Merry. "You couldn't walk on the sidewalk." To a newcomer, the sidewalks still look perilous, but the regulars see tremendous progress. Patrol cops agree. "These guys [the homeless task force] have done an incredible job," says officer Robert Duke. "If they stopped for two days, it would be out of control; patrol can't handle it."

Developers are taking note as well. They are converting abandoned Beaux Arts office buildings and factories into hotly sought-after lofts moving ever closer to the heart of the Nickel. If Bratton can continue to fend off the advocates and their judicial handmaidens, LA's architecturally rich downtown may eventually throb with round-the-clock living for the law-abiding.

What Bratton needs most for all these initiatives to succeed is more manpower. In New York, as he and his deputies rolled out one new strategy after another, the department had ample staffing to implement them, and crime plunged immediately—16 percent after six weeks. In Los Angeles, by contrast, Bratton has had to backtrack. He had to dismantle an anti-graffiti squad because he needed more patrol officers. He has scaled back his crime-reduction schedule from an originally promised 10 percent reduction in crime and a 25 percent cut in homicides in 2003 to a 5 percent drop in crime and a 20 percent cut in homicides. These goals are still exceedingly impressive, and he is already close to meeting them. As of September 13, homicides were down 23 percent compared with the year before, and all felonies were down 3.9 percent. But in his first year in New York, felonies dropped 12 percent.

When the city council refused Bratton's plea for 320 new officers this spring, the chief lashed out, citing the urgency of fighting gangs and defending against terrorism. Putting police hiring on hold, he said, is like "placing a telephone call to Osama and saying, 'Osama, hold off for nine months till we get our act together here.'" The council declared itself shocked by his tone. The *Los Angeles Times* told the legislators to get over it. When Bratton tried to free up existing cops by allowing them to ignore residential burglar alarms unless verified by the owner or alarm company, since over 90 percent of alarm calls are false, the council balked again, and the compromise that the mayor engineered—allowing homeowners two false alarms—will just engender more paperwork without unburdening patrol.

It is critical to LA's future that Bratton succeed. Effective policing is our most powerful urban reclamation tool: When cops make inner cities safe, commerce and homeownership revive, as happened in Central Harlem following its 80 percent drop in homicides and burglaries in the 1990s. Crime reduction also improves race relations. Bratton himself argued to a community meeting this June that as long as the black and Hispanic crime rate remains so high, whites and Asians—as well as some police officers—will continue to fear suspicious-looking blacks and Hispanics.

To get at least some of the manpower he needs, Bratton has a source at his fingertips: the 300-plus officers engaged full time in consent-decree duty. In addition, he could profitably redirect the thousands of hours that all other officers and commanders spend on consent-decree mandates, which undoubtedly add up to hundreds of full-time positions.

One of the best urban-policy moves that the Bush administration could make, since energetic policing is not a local issue but a national one, would be to free the LAPD from the consent decree. By doing so, the administration would also be boosting homeland security: Alert cops are the country's second most important defense against another terror attack, after robust intelligence. That defense is useless, however, without enough cops to go around.

The consent decree is based on outdated stereotypes about the LAPD. If Attorney General John Ashcroft thinks that, without federal control, the LAPD would abuse people's rights, he should send his Justice Department lawyers to talk to people like the Reverend Leonard Jackson of the First African-American Methodist Episcopal Church. Asked if the police treat innocent black men abusively, Jackson responds emphatically: "No, no, no. They don't still work like that. It's been drummed into the heads of officers that everybody has rights."

Urban policing could be raised to a new height of professionalism by taking the shackles off the LAPD and letting Bratton turn the department into a national model of twenty-first-century policing, as it once was for the twentieth century.

———

William Bratton finished his first full year as LAPD chief with a 23 percent drop in homicides and a 6 percent drop in serious crime—less than his original goals but impressive nevertheless. Across the city, subtler signs of a turnaround are visible as well: It now takes longer to score drugs in MacArthur Park, for example.

Bratton has ratcheted up the pressure on the department by pledging another 20 percent drop in homicides in 2004, even though the city council has not funded more cops and federal monitor Michael Cherkasky continues to plague managers with ignorant nit-picking. Cherkasky recently penalized the department for finding too many officers fit for duty after shooting incidents, unmoved by the fact that the officers had duly traipsed off to see a "licensed mental health care professional," per consent-decree requirements, after each shooting.

In a Machiavellian thrust, Bratton and the Police Commission have named one of Los Angeles's most strident police critics to investigate the Rampart scandal. Civil rights attorney Constance Rice has never shown the slightest understanding of police work in her frequent lawsuits and diatribes against the department, yet as head of this latest Rampart inquiry—the sixth to date—she can be counted on to blast former chief Bernard Parks for his handling of the scandal just in time for his likely challenge to Mayor James Hahn in late 2004.

For all the LAPD's progress in fighting crime, gangs continue to terrorize whole neighborhoods. Occasionally a retaliatory shooting hits a celebrity of sorts: Antoine Miller, one of the thugs who nearly beat Reginald Denny to death during the Rodney King riots, was fatally shot outside a Hollywood nightclub on Super Bowl Sunday 2004. Gang members are aiming at cops more often—shootings at LA officers jumped 21 percent in 2003—prompting black community leaders to finally denounce cop-targeted violence.

Politics still impede the department's performance—but the most serious drag at present is self-imposed. Illegal aliens commit a significant percentage of gang crime in Los Angeles: 95 percent of all outstanding homicide warrants and over 60 percent of all felony warrants in late 2003 targeted illegal immigrants. Yet the police cannot use the most obvious tool to get rid of illegal gangsters—their immigration status. A city ordinance—supported by top brass—prohibits officers from enforcing immigration crimes. As a result, previously deported gang members who have returned to Los Angeles know that they enjoy immunity from immigration law—even though reentry following deportation is a federal felony punishable by twenty years in prison. In Hollywood alone, officers have observed dozens of members of the bloody El Salvadoran prison gang Mara Salvatrucha back on the streets. "They just thumb their noses at you," says a frustrated patrol supervisor. "They know we can't put a finger on them."

WHO IS THE BOY IN THE BOX?

SABRINA RUBIN ERDELY

An old man sits on an aqua couch in a pink room. Soon he will visit a little boy's grave. But first he leafs through the white binder in his lap, turning its plastic pages with a patient hand. Here is the typewritten autopsy report, dated February the 25th, 1957. Here are fading aerial photographs of the farms and woodlands surrounding the crime scene, taken with his own Speedgraphic camera. Here are photos of the battered boy laid out on a metal gurney, nude but for a white handkerchief draped over his groin for modesty's sake. Here are copies of newspaper clippings from the 1950s, '60s, '70s, and so forth, the past bleeding into the present. And here are snapshots of the old man himself, and of his police department colleagues, through the years. Black-and-white pictures of them in the '50s, young and purposeful and efficient-looking in high-waisted pants and short ties. Color four-by-sixes of them today, in white slacks and baseball hats, thicker around the middle and a little worse for wear but still alive and kicking. Still searching for that thing—that one thing. It's the thing they have yet to resolve, the one thing they still haven't made right. It's the one thing the old man needs to take care of before it's too late.

The little boy would be fifty, fifty-one years old if he were alive today, but in Bill Kelly's mind he is still a child. Time has stood still for the boy, but not for the man. He has circulation problems now, and age spots on his skin, and white hair he combs neatly back each morning, and a plastic pillbox of medicines he takes daily, some with food, some on an empty stomach. He's been living on God's green earth for seventy-five years. He's seen a lot during that time—some of which he'd rather forget, frankly—and yet Kelly remains singularly haunted by this case, by this one little boy, who has been on his mind for the better part of forty-six years. It's the one case he couldn't close, the one mystery he couldn't solve. Kelly knows time is running out. He leans in to study a close-up of the boy's face for the umpteenth time. *Who are you?* he wants to ask. *What is your name?*

Time to go.

The ridges of the little boy's footprints are burned onto the insides of Bill Kelly's eyelids. Kelly can still see them clearly, can fix the image so he can zoom in on the loops and whorls that pattern the boy's flesh. It's like standing next to a painting on a wall and peering closely enough to make out the individual brushstrokes—the elements of creation. But take a giant step back, and the whole picture comes into terrible focus. The four round bruises stippling the boy's forehead. Blue eyes whose lids have fluttered partly open, as though the boy were waking from sleep. The small, dry lips parted and crusted with blood. Tiny ribs like chicken bones etched through the skin. The little tummy already greenish with rot.

That February day in 1957, twenty-nine-year-old fingerprint expert Bill Kelly had lifted a little foot from the metal gurney and examined its sole. Sometimes it's easier to step in as close as you can, to concentrate on details so small that you don't see the larger picture at all.

The boy had been found hours earlier. A La Salle College junior was tramping through the woods of Northeast Philly's Fox Chase neighborhood, checking on some rabbit traps—or so he said; more likely, he was trying to sneak a peek into the nearby House of the

Good Shepherd home for wayward girls. At the edge of the woods, he noticed a cardboard box with what looked like a doll inside. It spooked him enough that he telephoned police to make sure. Patrolman Elmer Palmer drove through a morning drizzle to the location, a secluded dirt path off of Veree and Susquehanna roads. Locals used the area as a dumping ground, and the place was strewn with garbage and rusting appliances. A large rectangular box lay on its side in a tangle of underbrush. One end was open. A head and small shoulder were sticking out. Palmer knew right away it was no doll.

The little boy was forty inches tall and just thirty pounds, with a full set of baby teeth, putting him between four and six years old—he was so malnourished, it was hard to tell his age for sure. His nude, badly bruised body was wrapped in an Indian-patterned blanket of rust and green. His blond hair had been recently cropped in a home-made crew cut; his torso was dusted with the clippings. Other than that, his body was clean; his nails were trimmed. The skin of his right hand and both feet was pruny, as though they'd been immersed in water immediately before or after death. There were surgical scars on the boy's ankle and groin, and an L-shaped scar under his chin. The chilly weather had preserved the body somewhat, but he'd been dead long enough—from three days to two weeks—that the pull of gravity had sunk his eyeballs back into their sockets.

By the time Bill Kelly arrived at the morgue, the entire police department was talking in low voices about the discovery. They were normally stoic guys, men of few words, most of them vets who'd served in World War II or Korea. Hardened guys, you might say. But they were also men raised in a simpler era, who as boys had worn sailor suits and played with marbles—raised during a time when trashmen came around in a horse and carriage, milkmen delivered bottles to your doorstep, and families spent evenings gathered around the radio. A gentler time. Children died, of course—of polio, scarlet fever, TB—but rarely were they murdered. They certainly never met their ends the way this boy had, thrown away like a piece of trash. And so he made a deep impression on the police force. One seasoned captain got sick at the crime scene.

Kelly methodically set his inks and rollers on the morgue table. He'd seen dead children before, in Korea, but tried not to think about that. He tried not to think of his own four-year-old son, who was towheaded like this boy, or of his three-year-old daughter, or of his wife, Ruth, five months pregnant with their third. The Kelly family was growing so fast that despite Bill's standing in the Philadelphia police force—he was head of the Identification Unit—he supplemented his earnings by moonlighting as a wedding photographer. It was all worthwhile, though; Kelly loved his children, loved children *period*, and wanted as many as God would grant him. At the end of his shift that day, the little unknown boy lingering on his mind, Kelly would return to his Northeast row home and hug his kids extra tight, their happy faces shining with holy innocence.

For now, though, Kelly was first and foremost a fingerprint expert, a coolheaded man of science and reason. He inked the little boy's fingertips and feet and pressed them onto paper. Someone would come forward to claim this boy; of that, Kelly and the police were certain. The case would no doubt be solved by Monday morning.

Bill Kelly steers his silver Grand Marquis westward from Northeast Philly, toward the boy's grave. His hand rests lightly on the wheel; the insignia on his gold Knights of Columbus ring is worn smooth with time. Too many graves to visit these days; an old man could fill his retirement years just paying his respects. There are the graves of his parents to see, the graves of relatives and dear friends. Old Rem's grave. The grave of—it gives Kelly's heart a squeeze to think of it— his little girl Irene, fourth of his six children, dead since September 2002, a stroke victim at forty-one. In his prayers, Kelly asks Irene to keep an eye out for him here on earth. He asks the same of the little unknown boy, who has been dead longer than Irene was ever alive. Kelly's sure both children are in a far better place now.

The boy's discovery created a nationwide sensation once an alert was broadcast to all forty-eight states via police teletype; headlines dubbed him "the Boy in the Box." Locally, the case was inescapable, with four hundred thousand fliers of the boy's likeness printed up courtesy of the *Inquirer* and handed out on street corners, hung in shop windows, enclosed with every gas bill. Hundreds of leads came in. A New York airman thought it might be his kidnapped son Steven. A West Philly boy was sure it was his kid brother. A Lancaster woman wondered if it was her son, who was supposed to be in the care of his good-for-nothing father. No, no, and no. A man called to say he'd driven past the Fox Chase location days earlier and had seen a woman and a boy of about twelve standing by the trunk of a car; when he called out asking if they needed help, the lady had shaken her head, and he'd driven off. No, he never saw her face, her back was turned—making his call just one more in a string of well-meaning but vague tips. Police canvassed neighborhoods and checked with every orphanage, foster home, and hospital in the region, but every last child was accounted for. Two hundred and seventy police-academy recruits combed the crime scene, finding a handkerchief, a child's scarf, and a dead cat wrapped in a man's sweater—trash, or clues? And what of a child-sized blue corduroy cap discovered nearby?

The leads soon fizzled, baffling police. It seemed impossible that no one would recognize this boy and come forward—no relative, no neighbor, no teacher, playmate, or doctor. Investigators redoubled their efforts. They ran an article in a pediatric journal describing the boy's surgical scars, but got no response. They figured out that the box originally held a baby's white bassinet, eleven of which had been sold for $7.50 apiece at the Upper Darby J.C. Penney. Police actually managed to track down nine of the purchasers—quite a feat in the days before credit cards—but got no closer to an answer. They tracked the blue cap to the Robbins Bald Eagle Hat & Cap company in South Philly, which had no meaningful customer records. "This case is written on ice," a detective told Bill Kelly; all traces had melted away.

Kelly, meanwhile, had begun his own volunteer mission. Nearly each day before or after work, he would spend two or three hours in hospital records departments and unheated warehouses, sifting through badly organized maternity files. All babies' footprints are recorded at birth; if the boy had been born anywhere in this area, Kelly reasoned, his footprints would be on file *somewhere*. The police department couldn't pay the overtime for such a needle-in-a-haystack search, but that was okay. The way Kelly saw it, the boy's murder was a crime almost beyond imagination, but his being robbed of an identity was a crime against the very order of things. Everyone deserved a name. Perhaps Kelly would be able to set things right again.

"Good luck, hon—maybe today you'll get a winner," Ruth would tell Kelly as she kissed him good-bye each morning. When he returned home at night, she'd shoot him an expectant look, and he'd wordlessly shake his head no. In the hours between, Kelly would go through the same routine over and over again: pulling a set of prints from a folder, laying them flat beside the boy's footprints, then staring hard at the images. Sometimes he could tell at a glance that they weren't a match, while others required close scrutiny through a magnifying glass. Occasionally the prints were nothing but an ink splotch, impossible to read, and Kelly would despair: *Is that you?* When his enthusiasm flagged, he would remind himself of Scripture: "Seek, and ye shall find." Religion and hard science were the twin pillars of Kelly's life; he aspired to respect both and keep them in balance. (Later in life, he would be astounded to learn that the science of fingerprinting is mentioned in the Book of

Job—"He sealeth the hand of every man, that all men may know his work"—thus uniting Kelly's two passions.) To cover his bases, when Kelly went to the Good Shepherd girls' home to request adoption records for out-of-wedlock babies born there, he asked the nun to pray for his success.

He wasn't the only person preoccupied with the boy. A medical examiner's investigator named Remington Bristow, a quiet man with a craggy face, had also been trying to solve the case on his own time. Drawn together by their shared interest, Kelly and Bristow would often meet in one or the other of their City Hall offices. They agreed on one thing from the start: The boy's abusive parents or caretakers must have killed him. Considering the boy's grooming, perhaps it had happened during bath time; he'd resisted, and been smacked around harder than usual. Certainly the four bruises across his forehead could have been dug in by rough fingers trying to keep his head still during a haircut. Or maybe his hair was cut postmortem, to disguise his identity.

But how to lure the parents out of the woodwork? A year or two into the case, Bristow cleverly planted an idea in the newspapers that perhaps the boy's death had been accidental and his loving family had been too poor to afford a funeral. Bristow didn't believe it, of course, but hoped to bring the killer forward. It didn't work. Even so, Bristow's determination grew with each passing year. In year five, he consulted a psychic, which raised some eyebrows. In year six, he offered a $1,000 reward from his own meager salary for any information leading to the boy's identity. To observe the ten-year mark, Rem Bristow organized a Christmastime cemetery visit with a group of ME investigators. Bill Kelly still cherishes a black-and-white picture taken that snowy day; it's in his white binder. The group is crowded around the grave, an American flag flapping behind them; Rem's expression is grim as he gazes down at the little boy's head-stone. Poor Rem. Somewhere along the line, Kelly learned that

Bristow had a daughter who died in infancy, of crib death. Maybe that explained some things.

As for Kelly, after nine years of poring through maternity records, he finally ran out of records to search. It had taken him countless hours—time he could have been earning extra cash as a shutterbug, or spending with his family. At least some good came of it, Kelly consoled himself: He became so well-known to the hospital staffs that he'd been called in to resolve a couple of delivery-room mix-ups. Could that have been the divine reason he'd been set on this case? If he couldn't find the boy's identity, maybe he'd been meant to restore the identities of those other little boys and girls. Kelly tried to find comfort in that notion. But he was deeply bothered by his defeat, and by a memory that had disturbed him throughout his years of searching. Four months after first visiting the nun at the Good Shepherd home, he'd gone back for a follow-up, bearing a box of Whitman's chocolates.

"By the way, Sister, did you say a prayer for me? Because I'm still searching," Kelly had said, half-joking. He was frozen by her response.

"Oh, every day, Mr. Kelly," the nun had answered serenely. "Maybe God said no."

A person can't go through all that Bill Kelly has—four years at war, first on a destroyer in World War II and then on the ground in Korea; sixteen years with the Philadelphia police department, and another fifteen with the adult probation department—without some things sticking with you, and not in a good way. Bill Kelly'd probably be on the funny farm by now if he hadn't found an outlet for his disquiet: He spends one long weekend each year in silence at the St. Joseph's-in-the-Hills Retreat House in Malvern. Kelly went on his first retreat right after Korea, and the ritual has kept him sane ever since. He's gotten even more involved with the retreat house since his 1984 retirement. In fact, Kelly had just left a board meeting in early '99 when he came home to something that threw him for a loop. Ruth was watching the evening news in her living room chair. Bill had barely hung up his coat when Jim Gardner appeared on-screen and said something about a breakthrough in the case of the Boy in the Box.

The hairs on Bill Kelly's arms stood on end. He'd heard that a couple of retired guys his age had revived the case: a detective named Sam Weinstein, and a guy from the medical examiner's office, Joe McGillen. Could they actually have done it? Kelly sank into his armchair and waited impatiently through a commercial.

He had never forgotten the boy. No one had, it seemed; each time Kelly visited the grave, it was strewn with flowers and toys. Some were from other investigators, but most were left by regular citizens, prompted by some shared sense of loss. Maybe they truly grieved for the boy; then again, perhaps he had become a symbol in their minds, a way of giving shape and expression to their individual sorrows. Sometimes Kelly wonders whether *that* was the boy's purpose, that he was meant to be a tragic reminder of the fragility and helplessness of little children. Kelly would always murmur a prayer at the grave: "Guide me where to seek, that I may find the identification of the little unknown boy. Or, as I've come to call him, Sean." Then, mindful of the Good Shepherd nun, he'd add, "Thy will be done." Sean was a good Irish name, just for use until the boy's true name surfaced. Oddly enough, when Kelly's daughter Eileen became pregnant with the sixth of his ten grandchildren, she told him she planned to name her baby Sean, a coincidence that had startled Kelly. Sean is seventeen years old now, president of his class at Father Judge.

Maybe the elderly detectives working the case had found the answer. But as the news flashed a black-and-white picture of a boy with a bowl haircut, Kelly was overwhelmed with disappointment.

"I know who that is," he told Ruth heavily. "I already identified him."

They'd been so sure of that lead back in '65. He and Bristow had brainstormed that since the boy had no vaccination scars, perhaps his parents had lived under the radar, were some sort of itinerants. For a while, they'd turned their attention to a family of carnival workers. Then they considered that maybe the boy had been a recent immigrant. Going through newspapers one day, Kelly came across a 1956 article about the tide of Hungarian refugees—and there, in the accompanying photo, was the little unknown boy. It *had* to be—the ear looked just like his. With the assistance of the Immigration and Naturalization Service, Kelly sifted through 11,200 passport photos before finding the Hungarian boy's picture, and located his family in North Carolina. State troopers found the family at home, the boy playing safely in the yard.

Well, it seemed that the investigators going through the old case file had come across that same photo, and got a little excited, and put it on TV. Kelly phoned the police department the next morning to set them straight. "I heard you were dead!" homicide detective Tom Augustine exclaimed. Kelly just laughed: "Rumors of my death have been greatly exaggerated." He unearthed his box of files from the basement, and he and Sam Weinstein and Joe McGillen met for coffee at a diner. And just like that, Bill Kelly was back on the case.

It didn't take long to bring him up to speed. After Rem Bristow's death in 1993, with the investigation still open but no one manning it, the Vidocq Society—a group of local investigators devoted to solving old murder cases—had suggested Weinstein and McGillen get on it. Their point person within the police department was Detective Augustine, who'd been but a boy himself when the Boy in the Box was murdered and never forgot the mutilated face on those posted fliers.

There was one danger Kelly was aware of as he plunged back into the case, one that Rem himself might have succumbed to: wanting an answer too badly, believing in a certain resolution despite its shaky logic. Bristow had grown more obsessed with each passing year. One time, while on vacation in Mexico, he was struck by the idea that perhaps the reason no one recognized the boy was because he'd been raised as a girl. Right then and there, Bristow paid a street artist to draw a picture of what the boy would have looked like dressed as a girl, working off of an autopsy photo he always carried. After retiring, Bristow had devoted himself to the case full-time, crisscrossing the country on any thin lead he found. He also paid repeat visits to the psychic, who Bristow became increasingly convinced was on to something. Bill Kelly once visited Rem Bristow at home after they'd both retired. There on a desk in Bristow's living room lay the boy's white plaster death mask, swiped from the office. Rem had cradled the little face in his hands and stroked its forehead as he told Kelly his latest theory. He'd grown positive that the boy died at a foster home near the crime scene. The psychic had visualized a log cabin near a body of water, and a wooden porch railing. Lo and behold, Bristow had discovered a small cabin and a pond behind the stone foster home, whose porch was bordered by a wooden railing. Years earlier, in '61, Rem had toured the home, and noticed a dusty baby's bassinet in the basement. Now Bristow was sure he'd come up with the answer. He'd convinced himself that the boy's death had been an accident after all. The foster-care boys had lived on the third floor of the home; the unknown boy could have fallen out a window and then, dazed, collapsed at the edge of the pond, with both feet and a hand immersed. When the caretakers found him, they panicked, and hastily prepared him for burial in a makeshift coffin. But on the verge of burying him, they'd been frightened off, and never returned.

Kelly had nodded along with Rem's theory, but was rather taken aback. It was as though Bristow had gotten too close to the boy, until he couldn't bear the idea of intentional harm coming to him. It seemed clear that he was bending the facts to fit his theory—after all, a bassinet and a pond do not a case make. Besides, police records showed the children at that foster home were accounted for. Perhaps all Rem really wanted by that point was a resolution, *any* resolution.

In 1998, though, there was new, hard science to pursue: The Vidocq Society arranged for the little boy's skeleton to be dug up for DNA testing. At the exhumation, Weinstein was struck by the disgraceful state of the boy's grave in the potter's field in Holmesburg, littered with condoms and beer bottles and Kotex pads. When it came time to rebury the boy, they decided to give him a little more dignity; Ivy Hill Cemetery in Mt. Airy donated a lovely triangular plot by the entrance.

By the time Bill Kelly joined up in '99, the elderly investigative team had its hands full. The reburial had attracted lots of attention, including a segment on *America's Most Wanted*, spawning dozens of leads for Weinstein, McGillen, and now Kelly to follow up on. They turned out to be nothing but nebulous recollections, viewer suggestions ("Did you check with hospitals?"), and nut jobs who sent drawings of what the "cult" had done to the boy. The DNA was a wash, too; they had a sample, but no one to match it to. Then Sam Weinstein fell ill, leaving Kelly and McGillen to work the case on their own. Hoping for inspiration, they managed to locate the crime scene—a challenge, considering how the lush, green Fox Chase of 1957 had changed. The patch of wooded ground where the boy once lay is now just to the left of someone's driveway, by the side of a wide paved road lined with brick homes; Kelly and McGillen were only able to find it thanks to a telephone pole that was still across the street. Standing there amid the whizzing traffic, Kelly thought about how much the world had changed through the years, and yet how little the case had. How were they supposed to name the little boy now? It seemed hopeless. Maybe the nun was right. Maybe Kelly wasn't meant to find the answers.

And then. And *then*. The morning of February 25, 2000, a Saturday, the homicide division received a call from an Ohio psychiatrist concerning one of her outpatients. Since Kelly is sworn to keep the patient's identity a secret, he'll call her Mary. In the still-dark hours of that very morning—the forty-third anniversary of the boy's discovery—Mary had awakened in a panic and picked up the phone. She wanted to report a murder. She needed to get it off her chest, after all these years.

With the psychiatrist acting as a middleman, the investigators began a two-year correspondence with Mary, slowly piecing together the details. She claimed to have grown up in Lower Merion, the only child of schoolteachers. She remembered being ten years old and driving with her mother to a house in a neighborhood she didn't recognize. The woman who answered the door held a toddler in a soaked diaper. A male voice came from inside the house: "Did you get the money?" Mary's mother handed over an envelope, and was given the child in return. She took the boy home, shut him in the basement, and never allowed him to leave the house. The boy never spoke a word. Something was physically wrong with him—Mary later wondered if he might have had cerebral palsy. He was terribly abused and underfed; they both were.

After such a long drought, Bill Kelly and Joe McGillen were ecstatic at this new stream of information, even if it *was* slightly bizarre. They rushed to verify the details as each fragment was revealed, nearly giddy with urgency. When they received a letter the day before Palm Sunday 2002, mentioning the name of Mary's childhood street, the pair couldn't wait; as soon as Mass let out, they drove to Lower Merion, still in their church suits, knocking on doors until they confirmed that Mary's family had indeed lived there. At long last, in June 2002, Mary agreed to a face-to-face meeting. Because of McGillen's fear of flying, they rented a van for the trip to Ohio, with McGillen driving, Tom Augustine riding shotgun with the directions, and Kelly with his legs up across the backseat for his circulation's sake.

It took Mary three hours to tell the whole story. She was twelve when it happened. She remembered the boy had thrown up after eating some baked beans. She remembered her mother, enraged at the mess, throwing the boy in the bathtub and then beating him, slamming his head again and again against the bathroom floor. The boy let out a shriek, the only sound Mary ever heard him utter. Then he was silent. Her mother cleaned him up, cut his untended hair, wrapped him in a blanket, and carried him out to the trunk of the car. Mary went with her, wearing her raincoat against the February drizzle. She remembered driving to a forlorn place, getting out and standing by the trunk. Her mother stiffening as a man stopped his car: "Do you need any help?" Her mother shaking her head no. After the man drove on, her mother stashed the dead boy in an empty box lying nearby. Mary had memorized the route home, so that one day she could return for him. He wasn't her real brother, but she loved him all the same.

The investigators were rapt. *What was his name?* they asked hungrily.

It comes down to this, an old man standing over a boy's grave. Bill Kelly is at ease here. He brushes some twigs from atop the headstone, crouches to straighten out a small flag someone has poked into the ground. As always, there's a new batch of toys around the stone: a soldier figurine, a race car, a ceramic teddy bear, a couple of plastic orange fish that are probably bath toys. Flowers, too—the Ivy Hill manager says that when people come to visit a loved one, they often pause by the boy's grave and pull out stems from their bouquets. Kelly once left a green ball belonging to his grandson Sean, thinking that if Unknown Sean were alive, he'd probably like to play with it. Kelly visits twice a year, usually. He'll be back again on November the 11th, when the Vidocq Society sponsors a memorial service to commemorate five years since the boy's reburial.

Kelly and McGillen have corroborated everything of Mary's story they can. They traced the route she described, and found it indeed leads between her Lower Merion home and where the boy was discovered in Fox Chase. They located a college roommate of Mary's who said Mary once confided that her mother had killed someone. For what it's worth, the psychiatrist believes Mary is sincere, and says her story has remained consistent over a decade of therapy. It all seems to add up. But the police department doesn't think the theory holds water. For one thing, Mary has been in and out of psychiatric care for much of her adult life—who's to say this isn't some crazy fantasy? Many of the details she provided are a matter of public record; the part about the Good Samaritan driving up, for example, was reported in the *Evening Bulletin* in 1957. She isn't a blood relative of the boy's, so the DNA does nothing to prove her claims. Her parents died years ago. Mary admitted that when they bought the boy, they were only told his first name—which may not have been his actual birth name, so there's no way to check his identity against a birth certificate. Anyhow, in Mary's old neighborhood, no one ever heard of a little boy living in her family's house. To Kelly and McGillen, that's proof the boy was kept prisoner in the basement, as Mary said, but to the cops it confirms that her tales are the delusions of a madwoman.

That frustrates Kelly. Of course Mary had mental problems—who wouldn't, after the things she witnessed as a child? But he wearily accepts that there's further work to be done. Not that he doesn't have other things to do with his golden years, mind you. He lives a good life. His days are filled with church activities, meetings of his various clubs, joyous visits with his grandchildren—everyone calls them "Kelly's Angels," and they in turn call him Pop-Pop—and too-frequent doctor appointments. But Kelly always finds time to spend a few hours each week going through his notes, flipping through his binders. He and McGillen have worked up an extensive genealogy of Mary's family in the hope of finding other living relatives. They've come up with yearbook photos of Mary's parents, and interviewed one of her mother's former co-workers. They tracked down and reinterviewed the Good Samaritan. Kelly and McGillen feel Mary is telling the truth. Bill Kelly looked her in the eye, and he firmly believes her. What choice does he have, really? Because if not this answer, what then?

Kelly understands now why Rem came to believe his theory about the foster home. Maybe sometimes what we call truth is simply the answer we choose to live with, a way to reassure ourselves that we've done all we can. In the end, maybe we all want to believe in *something*, even if we can't quite connect the dots, even if it's a belief in something we can't see. Maybe it all comes down to faith. Bill Kelly wants to have faith in Mary. He wants to have faith that the answers are close at hand, and that he will finally do right by this little boy. And he wants to have faith—in faith.

Perhaps it comes down to accepting that sometimes, life doesn't match up neatly like the loops and whorls of a fingerprint. In time, Kelly is sure he'll find the true answers to the mystery of the boy's identity—if not in this life, then in the next. And so maybe he has found a set of answers he's willing to live with, for now.

Bill Kelly lingers at the grave for a moment longer, then touches the headstone with an affectionate palm.

"Good-bye, Jonathan," he says gently. "I'll see you again soon."

———

Over the years, through my crime reporting, I kept hearing about the boy in the box. Law-enforcement agents would mention the case with a solemn nod, as though they expected me to be familiar with it; I read in the newspaper that mourners still left flowers at the boy's grave. I was surprised, frankly, that in a city like Philadelphia—a place where new murders happen every day—this decades-old case held such a macabre grip over the public. But when an investigator told me that a clutch of retired police officers was still actively pursuing the case—still obsessed with it, forty-six years later—I knew I had to go deeper.

Meeting Bill Kelly, I only became more fascinated by the nature of his search. His devotion to the boy was amazing to me; when we eventually visited the cemetery together and he sweetly bid the boy goodbye, my eyes filled with tears. I came to understand that Kelly's quest for the boy's identity had become inextricable from his own life story—giving up on the search would have meant giving up on a part of himself. But I was also acutely aware that Kelly's mission had a natural time limit, which was getting closer by the day. The clock was ticking on the one thing Kelly was determined to finally make right, the one thing in his life that had been left undone. And I've found myself wondering: What will that one thing be for me, when I'm older?

I hope Kelly finds what he's looking for. I hope we all do.

LORD OF THE DRUG RING
CHARLES BOWDEN

Listen to the silence. Bougainvilleas drip red in the parking area just off 10th Street in McAllen, Texas. The day will be warm, with little wind. At 10:53 AM, it is almost sixty-five degrees. Comandante Guillermo González Calderoni has been in the office of his lawyer, Roberto Yzaguirre, for almost an hour, talking. He desperately wants to buy a ranch and has, against all custom, come in early—he never stirs much before noon—with his sidekick, Chato. Yzaguirre calms him down, tells him no, we cannot look at the property today, but we can go out Saturday if you wish. Calderoni reluctantly agrees to wait. He is anxious for this ranch. He had many ranches in Mexico before he fled ten years ago and the government seized them.

This very morning, he has driven from the gated community where he lives, has left his beautiful young wife and has come here about this passion for a ranch. And now, the meeting over, he is standing in the lobby of Yzaguirre's office, with its stone wall and green leather mahogany furniture, saying good-bye to his gravelly voiced lawyer and flirting with the receptionist. Calderoni is a peacock of a man, dressed nattily in fine fabrics and handmade boots, quick eyed and fluent in English, Spanish, and French. He has a keen eye for women—his second wife was a beauty queen—and is a legendary shot with a .45, the weapon he is said to keep in his boot. He has lived for the past decade in McAllen, a few minutes from Mexico, a country that claims he is a major criminal and has sought his extradition. This hardly seems to concern him. No, at the moment he is all about this ranch he must have.

He has sixty seconds or so left as he steps outside and walks to his parked Mercedes. Calderoni slides behind the wheel; Chato sits beside him. There is the slam of brakes as a car pins the Mercedes into its slot; then a man leaps from the passenger side, takes two or three steps, and fires one shot into the Comandante's neck. The car roars away, and the Comandante's head rolls back. He will be declared dead at a hospital in just over an hour.

Only Chato witnesses the murder. He is sitting beside Calderoni in the car, yet no one harms him. At first he gives the police a description: two men with dark skin, a Chrysler with Louisiana plates. Later the police cast doubt upon his story, saying he is too upset to recall what he has seen. The next day, they find the Chrysler about a mile away. The plates turn out to be stolen. On the window is a decal for the Mexican Red Cross. At that, the trail goes dead.

There is a brief flurry of notice, and then the fantasies begin. Within days the Mexican press announces that the FBI beat local cops to the murder scene. A rumor hits the U.S. press that a Mexican drug leader paid $3 million for the hit. A magazine claims the Comandante was getting ready to return to Mexico and tell all. An old colleague of his says it was a contract killing from the ruling class of Mexico.

And then the footprints of Calderoni's life begin to blow away as the ground shifts in the secret world where he thrived. Just five days after his death, he is already well on his way to being a figure known by a few old cops, a story told in murderous cantinas, a memory to some beautiful women as they rest their heads against their fine pillows in those special moments just before sleep comes. He was the man who knew everything, and his death means that now things will never be known. That is the way of the world that produced him — a world that was not really Mexico or the border or the drug wars, but the world of spies, secrets, agents, networks—the basic elements governments have found so necessary as events overwhelmed simple customs and laws. Ask around and it's unlikely you'll find a man who even knows his name, unless he has entered certain rooms under certain conditions and tasted certain pains.

I can taste things sometimes.

In November 2001, I was in a border city where eight girls had been buried in a ditch splattered with sunflowers in bloom. I left the grave site and went to a country club in a gated community where the Mexican rich huddled. I entered the bar, which overlooked the golf course, ordered a drink, and began taking notes on what I'd seen. A couple of hundred yards away was the home of the head of a major drug cartel. This bar and this country club were his playground. I remember the anger rising in me over the dead girls, over the rich ignoring the poor, over the protection granted the drug merchant who lived a football field from where I sat. Calderoni had once been the boss of this town.

Sometimes when I'm in the mood in strange cities, I go to suicide bars—the kind of places where, by the second beer, someone is going to call you out. I do this because I am angry and looking for trouble. I felt the same way in this country club. As I sipped my drink and took notes, the waiters stared at me. Then I could hear them on the phone. I was with a Mexican, and as time passed he became very worried.

We got up and left. As we walked down the palatial steps fronting the clubhouse, an unmarked state-police car wheeled up, the two men in it staring at us with hard eyes. Someone had called them; the Mexican and I knew this in our bones. We walked past. Had we stayed five more minutes in the bar, things could have turned out differently.

I think of my drinks and note-making in the country-club bar as a kind of Calderoni moment. He lived in that zone where violence floods the air like lilacs in springtime, and he was at the beck and call of those who needed someone murdered or vanished pronto. Sometimes he answered the call and took care of business. On that warm Wednesday morning last February in McAllen, someone else got the call, and then someone took care of him.

That is how things happen in this world beneath our smug notice and official pieties. Americans, and I count myself among them, are fools, oblivious of the screams shredding the air. Mexicans drink darker truths.

The small metal statue of the steer and mounted cowboy sleeps on the huge wooden conference table in the dead man's office. It has been just five days since the Comandante's execution. The son's voice purls out soft words as he sits at his father's oak desk in the trading company near the border. He wears slacks, loafers, and a plaid cotton shirt and has all the élan of a bookkeeper. He is explaining that his father lived an honorable life and died an honorable death. One bullet to the neck and he was gone. The son sweeps his arms as if holding a machine gun, goes *ack! ack! ack!* as he demonstrates the gory alternatives and says he is grateful that his father was not disfigured by death, which, he notes once again, came swiftly, almost tranquilly. The office has the feeling of a place where decisions are made but papers seldom shuffled. The conference table squats, with no chairs. A desk gleams clean of paper. The phone rings only once during the hour we talk, and that with a call from the son's mother, Calderoni's first wife.

I'm here because I've just come off seven years in the drug world, writing a book, and during those years Calderoni has stalked my thoughts, a thread running through everything and yet refusing to explain anything. I talked to men who had been on raids with him, talked to a man who had been one of his pistoleros, saw the fear his name evoked wash across the faces of many along the border. For almost twenty years, nothing of consequence happened in Mexico's drug world without Calderoni's hand being present. But I never met or talked to the Comandante, who by nature did not answer questions but asked them. He had become a fantasy in my mind, living in his mansion in McAllen with his millions and his pack of blooded Rottweilers. His death offered the last open window into his life I was ever likely to see. So I flew to Texas, rented a car, and came down to the border before the body grew too cool.

The son explains that his father and he lived separate lives, that his father's business was his father's business, that he has followed a different path. He has spoken to no one in the press since his father's death, he rolls on, because he wants his father to rest in peace. But then, I know, everyone wants his father to rest in peace — and especially to stay silent. *Epoca*, a Mexican magazine, runs a simple graphic to announce the murder: Calderoni's face with a gun to his head and, imprinted on the mouth, the universal symbol of a circle with a slash across it. *The New York Times* dismisses the killing with seventy-odd words and then, twelve days later, runs an article explaining that Comandante Calderoni was a creature from the past, a footnote to an era that is now "as remote and romantic as cowboys and Indians." The world, the paper asserts, has moved on to an age of terror, a fact that makes the high jinks of a Calderoni both quaint and irrelevant.

The son, in his utter calm, seems to agree. Ah, he explains, he knows nothing of his father's activities; he simply runs the family business, this trading company where the phones hardly ever ring, this large building full of offices with nothing going on in them.

Just what does the firm export? An oil, yes, an oil, the son explains, a *special* oil, though he cannot quite remember what it is at the moment. And drinks, yes, wine and vodka, things like that also. There is no evidence of any samples in the silent building, nothing to indicate activity except numerous paper-shredding machines.

His father was shot on Wednesday, February 5, 2003, at 10:54 AM. The funeral was Friday, followed quickly by a cremation because, the son continues, his father had always expressed a wish to be free of the grave, to be part of the wind and the world. So as we sit on Monday in the late afternoon, everything is over; the era of cowboys and Indians has ended. There is only the desire for quiet, a desire shared by people in many places: in the FBI, in DEA, in the highest reaches of the Mexican government, in the largest drug organizations on earth, in the vaults of American secrets where clerks quietly bury unseemly sections of the history of the United States.

I nod at the son, say that I understand. And I do.

I learned about Comandante Calderoni the normal way you learn about things on the border—voices whispering with fear, heads bending low over cups of coffee in cheap cafés, people looking over their shoulders and softly saying his name. I'll get to the little facts on which we build our lies in a moment. But first I want to revisit the place where the real facts kill you dead.

Years ago I lived in a small town along the base of the Sierra Madre where most of the population survived by producing or shipping drugs. I met a widow there whose husband had been the Mexican equivalent of a county attorney. One day he and his wife had gone down to the plaza to buy ice cream cones. The air was full of laughter, the sidewalks packed with families and lovers promenading, the air sagging with the scent of flowers. Two men walked up, shot him dead, strolled down the block, and climbed into a taxi. No one got a good look at them. The taxi driver had no memory of where he took them. The widow eventually got a job with the Mexican federal police, or *federales*. Soon she owned nice houses in the capital, on the beach. I would see her at parties laughing, her lips red, her body wrapped in fine garments.

I told myself I did not understand. Now I do. There is a reason to forget.

I'll tell you irrelevant details. If you work in a border factory in Mexico, one most likely owned by an American corporation, you will work four hours and fifty minutes to buy one pound of beef. You will work three hours and nine minutes to buy a half gallon of milk. You will work fifty-five minutes for a bar of soap. You will work over eleven hours to buy your kid a new pair of pants. I've taught myself to say it is not my problem, to say it does not justify the drug trade, to say it will all work out in the end, just give it a spell. Most days I'm a fair hand at saying these things.

You will learn to forget things, too. You will learn things you will always remember. And after the blood dries, you will dance and want and try to get pretty things. And you will know in every cell of your being that nothing that happens to you will ever be known to your neighbors up north.

Calderoni came up in a well-off family, his father a success in the state-owned oil business. He mastered several languages, learned to be a good shot, and by the early 1980s was a *federale* on the border. Soon he was a comandante. He took a million-dollar contract from one drug lord to kill another. (The FBI unknowingly helped him with this murder.) He hobnobbed with DEA agents, helped them out when he needed to, and was flown to Washington for a personal tour of the inner sanctum of DEA intelligence. In the 1988 presidential election, he allegedly arranged the murders of key leaders of the opposition party and rigged the computers so that the ruling party's candidate, a man who almost certainly lost the popular vote, won the official vote. In 1992 he got in trouble and fled to the United States, across the Rio Grande. His official wealth was listed at about $7 million. While DEA protected him, it also knew he had more than a billion dollars in stashed assets. He had made his money by killing people. He had made his money by charging a toll to drug traffickers. He had made his money by doing the little dirty tasks commanded by the president of Mexico, Carlos Salinas. He had made his money by knowing how to forget and, of course, when to remember.

Calderoni had thrived while working for the *federales*, a law team that combines all the virtues of the FBI and the Mafia. I once attended a wedding where drug dealers and *federales* drank, did drugs, fucked, and celebrated together for five days. During the party, one *federale* major and a colleague left for a few hours, murdered two peasants who were smuggling drugs without paying them off, took the load of dope, and sold it.

A week later, that *federale* major was dead. When I asked what had happened to him, I was told "his heart stopped." It is, of course, not polite to pry. Just as when I drove by the state-police office each day and admired the towering marijuana plants that constituted the front lawn, I did not pry. Just as when I was run off the road by *federales* and had an AK-47 poked in my guts, I did not lose my civility.

But now, I think, I'll lose it.

You are holding this magazine, and you think, if you are a sane American, what does this obscure, dead comandante, Guillermo Calderoni, have to do with me? I'll tell you. He was a captain in an industry—the global dope business—that earns close to half a *trillion* dollars a year. He was an enforcer that made Mexico safe for your vacations and for your investments in factories where people work for next to nothing. Even if you don't have shares in some U.S. company with factories down in Mexico, you still get your slice of the pie every time you pick up some deal on a television or a VCR or thousands of other items made by people living in cardboard shacks all along the line.

I once was talking to a Mexican woman in her twenties whose sister had been kidnapped, raped, and murdered on the border. I asked, "Just what did your sister do?"

She looked at me with cold eyes and said, "She made things for you."

I keep going to Mexico, God knows why. Partly, I like the people. But mainly, things exist south of that river, on the other side of that fence. Big things, bloody things. Oh God, I love the ladies and the scent coming off their skin, the way they move in stiletto heels, nimble as goats. The beer's good, too, and I can't say enough about the beaches.

This other business, well, best not to talk about it. I'm sure that's what the Comandante would advise me if he were still around.

By the mid-eighties, a legend had begun to trail Calderoni, one that struck awe in American FBI and DEA agents and terror in Mexican citizens. Rumors had spread that he interrogated with a bolt cutter or with pliers on the teeth. He became the guy who was sent in to clean up the various Dodge Citys of Mexico. When a drug leader in Juárez roughed up an American newspaper photographer in 1986 and the U.S. press demanded justice, Calderoni was the one who made it right. He did several things. He told the previous comandante in Juárez that he had twenty-four hours to get out of town. Then he went to the mansion of the offending drug leader—getting past his pet tiger, alligators, and boa constrictors—and hauled the guy and his pistoleros off to prison. Then, as a separate venture, he flew through U.S. territory—escorted by FBI agents in American helicopters—to a small Mexican town near Ojinaga, Chihuahua, and killed Pablo Acosta, at that moment the major conduit of Colombian cocaine through Mexico into the United States. (The FBI was unaware that this was actually a contract killing for which Calderoni was paid

$1 million.) Acosta's mistake was being featured in the press; he'd given a front-page interview to an El Paso daily detailing his bribe payments to the Mexican government. This fame made him expendable. The FBI was so hungry for a headline blow against a major drug dealer that it kept its scheme with Calderoni a secret from DEA.

But to its consternation, the FBI also kept hearing of a different Calderoni from its snitches, information that the bureau buried in its files—in part because Calderoni was the kind of connection who could make a narc's career, a man who could hand over the big case all wrapped up in a ribbon with a bow, and in part because the FBI could not believe the truth, because it meant its Mexico was not the *real* Mexico, just as successive American administrations have ignored reports linking the Mexican president and the country's ruling class to the drug business. Just as the brother of one president of Mexico funneled roughly $100 million in drug money through one U.S. bank without anyone saying a word in the regulatory agencies. The U.S. government knows very little about Mexicans. Except, of course, that they continue to flee the country the U.S. government helps to sustain.

In 1996, Calderoni mysteriously erupted in a huge story in *The New York Times*, complete with a photo of him and President Carlos Salinas. The story explained that Calderoni's earlier warnings to the American government of links between Mexico's $30-billion-a-year drug world and the Salinas administration had been ignored lest they upset international relationships and trade deals. The Comandante, in this singular newspaper appearance, made his point: *I know, and if I'm bothered, I will remember what I know.*

Then the Comandante vanished from public notice and became a man left to his golf game in Texas. For years I heard rumors that he had not truly retired, that he retained his network in Mexico, that he continued to help in contract killings and other housekeeping matters. When I would mention these rumors to people in DEA, I'd receive a shrug and silence.

The agency wanted to forget what it really knew about Calderoni—about how, back in the '80s, when shipments of cocaine began to flood Mexico, the Comandante had prospered, and as he rose, so did his share of the action. During the Salinas years, an effort by U.S. operatives to pin down the Comandante's assets stalled when they reached $1 billion. And here the unreality returns as it always does in Mexico: a billion dollars flowing into the hands of a man who lived and died largely unknown to the American press and government. The Comandante prospered in this world of ignorance. He would work with DEA, seize loads left and right, and do this because a part of him wanted to be a supercop. And then the Comandante would blame the seizures on DEA, even when the agency had nothing to do with them. DEA made busts, got headlines, and had a valiant antidrug Comandante to celebrate. The billion dollars stashed away? A detail.

"DEA never looked for Calderoni's money," a retired U.S. government agent told me. "DEA was in love with him."

Retired to his mansion in McAllen, Calderoni continued to do what he had always done. He sold intelligence. He consulted with traffickers on how to bring drugs into the United States. He blackmailed leading Mexican politicians with his tapes. He flourished as if the flight from his police post and nation had never occurred.

The church is modern, sterile, and reeks of a germproof United States, a fortress built to block the aromas drifting across the border. People come from Mexico for the Comandante's funeral, and St. Joseph the Worker in McAllen is packed. Retired DEA agents show up, along with many other people who do not advertise who or what they are. In death, it seems, the Comandante is finally safe to visit. One former DEA agent tells the press that the Comandante never took dirty money or played both sides against each other. Or did murder for hire. Which is only more evidence of the fantasy history peculiar to the war on drugs.

I like to imagine the world of Comandante Calderoni: doing deep deals with the FBI and DEA and most likely the CIA; arresting, killing, and charging multibillion-dollar drug cartels; carrying out the crimes and desires of the leaders of Mexico; and betraying all of them to one another and somehow keeping his footing, never spinning out of control, never flinching as one thing led to another. Living in McAllen, playing golf right there on the banks of the Rio Grande, where he faced a nation of harsh and corrupt power that wanted to jail him, as well as large organizations of cutthroats whom he had beaten, tortured, arrested, and of course charged generously for the experience.

Now he becomes ash and dust, becomes a footnote in a few American newspapers, becomes a file sealed in various agencies. His tracks across Mexican history and our own history are at this very moment blowing away in the wind.

Time to open a cold beer, maybe head down to the playas. Mexico can be really colorful. Hell, you can't believe the parties—they go on for days. The water can be risky, some say, but you can bank on the beer and the women.

——

I got a call and the voice told me that Comandante Calderoni had been murdered. The caller was worried for a simple reason: He'd just finished a deal with Calderoni and been warned at that time by the

Comandante that he'd best vanish for his own safety due to the nature of their transaction. So when Calderoni was executed in the daylight parking lot of his lawyer's office, my caller kind of wondered if he was next on some list.

So we went down together. I wanted to discover if anything about the mysterious comandante would be revealed by death, my companion simply needed to know whether he was a marked man. What we found was silence and an adamant lack of curiosity by everyone about investigating the murder. My companion felt relieved as it became clear to him that the killing did not result from their recent business, and I felt history blowing away like dust in the wind.

Since then rumors have bubbled up and everyone has been fingered as a possible source of the murder contract. And nothing has come of any of these rumors, which is right and fitting. The Comandante lived in the shadows, and it would be almost immoral should his murder suddenly be solved by bright lights and sworn depositions.

One of these rumors did catch my eye. Earlier I had written about the downfall of a DEA agent, Salvador Martinez, an article republished in Best American Crime Writing, 2002 edition, edited by Otto Penzler. A year and a half after Martinez's arrest and imprisonment, his main accuser, a Mexican state cop, was executed on the border with $20,000 on the car seat beside him. Well, after Calderoni's death, a new tale began to be whispered, one that said the Mexican cop had spoken disrespectfully of Calderoni and these bad words had gotten back to him. The Comandante had then ordered his murder.

So it seems the Comandante continues to meddle with my life and understanding, even from the grave.

WHO SHOT MOHAMMED AL-DURA?

JAMES FALLOWS

The name Mohammed al-Dura is barely known in the United States. Yet to a billion people in the Muslim world it is an infamous symbol of grievance against Israel and—because of this country's support for Israel—against the United States as well.

Al-Dura was the twelve-year-old Palestinian boy shot and killed during an exchange of fire between Israeli soldiers and Palestinian demonstrators on September 30, 2000. The final few seconds of his life, when he crouched in terror behind his father, Jamal, and then slumped to the ground after bullets ripped through his torso, were captured by a television camera and broadcast around the world. Through repetition they have become as familiar and significant to Arab and Islamic viewers as photographs of bombed-out Hiroshima are to the people of Japan—or as footage of the crumbling World Trade Center is to Americans. Several Arab countries have issued postage stamps carrying a picture of the terrified boy. One of Baghdad's main streets was renamed the Martyr Mohammed Aldura Street. Morocco has an al-Dura Park. In one of the messages Osama bin Laden released after the September 11 attacks and the subsequent U.S. invasion of Afghanistan, he began a list of indictments against "American arrogance and Israeli violence" by saying, "In the epitome of his arrogance and the peak of his media campaign in which he boasts of 'enduring freedom,' Bush must not forget the image of Mohammed al-Dura and his fellow Muslims in Palestine and Iraq. If he has forgotten, then we will not forget, God willing."

But almost since the day of the episode evidence has been emerging in Israel, under controversial and intriguing circumstances, to indicate that the official version of the Mohammed al-Dura story is not true. It now appears that the boy cannot have died in the way reported by most of the world's media and fervently believed throughout the Islamic world. Whatever happened to him, he was not shot by the Israeli soldiers who were known to be involved in the day's fighting—or so I am convinced, after spending a week in Israel talking with those examining the case. The exculpatory evidence comes not from government or military officials in Israel, who have an obvious interest in claiming that their soldiers weren't responsible, but from other sources. In fact, the Israel Defense Forces, or IDF, seem to prefer to soft-pedal the findings rather than bring any more attention to this gruesome episode. The research has been done by a variety of academics, ex-soldiers, and Web-loggers who have become obsessed with the case, and the evidence can be cross-checked.

No "proof" that originates in Israel is likely to change minds in the Arab world. The longtime Palestinian spokesperson Hanan Ashrawi dismissed one early Israeli report on the topic as a "falsified version of reality [that] blames the victims." Late this spring Said Hamad, a spokesman at the PLO office in Washington, told me of the new Israeli studies, "It does not surprise me that these reports would come out from the same people who shot Mohammed al-Dura. He was shot of course by the Israeli army, and not by anybody else." Even if evidence that could revise the understanding of this particular death were widely accepted (so far it has been embraced by a few Jewish groups in Europe and North America), it would probably have no effect on the underlying hatred and ongoing violence in the region. Nor would evidence that clears Israeli soldiers necessarily support the overarching Likud policy of sending soldiers to occupy territories and protect settlements. The Israelis still looking into the al-Dura case do not all endorse Likud occupation policies. In fact, some strongly oppose them.

The truth about Mohammed al-Dura is important in its own right, because this episode is so raw and vivid in the Arab world and so hazy, if not invisible, in the West. Whatever the course of the occupation of Iraq, the United States has guaranteed an ample future supply of images of Arab suffering. The two explosions in Baghdad markets in the first weeks of the war, killing scores of civilians, offered an initial taste. Even as U.S. officials cautioned that it would take more time and study to determine whether U.S. or Iraqi ordnance had caused the blasts, the Arab media denounced the brutality that created these new martyrs. More of this lies ahead. The saga of Mohammed al-Dura illustrates the way the battles of wartime imagery may play themselves out.

The harshest version of the al-Dura case from the Arab side is that it proves the ancient "blood libel"—Jews want to kill gentile children—and shows that Americans count Arab life so cheap that they will let the Israelis keep on killing. The harshest version from the Israeli side is that the case proves the Palestinians' willingness to deliberately sacrifice even their own children in the name of the war against Zionism. In Tel Aviv I looked through hour after hour of videotape in an attempt to understand what can be known about what happened, and what it means.

THE DAY

The death of Mohammed al-Dura took place on the second day of what is now known as the second intifada, a wave of violent protests throughout the West Bank and Gaza. In the summer of 2000 Middle East peace negotiations had reached another impasse. On September 28 of that year, a Thursday, Ariel Sharon, then the leader of Israel's Likud Party but not yet prime minister, made a visit to the highly contested religious site in Jerusalem that Jews know as the Temple Mount and Muslims know as Haram al-Sharif, with its two mosques. For Palestinians this was the trigger—or, in the view of many Israelis, the pretext—for the expanded protests that began the next day.

On September 30 the protest sites included a crossroads in the occupied Gaza territory near the village of Netzarim, where sixty families of Israeli settlers live. The crossroads is a simple right-angle intersection of two roads in a lightly developed area. Three days earlier a roadside bomb had mortally wounded an IDF soldier there. At one corner of the intersection were an abandoned warehouse, two six-story office buildings known as the "twin towers," and a two-story building. (These structures and others surrounding the crossroads have since been torn down.) A group of IDF soldiers had made the two-story building their outpost, to guard the road leading to the Israeli settlement.

Diagonally across the intersection was a small, ramshackle building and a sidewalk bordered by a concrete wall. It was along this wall that Mohammed al-Dura and his father crouched before they were shot. (The father was injured but survived.) The other two corners of the crossroads were vacant land. One of them contained a circular dirt berm, known as the Pita because it was shaped like a pita loaf. A group of uniformed Palestinian policemen, armed with automatic rifles, were on the Pita for much of the day.

Early in the morning of Saturday, September 30, a crowd of Palestinians gathered at the Netzarim crossroads. TV crews, photographers, and reporters from many news agencies, including Reuters, AP, and the French television network France 2, were also at the ready. Because so many cameras were running for so many hours, there is abundant documentary evidence of most of the day's events—with a few strange and crucial exceptions, most of them concerning Mohammed al-Dura.

"Rushes" (raw footage) of the day's filming collected from these and other news organizations around the world tell a detailed yet confusing story. The tapes overlap in some areas but leave mysterious gaps in others. No one camera, of course, followed the day's events from beginning to end; and with so many people engaged in a variety of activities simultaneously, no one account could capture everything. Gabriel Weimann, the chairman of the communications department at the University of Haifa, whose book *Communicating Unreality* concerns the media's distorting effects, explained to me on my visit that the footage in its entirety has a *"Rashomon* effect." Many separate small dramas seem to be under way. Some of the shots show groups of young men walking around, joking, sitting and smoking and appearing to enjoy themselves. Others show isolated moments of intense action, as protesters yell and throw rocks, and shots ring out from various directions. Only when these vignettes are packaged together as a conventional TV news report do they seem to have a narrative coherence.

Off and on throughout the morning some of the several hundred Palestinian civilians at the crossroads mounted assaults on the IDF outpost. They threw rocks and Molotov cocktails. They ran around waving the Palestinian flag and trying to pull down an Israeli flag near the outpost. A few of the civilians had pistols or rifles, which they occasionally fired; the second intifada quickly escalated from throwing rocks to using other weapons. The Palestinian policemen, mainly in the Pita area, also fired at times. The IDF soldiers, according to Israeli spokesmen, were under orders not to fire in response to rocks or other thrown objects. They were to fire only if fired upon. Scenes filmed throughout the day show smoke puffing from the muzzles of M-16s pointed through the slits of the IDF outpost.

To watch the raw footage is to wonder, repeatedly, What is going on here? In some scenes groups of Palestinians duck for cover from gunfire while others nonchalantly talk or smoke just five feet away. At one dramatic moment a Palestinian man dives forward clutching his leg, as if shot in the thigh. An ambulance somehow arrives to collect him exactly two seconds later, before he has stopped rolling from the momentum of his fall. Another man is loaded into an ambulance—and, in footage from a different TV camera, appears to jump out of it again some minutes later.

At around 3:00 PM Mohammed al-Dura and his father make their first appearance on film. The time can be judged by later comments from the father and some journalists on the scene, and by the length of shadows in the footage. Despite the number of cameras that were running that day, Mohammed and Jamal al-Dura appear in the footage of only one cameraman—Talal Abu-Rahma, a Palestinian working for France 2.

Jamal al-Dura later said that he had taken his son to a used-car market and was on the way back when he passed through the crossroads and into the crossfire. When first seen on tape, father and son are both crouched on the sidewalk behind a large concrete cylinder, their backs against the wall. The cylinder, about three feet high, is referred to as "the barrel" in most discussions of the case, although it appears to be a section from a culvert or a sewer system. On top of the cylinder is a big paving stone, which adds another eight inches or so of protection. The al-Duras were on the corner diagonally opposite the Israeli outpost. By hiding behind the barrel they were doing exactly what they should have done to protect themselves from Israeli fire.

Many news accounts later claimed that the two were under fire for forty-five minutes, but the action captured on camera lasts a very brief time. Jamal looks around desperately. Mohammed slides down behind him, as if to make his body disappear behind his father's. Jamal clutches a pack of cigarettes in his left hand, while he alternately waves and cradles his son with his right. The sound of gunfire is heard, and four bullet holes appear in the wall just to the left of the pair. The father starts yelling. There is another burst. Mohammed goes limp and falls forward across his father's lap, his shirt stained with blood. Jamal, too, is hit, and his head starts bobbing. The camera cuts away. Although France 2 or its cameraman may have footage that it or he has chosen not to release, no other visual record of the shooting or its immediate aftermath is known to exist. Other Palestinian casualties of the day are shown being evacuated, but there is no known on-tape evidence of the boy's being picked up, tended to, loaded into an ambulance, or handled in any other way after he was shot.

The footage of the shooting is unforgettable, and it illustrates the way in which television transforms reality. I have seen it replayed at least a hundred times now, and on each repetition I can't help hoping that this time the boy will get himself down low enough, this time the shots will miss. Through the compression involved in editing the footage for a news report, the scene acquired a clear story line by the time European, American, and Middle Eastern audiences saw it on television: Palestinians throw rocks. Israeli soldiers, from the slits in their outpost, shoot back. A little boy is murdered.

What is known about the rest of the day is fragmentary and additionally confusing. A report from a nearly hospital says that a dead boy was admitted on September 30, with two gun wounds to the left side of his torso. But according to the photocopy I saw, the report also says that the boy was admitted at 1:00 PM; the tape shows that Mohammed was shot later in the afternoon. The doctor's report also notes, without further explanation, that the dead boy had a cut down his belly about eight inches long. A boy's body, wrapped in a Palestinian flag but with his face exposed, was later carried through the streets to a burial site (the exact timing is in dispute). The face looks very much like Mohammed's in the video footage. Thousands of mourners lined the route. A BBC TV report on the funeral began, "A Palestinian boy has been martyred." Many of the major U.S. news organizations reported that the funeral was held on the evening of September 30, a few hours after the shooting. Oddly, on film the procession appears to take place in full sunlight, with shadows indicative of midday.

THE AFTERMATH

Almost immediately news media around the world began reporting the tragedy. Print outlets were generally careful to say that Mohammed al-Dura was killed in "the crossfire" or "an exchange of fire" between Israeli soldiers and Palestinians. *The New York Times,* for instance, reported that he was "shot in the stomach as he crouched behind his father on the sidelines of an intensifying battle between Israeli and Palestinian security forces." But the same account included Jamal al-Dura's comment that the fatal volley had come from Israeli soldiers. Jacki Lyden said on NPR's *Weekend All Things Considered* that the boy had been "caught in crossfire." She then interviewed the France 2 cameraman, Talal Abu-Rahma, who said that he thought the Israelis had done the shooting.

> ABU-RAHMA: I was very sad. I was crying. And I was remembering my children. I was afraid to lose my life. And I was sitting on my knees and hiding my head, carrying my camera, and I was afraid from the Israeli to see this camera, maybe they will think this is a weapon, you know, or I am trying to shoot on them. But I was in the most difficult situation in my life. A boy, I cannot save his life, and I want to protect myself.
>
> LYDEN: Was there any attempt by the troops who were firing to cease fire to listen to what the father had to say? Could they even see what they were shooting at?
>
> ABU-RAHMA: Okay. It's clear it was a father, it's clear it was a boy over there for ever who [presumably meaning "whoever"] was shooting on them from across the street, you know, in front of them. I'm sure from that area, I'm expert in that area, I've been in that area many times. I know every [unintelligible] in that area. Whoever was shooting, he got to see them, because that base is not far away from the boy and the father. It's about a hundred and fifty meters [about 500 feet].

On that night's broadcast of *ABC World News Tonight*, the correspondent Gillian Findlay said unambiguously that the boy had died "under Israeli fire." Although both NBC and CBS used the term "crossfire" in their reports, videos of Israeli troops firing and then the boy dying left little doubt about the causal relationship. Jamal al-Dura never wavered in his view that the Israelis had killed his son. "Are you sure they were Israeli bullets?" Diane Sawyer, of ABC News, asked him in an interview later that year. "I'm a hundred percent sure," he replied, through his translator. "They were Israelis." In another interview he told the Associated Press, "The bullets of the Zionists are the bullets that killed my son."

By Tuesday, October 3, all doubt seemed to have been removed. After a hurried internal investigation the IDF concluded that its troops were probably to blame. General Yom-Tov Samia, then the head of the IDF's Southern Command, which operated in Gaza, said, "It could very much be—this is an estimation—that a soldier in our position, who has a very narrow field of vision, saw somebody hiding behind a cement block in the direction from which he was being fired at, and he shot in that direction." General Giora Eiland, then the head of IDF operations, said on an Israeli radio broadcast that the boy was apparently killed by "Israeli army fire at the Palestinians who were attacking them violently with a great many petrol bombs, rocks, and very massive fire."

The further attempt to actually justify killing the boy was, in terms of public opinion, yet more damning for the IDF. Eiland said, "It is known that [Mohammed al-Dura] participated in stone throwing in the past." Samia asked what a twelve-year-old was doing in such a dangerous place to begin with. Ariel Sharon, who admitted that the footage of the shooting was "very hard to see," and that the death was "a real tragedy," also said, "The one that should be blamed is only the one . . . that really instigated all those activities, and that is Yasir Arafat."

Palestinians, and the Arab-Islamic world in general, predictably did not agree. Sweatshirts, posters, and wall murals were created showing the face of Mohammed al-Dura just before he died. "His face, stenciled three feet high, is a common sight on the walls of Gaza," Matthew McAllester, of *Newsday*, wrote last year. "His name is known to every Arab, his death cited as the ultimate example of Israeli military brutality." In modern warfare, Bob Simon said on CBS's *60 Minutes*, "one picture can be worth a thousand weapons," and the picture of the doomed boy amounted to "one of the most disastrous setbacks Israel has suffered in decades." Gabriel Weimann, of Haifa University, said that when he first heard of the case, "it made me sick to think this was done in my name." Amnon Lord, an Israeli columnist who has investigated the event, told me in an e-mail message that it was important "on the mythological level," because it was "a framework story, a paradigmatic event," illustrating Israeli brutality. Dan Schueftan, an Israeli strategist and military thinker, told me that the case was uniquely damaging. He said, "[It was] the ultimate symbol of what the Arabs want to think: The father is trying to protect his son, and the satanic Jews—there is no other word for it—are trying to kill him. These Jews are people who will come to kill our children, because they are not human."

Two years after Mohammed al-Dura's death his stepmother, Amal, became pregnant with another child, the family's eighth. The parents named him Mohammed. Amal was quoted late in her pregnancy as saying, "It will send a message to Israel: 'Yes, you've killed one, but God has compensated for him. You can't kill us all.'"

SECOND THOUGHTS

In the fall of last year Gabriel Weimann mentioned the Mohammed al-Dura case in a special course that he teaches at the Israeli Military Academy, National Security and Mass Media. Like most adults in Israel, Weimann, a tall, athletic-looking man in his early fifties, still performs up to thirty days of military-reserve duty a year. His reserve rank is sergeant, whereas the students in his class are lieutenant colonels and above.

To underscore the importance of the media in international politics, Weimann shows some of his students a montage of famous images from past wars: for World War II the flag raising at Iwo Jima; for Vietnam the South Vietnamese officer shooting a prisoner in the head and the little girl running naked down a path with napalm on her back. For the current intifada, Weimann told his students, the lasting iconic image would be the frightened face of Mohammed al-Dura.

One day last fall, after he discussed the images, a student spoke up. "I was there," he said. "We didn't do it."

"Prove it," Weimann said. He assigned part of the class, as its major research project, a reconsideration of the evidence in the case. A surprisingly large amount was available. The students began by revisiting an investigation undertaken by the Israeli military soon after the event.

Shortly after the shooting General Samia was contacted by Nahum Shahaf, a physicist and engineer who had worked closely with the IDF on the design of pilotless drone aircraft. While watching the original news broadcasts of the shooting, Shahaf had been alarmed, like most viewers inside and outside Israel. But he had also noticed an apparent anomaly. The father seemed to be concerned mainly about a threat originating on the far side of the barrel behind which he had taken shelter. Yet when he and his son were shot, the barrel itself seemed to be intact. What, exactly, did this mean?

Samia commissioned Shahaf and an engineer, Yosef Duriel, to work on a second IDF investigation of the case. "The reason from my side is to check and clean up our values," Samia later told Bob Simon, of CBS. He said he wanted "to see that we are still acting as the IDF." Shahaf stressed to Samia that the IDF should do whatever it could to preserve all physical evidence. But because so much intifada activity continued in the Netzarim area, the IDF demolished the wall and all related structures. Shahaf took one trip to examine the crossroads, clad in body armor and escorted by Israeli soldiers. Then, at a location near Beersheba, Shahaf, Duriel, and others set up models of the barrel, the wall, and the IDF shooting position, in order to reenact the crucial events.

Bullets had not been recovered from the boy's body at the hospital, and the family was hardly willing to agree to an exhumation to reexamine the wounds. Thus the most important piece of physical evidence was the concrete barrel. In the TV footage it clearly bears a mark from the Israeli Bureau of Standards, which enabled investigators to determine its exact dimensions and composition. When they placed the equivalent in front of a concrete wall and put mannequins representing father and son behind it, a conclusion emerged: soldiers in the Israeli outpost could not have fired the shots whose impact was shown on TV. The evidence was cumulative and reinforcing. It involved the angle, the barrel, the indentations, and the dust.

Mohammed al-Dura and his father looked as if they were sheltering themselves against fire from the IDF outpost. In this they were successful. The films show that the barrel was between them and the Israeli guns. The line of sight from the IDF position to the pair was blocked by concrete. Conceivably, some other Israeli soldier was present and fired from some other angle, although there is no evidence of this and no one has ever raised it as a possibility; and there were Palestinians in all the other places, who would presumably have noticed the presence of additional IDF troops. From the one location where Israeli soldiers are known to have been, the only way to hit the boy would have been to shoot through the concrete barrel.

This brings us to the nature of the barrel. Its walls were just under two inches thick. On the test range investigators fired M-16 bullets at a similar barrel. Each bullet made an indentation only two-fifths to four-fifths of an inch deep. Penetrating the barrel would have required multiple hits on both sides of the barrel's wall. The videos of the shooting show fewer than ten indentations on the side of the barrel facing the IDF, indicating that at some point in the day's exchanges of fire the Israelis did shoot at the barrel. But photographs taken after the shooting show no damage of any kind on the side of the barrel facing the al-Duras—that is, no bullets went through.

Further evidence involves the indentations in the concrete wall. The bullet marks that appear so ominously in the wall seconds before the fatal volley are round. Their shape is significant because of what it indicates about the angle of the gunfire. The investigators fired volleys into a concrete wall from a variety of angles. They found that in order to produce a round puncture mark, they had to fire more or less straight on. The more oblique the angle, the more elongated and skidlike the hole became.

The dust resulting from a bullet's impact followed similar rules. A head-on shot produced the smallest, roundest cloud of dust. The more oblique the angle, the larger and longer the cloud of dust. In the video of the shooting the clouds of dust near the al-Duras' heads are small and round. Shots from the IDF outpost would necessarily have been oblique.

In short, the physical evidence of the shooting was in all ways inconsistent with shots coming from the IDF outpost—and in all ways consistent with shots coming from someplace behind the France 2 cameraman, roughly in the location of the Pita. Making a positive case for who might have shot the boy was not the business of the investigators hired by the IDF. They simply wanted to determine whether the soldiers in the outpost were responsible. Because the investigation was overseen by the IDF and run wholly by Israelis, it stood no chance of being taken seriously in the Arab world. But its fundamental point—that the concrete barrel lay between the outpost and the boy, and no bullets had gone through the barrel—could be confirmed independently from news footage.

. . .

It was at this point that the speculation about Mohammed al-Dura's death left the realm of geometry and ballistics and entered the world of politics, paranoia, fantasy, and hatred. Almost as soon as the second IDF investigation was under way, Israeli commentators started questioning its legitimacy and Israeli government officials distanced themselves from its findings. "It is hard to describe in mild terms the stupidity of this bizarre investigation," the liberal newspaper *Ha'aretz* said in an editorial six weeks after the shooting. The newspaper claimed that Shahaf and Duriel were motivated not by a need for dispassionate inquiry but by the belief that Palestinians had staged the whole shooting. (Shahaf told me that he began his investigation out of curiosity but during the course of it became convinced that the multiple anomalies indicated a staged event.) "The fact that an organized body like the IDF, with its vast resources, undertook such an amateurish investigation—almost a pirate endeavor—on such a sensitive issue, is shocking and worrying," *Ha'aretz* said.

As the controversy grew, Samia abbreviated the investigation and subsequently avoided discussing the case. Most government officials, I was told by many sources, regard drawing any further attention to Mohammed al-Dura as self-defeating. No new "proof" would erase images of the boy's death, and resurrecting the discussion would only ensure that the horrible footage was aired yet again. IDF press officials did not return any of my calls, including those requesting to interview soldiers who were at the outpost.

So by the time Gabriel Weimann's students at the Israeli Military Academy, including the one who had been on the scene, began looking into the evidence last fall, most Israelis had tried to put the case behind them. Those against the Likud policy of encouraging settlements in occupied territory think of the shooting as one more illustration of the policy's cost. Those who support the policy view Mohammed al-Dura's death as an unfortunate instance of "collateral damage," to be weighed against damage done to Israelis by Palestinian terrorists. Active interest in the case was confined mainly to a number of Israelis and European Jews who believe the event was manipulated to blacken Israel's image. Nahum Shahaf has become the leading figure in this group.

Shahaf is a type familiar to reporters: the person who has given himself entirely to a cause or a mystery and can talk about its ramifications as long as anyone will listen. He is a strongly built man of medium height, with graying hair combed back from his forehead. In photos he always appears stern, almost glowering, whereas in the time I spent with him he seemed to be constantly smiling, joking, having fun. Shahaf is in his middle fifties, but like many other scientists and engineers, he has the quality of seeming not quite grown-up. He used to live in California, where, among other pursuits, he worked as a hang-gliding instructor. He moves and gesticulates with a teenager's lack of self-consciousness about his bearing. I liked him.

Before getting involved in the al-Dura case, Shahaf was known mainly as an inventor. He was only the tenth person to receive a medal from the Israel Ministry of Science, for his work on computerized means of compressing digital video transmission. "But for two and a half years I am spending time only on the al-Dura case," he told me. "I left everything for it, because I believe that this is most important." When I arrived at his apartment, outside Tel Aviv, to meet him one morning, I heard a repeated sound from one room that I assumed was from a teenager's playing a violent video game. An hour later, when we walked into that room—which has been converted into a video-research laboratory, with multiple monitors, replay devices, and computers—I saw that it was one mob scene from September 30, being played on a continuous loop.

Shahaf's investigation for the IDF showed that the Israeli soldiers at the outpost did not shoot the boy. But he now believes that everything that happened at Netzarim on September 30 was a ruse.

The boy on the film may or may not have been the son of the man who held him. The boy and the man may or may not actually have been shot. If shot, the boy may or may not actually have died. If he died, his killer may or may not have been a member of the Palestinian force, shooting at him directly. The entire goal of the exercise, Shahaf says, was to manufacture a child martyr, in correct anticipation of the damage this would do to Israel in the eyes of the world — especially the Islamic world. "I believe that one day there will be good things in common between us and the Palestinians," he told me. "But the case of Mohammed al-Dura brings the big flames between Israel and the Palestinians and Arabs. It brings a big wall of hate. They can say this is the proof, the ultimate proof, that Israeli soldiers are boy-murderers. And that hatred breaks any chance of having something good in the future."

The reasons to doubt that the al-Duras, the cameramen, and hundreds of onlookers were part of a coordinated fraud are obvious. Shahaf's evidence for this conclusion, based on his videos, is essentially an accumulation of oddities and unanswered questions about the chaotic events of the day. Why is there no footage of the boy after he was shot? Why does he appear to move in his father's lap, and to clasp a hand over his eyes after he is supposedly dead? Why is one Palestinian policeman wearing a Secret Service–style earpiece in one ear? Why is another Palestinian man shown waving his arms and yelling at others, as if "directing" a dramatic scene? Why does the funeral appear — based on the length of shadows — to have occurred before the apparent time of the shooting? Why is there no blood on the father's shirt just after they are shot? Why did a voice that seems to be that of the France 2 cameraman yell, in Arabic, "The boy is dead" before he had been hit? Why do ambulances appear instantly for seemingly everyone else and not for al-Dura?

A handful of Israeli and foreign commentators have taken up Shahaf's cause. A Web site called musada2000.org says of the IDF's initial apology, "They acknowledged guilt, for never in their collective minds would any one of them have imagined a scenario whereby Mohammed al-Dura might have been murdered by his *own* people . . . a cruel plot staged and executed by Palestinian sharpshooters and a television cameraman!" Amnon Lord, writing for the magazine *Makor Rishon*, referred to a German documentary directed by Esther Schapira that was "based on Shahaf's own decisive conclusion" and that determined "that Mohammed al-Dura was not killed by IDF gunfire at Netzarim junction." "Rather," Lord continued, "the Palestinians, in cooperation with foreign journalists and the UN, arranged a well-staged production of his death." In March of this year a French writer, Gérard Huber, published a book called *Contre expertise d'une mise en scène* (roughly, *Re-evaluation of a Reenactment*). It, too, argues that the entire event was staged. In an e-mail message to me Huber said that before knowing of Shahaf's studies he had been aware that "the images of little Mohammed were part of the large war of images between Palestinians and Israelis." But until meeting Shahaf, he said, "I had not imagined that it involved a fiction"—a view he now shares. "The question of 'Who killed little Mohammed?'" he said, "has become a screen to disguise the real question, which is: 'Was little Mohammed actually killed?'"

The truth about this case will probably never be determined. Or, to put it more precisely, no version of truth that is considered believable by all sides will ever emerge. For most of the Arab world, the rights and wrongs of the case are beyond dispute: An innocent boy was murdered, and his blood is on Israel's hands. Mention of contrary evidence or hypotheses only confirms the bottomless dishonesty of the guilty parties—much as Holocaust-denial theories do in the Western world. For the handful of people collecting evidence of a staged event, the truth is also clear, even if the proof is not in hand. I saw Nahum Shahaf lose his good humor only when I asked him what he thought explained the odd timing of the boy's funeral, or the contradictions in eyewitness reports, or the other loose ends in the case. "I don't 'think,' I know!" he said several times. "I am a physicist. I work from the evidence." Schapira had collaborated with him for the German documentary and then produced a film advancing the "minimum" version of his case, showing that the shots did not, could not have, come from the IDF outpost. She disappointed him by not embracing the maximum version—the all-encompassing hoax—and counseled him not to talk about a staged event unless he could produce a living boy or a cooperative eyewitness. Shahaf said that he still thought well of her, and that he was not discouraged. "I am only two and a half years into this work," he told me. "It took twelve years for the truth of the Dreyfus case to come out."

For anyone else who knows about Mohammed al-Dura but is not in either of the decided camps—the Arabs who are sure they know what happened, the revisionists who are equally sure—the case will remain in the uncomfortable realm of events that cannot be fully explained or understood. "Maybe it was an accidental shooting," Gabriel Weimann told me, after reading his students' report, which, like the German documentary, supported the "minimum" conclusion—the Israeli soldiers at the outpost could not have killed the boy. (He could not show the report to me, he said, on grounds of academic confidentiality.) "Maybe even it was staged—although I don't think my worst enemy is so inhuman as to shoot a boy for the sake of publicity. Beyond that, I do not know." Weimann's recent work involves the way that television distorts reality in attempting to reconstruct it, by putting together loosely related or even random events in what the viewer imagines is a coherent narrative flow. The contrast between the confusing, contradictory hours of raw footage from the Netzarim crossroads and the clear, gripping narrative of the evening news reports assembled from that footage is a perfect example, he says.

The significance of this case from the American perspective involves the increasingly chaotic ecology of truth around the world. In Arab and Islamic societies the widespread belief that Israeli soldiers shot this boy has political consequences. So does the belief among some Israelis and Zionists in Israel and abroad that Palestinians will go to any lengths to smear them. Obviously, these beliefs do not create the basic tensions in the Middle East. The Israeli policy of promoting settlements in occupied territory, and the Palestinian policy of terror, are deeper obstacles. There would never have been a showdown at the Netzarim crossroads, or any images of Mohammed al-Dura's shooting to be parsed in different ways, if there were no settlement nearby for IDF soldiers to protect. Gabriel Weimann is to the left of Dan Schueftan on Israel's political spectrum, but both believe that Israel should end its occupation. I would guess that Nahum Shahaf thinks the same thing, even though he told me that to preserve his "independence" as a researcher, he wanted to "isolate myself from any kind of political question."

The images intensify the self-righteous determination of each side. If anything, modern technology has aggravated the problem of mutually exclusive realities. With the Internet and TV, each culture now has a more elaborate apparatus for "proving," dramatizing, and disseminating its particular truth.

In its engagement with the Arab world the United States has assumed that what it believes are noble motives will be perceived as such around the world. We mean the best for the people under our control; stability, democracy, prosperity are our goals; why else would we have risked so much to help an oppressed people achieve them? The case of Mohammed al-Dura suggests the need for much more modest assumptions about the way other cultures — in particular today's embattled Islam — will perceive our truths.

———

The case of Mohammed al-Dura would seem to be ideal for the movies. The central event was unforgettably vivid. The later attempts to investigate, reassess, and explain what had happened followed the course of the best cinematic mysteries. Scenes were reconstructed; video footage was endlessly replayed and analyzed; committed and often obsessed characters thought of nothing except discovering the truth.

But one aspect of a successful mystery story was missing from this case: a satisfying resolution. When I reported on the story, early in 2003, the available evidence convinced me that the official explanation of events could not be true. Soldiers from the Israeli Defense Force, firing from their known positions, could not have shot the boy to death. Who might have shot him, or whether he was shot at all, seemed to me to be unknowable at that time.

And so, at this writing, they remain. The parties with a stake in the final truth of the case have taken different courses. In the Palestinian world, the truth of the official story and the perfidy of the Israeli troops are so taken for granted that further discussion is uninteresting. After my article came out, the hostile mail I received was mainly from people in this camp, and their American and European supporters, who thought I had naively fallen for the Israeli Big Lie in my reporting. As I suggested in the story, the details of the case matter less and less on the Palestinian side. Even if the official account were someday conclusively proven to be false, the idea and image of the boy's martyrdom would live on. Since the time of this article, the supply of potential Arab and Islamic martyr figures has steadily increased because of conflicts between U.S. forces and Iraqi civilians and between Israeli soldiers and Palestinians.

In Israel, the mainstream media have kept a healthy distance from the case. The same is true of the Israeli government and its military. They apparently believe that nothing good can come from calling further attention to the horrifying video of the boy and his father—even if the replays were accompanied by announcements that it hadn't been as bad as it looked, or even that the boy was still alive.

Apart from Nahum Shahaf, who with good humor but absolute determination continues his al-Dura studies, the case has claimed the continuing attention mainly of a few groups in France with allies in the United States and elsewhere. These people generally see the case in the context of a worldwide rise of anti-Semitism; like Dan Schueftan, whom I interviewed for my article, they say that the blame cast on the Israeli soldiers in the al-Dura episode confirms the "blood libel" of Jews killing non-Jewish children. Like Nahum Shahaf, and distinctly unlike Gabriel Weimann and some others I quote in my article, most of those still involved in al-Dura research believe that the entire event was a ruse. The boy was not shot; he did not die; the episode was a staged event to discredit Israel. They admit that this sounds far-fetched but point out that other whole-cloth stagings have occurred. The best known is the phony funeral procession in Jenin in 2002, which ended when a supposedly martyred Palestinian finally climbed out of his coffin and ran away. This was all captured on videotape. About al-Dura, I remain unconvinced. It would help if any unambiguous evidence for what French researchers call the mise-en-scène proposition had turned up—footage of young Mohammed walking and talking after his apparent "death," for instance, or a comment from any of the hundreds of eyewitnesses that indeed it was a deception.

Conceivably, such proof will emerge someday. If and when it does, the story of Mohammed al-Dura will qualify not simply for cinematic treatment but also for careful study as one of the most successful public deceptions ever carried out. In the meantime, it retains the quality not of movies but of real life, being frustratingly difficult to understand.

NIGHT OF THE BULLIES
ROBERT DRAPER

"I never set out to make my life a violent one. But I have crime happen around me *all the time*." Michael takes a meager sip from his tall glass of orange juice. "This business of what happened in 1978—I was just a kid walking down the street when all this happened to me."

"You think it's predestined, then," prods the stranger—a man his age, of similar background, who has traveled a thousand miles to wrench Michael out of his anonymous torpor with twenty-five-year-old questions.

"I've come to that conclusion, yes."

As the evening dwindles, the barroom jabber gives way to Michael's voice like the sputtering of trumpets to the keening of a single undying oboe. These are his hours now. His frame is largely inert, an alabaster cocoon. Through his pinkish eyes, he considers the intruder's skepticism about predestiny and adds: "See, I've had a life that's totally different than that which I would've chosen to have. I would've had a more conventional life, if I'd had the option of choosing it."

Then he laughs, a soft but elaborate chuckle, which is how he responds to any number of things that aren't particularly funny. Michael has been laughing throughout the evening. The subject is his life. Michael hasn't been sleeping well for the past quarter century or so. His troubles did not begin immediately after the two future oilmen and the future dentist assaulted him. For at least a year after that, he resumed his path to adulthood as if in a sleepwalk. The recurring nightmare put a stop to that. Michael would dream that he was awakened by the sound of strange men pressing against his windows, rustling through the shrubs, jostling the doorknob. As he bolted from his bed, a sickness embraced him. The bed was not his. The house was wholly unfamiliar to him. The strange men knew the place better than he did.

As they lunged for him, Michael would awaken and disentangle himself from the bedsheets. Only a bad dream. Only that. Unless . . . Was he safe? Was he? In fact, when he listened, there *were* sounds outside. Obscure noises in the dark. Signals. Danger. God, yes. August 31, 1978. He *had* been taken to a strange house. He *had* been surrounded by more than a dozen young men. These things had actually occurred. There were arrests, a lawsuit, scrutiny by *The New York Times* and *Rolling Stone.* For many weeks, the incident had been the talk of Austin, Texas, a college town that had seen campus rapists, campus murderers—but never something quite so inexplicable as the seizure by fraternity members of a seventeen-year-old boy not of their tribe. Eventually, of course, everyone got over it—except Michael and, apparently, this unexpected intruder.

The tape recorder crouches between them, hissing, gleaming red as it digests Michael's chuckling ruminations: "You've got to understand. This whole thing was so unreal. There were so many witnesses that I couldn't figure out what the hell reality was." And because this true event unspooled like a dream—shady, haphazardly sequenced, preposterous—who was to say that his recurring nightmare was the mere authorship of his subconscious? And so he would not go back to sleep after dreaming that night or in the nights to follow. Darkness finds him alert, alone. At a twenty-four-hour gym, he works his biceps. At an all-night diner, he takes his place among the hipsters and the truckers and orders lunch. "When normal people are out doing their business, I'm asleep. And when I'm up and ready to go, the normal world is *dead*. I mean"—his voice is both amused and amazed—"I drive around town at three or four in the morning, listening to a talk show on the radio, and everyone's asleep. I'm completely outside of society. Completely disconnected."

Michael is forty-three and lives with his mother in one of those gated apartment stalags no one resides in very long. His ear is cocked to the pitch of malevolence. Shotgun slayings where he once lived. Two women screaming for help at his new complex. Felons where he once worked, crooked policemen, lawyers playing both sides, daily depredations engulfing his field of vision . . . and though he hasn't a clue why, it is not random; it is not coincidence. It is the shadow world into which he has been thrust. He knows it all goes back to the two oilmen and the dentist. But their role was merely to supply the rude awakening. The truth is, he had not thought of them in quite some time—their kind, yes, but not them individually, and certainly not what they did to him—until the intruder tracked him down. And now he would rather not talk about the particular indignities of that evening.

"I'm not the same guy I was in 1978. I get by. . . . My life is what it is."

The intruder writes down: *His life is what it isn't.*

"These guys are first-class citizens. I thought so then, and I think so now."

As he sits dozens of floors above the city of Dallas, the attorney's eyes are steeped in pain and worry. He is a partner in one of the nation's most powerful law firms and quite at home at this elevation—but he is also a man of almost palpable decency, measured in his views, humble in his bearing. The intruder pulls out his tape recorder. The attorney asks that it remain off. Only with the greatest reluctance has he agreed to this meeting. The intruder has spoken at length about the humanistic value of his project: reconciling decent people with the indecencies they commit, examining the psychic life span of trauma, and so forth. To the attorney, no good can come of it. The two oilmen and the dentist were his fraternity brothers at Alpha Tau Omega. "I never once, to this day, asked them what occurred," he tells the intruder. "And twenty-four years later, that's not important. What happened that night was harmful, and revisiting it today is not going to help anything. . . . They are absolutely paranoid that this will destroy their lives."

The intruder assures the attorney that he is not out to inflict damage. He is well aware that in addition to the two oilmen and the dentist, the roster of ATO members and pledges who were present for at least some of the events of August 31, 1978, reads today like a roll call of Texas gentility: petroleum and insurance executives, cattle ranchers, car dealers, stock traders, a movie director, the inevitable Enron climber. The fraternity president, who so nimbly wriggled his way through his deposition—"I don't remember anything specific or not specific regarding this incident that could be distinguished from anything that I may have heard since then"—is today the head physician for one of Texas's professional sports teams. Two rush captains in charge of that evening's festivities are titans of commercial real estate. The pledge trainer, who supervised two of Michael's three accused tormentors, is among the fraternity's many stalwarts of the Texas legal community. Gentlemen all. Foes of barbarism, surely.

And this is what intrigues the intruder. He does not obsess about evil but, rather, deliverance from it. He would very much like to believe that these men look back with shame, that their present success rests on a bedrock of humility. "And if they witnessed such a thing today," he tells the attorney, "I would hope they'd put a stop to it."

"And the thing is?" interjects the attorney, leaning across the memos and briefs obscuring his desk. "*They*"—meaning the two oilmen and the dentist—"would put a stop to it."

As it happens, the attorney was not present that August evening. His placid face curdles as he listens to what the intruder has learned. "You've given me a horrific set of facts," the attorney gravely admits. "One that would shock anyone's conscience." But, he then says, what if the intruder has it wrong? Eyewitnesses, the attorney knew from years of experience, were often in error. Perhaps the two future oilmen and the future dentist weren't there after all. In fact—and now the attorney's eyes are alight with revelation—what if the actual assailants were in fact not even ATO brothers? He'd often seen outsiders hanging out at the frat house. Maybe, just maybe, the two oilmen and the dentist took the fall for someone else. Now *that's* the kind of guys they are. Men in keeping with other Alpha Tau Omega difference makers: Steve Spurrier, former senator Alan Simpson, former secretary of the interior James Watt, Art Linkletter, Lee Atwater, James P. Hoffa, and H. Ross Perot's former running mate Vice Admiral James "Who am I? Why am I here?" Stockdale.

The attorney offers his assistance in arranging an audience with the two oilmen and the dentist—that the intruder might glean the virtuousness Michael could not readily discern on August 31, 1978. "Respected by their peers." Possessing the "moral fiber, character, and empathy of those I am proud to call friend." He could go on forever. But when asked if he has ever given a moment's thought to Michael, the attorney's verbiage fails him. He stares at his cluttered desk. "Yes," he glumly responds. And that is all.

Whereupon the intruder proffers a document. It is a lawsuit, brought in the summer of 2002 against yet another University of Texas ATO member—no doubt a first-class citizen himself, no doubt with brothers ready to rally to his defense against allegations that he drugged a young woman with Rohypnol and raped her in the ATO frat house while she lay semiconscious. The intruder has spoken to the young woman; it was an agonizing conversation. "He said I instigated the sex act," she recalled bitterly. "He said it was my fault." She added that she had been a virgin. After her account trailed off into sobs, the intruder thought he should say something. So he said that she was not alone—thinking, of course, of Michael and of other scattered souls awake in the dark, a fraternity of stolen innocence.

The attorney grimaces as he scans the allegations. "This is going to hurt," he says quietly. Of course, he has no idea.

"No, I wasn't inclined to talk to anyone about this," says Michael late one night as he bites down on a tortilla chip. He shrugs helplessly. "What is there to say about it? There was nothing to discuss. That's the way I felt about it. I still feel about it that way. What good would it have done? What am I supposed to gain at all?" He's laughing.

"Not even to a close friend?" the intruder presses.

"There's nobody around me that I had respect for. That's the truth of it." Michael smirks as he studies the contents of his glass. It's not the orange juice he ordered but some Mexican concoction instead. At least it's the right color. "Beyond that, I'm missing the— I mean, what is there I'm *supposed* to talk to a friend about? What is there to talk about? I don't know what that's about."

"Sharing feelings," says the intruder. "It's a human need."

"I don't have that. I don't have that. I mean, I sit around when people are having discussions about their personal lives. All these personal conversations about their emotions—I just end up thinking that they're jerks or they're wrong or self-indulgent or, what're you talking to *me* about that for? I don't have any impulse to want to talk to others."

The intruder is at a loss. "That's unusual," he finally says.

"Perhaps it is," says Michael indifferently. "But I don't have that impulse at all."

Being August in Austin, it was a hot evening. He did not know that it was Pledge Night. He did not know much of anything, except that he was a kid from the Texas-hill-country province of New Braunfels and glad to be here in the big city, an incoming freshman walking along 24th Street with his new roommate, headed for a bar. He was strolling and scatter-shooting ideas, this gentle kid who struck the roommate as exceedingly bright and somewhat naive and obviously not attentive to the group on the sidewalk up ahead: young men, or perhaps boys, but much bigger than they and, even from the distance of a block, so outlandishly drunk the roommate thought to suggest—and later wished desperately he had suggested—that they cross the street.

The young men up ahead were Alpha Tau Omega brothers, most of them freshly pledged, and their house sat on the corner. For them it was a night both memorable and vaguely incomplete. They had begun it as elite initiates warmly welcomed by the elders, who then led them into a cavernous living room vacant of anything except a keg of beer and a hardwood floor slicked down with shampoo. The pledges were then instructed to play tackle football. And so they had, swilling and sliding, two dozen young athletic male bodies colliding, friend piled beneath everlasting friend. When it was over, two pledges were dispatched to the hospital: one with a broken nose, another with his two front teeth in his pocket. The rest emerged from the frat house sweaty, lather-haired, and shitfaced, and they proceeded across the street to a bar to drink some more. By the time they'd paid the tab and spilled out onto the sidewalk, the night was still young, the air still hot, the girls still out celebrating their sorority pledgeships. All that testosterone careening beneath their wet clothes. How to release it? How to complete this memorable night?

The sidewalk teemed with youthful pedestrians, a languid confederation. Michael and his roommate strolled among them. An instant later, rough hands jerked them away. Their world was suddenly claustrophobic with the odors of beer and sweat, with bellowed obscenities—and, most of all, with large male bodies clamped against their frail musculatures. The roommate saw Michael being dragged off the sidewalk toward the fraternity house lawn, felt himself being tugged as well. At that moment the roommate experienced a most improbable vision: a host of princesses gliding past in lavish Southern regalia. Sorority pledges. His detainers saw them, too. They commenced to whistle and spew out bleak flirtations. The roommate broke free and ran. The ATOs gave chase, but the roommate had been a long-distance runner in high school. After several blocks, he felt safe enough to stop. Minutes later, he warily jogged back to the frat-house corner. Michael had been taken away.

As Michael would remember it, they dragged him to the lawn—*they* being three young men, all well built, five feet ten to six feet one, garbed in denim, hair styled wispily in the manner of Lee Majors. Michael screamed back at the sidewalk procession from which he had been plucked. A policeman idled past. A swarm of young men now gathered around him. He felt a punch, then another. "Suck my dick," somebody said.

"Please let me go," he begged. Then he saw a cock unsheathed from the sea of denim. Piss sprayed against him. Someone else called out for sex. Fists torpedoed into him from all sides.

Then: "Yeah, him. We'll use him." Spoken not by either of the pledges but by an older, more authoritative face. *Use me? Use me for what?* Again he was propelled by force, this time deeper into darkness, away from the lawn and across an alley and into a garage. It was now the two pledges, the elder brother, and Michael. Two of them threw him to the ground and proceeded to beat him. One of the three, sloe-eyed and anvil-shouldered, was especially rough with his fists. Another stomped Michael with his cowboy boots. Meanwhile, the eldest supervised with pleasure. This night was for the pledges.

A man from the apartment upstairs poked his head in, hollered, "You guys get out of here!" and promptly disappeared. The three merrily continued. They stripped off Michael's oxford shirt, his corduroys, his underwear, and his canvas sneakers, everything but his socks, and flung them in the alley. One of them yanked him hard by the balls. A cock was thrust in his face. "Suck it!" The other two joined in. "Make him suck it!" Michael recoiled from the waggled cock, was punched and kicked. Then they whisked him off the floor, ferrying him back across the alley, where male and female pedestrians alike gaped at him and he at them—a pallid and glassy-eyed creature on the wrong side of the looking glass.

And now, inside a house. *Their* house. In a vast room as naked as he was. Loud music, a chaotic melody. The floor syrupy, puddled with spent beer. Now there were more than a dozen of them. They grabbed him by his wrists and ankles and slid him across the viscous floor. Laughing, cursing, taking turns with their blows—a kind of elemental siege, acutely specific and at the same time brutally impersonal, a horde of apes flailing in the jungle, their odor filthy, wetness, screeches, surging further and further out of control, further out of drunkenness and into a panting omnivorous hysteria, bodies and obscenities in wild orbit, the music crazed and Michael swinging through the slop and into their knuckles and boots like a sacrificial carcass onto the banquet table, feeling no pain, none whatsoever, only a humming terror; while outside his roommate stood impotently and watched through a window for an uncomprehending moment before running off again.

And who knows where this would have ended had not, out of nowhere, a new face appeared—swarthy, somewhat eccentric, older than the others. A senior member. He was not happy. "You guys have got to stop this," he yelled. "You've got to *do* something about this guy." The others pretended at first not to hear him. Then, from across the vast room, came some other distraction. The others staggered off to greet it. Michael slowly rose up from the debris-strewn floor.

"You should go," advised the senior member in a thick but urgent drawl. The words took a moment to register. Michael considered his nakedness. Then he saw the open double doors. He sprang through the doorway, his socks squishing from beer as he ran across the yard, through a parking lot, and into a dormitory parking garage, where he curled up into a fetal ball behind the hood of a car.

A young couple coming back from a party were startled to see a naked male lunge out from the shadows. He guessed what they were thinking—but no, he explained breathlessly, he was not a member of a fraternity. Only their victim. Wet-haired, redolent of beer and sweat and urine, profoundly agitated, he begged the couple for a ride. The girl ran upstairs to get a pair of gym shorts he could wear. Michael crouched on the floorboards of the backseat until she returned. They did not speak much on the brief drive to his dorm. He did, however, ask for their phone number so he could someday return the gym shorts.

He had no keys, and his roommate was not home, so he waited in the dorm bathroom. At one point, the door flew open and a throng of males marched in. Michael cringed against a wall. But they were only there to piss, and not on him.

The next day he moved back to New Braunfels.

"When I started doing the intelligence work," says Michael as he drives through the night in search of a place still open where he can drink orange juice and the intruder can drink wine, "one of the first people I worked with is a guy who wrote the first CIA assassination manual, in 1952 or 1953. I mean, these are the people I do business with. That's the life I drifted into. That milieu is the same as the one my father was in. There's no particular point at which I said, 'God-damn, my father was right all along.' But the more involved I got, the more I found myself living in that world and realizing that these things are not dealt with legally. We refer to it as *extrajudicial*."

His father, a prisoner of war in Korea and a licensed gun dealer who had ties to criminal elements in the San Antonio area, did not believe his son's assault was a matter for the courtroom. According to Michael, his father spoke with some friends about disposing of the two future oilmen and the future dentist. They selected a remote location. When the father asked Michael if he would like to participate, the son insisted that they let the justice system handle it, and he pressed criminal charges and also filed suit against the three individuals identified to the police by ATO members as his chief tormentors. The three defendants promptly hired one of the most skillful trial lawyers in Texas, who convinced Michael's attorney that a cash settlement was in the best interest of all parties. Michael was chagrined to learn that the young men's parents had very little money. He took the $30,000 offered in exchange for dropping the lawsuit and all criminal charges, returned to the University of Texas, then attended MIT for graduate work in defense and international relations. Somewhere along the way, he found out that the youngest defendant's father was in fact exceedingly wealthy. By then, Michael was already an insomniac, already spending his late evenings scribbling academic papers about strategic forces in the Persian Gulf while developing contacts with the intelligence community—a fraternity in keeping with his hours and with his dimming worldview.

He is not at liberty to discuss his activity. But his passport is a clamor of overseas entries and exits: Eastern and Western Europe, Africa, South America. The work is not steady and not of monumental consequence—"just one simple thing in a larger picture," he offers cryptically in his reedy tenor. "Someone who's been defrauded in an overseas scam and needs to be put in touch with people to make it right. Or a competitor of a company wants to know its manufacturing process. I was never a candidate to do government work. But I have contacts, and"—he makes the slightest hand gesture out to the empty thoroughfares, the urban jungle in repose—"I'm available."

Available, yes, and more than just willing. Michael has bulked up fifty pounds since he was carried from the sidewalk. He keeps two pistols in his apartment. "In my network of buddies all over the world," he tells the intruder while chortling, "they think I'm a man of action. I'm willing to do things that other people are not willing to do. When I go into a situation like that, and I come out of it, I just have this strange idea that I've conquered the risk. When I come out of it, I feel *so fucking smart.* There are situations that have been scary, and I've feared for my life. And then, when it was over, I felt this great accomplishment.

"But I'm wrong," and he sings out a laugh. "I'm wrong. There're so many fucking things that can happen. I mean, just walking down the street in Austin, Texas, in August of 1978, there're 40,000 people, and I'm the one who gets snatched. I'm fooling myself. And it's ironic, because I live with this feeling that my life is at risk. All the time. I'm never safe."

Throughout the seething Texas summer, the intruder drives door-to-door, slipping business cards through crevices, leaving messages on telephone answering machines. The neighborhoods he visits are havens from disorder. The street names — Tanglewood, Cooling Breeze, Fountainview, Briargrove, Hickory Hollow — stand outside of history, watchwords of timeless bliss. Treading past the parked SUVs, haloed by basketball rims, observed by Hispanic gentlemen tending to the lawns, he cannot help but feel like some rapacious predator whose very presence is a blasphemy.

Naturally, the intruder did not expect the twenty-four-year-old topic to be fresh on anyone's mind. Arriving unannounced on door-steps, barging in on people's weekend reprieves, he is first regarded as a huckster, a cop, or some kind of fiendish stalker. Why now? they want to know. Because, he replies, these things have a psychic life span. The past does not readily surrender. Michael lives with his mother and cannot sleep. The investigating officer who told Michael, "I wouldn't treat a dog the way they treated you," today winces his sympathies. The woman who fetched him a pair of gym shorts murmurs in recollection, "He was monumentally desperate," and she hands the intruder a sealed envelope containing a note for Michael. Over beers, the roommate, now an attorney and elected official on the Gulf Coast, tells about a female client who recently sought a divorce from her husband, an ATO brother. Why, yes, she'd heard about the 1978 incident . . . but, it was just a couple of queers, wasn't it, and then she saw the roommate's family portrait, the wife and kids, and he smiled grimly at her expense. But he does not laugh the way Michael does. He ran, after all. "It's not my proudest moment," the roommate confesses to the intruder. "Something bad happened to a nice guy, and there was nothing I could do. Maybe that's why I'm in family law now."

From among the brothers, the intruder elicits a single regretful voice—that of the one individual who saw fit to halt the escalating Caligulan frenzy: *You've got to do something about this guy!* Now living a modest life as a carpet salesman in the Dallas–Fort Worth Metroplex, he drawls wistfully, "I wished I'd gotten him some clothes to wear."

His fellow brothers offer no such misgivings, however. Most say nothing at all. "You don't talk about what goes on inside the house," one of them nervously explains. "I don't want my kids to get beat up in the schoolyard because of anything I've said." Thus are e-mails and phone calls relayed from brother to brother about the man on the prowl with his old kit bag bulging with scandal—a man who looks like them, who knows a great deal about them, who in fact lived three blocks away from them as a UT student a quarter century ago, but who is not—repeat, *is not*—their brother. By now, the boys of that summer are well disabused of their invincibility. They cannot control the stock market, the terrorists, their children, or their own advancing decrepitude. But they can keep things in the house, can't they? They can stave off this intruder. Bury the past. And God save them from all the rest.

Such callous behavior he inspires! The brothers' toothy faces collapse into scowls. They briskly propel their golfers' tans past him. Their perky wives hang up without a good-bye.

Still, nothing compares to the evasiveness of the three men he longs to meet, those three brave lads who stood accused of publicly dragging a naked weakling into their spewing volcano. Now it is they who are running scared. The dentist has a wife and children, along with a practice that thrives, due in part to the brothers who file in for root-canal work. The two oilmen have struggled to meet the standards of their fathers, a major general and a rich petroleum entrepreneur. Both floundered in the years after 1978, accumulating criminal records for drunk driving before at last leaning on their brothers yet again: The younger joined a drilling firm in a building leased by an ATO alumnus; the elder worked for an ATO brother who inherited the family oil business. The intruder can only destabilize the fulcrum upon which they at last luxuriate. When he informs them of his pending arrival in their city of Houston, they make themselves scarce, peeking out of doorways at night, furtively creeping off to work in the morning, and in the elder oilman's case, staying away from home altogether. They will return no calls, no computer messages, not even those of their brother, the attorney in Dallas who continues to extol their love of country and devotion to society's betterment until finally, the intruder turns his ear away. He at last hears their silence for the statement it is. *Go away. Please.* An echo of Michael. A plea for peace. And so, the intruder withdraws.

Yet in the days and nights that follow, he continues to wrestle with the nature of his obsession. Why, long after the ATO incident was chased off the front page, did it reverberate in his subconscious, as if he were much, much closer than three blocks away? Perhaps because he used to be Michael. First in elementary school, when the hotshot on his basketball team repeatedly thrashed his face with a towel in front of the others, for no reason at all other than the hotshot's delight in—and disdain of—the intruder's puniness. The intruder had not lifted a finger in his own defense, nor would he in junior-high gym class, when two losers bedeviled him from bell to bell, taking inventory of his every shortcoming, from his last name to his wobbly voice to his insurmountable gutlessness. A day came when all the thugs disappeared, however. The intruder was stronger now, surer in his stride. But when he ponders the horror show of Michael prone and naked in the frat house, his own face courses red from injuries past, while loathing rattles in his ribs like a prehistoric demon.

Loathing, but for whom? The intruder has himself sipped from the tribal cup. Long before 1978, he descended into the valley of the brain-dead, risking life and limb to bond with fellow hairy-chested morons, this selfsame boy who had been tormented—and indeed, concurrent with his own miseries—had laughed as the absolute rock-bottom doggies of the schoolyard were de-pantsed and slapped and rattailed and sprayed with fungus repellent, hazed into oblivion; had laughed guiltily, and had later offered a few kind words, but all too late, and he knew it, and so did the rock-bottom doggies. There he was, a coconspirator. And here he is today, a prosperous white American male, member in good standing of the most bullying cabal on earth. Meanwhile, everywhere he looks, from the soccer stands of London to the public squares of Peshawar to the projects of East LA, he sees the tribes gather, hears whispers become howls. Evolution? It's for sissies. To the victor go the spoils, until to the tar pit go we all.

Back home, the intruder lies sweating in bed beside his sleeping wife. Well after midnight, the hippie undergraduates next door are playing their bongos. He listens to his heart join in. Tries to bury his head in his pillow, but the pounding won't go away. It's in his head now. Temples swelling into fists. The pulse of a monster. Nothing is louder. So he rolls onto his back, feels the sweat drip from his ankles. The neighbors won't go on forever, he reasons. Everyone has to sleep at some point.

Michael has a surprise for the intruder: He's married.

He leads his guest into his clean but barren north Austin apartment, where his mother sits in darkness watching late-night television with Charles, a slender middle-aged Sierra Leone refugee Michael brought to the United States after one business trip and who now sleeps on a mattress on the floor of Michael's bedroom. Michael has been to Africa often, particularly to Sierra Leone, where the diamond mines bring out the worst in all who draw near. He proclaims it "hell on earth." But the violence-prone nation is not without its attractions.

Michael walks into his bedroom closet. From the top shelf, he removes two framed color photographs and hands one of them over. She is in her twenties, dressed in a bright yellow pantsuit of her own making, with lively eyes and smooth walnut-colored skin. "I'm always sick when I'm over there," he begins. "I met her in '95. She was my nurse, and she would go out and get my medication and hang around my hotel room. She had a civilized mind. Here's this person in the midst of that hell who has every quality you'd want to find in a human being. Her father died before she met me. She has a mother and a brother and a couple of sisters, and now she's adopted a couple of kids. She's nothing at all like any other African woman. The last thing she'd want to do is bring another kid into this world. I talk to her on the phone a couple of times a week. I can't afford that much. Five or ten minutes each time."

He hands the intruder the other frame, which contains a photo of an extended African family. "That's her," he says, pointing. "She's wearing frayed jeans and a T-shirt, a sleek Western counterpart to those stooped in rags beside her. "I like this particular photograph because you can see so many different personalities among the children. Some are very timid, and some are bold. This little guy's really sad-looking. And this little girl, she's starting to walk around with a pan on her head."

The intruder observes, "You love her."

"Well," Michael backs off, "I'm her means of support." He sends her $200 to $400 a month, whatever he can afford at the time. They married, he explains, so she could benefit from his life-insurance policy and so her relatives don't pressure her into marrying some ogre in Freetown who would demand offspring destined to starve in the street. He doesn't think America would be right for her. Perhaps Canada, where she knows other Sierra Leoneans. "We have purely practical conversations," he goes on. "How is your mother? What are you going to eat today? Have the riots subsided so people can go out now?"

But the intruder's eyes are wide as he watches the curious man with the bittersweet voice fix his pale smile upon the images before replacing them on the shelf and closing his closet door. Now he sees: Michael's life, in fact, *is* what it is, not what it isn't. From this angle, his maladies—the chronic insomnia, the "repetition compulsion" to reorder the past by courting danger in the present— recede into psychic dueling scars. He is, finally, the man he has made of himself. A fraternity of one. One day, he tells the intruder as they walk together to the apartment parking lot, he may even give back the settlement to the two oilmen and the dentist. Give 'em their damn money. Why not? Although first he must tend to his mother and Charles and the girl on the other side of the world.

"Does she know about what happened?" the intruder asks, if only to hear Michael's laugh one final time.

Michael doesn't disappoint. "Why would I burden her with *my* problems?" he exclaims. "She's been through two coups!"

Very true, thinks the intruder as he steps into his car. Still, even as the rearview image of the man beside the apartment gates fast becomes a speck of ivory, the man behind the wheel falls victim to the notion of that solitary white knight and his distressed damsel stranded in awful evening, his reaching out to the sky with trembling fingers and, with those mortal digits, inscribing stars into the darkness.

———

Is a story a story simply because the writer yearns to tell it? Fully twenty-five years after Michael was attacked by ATO pledges, the horrific incident had lost all significance to everyone but me. And yet there was no denying the almost mythic resonance of that event in my life. I had two formidable hurdles to clear: First, to convince my editors at GQ that this obscure crime remained somehow a vital subject; and second, to convince those who were involved that a revisitation was in order. It's a testament to the late, great Art Cooper's faith in a writer's passion that he approved the story idea without lengthy discussion. Getting to the principal characters was another matter.

It took great effort to locate Michael. Once I did, I was stunned to find him so cooperative, though he would not at first disclose the grim specifics of the assault itself. His tormentors, however, huddled under a fraternal cone of silence. They, unlike Michael, now had wives and children, had attained prestige and social stability—all of which would be put at risk by reexamining this singular "youthful indiscretion." Out of the dozens of ATO members I contacted, only seven would speak to me, and always with trepidation. "Why now?" everyone wanted to know. I had an answer—"Trauma has its own psychic life span; if you don't believe me, ask Michael"—but the parallel truth, uttered with some embarrassment, was that fraternity brothers just didn't rat out, not even a quarter-century after the fact.

In such cases, a journalist has to fight the temptation to reward the compliant while punishing the reticent. I think I succeeded by exam-

ining my own complicity. After all, I'd grown up in the same neighborhood as several of the ATO members and on various levels had more in common with them than with Michael. More to the point, as a kid I'd stood by several times and watched some poor geek undergo the ritual humiliation of some male tribe or other. Stood by in mute horror, but letting it happen, and thus as guilty as every other dog in the pack. Furthermore, the writer's privilege of having the last word is itself a kind of bullying. If this exploration was about truth rather than brute vengeance, than I had to overcome my dismay that not one single male who was there that evening would today profess any regret over what had taken place.

Victimization does not confer perfection. Both before and after the assault, Michael was himself flawed. Nonetheless, I came to admire how he had cobbled together a life that was his own, complete with psychic dueling scars. If he comes off as a hero in "Night of the Bullies," so be it. But I'd also like to cite a cameo player in this saga. While researching Michael's story, I came to learn of a young woman who had been sexually assaulted by yet another ATO member and had taken civil action after the DA in Austin, Texas, had decided not to pursue an indictment. After months of protestations and counter-accusations, the ATO and his fraternity quietly settled matters with the victim. Like Michael, she has no doubt learned that banishing the demons is not an overnight proposition. Still, she mustered the courage to fight them; and so in the event that her travails are also forgotten twenty-five years hence, I offer her now as a hero, albeit an anonymous one.

POSSESSED

LUKE DITTRICH

H e's back. For days now the stranger has been showing up on her doorstep, ringing her doorbell, pounding his fist against her door.

She's found that if she stays quiet, turns off the lights and the TV, and pretends she's not there, he'll eventually return to his old pickup truck. He'll sit in it for five, ten, fifteen minutes, staring at her house, then drive away.

But he always comes back.

And here he is again, walking through the mottled mid-afternoon shadows cast by the maple trees in her front yard. She turns off her television and peers through her blinds. It's a clear winter day in West Georgia, and she sees him fine. He's wearing black boots, black sweatpants, a black leather motorcycle jacket, and a black skullcap. He's at least six feet tall, and has a long, dark, graying beard. Above the beard, a thin, weather-reddened nose supports a pair of cloudy bifocals. His arm rises. Is that a swastika on his sleeve? The door shakes as he pounds on it.

"This is Tom Bronson! Is anybody home? I need to speak to you!"

His voice is deep and strong and loud.

"Hello! Tom Bronson here! I'm looking for Anthony and Robin Lea! I have some questions for you!"

And that's enough for her. She can't take this anymore. Her husband, Anthony, works for the power company and has been out of town for the last several days. She is all alone.

Robin Lea picks up the telephone and dials 911.

. . .

Excerpt from the direct examination of a police officer who responded to Robin Lea's 911 call, taken from the transcript of Tom Bronson's stalking trial:

> PROSECUTOR S. JAMES TUGGLE: What specifically did you do when you arrived on the scene?
>
> OFFICER FIDEL ESPINOSA JR.: I made my way around to the passenger side of the vehicle, kind of to look inside the cab of the vehicle.
>
> Q: Did you see anything in the vehicle that caused you some alarm?
>
> A: Yes, there was in between the two, the driver and the passenger seats, there was a semiautomatic rifle kind of laid in between the seats.
>
> Q: Do you know specifically what type of weapon this was?
>
> A: I believe it was a SKS rifle, it was equipped with some other . . .
>
> Q: What was it equipped with?
>
> A: It had a laser sight, it also had a scope, and two fully loaded magazines with it.
>
> Q: Did you notice anything unusual about the rounds themselves?
>
> A: The rounds themselves, they were what is called a full-metal jacket.
>
> Q: And based on your training and experience is there any particular use for a full-metal jacket bullet or round?
>
> A: From military and my police training they are commonly used to penetrate . . . high penetration, automobile doors, houses, things of that nature.

. . .

The bullet passes through the plank of wood, through the small tree the plank of wood is leaning against, through a smaller tree behind it, and then burrows with a kick of dirt into the ground. The red circle from the laser sight still wavers on the plank, a couple of inches away from the hole the bullet just made.

"It's a piece of shit," Tom Bronson tells me. "Chinese assault rifle. Made for peasants who have never even seen shoes."

He says he was surprised when the authorities gave him his gun back. Apart from the time spent in court during his stalking trial, he spent the 219 days following Robin Lea's call to 911 in the Carroll County Jail, and he half-expected to never see his gun again. But when they let him out there it was, full-metal jacket ammo and all.

Actually, if the authorities had examined all of his bullets they'd have seen that they weren't all full-metal jacket. He cuts bowls into the points of some of his rounds, so that they expand after hitting their targets, causing more damage. And some of those hollow points he modifies even further, cutting crosses into the bowls, making them "dum-dums," giving them the potential to literally explode on impact.

There's a loud report from the barrel and the collapsible stock pulses against his shoulder. I flinch. The hand-painted white swastika on the sleeve of Tom's black leather jacket jerks in the sun. Another bullet penetrates the plank of wood.

It's been almost three years since Tom Bronson was set free. He doesn't want to lose his freedom again, but there are still things he must do.

It's time to get on with his mission.

He lowers his gun and looks at me.

"You ready to go?" he asks.

. . .

Tom Bronson's mission began in the first few days of a new year, when he went to his post office box and found a letter waiting for him there:

1-3-2000

Dear Mr. Bronson,

I received your letter concerning my daughter, Betty Jean Farris.

I need for you to come see me or call me as soon as possible.

I need your help.

Sincerely yours,

Katherine Phillips

Katherine Phillips lives alone in a small apartment on the periphery of Carrollton, the county seat of Carroll County, Georgia, an hour's drive west of Atlanta. She keeps her home fastidiously clean, and decorates it with plastic fruit, ceramic figurines, embroidered pillows, and framed photographs. With the exception of the Elvis headshot hanging just inside her bedroom door, all of the photographs are of her or her family. The oldest shows Katherine Phillips sixty-eight years ago, at the age of four, standing barefoot between her two slightly older siblings in her hometown of Sand Mountain, Alabama, shortly before her family moved to Carrollton.

Katherine Phillips stayed in school until the sixth grade, gave birth to her first child at fifteen, and started working full-time a short while later. She spent her working life in Lawler Hosiery Mill, "making bobby socks." During her career there she had many different jobs. She was a pairer, matching appropriate socks to each other as they came down the line. She was a packer, rubber-banding socks and stuffing them into plastic bags. She was a trimmer, cutting and discarding loose threads. When she retired in 1991, she was a floor lady, a sort of low-level supervisor who makes sure the socks are flowing smoothly from one station to the next. She was earning her highest salary ever, $5.75 an hour. Upon her retirement, the mill gave her a special pin for her long and faithful service.

Katherine Phillips doesn't care to talk about her working life.

What she likes to talk about are her children:

Diane.

Patsy Ann.

Kathy.

Betty Jean.

If you bring up Diane, Patsy Ann, or Kathy, she like as not will tell you long and lively stories about them.

If you bring up Betty Jean, she like as not will light a Doral Ultra Light 100, draw from it as deeply as her old lungs will allow, and then fix you with watery eyes and say much the same thing she said to Tom Bronson three years ago when he came to her house after receiving her letter. She will say much the same thing she said before he went out on the mission that led him to Robin Lea's door and from there to the Carroll County Jail.

"Betty Jean was my baby. Thirty-two years old but she was my baby. The day she died I told Gary, I told him, 'Gary Farris, you've been killing my baby for eleven years, you sonofabitch.'"

Then, while her unproven and emotionally charged allegation still rings in your ears, she will apologize for her language, bring the Doral back to her lips, and cry silently for a while.

Excerpt from an obituary that ran in the July 27, 1999, edition of the *Carrollton Times-Georgian*:

Mrs. Betty Jean Farris, 32, died July 24, 1999, following a brief illness.

Survivors include her husband, Gary Farris . . .

. . .

Tom Bronson lives in the woods.

He has no electricity and no running water.

He does, however, have a Web site.

I stumbled across it a few weeks ago. I was in my office, scavenging the Internet for crime-related story ideas, typing various combinations of words like "Georgia," "trial," and "transcript" into search engines. While scrolling through the responses to one of my queries, my eye caught on the word "Nazi," highlighted in blue hypertext. I clicked on it and found myself reading the transcript of a stalking trial that took place in Carrollton. The defendant was a man named Tom Bronson, and the transcript was a small part of a larger site, one apparently built by the defendant himself. I read the transcript and then I read the rest of the site. This took me several hours, and by the time I was done I knew I'd found a story.

Here are some things I learned from Tom Bronson's Web site:

1. Tom Bronson is a neo-Nazi. His home page is topped with both a swastika and an iron cross, and he describes himself as a National Socialist Party activist. His political beliefs form the foundation for a particularly hateful brand of paranoia, and he often alludes to the vast homosexual conspiracies that he believes have kept him from finding steady work.

2. Tom Bronson is highly intelligent, but his intelligence appears to skirt the edge of sanity. One part of his site is taken up by papers he's written on topics like the universal gravitational field theorem. Another part contains a glossary of the scientific terms he invented for use in these papers.

3. Tom Bronson has been investigating the death of Betty Jean Farris for almost four years now. Betty Jean's mother, Katherine Phillips, is helping with this investigation. Through a series of events that the site does not fully illuminate, Tom's investigation led him to Robin Lea's front door.

The Web site gave a phone number. I dialed it. The person who answered took my name and number and told me that Tom Bronson didn't live there, but lived nearby, and checked his messages often. A few hours later my phone rang.

"This is Tom Bronson. B-R-O-N-S-O-N. You called me."

His voice was deep and strong and loud.

I explained that I write for *Atlanta* magazine, had seen his Web site, and would like to meet him.

"When?"

"Tomorrow."

He gave me directions to the house he was calling from, a house near Carrollton, on the outskirts of John Tanner State Park. He explained that he didn't live at the house itself, but rather in the woods nearby, he'd rather not say exactly where. But he could meet me at the house, no problem. He'd be in the garden out back, tending to the small crops that the property's owners let him plant there.

"I'll hang a fluorescent orange flag on the mailbox so you can find it easy," he said, "and I'll call you early tomorrow if I need to abort."

"Any reason you wouldn't be able to make it?" I asked.

"No," he said. "But things happen. Bears appear and kill us all the time."

He is shirtless when I first see him, hunched over a patch of hot peppers. He's wearing an old pair of sweatpants, a sagging fanny pack, and stained leather boots. The flesh on his torso is loose around the midsection, but there's not much fat on him, and the muscles on his arms are well defined. For a fifty-year-old, he is in good shape.

He stands when I get out of the car, walks over, extends a hand.

"Tom Bronson," he says.

We had decided over the phone to meet here and then go right away to a nearby library that has a conference room where we can talk in private. Tom walks to the mailbox and unties the fluorescent orange T-shirt that had served as a flag. He puts it on and gets into my car. I pull out of the driveway and start following his directions to the library.

As we drive, he launches into an impromptu travelogue. After about a minute I reach into the backseat, grab my microcassette recorder, press record, and give it to Tom to hold. Despite the heat, I roll up my window, so the wind noise doesn't ruin the recording.

"May I suggest," Tom says, nodding toward my recorder, "that you look into getting a digital one."

Then he continues his travelogue.

"Right in front of us, that's old Highway 78, used to be the main highway between Birmingham and Atlanta. Used to be full of oxen, pulling oxcarts. It matters. You're about to see an old railroad line between Birmingham and the city of Atlanta. That railroad figures into Civil War history. It matters. I mean this is cultural history, right, but around here it matters. Go right through here. This is Bremen, a very old cotton picking town. This is the sort of town where the old Negroes shambled along barefoot. Hang a left. Go right through that little area. You can't hardly get more Old South than right here. Looks it, doesn't it? It matters. Go straight through here, just go right on through. And there's the new Wal-Mart. The brand-new Wal-Mart Supercenter. That matters, too, but you know, that ain't history, that's current, right now, what's going on. . . ."

The woman at the library front desk knows Tom, greets him by name. Tom spends a lot of time in libraries. He reads their books and magazines and uses their computers. That's how he built his Web site: public access Internet terminals at public libraries.

Tom leads me to the empty conference room at the back. There is a poster of a lion leaning against a wall, several bound census books on the shelves, light shining through dimpled ceiling plastic, a brown table, and comfortable chairs. We sit across from each other.

I tell Tom I want to know exactly what led him to Robin Lea's door.

"Then you need to know about Gary Farris," he says. "Gary is a wall-walker. He can walk on a two-by-four stud wall eight feet off the ground, nimble as a cat. He's a dog as a person, but he's a cat as far as his physical skills. . . ."

Several years ago, Tom continues, he met Gary on a construction site the two of them were working near Carrollton. That's what both men do for a living. They're carpenters. On that particular site, the two were framing row houses in one of the new subdivisions that are starting to proliferate like kudzu around here, on the western frontier of Metro Atlanta's encroaching sprawl. One day after work, Tom asked Gary if he could use his shower. Then as now, Tom didn't have running water. Gary said sure he could, anytime, for $2. Tom started showering at Gary's place three or four times a week. Sometimes he would shower and leave immediately. Sometimes he would shower and stay for an hour or two.

He got to know Gary's family. His wife, Betty Jean, and their three kids, infant Star, two-year-old Gary Jr., and four-year-old Shandi.

Got to know the family and got to hate the way Gary treated the family. Gary whipped the kids, Tom says. Gary slammed Betty Jean against a wall, Tom says.

But what could he do? They weren't his kids. It wasn't his family.

So he didn't do anything.

Not until the day he was working on another construction site and a co-worker came up and asked him if he'd heard that Betty Jean Farris was dead.

. . .

Betty Jean's mother, Katherine Phillips, pulls out one, two, three, half a dozen shoe boxes from a closet near her kitchen. She piles them on her kitchen table and starts going through them, one at a time. Finds insurance policies on her life and her car, a Bible containing pressed flowers, a whole stack of documents related to her recent bankruptcy filing, scrips for her prescriptions of Paxil, Prolex, Furosemide, Bextran, Allegra, and Zanaflex. And then, finally, she finds what she is looking for.

She unfolds a sheet of paper and lays it out flat in front of me. I take note of the salient lines.

Certificate of Death/State of Georgia
Decedent's Name (First, Middle, Last): Betty Jean Farris
Race: White
Origin of Decedent (Italian, Mex., French, English, Etc.): American
Immediate Cause: Cardiopulmonary arrest
Due to, or as a consequence of: Cerebral edema
Due to, or as a consequence of: Subarachnoid hemorrhage
Was operation performed (Yes or No): No
Autopsy (Yes or No): No

"For about two months before she died, she'd been having bad headaches," Katherine tells me, then explains how on that late July morning in 1999 Betty Jean had complained to her eldest daughter, Shandi, about her head hurting extra bad. A few moments later she had lain back on her bed and closed her eyes. She never opened them of her own volition again.

"They had her on life support when I got to the hospital, had a tube down her throat," Katherine says. "The nurse told me Betty

Jean could hear me but she couldn't speak. Her eyes were swelled and sticking way out and I opened her lids and her eyes were just bloodshot, full of it. Her eyes looked like they were going to pop out of her head."

Betty Jean had chosen to be listed as an organ donor on her driver's license, and while she was lying there with her heart still beating but her eyes all swollen and red, the doctors asked Katherine if they should comply with Betty Jean's wishes and reap her body parts. Katherine told them they should not, told them that Betty Jean had suffered enough and now she should just be left alone.

And that was about it.

"She died on Saturday," Katherine says, "and on Sunday we went to pick her coffin out."

She keeps the pictures from Betty Jean's funeral in another shoe box.

In these photos, Betty Jean lies in a white linen–lined coffin, hands across her midsection, eyes closed, head propped up on a pillow so that she has the hint of a double chin. She holds a red rose in one hand, and a small bouquet of white carnations rests on her chest. She wears a black short-sleeved top that shines a bit in the light of the camera flash. The mortician applied darker makeup to her hands and forearms than to her face, making the latter look deader than the former.

For Katherine, the months following the funeral were very difficult, as the shattering loss of her daughter was compounded by the second, more gradual loss of her daughter's children.

Katherine's relationship with her son-in-law, Gary Farris, had always been strained. She met him the same day Betty Jean had, many years ago, when all three briefly worked together at Lawler

Hosiery Mill. Katherine never thought Gary was the right man for Betty Jean—"I told her, I said, 'Honey, that's not the guy for you, you don't need him.'" As the years went by and Gary and Betty Jean's relationship evolved, dragging the young couple into the roles first of husband and wife and then of mother and father, Katherine's low opinion of Gary hardened into something darker. She even called the cops on him once, claiming he broke down the door of her apartment looking for Betty Jean, and grabbed Katherine's forearm hard enough to leave deep welts on it. She did not press charges, and the dislike between her and her son-in-law mostly just simmered below the surface, kept in check by their mutual link, Betty Jean.

But with Betty Jean gone, there was nothing to stop their antipathy from blossoming. Following Katherine's first post–Betty Jean visit with her grandchildren, she called the Division of Family and Children Services on Gary, told them that Gary's home was an unsafe environment to raise children in. After DFCS officers visited and found the home to be in acceptable shape, Gary took Katherine to court and tried unsuccessfully to convince a judge to issue a restraining order to keep her off his property in the future. Her access to her grandchildren became more and more limited, and Katherine worried that Gary might eventually take the kids away for good by moving back to his home state of Oklahoma.

It was at the height of all this anxiety that Katherine remembered a letter she had received from Tom Bronson shortly after Betty Jean's death. She had met Tom several times during the years that he was paying to take showers at her daughter's home, but had never really gotten to know him. The letter had initially disturbed Katherine: It basically laid out some complicated theory of Tom's about how he thought Gary had killed Betty Jean. At the time she'd received the letter, Katherine had brushed Tom off, called him and told him to stay out of it, warned him that his mucking around might make things worse, might turn Gary further against her. But now, at the beginning of her first year in thirty-two years without her daughter, things had gotten worse on their own and Gary was about as far against her as possible.

On January 3, 2000, Katherine wrote a letter to Tom Bronson. And it was this letter, the one asking for his help, the one telling him to please come see her as soon as possible, that Tom Bronson found waiting for him in his P.O. box a few days later.

When he arrived at Katherine Phillips's house after receiving her letter, Tom Bronson came prepared like a salesman, full of facts, armed with diagrams and documents. He brought along pictures of skulls and brains and stabbed his finger at them, showing the weak points where a blow to the head might cause a skull to crack, an artery to burst, blood to flow.

Tom has always been fascinated by neurology. For example, when he first began spending those post-work, post-shower evenings at Betty Jean Farris's home, Betty Jean's four-year-old daughter Shandi was just beginning to learn the alphabet. Tom had enjoyed thinking about the changes taking place in Shandi's tender young cerebrum; he imagined it silently exploding with new connections, growing to meet the needs of the new task. In a way, Tom had been jealous of Shandi. He wished he could relive, as he put it, "the equivalent of puberty linguistically, when those cells first proliferate in the brain." In order to approximate the experience for himself, he went to the library and checked out a book on Cyrillic, a Slavic alphabet. For the next few weeks, every time he went to the Farris's house, Tom Bronson would flop on the living room floor and study Cyrillic while Shandi studied English.

But years later, standing there in Shandi's bereaved grandmother's living room, armed with his props and his enthusiasm, Tom was not talking about how a brain develops. He was talking about how a brain dies.

Perhaps it began with an aneurysm, he told Katherine. He explained to her what that was. An aneurysm was a swelling of an artery, "like a balloon forming on a water hose; like a blister on a tire; like a blood blister on your skin." Eventually the balloon would pop. That would lead to the first cause on the three-tiered list of causes on Betty Jean's death certificate: subarachnoid hemorrhage. Those seven syllables describe bleeding into the spinal fluid–filled space between the pia mater and arachnoid membranes, two quilts of tissue that help cushion the brain. As the bleeding continued, Tom told Katherine, the space between the membranes would swell with blood, leading to the second condition listed on the death certificate: cerebral edema. That's all cerebral edema is: an overaccumulation of fluids in the cranium. The blood would then mix with the spinal fluid and be pumped from between the membranes into the brain itself, besieging the tender organ and initiating the fatal damage. The parts of the brain that controlled Betty Jean's lungs would shut down, and then, eventually, her heart would stop. Cardiopulmonary arrest. The final cause listed on the death certificate. The last of Betty Jean's many killers.

But what was still unknown, Tom told Katherine, was Betty Jean's first killer. What caused the artery to swell, the blood to flow, the heart to stop? What sparked the lethal chain reaction inside her head? What killed her? Or the question might be posed with a different pronoun: Who. Who killed her?

The doctor had ruled that Betty Jean died of natural causes. And it's true, Tom said, that cerebral aneurysms can rupture naturally, spontaneously, through no fault of anyone but God. But there can be other causes as well. A violent blow to the head, say. A rough jostle, a hard smack, a closed fist.

Katherine had always, in some prerational way, held Gary somehow responsible for her daughter's death. Now Tom was outlining a scenario that propped up her rickety belief in her son-in-law's guilt, a theoretical vision of Gary Farris hitting Betty Jean in the head, jostling her brain, damaging something delicate and essential. Tom shared his theory with Katherine, and his theory quickly entered her gut. Her gut now told her, despite the lack of any substantiating evidence, what had happened to her daughter's brain.

But how to prove it? Tom told Katherine that if Gary had struck Betty Jean in the head her body probably still bore traces of the assault. Minute abrasions on the scalp, perhaps, or tiny fissures in the skull, some traces of violence overlooked by the attending physician who had no reason to suspect anything untoward, who declared her death natural and then decided not to perform an autopsy. Tom told Katherine that they must convince the authorities to turn over all of Betty Jean's medical records and then, if necessary, dig her up, cut her open, look inside. Only Gary Farris, as Betty Jean's next of kin, had legal access to her medical records, but a court order could change that, just as a court order could set the shovels moving for an exhumation. The first priority, then, was to gather testimony and present it to a judge.

Tom had come to Katherine's home because she had sent for him and told him she needed his help. Now, he told her, he needed hers. The judge would want more than general testimony about Betty Jean having been an abused woman. The judge would demand something stronger and rarer: specific testimony related to a specific event that could have caused Betty Jean sufficient head trauma to kill her. Did Katherine know, Tom asked her, of anyone who might have witnessed Gary abusing Betty Jean shortly prior to death?

So Katherine told Tom about Anthony Lea.

Anthony is Katherine's son and Anthony is not her son. She gave birth to him at a time when she was stretched too thin for another child, and so she offered him to her older brother and his wife to raise as their own. Anthony didn't learn that Katherine was his mother until he was twelve years old, and his relationship with her had never been better than strained. But he did get along well with Katherine's daughters, his cousins/sisters. He got along particularly well with Betty Jean. In fact, not long before Betty Jean died, Anthony Lea and his wife had accompanied Betty Jean and her husband to a local tavern, T. C. Rose, on Brumbelow Road, in Carrollton. According to what Katherine heard later from Betty Jean, the night had ended badly.

"Gary attacked Betty Jean, slinging her around, and slung her against the wall, and was slapping her upside the head," Katherine told Tom. This happened, according to what Katherine recalled of Betty Jean's account, in front of Anthony and his wife.

Tom heard this and something inside him clicked, "like a key in a lock."

Do you have a phone number for Anthony? Tom asked Katherine.

No, she told him, but she did have a home address. She gave it to him. She also gave him the name of Anthony's wife: Robin.

Robin Lea.

. . .

What happened between Tom Bronson's arrest at Anthony and Robin Lea's house and his release seven months later is a matter of public record.

He went on trial for stalking.

In order to prove stalking, you have to prove that the perpetrator is contacting the victim for no good reason other than to terrorize or antagonize him or her. The case against Tom Bronson fell apart quickly, for though it was clear that Robin Lea was scared of Tom Bronson, it also was clear that Tom went to her house for reasons other than to scare her. That became evident as soon as a tearful Katherine Phillips took the stand:

S. JAMES TUGGLE: How long have you known Thomas Bronson?
KATHERINE PHILLIPS: Approximately five years. He was a friend of my daughter and her husband.

Q: I believe there's some Kleenex there.

A: The man was just trying to help me. . . . He was just good enough to, you know, he was going to find out some things. He's a good person. Tom Bronson is a wonderful person.

Later, a cross-examination by Tom's public defender, Dennis Blackmon, of the arresting officer in the case, Sergeant Steve Daniel, weakened the prosecution's case even further.

DENNIS BLACKMON: Tell me by what authority in the criminal code do you cite that would indicate that a person can't investigate?

SERGEANT STEVE DANIEL: There's not one that I know of that you can't investigate.

Q: So, in fact, Mr. Bronson's investigation was not in any way illegal, was it?

A: The investigation itself, I'm assuming, is not illegal.

Q: Is there anything illegal about knocking on somebody's door?

A: Just to knock on their door, no, sir.

Q: How about ring(ing) their doorbell?

A: No, sir.

Q: Do you have any indication . . . that Mr. Bronson was at Mrs. Lea's house for any other purpose than to ask her questions about this investigation?

A: No, sir, just strictly asking questions.

BLACKMON: Thank you, no further questions at this time, Judge.

As for Robin Lea, when she took the stand she testified about how intimidating Tom had appeared to her. "He just seemed to be a strange person," she said. Regarding Tom Bronson's investigation, the investigation that led him to her door, Robin Lea testified that she herself had never witnessed any incident of violence committed by Gary Farris against Betty Jean. "The only thing I knew about their relationship was hearsay," she said.

The jury found Tom innocent.

But on the day of the verdict, before he could be released, the state brought a new charge against him: aggravated stalking. This charge related to several letters that Tom had written to Anthony and Robin Lea from jail before the trial. In tone, the letters veered between equanimity and anger, and several of them contained paranoid ramblings about Sergeant Steve Daniel's sexuality. Here's the full text of one of Tom's letters:

> February 4, 2K
>
> Dear Robin and Anthony Lea:
>
> My attempts to contact you folks was to obtain an affidavit concerning your witness to an act of violence against Betty Farris by her husband Gary. I need this to obtain a court order for the release of the medical records concerned to Katherine Phillips.
>
> Please contact Katherine immediately. She will assure you of the innocence of my activities.
>
> Be aware that I am a National Socialist activist and that the party's long history of fascism is deeply obnoxious to homosexuals generally, and to homosexual officers of state especially. I must suspect that Sergeant Steve Daniel is motivated to malice of this cause, particularly because he encouraged you to file this charge without insisting on a meeting between you and I.
>
> I am more than innocent Mrs. Lea. Please have me released immediately!
>
> Most Sincerely,
>
> Your Prisoner
> Tom Bronson

Despite the new charges, the district attorney eventually decided not to retry Tom Bronson. Tom stayed in jail for another five months, and then the state "dead-docketed" his case. "Dead-docketing" is a legal procedure whereby a case is indefinitely suspended but can be reopened at any time.

On August 30, 2000, Tom Bronson left cell 57 of the Carroll County Jail and quickly got back to his old life.

Three years on, not much has changed.

He still lives in the woods.

He still takes whatever construction work he can find.

And he still, in a continuation of a mission that has remained an "immediate current objective" for almost four years now, investigates the death of Betty Jean Farris.

. . .

I am following Tom Bronson down a path through the woods.

The forest is thick, heavy with new-growth bramble, but the path is worn and easy to navigate. It rained recently, and water droplets weigh down the maple and oak leaves around us. The air smells clean and earthy.

A dog runs down the path toward us, a young black Labbish mutt with a loop of twine around her neck instead of a collar, wagging her tail energetically. She runs straight to Tom, who strokes her head and rubs her ears.

"Hey Baby," he says.

Baby then walks a bit hesitantly over to me. I let her smell the back of my hand and then pet her.

Tom stiffens. "I'd prefer you not do that," he says. "If you wouldn't mind, as a courtesy to me, I'd like you to slap her."

I ask him why.

"Because," he says, "I don't want her to like strangers."

I don't hit Baby but I stop petting her, and we continue on until we come to a small clearing. I see an old Winnebago trailer and a battered Toyota pickup truck, both painted red and green and black in a camouflage pattern. I see a wooden shack containing books, pots, tools, a couple of tables, a Kawasaki motorcycle, and a Huffy bicycle. I see a tall post lodged in the ground and wrapped in pillows and scraps of cloth — a makeshift punching bag. I see a circular pit, six feet across, that seems to be both a compost heap and a toilet. I see thick corn tortillas, cooked over a butane cooker and left to cool on a plastic wide-gapped screen taken from a fan. I see, next to the motorcycle, a twenty-gallon metal tin. Tom has affixed a strip of masking tape to the tin and written the following word on it: ГАЗОЛЕН. Readers of Cyrillic would pronounce that word like this: Gah-Zoh-Leen.

Tom has lived out of this trailer, in this and other clearings in the woods, for more than fifteen years now. He lives on food stamps and the meager earnings he makes from his occasional carpentry work, lives much the same way he's lived since a messy divorce on the West Coast, where he's from, propelled him onto the road and into the wild. He often says it was his divorce that sent him into a tailspin, hurled him and his dreams to this patch of earth in West Georgia, but I don't think his life ever got very far off the ground to begin with.

Ask him where he was born and he'll tell you, in a flat baritone: "Watsonville, California, a Mexicanized agricultural community, January 24, 1953, at 3:30 AM." His parents split up when he was ten years old, and he lived with his mother until the age of fourteen, after which point he started living in foster homes. Push him for more details about his childhood and he'll give them to you slowly, holding back heaps. Frustrated by his reticence and hoping that he might be more open on paper, I once asked Tom to write me a short autobiographical sketch. Here are the first few lines of the essay he wrote for me: *"In 1984, at the age of 31, I solved the 'Riddle of Gravitation' and proceeded to resolve my ideas on the subject in the con-*

text of pre-existing field theory. The resolution of the gravitation field with the other observed fields constitutes 'general' field theory. At the same time I continued to develop my ideas concerning spallation fission in magnetic confinement and particle/plasma dynamics in general. . . ." The document continued in that vein, laying out the various contributions Tom claims to have made to the sciences. Apart from a couple of passing references to his "problems with the police and judiciary" his entire "autobiography" was entirely impersonal.

Tom's reluctance to talk about his past is probably appreciated by his mother, Pat Collier, who lives in California with Tom's step-father, Jack. The now-elderly couple are active members of the False Memory Syndrome Foundation, an organization devoted to helping parents defend themselves against accusations of child abuse. Jack Collier is something of a poster child for the organization, and has appeared on both *Oprah* and *Prime-Time Live*, claiming that the sex abuse charges brought against him by his daughter, Tom's stepsister, were false.

Whatever it was that destroyed Tom's family, whatever explosion tore his home apart, it spread him and most of his five siblings like shrapnel across the globe, about as far as they could get from their birthplace and each other as possible. One brother lives in Alaska, works as an environmental consultant for Exxon. Another brother lives in Hawaii, makes furniture. One of his other siblings he hardly talks about. That one converted from Catholicism to Judaism and lives in Israel, a nation Tom wishes could be wiped off the face of the earth, on a kibbutz named Givat Oz.

Tom says he felt like a Nazi ever since he read an illustrated history of World War II at the age of six. He saw a photograph of a Nazi youth rally, a photograph spread out over two pages in grim black and white, and said, "That's me." Tom felt a kinship with the jack-booted hordes, felt a passion for the rhetoric of their leaders. When he grew up he found that others shared his passion, offered their own kinship. But although at different times in his life he's fallen in with a variety of the clans and networks and groups and gangs that make up the American white supremacist movement, Tom eventually, invariably, falls out with any group he joins. Falls out because of some or other stubborn idiosyncrasy in his personal belief system. Falls out for expressing a favorable opinion about, say, Josef Stalin.

"Josef Stalin was an outstandingly good leader," Tom once told me. "I'm not going to spit on his grave. This caused me problems in Nazi circles because most Nazis are extreme anti-Soviets and extreme anti-Stalinists. In some ways it's like you're standing in the grass, this is your high school, right, and you have one good thing to say about one guy out there on the football field on the other high school team, and now they're calling you a traitor and splitting your lip. Well, that's bullshit. That doesn't make you untrue to your school, does it? It's bullshit. You say one good thing about Josef Stalin and they say fuck you, they call you a communist. . . ."

So Tom Bronson doesn't have many friends in white supremacist groups anymore. Doesn't have, really, many friends anywhere.

This is my first visit to Tom's home, and the first thing he shows me is a brown belt. It is a leather belt, sunbaked and stiff. He keeps it looped like a noose around the headrest of the passenger seat in his Toyota pickup truck. He says that the belt is a "magical item." What he means by that . . . well, I'm not exactly sure what he means by that, but I do know that the belt plays into the story. Or, as he says, "It doesn't have any bearing on this case, except it does, and everything does."

Tom claims that he took this belt from Betty Jean Farris's home one afternoon after he witnessed Gary Farris using it to whip Shandi Farris for not finishing a slice of pizza.

"She was just a little bitty kid," Tom says. "I was outraged by it and I stand here being outraged by it right now. And she'll be outraged by it her whole life. You know she'll hate the bastard."

He pauses. His gun lies, as it always does, nearby. He considers his gun one of the basic staples of life, a tool to protect him from the dangers he feels surround him. Someday, when the Final War begins, Tom believes he will have to use this gun to kill. He will need to take up arms against the faggots and the Jews and the Negroes. He is not eager to do this, but when he has to, he will. (His eschatological perspective, he once told me, comes from his reading of the Bible's book of Revelation. He considers himself a Catholic, though he admits that his Catholicism "doesn't mean that I wouldn't burn priests at the stake if they suck little boys' pee-pees.")

Tom holds the belt out in front of him and runs his eyes slowly down its length.

"Brutality against children, great, excessive violence against children, happens all the time," he muses, then pulls the belt tight between his hands, the middle looped around his knuckles, the two loose ends gripped in a stiff fist.

"That's what turns people into monsters," he says.

"He talks about my kids being thrashed with a belt, bruises left on their legs and all that. Man, I'm just a typical dad that whups their kids when they do something wrong. They got whupped just like I got whupped, probably just like you got whupped when you was a kid. When you did something wrong you got whupped."

I reach Gary Farris by phone at his father's house in Oklahoma. Gary left Georgia while Tom was in jail, took his three kids with him. He also took his new wife, Cassie, a woman he met at a Waffle House. Cassie already had one kid of her own; since marrying Gary she's given birth again, to a boy named Jeremiah, born on the two-year anniversary of Betty Jean's death.

I was lucky to reach Gary at his father's house, as his own phone number and address are unlisted. He made them unlisted because he doesn't ever want to see or speak with his former mother-in-law, Katherine Phillips, again. He doesn't want to ever see Tom Bronson again, either.

"I'm scared of him," he says. "I think he wants to kill me. And him and [Katherine] think I killed Betty. It's so stupid. I think I slapped Betty twice in thirteen years. Why do they think I would kill my wife? I just had bought a double-wide and five acres of land, had three kids and not a bit of insurance on any of it. Tom has a brain but he doesn't know how to use it. I think he used to be a very intelligent man. Then I think he did something bad somewhere. You know, like one of these murderers that just murdered masses of people for no reason. I mean, that's just the kind of feeling I get just even thinking about him. When this guy gets on you he don't let go.

"It's crazy, you know, and it just won't end. It just won't end."

Actually, Gary Farris can imagine one ending, though it's grim.

"If Tom ever come out here, there's only one of two things gonna happen," he says. "One of us is gonna die."

"Hello, you have visitors in the yard! Hello! Are you home?"

KNOCK KNOCK KNOCK.

"Hello! I'm looking for Anita McIntyre!"

KNOCK KNOCK KNOCK.

"I have some questions for you! Hello!"

Tom Bronson is at another front door.

A county water tower peeks above the tops of some nearby trees. It was the water tower that led Tom and me to this house.

About an hour ago we'd been in Katherine Phillips's living room, where she and Tom once again searched the worn tracks made in their memories by Betty Jean Farris's life and death. They scrounged each other's minds for leads, clues, lost scraps of information that might help them advance this investigation of theirs. Thwarted in his attempt to track down Robin Lea, to follow that lead, Tom has been hunting a new witness. In the past several years he has talked to so many people, filled dozens of notebooks, and for what? The authorities never respond to the letters he sends them anymore, and he's no closer than he ever was to finding the smoking gun that might convince them to seize shovels and dig Betty Jean up. Nor has he had much luck pursuing what has become a second prong of his investigation: finding out where Gary Farris lives in Oklahoma.

But maybe the investigation is an end, not a means. It gives Tom energy, purpose, something to occupy his fierce and sprawling mind. While questioning Katherine Phillips this afternoon, trying to spur her to recollect something new, he was more animated than I'd ever seen him, more energetic even than when he's denouncing the evils of faggotry or extolling the virtues of Stalin.

As for Katherine, when Tom isn't with her, she says, her days run on and on and don't even end at night because she can't sleep. She hasn't spoken with her grandchildren in eighteen months. The last communication of any sort she's had with them was a letter Shandi sent her more than a year ago. The pain has worn away at Katherine, and sometimes her face is flat, scrubbed free of emotion. This afternoon, though, with Tom by her side, Katherine's face had flushed with color and grief and anger and something else. Hope?

Their meeting didn't produce any new leads, but, as we drove back toward Tom's camp, Tom had spotted the water tower peeking above the trees, and it reminded him of something Katherine had told him during one of his innumerable other visits to her home. Something about a woman, Anita McIntyre, who occasionally baby-sat Betty Jean's children and might, who knows, have witnessed something relevant to the investigation. No reason to think she had, but no reason to think she hadn't, either. Katherine didn't know Anita McIntyre's address, but she had given Tom a description of her home—"a fine gray house with burgundy trim near a water tower"—and Tom had filed this description away in the recesses of his brain, where it resided peacefully until his sighting of the water tower jerked it back up into his immediate consciousness and propelled him to the front door of this house.

"I have no reason not to just stop and knock just like this," Tom explains between his bellowed hellos. "It might definitely yield some good apples."

Eventually, when it becomes clear that no one is inside, at least no one courageous enough to answer the door, Tom starts walking around the property, commenting as he writes in his notebook.

"I see a Chevrolet Lumina, dark blue, Georgia plate, Haralson County, 459CKS. I see a real nice modern Hyundai, being silver-gray, got a Georgia Haralson plate 5438AKW. I see a real old, flat black, or real dark blue, looks like a European vehicle, being scrapped out in the yard. The house is apparently brand-new, over $200,000, with vinyl above and wainscoting below. A real fancy main door entry with a long vertical old etched glass window with flower design. The house is not gray, it's actually beige, and it's got black or extremely dark, real dark, maybe black or forest green shutters. I see a for-sale sign out front. Re/Max. That's all I see for signs. We are immediately north of a blue and white water tower. . . ."

Two boys, aged maybe eleven or twelve and riding BMX bikes by the house, stop to look at Tom and the figure he cuts in his camouflage shorts and camouflage tank top. Tom calls out to them.

"Is this the McIntyre residence?"

The boys don't say anything. Tom approaches, looms over them.

"Does Anita McIntyre live here?"

No, one of the boys says, not anymore. She and her husband split up.

"Do you know where she lives now?"

They shrug.

Tom's shoulders wilt. Another lead is slipping away.

"Do you know a girl by the name of Shandi Farris?" he asks, and there's something soft, the hint of a plea, in his voice. "A girl about your age. She'd be about twelve years old now. She used to live near here. Does that sound familiar to you? Her mother died. Which is the reason I want to talk to this Anita McIntyre. About what happened. What happened to Shandi's mom."

The boys shrug again, then ride off down the street together, away from Tom.

———

After this article came out, Tom Bronson e-mailed me and requested that I send a few extra copies of the magazine to his P.O. box. I complied, then didn't hear from him again for a couple of months. Finally, I received a lengthy e-mailed critique. "Why did you choose this title?" it began. "'Obsessed' would have been far more appropriate if it was your intention to imply that I spent an excessive amount of time on the project."

While I don't entirely agree with Tom, I will say that my original title, a title that ended up as a cover line for the issue of the magazine in which the article ran, was "The Nazi and the Floor Lady." I still like that title. The relationship between Tom Bronson (the Nazi) and Katherine Phillips (the Floor Lady) is the crux of this story. Tom and Katherine are each, in their own way, outcasts, but their investigation into the death of Katherine's daughter has given them an empowering sense of purpose. It has also evolved into a seemingly endless quest that can only be called (yes, Tom) obsessive.

THE DARK ART OF INTERROGATION
MARK BOWDEN

RAWALPINDI, PAKISTAN

On what may or may not have been a Saturday, on what may have been March 1, in a house in this city that may have been this squat two-story white one belonging to Ahmad Abdul Qadoos, with big gray-headed crows barking in the front yard, the notorious terrorist Khalid Sheikh Mohammed was roughly awakened by a raiding party of Pakistani and American commandos. Anticipating a gunfight, they entered loud and fast. Instead they found him asleep. He was pulled from his bed, hooded, bound, hustled from the house, placed in a vehicle, and driven quickly away.

Here was the biggest catch yet in the war on terror. Sheikh Mohammed is considered the architect of two attempts on the World Trade Center: the one that failed, in 1993, and the one that succeeded so catastrophically, eight years later. He is also believed to have been behind the attacks on the U.S. embassies in Kenya and Tanzania in 1998, and on the USS *Cole* two years later, and behind the slaughter last year of *The Wall Street Journal* reporter Daniel Pearl, among other things. An intimate of Osama bin Laden's, Sheikh Mohammed has been called the operations chief of al-Qaeda, if such a formal role can be said to exist in such an informal organization. Others have suggested that a more apt designation might be al-Qaeda's "chief franchisee." Whatever the analogy, he is one of the terror organization's most important figures, a burly, distinctly modern, cosmopolitan thirty-seven-year-old man fanatically devoted to a medieval form of Islam. He was born to Pakistani parents, raised in Kuwait, and educated in North Carolina to be an engineer before he returned to the Middle East to build a career of bloody mayhem.

Some say that Sheikh Mohammed was captured months before the March 1 date announced by Pakistan's Inter-Services Intelligence (ISI). Abdul Qadoos, a pale, white-bearded alderman in this well-heeled neighborhood, told me that Sheikh Mohammed was not there "then or ever." The official video of the takedown appears to have been faked. But the details are of minor importance. Whenever, wherever, and however it happened, nearly everyone now agrees that Sheikh Mohammed is in U.S. custody, and has been for some time. In the first hours of his captivity the hood came off and a picture was taken. It shows a bleary-eyed, heavy, hairy, swarthy man with a full black mustache, thick eyebrows, a dark outline of beard on a rounded, shaved face, three chins, long sideburns, and a full head of dense, long, wildly mussed black hair. He stands before a pale tan wall whose paint is chipped, leaning slightly forward, like a man with his hands bound behind him, the low cut of his loose-fitting white T-shirt exposing matted curls of hair on his chest, shoulders, and back. He is looking down and to the right of the camera. He appears dazed and glum.

Sheikh Mohammed is a smart man. There is an anxious, searching quality to his expression in that first post-arrest photo. It is the look of a man awakened into nightmare. Everything that has given his life meaning, his role as husband and father, his leadership, his stature, plans, and ambitions, is finished. His future is months, maybe years, of imprisonment and interrogation; a military tribunal; and almost certain execution. You can practically see the wheels turning in his head, processing his terminal predicament. How will he spend the last months and years? Will he maintain a dignified, defiant silence? Or will he succumb to this enemy and betray his friends, his cause, and his faith?

If Sheikh Mohammed felt despair in those first hours, it didn't show. According to a Pakistani officer who sat in on an initial ISI questioning, the al-Qaeda sub-boss seemed calm and stoic. For his first two days in custody he said nothing beyond confirming his name. A CIA official says that Sheikh Mohammed spent those days "sitting in a trancelike state and reciting verses from the Koran." On the third day he is said to have loosened up. Fluent in the local languages of Urdu, Pashto, and Baluchi, he tried to shame his Pakistani interrogators, lecturing them on their responsibilities as Muslims and upbraiding them for cooperating with infidels.

"Playing an American surrogate won't help you or your country," he said. "There are dozens of people like me who will give their lives but won't let the Americans live in peace anywhere in the world." Asked if Osama bin Laden was alive, he said, "Of course he is alive." He spoke of meeting with bin Laden in a "mountainous border region" in December. He seemed smug about U.S. and British preparations for war against Saddam Hussein. "Let the Iraq War begin," he said. "The U.S. forces will be targeted inside their bases in the Gulf. I don't have any specific information, but my sixth sense is telling me that you will get the news from Saudi Arabia, Qatar, and Kuwait." Indeed, in the following months al-Qaeda carried out a murderous attack in Saudi Arabia.

On that third day, once more hooded, Sheikh Mohammed was driven to Chaklala Air Force base, in Rawalpindi, and turned over to U.S. forces. From there he was flown to the CIA interrogation center in Bagram, Afghanistan, and from there, some days later, to an "undisclosed location" (a place the CIA calls "Hotel California") — presumably a facility in another cooperative nation, or perhaps a specifically designed prison aboard an aircraft carrier. It doesn't much matter where, because the place would not have been familiar or identifiable to him. Place and time, the anchors of sanity, were about to come unmoored. He might as well have been entering a new dimension, a strange new world where his every word, move, and sensation would be monitored and measured; where things might be as they seemed but might not; where there would be no such thing as day or night, or normal patterns of eating and drinking, wakefulness and sleep; where hot and cold, wet and dry, clean and dirty, truth and lies, would all be tangled and distorted.

Intelligence and military officials would talk about Sheikh Mohammed's state only indirectly, and conditionally. But by the time he arrived at a more permanent facility, he would already have been bone-tired, hungry, sore, uncomfortable, and afraid—if not for himself, then for his wife and children, who had been arrested either with him or some months before, depending on which story you believe. He would have been warned that lack of cooperation might mean being turned over to the more direct and brutal interrogators of some third nation. He would most likely have been locked naked in a cell with no trace of daylight. The space would be filled night and day with harsh light and noise, and would be so small that he would be unable to stand upright, to sit comfortably, or to recline fully. He would be kept awake, cold, and probably wet. If he managed to doze, he would be roughly awakened. He would be fed infrequently and irregularly, and then only with thin, tasteless meals. Sometimes days would go by between periods of questioning, sometimes only hours or minutes. The human mind craves routine, and can adjust to almost anything in the presence of it, so his jailers would take care that no semblance of routine developed.

Questioning would be intense—sometimes loud and rough, sometimes quiet and friendly, with no apparent reason for either. He would be questioned sometimes by one person, sometimes by two or three. The session might last for days, with interrogators taking turns, or it might last only a few minutes. He would be asked the same questions again and again, and then suddenly be presented with something completely unexpected—a detail or a secret that he would be shocked to find they knew. He would be offered the opportunity to earn freedom or better treatment for his wife and children. Whenever he was helpful and the information he gave proved true, his harsh conditions would ease. If the information proved false, his treatment would worsen. On occasion he might be given a drug to elevate his mood prior to interrogation; marijuana, heroin, and sodium pentothal have been shown to overcome a reluctance to speak, and methamphetamine can unleash a torrent of talk in the stubbornest subjects, the very urgency of the chatter making a complex lie impossible to sustain. These drugs could be administered surreptitiously with food or drink, and given the bleakness of his existence, they might even offer a brief period of relief and pleasure, thereby creating a whole new category of longing— and new leverage for his interrogators.

Deprived of any outside information, Sheikh Mohammed would grow more and more vulnerable to manipulation. For instance, intelligence gleaned after successful al-Qaeda attacks in Kuwait and Saudi Arabia might be fed to him, in bits and pieces, so as to suggest foiled operations. During questioning he would be startled regularly by details about his secret organization—details drawn from ongoing intelligence operations, new arrests, or the interrogation of other captive al-Qaeda members. Some of the information fed to him would be true, some of it false. Key associates might be said to be cooperating, or to have completely recanted their allegiance to *jihad*. As time went by, his knowledge would decay while that of his questioners improved. He might come to see once-vital plans as insignificant, or already known. The importance of certain secrets would gradually erode.

Isolated, confused, weary, hungry, frightened, and tormented, Sheikh Mohammed would gradually be reduced to a seething collection of simple needs, all of them controlled by his interrogators.

The key to filling all those needs would be the same: *to talk*.

SMACKY-FACE

We hear a lot these days about America's overpowering military technology; about the professionalism of its warriors; about the sophistication of its weaponry, eavesdropping, and telemetry; but right now the most vital weapon in its arsenal may well be the art of interrogation. To counter an enemy who relies on stealth and surprise, the most valuable tool is information, and often the only source of that information is the enemy himself. Men like Sheikh Mohammed who have been taken alive in this war are classic candidates for the most cunning practices of this dark art. Intellectual, sophisticated, deeply religious, and well trained, they present a perfect challenge for the interrogator. Getting at the information they possess could allow us to thwart major attacks, unravel their organization, and save thousands of lives. They and their situation pose one of the strongest arguments in modern times for the use of torture.

Torture is repulsive. It is deliberate cruelty, a crude and ancient tool of political oppression. It is commonly used to terrorize people, or to wring confessions out of suspected criminals who may or may not be guilty. It is the classic shortcut for a lazy or incompetent investigator. Horrifying examples of torturers' handiwork are cataloged and publicized annually by Amnesty International, Human Rights Watch, and other organizations that battle such abuses worldwide. One cannot help sympathizing with the innocent, powerless victims showcased in their literature. But professional terrorists pose a harder question. They are lockboxes containing potentially lifesaving information. Sheikh Mohammed has his own political and religious reasons for plotting mass murder, and there are those who would applaud his principled defiance in captivity. But we pay for his silence in blood.

The word "torture" comes from the Latin verb *torquere*, "to twist." *Webster's New World Dictionary* offers the following primary definition: "The inflicting of severe pain to force information and confession, get revenge, etc." Note the adjective "severe," which summons up images of the rack, thumbscrews, gouges, branding irons, burning pits, impaling devices, electric shock, and all the other devilish tools devised by human beings to mutilate and inflict pain on others. All manner of innovative cruelty is still commonplace, particularly in Central and South America, Africa, and the Middle East. Saddam Hussein's police force burned various marks into the foreheads of thieves and deserters, and routinely sliced tongues out of those whose words offended the state. In Sri Lanka prisoners are hung upside down and burned with hot irons. In China they are beaten with clubs and shocked with cattle prods. In India the police stick pins through the fingernails and fingers of prisoners. Maiming and physical abuse are legal in Somalia, Iran, Saudi Arabia, Nigeria, Sudan, and other countries that practice *sharia*; the hands of thieves are lopped off, and women convicted of adultery may be stoned to death. Governments around the world continue to employ rape and mutilation, and to harm family members, including children, in order to extort confessions or information from those in captivity. Civilized people everywhere readily condemn these things.

Then there are methods that, some people argue, fall short of torture. Called "torture lite," these include sleep deprivation, exposure to heat or cold, the use of drugs to cause confusion, rough treatment (slapping, shoving, or shaking), forcing a prisoner to stand for days at a time or to sit in uncomfortable positions, and playing on his fears for himself and his family. Although excruciating for the victim, these tactics generally leave no permanent marks and do no lasting physical harm.

The Geneva Convention makes no distinction: It bans any mistreatment of prisoners. But some nations that are otherwise committed to ending brutality have employed torture lite under what they feel are justifiable circumstances. In 1987 Israel attempted to codify a distinction between torture, which was banned, and "moderate physical pressure," which was permitted in special cases. Indeed, some police officers, soldiers, and intelligence agents who abhor "severe" methods believe that banning all forms of physical pressure would be dangerously naive. Few support the use of physical pressure to extract confessions, especially because victims will often say anything (to the point of falsely incriminating themselves) to put an end to pain. But many veteran interrogators believe that the use of such methods to extract information is justified if it could save lives—whether by forcing an enemy soldier to reveal his army's battlefield positions or forcing terrorists to betray the details of ongoing plots. As these interrogators see it, the well-being of the captive must be weighed against the lives that might be saved by forcing him to talk. A method that produces lifesaving information without doing lasting harm to anyone is not just preferable; it appears to be morally sound. Hereafter I will use "torture" to mean the more severe traditional outrages, and "coercion" to refer to torture lite, or moderate physical pressure.

There is no clear count of suspected terrorists now in U.S. custody. About 680 were detained at Camp X-Ray, the specially constructed prison at Guantánamo, on the southeastern tip of Cuba. Most of these are now considered mere foot soldiers in the Islamist movement, swept up in Afghanistan during the swift rout of the Taliban. They come from forty-two different nations. Scores of other detainees, considered leaders, have been or are being held at various locations around the world: in Pakistan, Saudi Arabia, Egypt, Sudan, Syria, Jordan, Morocco, Yemen, Singapore, the Philippines, Thailand, and Iraq, where U.S. forces now hold the top echelon of Saddam Hussein's dismembered regime. Some detainees are in disclosed prisons, such as the facility at Bagram and a camp on the island of Diego Garcia. Others—upper-tier figures such as Sheikh Mohammed, Abu Zubaydah, Abd al-Rashim al-Nashiri, Ramzi bin al-Shibh, and Tawfiq bin Attash—are being held at undisclosed locations.

It is likely that some captured terrorists' names and arrests have not yet been revealed; people may be held for months before their "arrests" are staged. Once a top-level suspect is publicly known to be in custody, his intelligence value falls. His organization scatters, altering its plans, disguises, cover stories, codes, tactics, and communication methods. The maximum opportunity for intelligence gathering comes in the first hours after an arrest, before others in a group can possibly know that their walls have been breached. Keeping an arrest quiet for days or weeks prolongs this opportunity. If March 1 was in fact the day of Sheikh Mohammed's capture, then the cameras and the headlines were an important intelligence failure. The arrest of the senior al-Qaeda figure Abu Anas Liby, in Sudan in February of 2002, was not made public until a month later, when U.S. efforts to have him transferred to custody in Egypt were leaked to the *Sunday Times* of London. So, again, there is no exact count of suspected terrorists in custody. In September of last year, testifying before the House and Senate Intelligence Committees, Cofer Black, the State Department's coordinator for counterterrorism, said that the number who have been detained was about 3,000.

All these subjects are questioned rigorously, but those in the top ranks get the full coercive treatment. And if official and unofficial government reports are to be believed, the methods work. In report after report hard-core terrorist leaders are said to be either cooperating or, at the very least, providing some information—not just vague statements but detailed, verifiable, useful intelligence. In late March, *Time* reported that Sheikh Mohammed had "given the U.S. interrogators the names and descriptions of about a dozen key al-Qaeda operatives believed to be plotting terrorist attacks on America and other western countries" and had "added crucial details to the descriptions of other suspects and filled in important gaps in what U.S. intelligence knows about al-Qaeda's practices." In June, news reports suggested that Sheikh Mohammed was discussing operational planning with his captors and had told interrogators that al-Qaeda did not work with Saddam Hussein. And according to a report in June of last year, Abu Zubaydah, who is said to be held in solitary confinement somewhere in Pakistan, provided information that helped foil a plot to detonate a radioactive bomb in the United States.

Secretary of Defense Donald Rumsfeld said in September of last year that interrogation of captured terrorist leaders had yielded "an awful lot of information" and had "made life an awful lot more difficult for an awful lot of folks." Indeed, if press accounts can be believed, these captured Islamist fanatics are all but dismantling their own secret organization. According to published reports, Sheikh Mohammed was found in part because of information from bin al-Shibh, whose arrest had been facilitated by information from Abu Zubaydah. Weeks after the sheikh's capture Bush administration officials and intelligence experts told *The Washington Post* that the al-Qaeda deputy's "cooperation under interrogation" had given them hopes of arresting or killing the rest of the organization's top leadership.

How much of this can be believed? Are such reports wishful

thinking, or deliberate misinformation? There is no doubt that intelligence agencies have scored big victories over al-Qaeda in the past two years, but there is no way to corroborate these stories. President Bush himself warned, soon after 9/11, that in war mode his administration would closely guard intelligence sources and methods. It would make sense to claim that top al-Qaeda leaders had caved under questioning even if they had not. Hard men like Abu Zubayhad, bin al-Shibh, and Sheikh Mohammed are widely admired in parts of the world. Word that they had been broken would demoralize their followers, and would encourage lower-ranking members of their organization to talk; if their leaders had given in, why should they hold out?

To some, all this jailhouse cooperation smells concocted. "I doubt we're getting very much out of them, despite what you read in the press," says a former CIA agent with experience in South America. "Everybody in the world knows that if you are arrested by the United States, nothing bad will happen to you."

Bill Cowan, a retired marine lieutenant colonel who conducted interrogations in Vietnam, says, "I don't see the proof in the pudding. If you had a top leader like Mohammed talking, someone who could presumably lay out the whole organization for you, I think we'd be seeing sweeping arrests in several different countries at the same time. Instead what we see is an arrest here, then a few months later an arrest there."

These complaints are all from people who have no qualms about using torture to get information from men like Sheikh Mohammed. Their concern is that merely using coercion amounts to handling terrorists with kid gloves. But the busts of al-Qaeda cells worldwide, and the continuing roundup of al-Qaeda leaders, suggest that some of those in custody are being made to talk. This worries people who campaign against all forms of torture. They believe that the rules are being ignored. Responding to rumors of mistreatment at Bagram and Guantánamo, Amnesty International and Human Rights Watch have written letters and met with Bush administration officials. They haven't been able to learn much.

Is the United States torturing prisoners? Three inmates have died in U.S. custody in Afghanistan, and reportedly eighteen prisoners at Guantánamo have attempted suicide; one prisoner there survived after hanging himself but remains unconscious and is not expected to revive. Shah Muhammad, a twenty-year-old Pakistani who was held at Camp X-Ray for eighteen months, told me that he repeatedly tried to kill himself in despair. "They were driving me crazy," he said. Public comments by administration officials have fueled further suspicion. An unnamed intelligence official told *The Wall Street Journal*, "What's needed is a little bit of smacky-face. Some al-Qaeda just need some extra encouragement." Then there was the bravado of Cofer Black, the counterterrorism coordinator, in his congressional testimony last year. A pudgy, balding, round-faced man with glasses, who had served with the CIA before taking the State Department position, Black refused to testify behind a screen, as others had done. "The American people need to see my face," he said. "I want to look the American people in the eye." By way of presenting his credentials he said that in 1995 a group of "Osama bin Laden's thugs" were caught planning "to kill me."

Describing the clandestine war, Black said, "This is a highly classified area. All I want to say is that there was 'before 9/11' and 'after 9/11.' After 9/11 the gloves came off." He was referring to the overall counterterrorism effort, but in the context of detained captives the line was suggestive. A story in December of 2002 by *The Washington Post* reporters Dana Priest and Barton Gellman described the use of "stress and duress" techniques at Bagram, and an article in *The New York Times* in March described the mistreatment of prisoners there. That month Irene Kahn, the secretary-general of Amnesty International, wrote a letter of protest to President Bush.

The treatment alleged falls clearly within the category of torture and other cruel, inhuman or degrading treatment or punishment which is absolutely prohibited under international law. . . . [We] urge the US government to instigate a full, impartial inquiry into the treatment of detainees at the Bagram base and to make the findings public. We further urge the government to make a clear public statement that torture and other cruel, inhuman or degrading treatment of suspects in its custody will not be tolerated under any circumstances, and that anyone found to have engaged in abuses will be brought to justice.

In June, at the urging of Amnesty and other groups, President Bush reaffirmed America's opposition to torture, saying, "I call on all governments to join with the United States and the community of law-abiding nations in prohibiting, investigating, and prosecuting all acts of torture . . . and we are leading this fight by example." A slightly more detailed response had been prepared two months earlier by the Pentagon's top lawyer, William J. Haynes II, in a letter to Kenneth Roth, the executive director of Human Rights Watch. (My requests for interviews on this subject with the Pentagon, the White House, and the State Department were declined.) Haynes wrote,

The United States questions enemy combatants to elicit information they may possess that could help the coalition win the war and forestall further terrorist attacks upon the citizens of the United States and other countries. As the President reaffirmed recently to the United Nations High Commissioner for Human Rights, United States policy condemns and prohibits torture. When questioning enemy combatants, US personnel are required to follow this policy and applicable laws prohibiting torture.

As we will see, Haynes's choice of words was careful—and telling. The human-rights groups and the administration are defining terms differently. Yet few would argue that getting Sheikh Mohammed to talk doesn't serve the larger interests of mankind. So before tackling the moral and legal questions raised by interrogation, perhaps the first question should be, What works?

ACID TESTS AND MONKEY ORGASMS

The quest for surefire methods in the art of interrogation has been long, ugly, and generally fruitless. Nazi scientists experimented on concentration-camp inmates, subjecting them to extremes of hot and cold, to drugs, and to raw pain in an effort to see what combination of horrors would induce cooperation. The effort produced a long list of dead and maimed, but no reliable ways of getting people to talk.

In 1953 John Lilly, of the National Institute of Mental Health, discovered that by placing electrodes inside the brain of a monkey, he could stimulate pain, anger, fear—and pleasure. He placed one inside the brain of a male monkey and gave the monkey a switch that would trigger an immediate erection and orgasm. (The monkey hit the switch roughly every three minutes, thus confirming the gender stereotype.) The idea of manipulating a brain from the inside promptly attracted the interest of the CIA, which foresaw, among other things, the possibility of sidestepping a reluctant informant's self-defenses. But Lilly dropped the line of research, pointing out that merely inserting the electrodes caused brain damage.

These experiments and others are recorded in detail in John Marks's somewhat overheated book *The Search for the "Manchurian Candidate": The CIA and Mind Control* (1979) and in George Andrews's book *MKULTRA: The CIA's Top Secret Program in Human Experimentation and Behavior Modification* (2001). Andrews summarized information revealed in congressional probes of CIA excesses. Marks was more sensational. In the spirit of the times, he tended to interpret the agency's interest in behavioral science, hypnosis, and mind-altering drugs as a scheme to create zombielike secret agents, although it appears that the real goal was to make people talk.

There was a lot of hope for LSD. Discovered by accident in a Swiss pharmaceutical lab in 1943, it produced powerful mindaltering effects in very small doses. It was more powerful than mescaline, which had its own adherents, and could easily be administered without the victim's knowledge, slipped into food or drink. The hope was than an informant in such an artificially openminded state would lose sight of his goals and sense of loyalty and become putty in the hands of a skilled interrogator. Studies on LSD began at a number of big universities, and as word of the drug's properties spread, it started to attract a broad range of interest. Theologians, scholars, and mental-health workers visited the Maryland Psychiatric Research Institute, just outside Baltimore, to turn on and tune in, and similar programs began in Boston, New York, Chicago, and other cities. Almost twenty years ago I interviewed a number of those who took part in these experiments; all of them were apparently motivated only by professional curiosity. The CIA's role was kept quiet. But the most notorious of its efforts at LSD experimentation involved Frank Olson, an army scientist who was dosed without his knowledge and subsequently committed suicide. The U.S. Army conducted field tests of LSD as an interrogation tool in 1961 (Operation Third Chance), dosing nine foreigners and an American soldier named James Thornwell, who had been accused of stealing classified documents. Thornwell subsequently sued the government and was awarded $650,000. Most of these efforts led to little more than scandal and embarrassment. The effects of the drug were too widely unpredictable to make it useful in interrogation. It tended to amplify the sorts of feelings that inhibit cooperation. Fear and anxiety turned into terrifying hallucinations and fantasies, which made it more difficult to elicit secrets, and added a tinge of unreality to whatever information was divulged. LSD may have unlocked the mind in some esoteric sense, but secrets tended to ride out the trip intact.

Experiments were also conducted with heroin and psychedelic mushrooms, neither of which reliably delivered up the secrets of men's souls. Indeed, drugs seemed to enhance some people's ability to be deceptive. Scopolamine held out some early hope, but it often induced hallucinations. Barbiturates were promising, and were already used effectively by psychiatrists to help with therapy. Some researchers advocated electroshock treatments, to, as it were, blast information from a subject's brain. Drugs such as marijuana, alcohol, and sodium pentothal can lower inhibitions, but they do not erase deep-seated convictions. And the more powerful the drug, the less reliable the testimony. According to my intelligence sources, drugs are today sometimes used to assist in critical interrogations, and the preferred ones are methamphetamines tempered with barbiturates and cannibis. These tools can help, but they are only as effective as the interrogator.

Better results seemed to come from sensory deprivation and solitary confinement. For most people severe sensory deprivation quickly becomes misery; the effects were documented in the notorious 1963 CIA manual on interrogation, called the *Kubark Manual*. It remains the most comprehensive and detailed explanation in print of coercive methods of questioning—given the official reluctance to discuss these matters or put them in writing, because such things tend to be both politically embarrassing and secret. Treatises on interrogation in the public domain are written primarily for police departments and address the handling of criminal defendants—with all necessary concern for protecting a defendant's rights. Unearthed in 1997, through the Freedom of Information Act, by *The Baltimore Sun* reporters Gary Cohn, Ginger Thompson, and Mark Matthews, the *Kubark Manual* reveals the CIA's insights into the tougher methods employed by the military and intelligence agencies. Much of the practice and theory it details is also found unchanged in the 1983 *Human Resource Exploitation Training Manual*, usually known as the *Honduras Manual*—which the CIA had tried to soften with a hasty edit prior to releasing it. The manual was shaken loose at the same time by Cohn and Thompson. And the more summary discussions of technique in later U.S. Army manuals on interrogation, including the most recent, also clearly echo *Kubark*. If there is a bible of interrogation, it is the *Kubark Manual*.

The manual cites a 1954 study at the National Institute of Mental Health (again led by John Lilly) in which two volunteers attempted to see how long they could stay suspended in water wearing blackout masks and hearing only the sound of their own breathing and "some faint sounds of water from the piping." Neither lasted more than three hours. According to the study, "Both passed quickly from normally directed thinking through a tension resulting from unsatisfied hunger for sensory stimuli and concentration upon the few available sensations to provide reveries and fantasies and eventually to visual imagery somewhat resembling hallucinations." John Marks reported in his book that in a similar experiment a volunteer kicked his way out of a sensory-deprivation box after an hour of tearful pleas for release had been ignored.

The summary of another experiment concluded,

The results confirmed earlier findings. 1) The deprivation of sensory stimuli induces stress; 2) the stress becomes unbearable for most subjects; 3) the subject has a growing need for physical and social stimuli; and 4) some subjects progressively lose touch with reality, focus inwardly, and produce delusions, hallucinations, and other pathological effects.

But these effects didn't trouble everyone. One man's misery is another man's mind-altering experience. Some people found they liked sensory-deprivation tanks; indeed, in later years people would pay for a session in one. Lilly was fond of injecting himself with LSD and then closing himself off in his tank—a series of experiments made famous in the 1980 film *Altered States*. In Canada a scientist put a fifty-two-year-old woman identified only as Mary C. in a sensory-deprivation chamber for thirty-five days. She never asked to be let out.

One thing all these experiments made clear was that no matter what drugs or methods were applied, the results varied from person to person. So another major area of inquiry involved trying to define certain broad personality types and discover what methods would work best for each. The groups were ridiculously general—the *Kubark Manual* lists "the Orderly-Obstinate Character," "the Greedy-Demanding Character," "the Anxious, Self-Centered Character"—and the prescriptions for questioning them tended to vary little and were sometimes silly (the advice for questioning an Orderly-Obstinate Character recommends doing so in a room that is especially neat). The categories were useless. Everyone, and every situation, is different; some people begin a day greedy and demanding and end it orderly and obstinate.

The one constant in effective interrogation, it seems, is the interrogator. And some interrogators are just better at it than others.

"You want a good interrogator?" Jerry Giorgio, the New York Police Department's legendary third-degree man, asks. "Give me somebody who people like, and who likes people. Give me somebody who knows how to put people at ease. Because the more comfortable they are, the more they talk, and the more they talk, the more trouble they're in—the harder it is to sustain a lie."

Though science has made contributions, interrogation remains more art than science. Like any other subject, Sheikh Mohammed presented his interrogators with a unique problem. The critical hub of a worldwide secret network, he had a potential road map in his head to the whole shadow world of *jihad.* If he could be made to talk, to reveal even a few secrets, what an intelligence bonanza that would be! Here was a man who lived to further his cause by whatever means, who saw himself as morally, spiritually, and intellectually superior to the entire infidel Western world, a man for whom capitulation meant betraying not just his friends and his cherished cause but his very soul.

What makes a man like that decide to talk?

ALLIGATOR CLIPS

Bill Cowan spent three and a half years fighting the war in Vietnam. He was a young marine captain assigned to the Rung Sat Special Zone, a putrid swamp that begins just south of Saigon. Miles and miles of thick, slurping mud that swallowed soldiers to their waists, it is populated by galaxies of mosquitoes and other biting insects, snakes, crocodiles, and stands of rotting mangrove. It is intersected by the saltwater rivers of the Mekong Delta, and features occasional stretches of flat, open farmland. The marines knew that several battalions of Vietcong were in the Rung Sat. The enemy would lie low, building strength, and then launch surprise attacks on South Vietnamese or U.S. troops. The soldiers in Cowan's unit played cat-and-mouse with an enemy that melted away at their approach.

So when he captured a Vietcong soldier who could warn of ambushes and lead them to hidden troops but who refused to speak, wires were attached to the man's scrotum with alligator clips and electricity was cranked out of a 110-volt generator.

"It worked like a charm," Cowan told me. "The minute the

crank started to turn, he was ready to talk. We never had to do more than make it clear we could deliver a jolt. It was the fear more than the pain that made them talk."

Fear works. It is more effective than any drug, tactic, or torture device. According to unnamed scientific studies cited by the *Kubark Manual* (it is frightening to think what these experiments might have been), most people cope with pain better than they think they will. As people become more familiar with pain, they become conditioned to it. Those who have suffered more physical pain than others—from being beaten frequently as a child, for example, or suffering a painful illness—may adapt to it and come to fear it less. So once the interrogators resort to actual torture, they are apt to lose ground.

"The threat of coercion usually weakens or destroys resistance more effectively than coercion itself," the manual says.

The threat to inflict pain, for example, can trigger fears more damaging than the immediate sensation of pain. . . . Sustained long enough, a strong fear of anything vague or unknown induces regression, whereas the materialization of the fear, the infliction of some form of punishment, is likely to come as a relief. The subject finds that he can hold out, and his resistances are strengthened.

Furthermore, if a prisoner is subjected to pain after other methods have failed, it is a signal that the interrogation process may be nearing an end. "He may then decide that if he can just hold out against this final assault, he will win the struggle and his freedom," the manual concludes. Even if severe pain does elicit information, it can be false, which is particularly troublesome to interrogators seeking intelligence rather than a confession. Much useful information is time-sensitive, and running down false leads or arresting innocents wastes time.

By similar logic, the manual discourages threatening a prisoner with death. As a tactic "it is often found to be worse than useless," the manual says, because the sense of despair it induces can make the prisoner withdraw into depression—or, in some cases, see an honorable way out of his predicament.

Others disagree.

"I'll tell you how to make a man talk," a retired Special Forces officer says. "You shoot the man to his left and the man to his right. Then you can't shut him up."

John Dunn found the truth to be a little more complicated. In his case the threat of execution forced him to bend but not break. He was a U.S. Army intelligence officer in the Lam Dong Province of Vietnam, in March of 1968, when he was captured by the Vietcong. He and other captives were marched for weeks to a prison camp in the jungle, where initially he was treated quite well. The gentle treatment lulled him, Dunn says, and contributed to his shock when, in his first interrogation session, he was calmly told, 'We don't need you. We did not sign the Geneva Convention, and you are not considered a prisoner of war anyway. You are a war criminal. If you don't cooperate with us, you will be executed."

He was sent back to his hammock to think things over. Dunn had never considered himself a superaggressive soldier, a "warrior type," and had never imagined himself in such a situation. His training for captivity had been basic. He had been instructed to tell his captors only his name, rank, and serial number. Anything beyond that was considered a breach of duty—a betrayal of his country, his role as a soldier, and his personal honor. Faced with death, Dunn weighed his devotion to this simple code. He felt it was unrealistic. He wrestled to come up with a solution that would keep him alive without completely compromising his dignity. He figured there were certain details about his life and service that were not worth dying to protect. Some things needed to be kept secret, and others did not. Struggling with shame, he decided to answer any questions that did not intrude on that closed center of secrecy. He would not tell them he was an intelligence officer. ("Not out of patriotism," he says. "Out of fear, strictly self-preservation.") He would not reveal accurate details about fortifications around his company's headquarters, in Di Linh. He would not tell them about upcoming plans, such as the Phoenix Program (an assassination program targeting Vietcong village leaders), and above all, he would not make any public statements. But he would talk. The threat of execution in his case was not "worse than useless." It shook Dunn to his core.

In a subsequent session he talked, but not enough to satisfy his captors. Again and again he refused to make a public statement. Starved, sore, and still frightened, Dunn was told, "You will be executed. After dark."

When the sun set, the interrogator, his aide, and the camp commander came for Dunn with a group of soldiers. They unlocked his chain, and he carried it as they led him away from the encampment into the jungle. They stopped in front of a pit they had dug for his grave and put a gun to his head. The interrogator gave him one more chance to agree to make a statement.

"No," Dunn said. He had gone as far as he was willing to go.

"Why do you want to die?" he was asked.

"If I must, I must," Dunn said. He felt resigned. He waited to be killed.

"You will not be executed," the camp commander said abruptly, and that was that.

Judging by Dunn's experience, the threat of death may be valuable to an interrogator as a way of loosening up a determined subject. But, as with pain, the most important factor is fear. An unfrightened prisoner makes an unlikely informer.

. . .

If there is an archetype of the modern interrogator, it is Michael Koubi. The former chief interrogator for Israel's General Security Services, or Shabak, Koubi probably has more experience than anyone else in the world in the interrogation of hostile Arab prisoners, some of them confirmed terrorists and religious fanatics — men, he says, "whose hatred of the Jews is unbridgeable." He has blue eyes in a crooked face: time, the greatest caricaturist of all, has been at work on it for more than sixty years, and has produced one that is lean, browned, deeply lined, and naturally concave. His considerable nose has been broken twice, and now ends well to the right of where it begins, giving him a look that is literally off-center. His wisdom, too, is slightly off-center, because Koubi has been given a uniquely twisted perspective on human nature. For decades he has been experimenting with captive human beings, cajoling, tricking, hurting, threatening, and spying on them, steadily upping the pressure, looking for cracks at the seams.

I met Koubi at his home on the beach in Ashkelon, just a short drive north of the border with the Gaza Strip, in whose prisons he worked for much of his career. His is comfortably retired from his Shabak job now, a grandfather three times over, and works for the municipal Inspection and Sanitation Department. There are still many things he is not free to discuss, but he is happy to talk about his methods. He is very proud of his skills, among them an ability to speak Arabic so fluently that he can adopt a multitude of colloquial flavors. Koubi came to his career as an interrogator through his love of language. He grew up speaking Hebrew, Yiddish, and Arabic, and he studied Arabic in high school, working to master its idiom and slang. He also had a knack for reading the body language and facial expressions of his subjects, and for sensing a lie. He is a skilled actor who could alternately befriend or intimidate a subject, sometimes turning on a dime. Blending these skills with the tricks he had learned over the years for manipulating people,

Koubi didn't just question his subjects, he orchestrated their emotional surrender.

To many, including many in Israel, Koubi and the unit he headed are an outrage. The games they played and the tactics they employed are seen as inhumane, illegal, and downright evil. It is hard to picture this pleasant grandfather as the leader of a unit that critics accuse of being brutal; but then, charm has always been as important to interrogation work as toughness or cruelty—perhaps more important. Koubi says that only in rare instances did he use force to extract information from his subjects; in most cases it wasn't necessary.

"People change when they get to prison," Koubi says. "They may be heroes outside, but inside they change. The conditions are different. People are afraid of the unknown. They are afraid of being tortured, of being held for a long time. Try to see what it is like to sit with a hood over your head for four hours, when you are hungry and tired and afraid, when you are isolated from everything and have no clue what is going on." When the captive believes that *anything* could happen—torture, execution, indefinite imprisonment, even the persecution of his loved ones—the interrogator can go to work.

Under pressure, he says, nearly everyone looks out first and foremost for number one. What's more, a very large part of who a man is depends on his circumstances. No matter who he is before his arrest, his sense of self will blur in custody. Isolation, fear, and deprivation force a man to retreat, to reorient himself, and to reorder his priorities. For most men, Koubi says, the hierarchy of loyalty under stress is 1) self, 2) group, 3) family, 4) friends. In other words, even the most dedicated terrorist (with very rare exceptions), when pushed hard enough, will act to preserve and protect himself at the expense of anyone or anything else. "There's an old Arab saying," Koubi says. "Let one hundred mothers cry, but not my mother—but better my mother than me."

With older men the priorities shift slightly. In middle age the family often overtakes the group (the cause) to become the second most important loyalty. Young men tend to be fiercely committed and ambitious, but older men—even men with deeply held convictions, men admired and emulated by their followers—tend to have loves and obligations that count for more. Age frays idealism, slackens zeal, and cools ferocity. Abstractions lose ground to wife, children, and grandchildren. "Notice that the leaders of Hamas do not send their own sons and daughters, and their own grandchildren, to blow themselves up," Koubi says.

So it is often the top-level men, like Sheikh Mohammed, who are easier to crack. Koubi believes that having the al-Qaeda leader's wife and children in custody gives his interrogators powerful leverage. The key is to find a man's weak point and exploit it.

For Koubi the three critical ingredients of that process are preparation, investigation, and theater.

Preparing a subject for interrogation means softening him up. Ideally, he has been pulled from his sleep—like Sheikh Mohammed—early in the morning, roughly handled, bound, hooded (a coarse, dirty, smelly sack serves the purpose perfectly), and kept waiting in discomfort, perhaps naked in a cold, wet room, forced to stand or to sit in an uncomfortable position. He may be kept awake for days prior to questioning, isolated and ill-fed. He may be unsure where he is, what time of day it is, how long he has been or will be held. If he is wounded, as Abu Zubaydah was, pain medication may be withheld; it is one thing to cause pain, another to refuse to relieve it.

Mousa Khoury, a Palestinian businessman, knows the drill all too well. A slender thirty-four-year-old man with a black goatee and thinning hair, he is bitter about the Israeli occupation and his experiences in custody. He has been arrested and interrogated six times by Israeli forces. He was once held for seventy-one days.

"My hands were cuffed behind my back, and a potato sack was over my head," he says. "My legs were cuffed to a tiny chair. The chair's base is ten centimeters by twenty centimeters. The back is ten centimeters by ten centimeters. It is hard wood. The front legs are shorter than the back ones, so you are forced to slide forward in it, only your hands are bound in the back. If you sit back, the back of the chair digs into the small of your back. If you slump forward, you are forced to hang by your hands. It is painful. They will take you to the toilet only after screaming a request one hundred times." He could think about only one thing: how to make the treatment stop. "Your thoughts go back and forth and back and forth, and you can no longer have a normal stream of consciousness," he says.

Preparing an interrogator means arming him beforehand with every scrap of information about his subject. U.S. Army interrogation manuals suggest preparing a thick "dummy file" when little is known, to make it appear that the interrogator knows more than he does. Nothing rattles a captive more than to be confronted with a fact he thought was secret or obscure. It makes the interrogator seem powerful, all-knowing. A man's sense of importance is wounded, and he is slower to lie, because he thinks he might be caught at it. There are many ways that scraps of information — gathered by old-fashioned legwork or the interrogation of a subject's associates — can be leveraged by a clever interrogator into something new. Those scraps might be as simple as knowing the names of a man's siblings or key associates, the name of his girlfriend, or a word or phrase that has special meaning to his group. Uncovering privileged details diminishes the aura of a secret society, whether it is a social club, a terrorist cell, or a military unit. Joining such a group makes an individual feel distinct, important, and superior, and invests even the most mundane of his activities with meaning. An interrogator who penetrates that secret society, unraveling its shared language, culture, history, customs, plans, and pecking order, can diminish its hold on even the staunchest believer. Suspicion that a trusted comrade has betrayed the group—or the subject himself—undermines the sense of a secretly shared purpose and destiny. Armed with a few critical details, a skilled interrogator can make a subject doubt the value of information he has been determined to withhold. It is one thing to suffer in order to protect a secret, quite another to cling to a secret that is already out. This is how a well-briefed interrogator breaches a group's defenses.

Koubi believes that the most important skill for an interrogator is to know the prisoner's language. Working through interpreters is at best a necessary evil. Language is at the root of all social connections, and plays a critical role in secret societies like Hamas and al-Qaeda. A shared vocabulary or verbal shorthand helps to cement the group.

"I try to create the impression that I use his mother tongue even better than he does," Koubi says. "No accent, no mistaken syntax. I speak to him like his best friend speaks to him. I might ask him a question about a certain word or sentence or expression, how it is used in his culture, and then demonstrate that I know more about it than he does. This embarrasses him very much."

Once a prisoner starts to talk, rapid follow-up is needed to sort fact from fiction, so that the interrogator knows whether his subject is being cooperative or evasive, and can respond accordingly. Interrogation sessions should be closely observed (many rooms designed for this purpose have one-way mirrors), and in a well-run unit a subject's words can sometimes be checked out before the session is over. Being caught so quickly in a lie demonstrates the futility of playing games with the interrogator, and strengthens his hand. It shames and rattles the subject. When information checks out, the interrogator can home in for more details and open up new avenues of exploration.

Religious extremists are the hardest cases. They ponder in their own private space, performing a kind of self-hypnosis. They are usually well educated. Their lives are financially and emotionally tidy. They tend to live in an ascetic manner, and to look down on nonbelievers. They tend to be physically and mentally strong, and not to be influenced by material things—by either the incentives or the disincentives available in prison. Often the rightness of their cause trumps all else, so they can commit any outrage—lie, cheat, steal, betray, kill—without remorse. Yet under sufficient duress, Koubi says, most men of even this kind will eventually break—most, but not all. Some cannot be broken.

"They are very rare," he says, "but in some cases the more aggressive you get, and the worse things get, the more these men will withdraw into their own world, until you cannot reach them."

Mousa Khoury, the Palestinian businessman who has been interrogated six times, claims that he never once gave in to his jailers. Koubi has no particular knowledge of Khoury's case, but he smiles his crooked, knowing smile and says, "If someone you meet says he was held by our forces and did not cooperate at all, you can bet he is lying. In some cases men who are quite famous for their toughness were the most helpful to us in captivity."

Interrogation is also highly theatrical. The *Kubark Manual* is very particular about setting the stage.

The room in which the interrogation is to be conducted should be free of distractions. The colors of the walls, ceiling, rugs, and furniture should not be startling. Pictures should be missing or dull. Whether the furniture should include a desk depends not upon the interrogator's convenience but rather upon the subject's anticipated reaction to the connotations of superiority and officialdom. A plain table may be preferable. An overstuffed chair for the use of the interrogatee is sometimes preferable to a straight-backed, wooden chair because if he is made to stand for a lengthy period or is otherwise deprived of physical comfort, the contrast is intensified and increased disorientation results.

The manual goes on to recommend lighting that shines brightly in the face of the subject and leaves the interrogator in shadow. There should be no phone or any other means of contact with those outside the room, to enhance concentration and the subject's feeling of confinement. In Koubi's experience it was sometimes helpful to have associates loudly stage a torture or beating session in the next room. In old CIA interrogation training, according to Bill Wagner, a retired agent, it was recommended that mock executions take place outside the interrogation room.

A good interrogator is a deceiver. One of Koubi's tricks was to walk into a hallway lined with twenty recently arrested, hooded, uncomfortable, hungry, and fearful men, all primed for interrogation, and shout commandingly, "Okay, who wants to cooperate with me?" Even if no hands, or only one hand, went up, he would say to the hooded men, "Okay, good. Eight of you. I'll start with you, and the others will have to wait." Believing that others have capitulated makes doing so oneself much easier. Often, after this trick, many of the men in the hall would cooperate. Men are herd animals, and prefer to go with the flow, especially when moving in the other direction is harsh.

In one case Koubi had information suggesting that two men he was questioning were secretly members of a terrorist cell, and knew of an impending attack. They were tough men, rural farmers, very difficult to intimidate or pressure, and so far neither man had admitted anything under questioning. Koubi worked them over individually for hours. With each man he would start off by asking friendly questions and then grow angrier and angrier, accusing the subject of withholding something. He would slap him, knock him off his chair, set guards on him, and then intervene to pull them off. Then he would put the subject back in the chair and offer him a cigarette, lightening the mood. "Let him see the difference between the two atmospheres, the hostile one and the friendly one," Koubi says. Neither man budged.

Finally Koubi set his trap. He announced to one of the men that his interrogation was over. The man's associate, hooded, was seated in the hallway outside the room. "We are going to release you," Koubi said. "We are pleased with your cooperation. But first you must do something for me. I am going to ask you a series of questions, just a formality, and I need you to answer 'Yes' in a loud, clear voice for the recorder." Then, in a voice loud enough for the hooded man outside in the hall to hear, but soft enough so that he couldn't make out exactly what was being said, Koubi read off a long list of questions, reviewing the prisoner's name, age, marital status, date of capture, length of detainment, and so forth. These were regularly punctuated by the prisoner's loud and cooperative "Yes." The charade was enough to convince the man in the hall that his friend had capitulated.

Koubi dismissed the first man and brought in the second. "There's no more need for me to question you," Koubi said. "Your friend has confessed the whole thing." He offered the second prisoner a cigarette and gave him a good meal. He told him that the information provided by his friend virtually ensured that they would both be in prison for the rest of their lives . . . unless, he said, the second prisoner could offer him something, anything, that would dispose the court to leniency in his case. Convinced that his friend had already betrayed them both, the second prisoner acted promptly to save himself. "If you want to save Israeli lives, go immediately," he told Koubi. "My friends went with a car to Yeshiva Nehalim [a religious school]. They are going to kidnap a group of students. . . ." The men were found in Erez, and the operation was foiled.

There are other methods of keeping a prisoner confused and off balance, such as rapidly firing questions at him, cutting off his responses in mid-sentence, asking the same questions over and over in different order, and what the manual calls the "Silent" technique, in which the interrogator "says nothing to the source, but looks him squarely in the eye, preferably with a slight smile on his face." The manual advises forcing the subject to break eye contact first. "The source will become nervous, begin to shift around in his chair, cross and recross his legs, and look away," the manual says. "When the interrogator is ready to break silence, he may do so with some quite nonchalant questions such as 'You planned this operation a long time, didn't you? Was it your idea?'"

Then there is "Alice in Wonderland."

> The aim of the Alice in Wonderland or confusion technique is to confound the expectations and conditioned reactions of the interrogatee. . . . The confusion technique is designed not only to obliterate the familiar but to replace it with the weird. . . . Sometimes two or more questions are asked simultaneously. Pitch, tone, and volume of the interrogators' voices are unrelated to the import of the questions. No pattern of questions and answers is permitted to develop, nor do the questions themselves relate logically to each other.

If this technique is pursued patiently, the manual says, the subject will start to talk "just to stop the flow of babble which assails him." Easily the most famous routine is "Good Cop/Bad Cop," in which one interrogator becomes the captive's persecutor and the other his friend. A lesser-known but equally effective technique is "Pride and Ego," "Ego Up/Ego Down," or (as the more pretentious *Kubark Manual* puts it) "Spinoza and Mortimer Snerd," in which the "Ego Down" part involves repeatedly asking questions that the interrogator knows the subject cannot answer. The subject is continually berated or threatened ("How could you not know the answer to that?") and accused of withholding, until, at long last, he is asked a simple question that he can answer. An American POW subjected to this technique has said, "I know it seems strange now, but I was positively grateful to them when they switched to a topic I knew something about."

CIA psychologists have tried to develop an underlying theory for interrogation—namely, that the coercive methods induce a gradual "regression" of personality. But the theory is not convincing. Interrogation simply backs a man into a corner. It forces difficult choices, and dangles illusory avenues of escape.

A skillful interrogator knows which approach will best suit his subject; and just as he expertly applies stress, he continually opens up these avenues of escape or release. This means understanding what, at heart, is stopping a subject from cooperating. If it is ego, that calls for one method. If it is fear of reprisal or of getting into deeper trouble, another method might work best. For most captives a major incentive to keep quiet is simply pride. Their manhood is being tested, not just their loyalty and conviction. Allowing the subject to save face lowers the cost of capitulation, so an artful interrogator will offer persuasive rationales for giving in: others already have, or the information is already known. Drugs, if administered with the subject's knowledge, are helpful in this regard. If a subject believes that a particular drug or "truth serum" renders him helpless, he is off the hook. He cannot be held accountable for giving in. A study cited in George Andrews's book *MKULTRA* found that a placebo—a simple sugar pill—was as effective as an actual drug up to half of the time.

Koubi layered his deception so thick that his subjects never knew exactly when their interrogation ended. After questioning, captives usually spent time in a regular prison. The Israelis had bugged the prison with a system that was disguised well enough to *appear* hidden but not well enough to avoid discovery. In this way prisoners were led to believe that only certain parts of the prison were bugged. In fact, all of the prison was bugged. Conversations between prisoners could be overheard anywhere, and were closely monitored. They were an invaluable source of intelligence. Prisoners who could hold out through the most intense interrogation often let their guard down later when talking to comrades in jail.

To help such inadvertent confessions along, Koubi had yet another card to play. Whenever an interrogated subject was released to the general prison, after weeks of often grueling questioning, he was received with open arms by fellow Palestinians who befriended him and congratulated him for having endured interrogation. He was treated like a hero. He was fed, nursed, even celebrated. What he didn't know was that his happy new comrades were working for Koubi.

Koubi calls them "birdies." They were Palestinians who, offered an incentive such as an opportunity to settle with their families in another country, had agreed to cooperate with Shabak. Some days or weeks after welcoming the new prisoner into their ranks, easing his transition into the prison, they would begin to ask questions. They would debrief the prisoner on his interrogation sessions. They would say, "It is very important for those on the outside to know what you told the Israelis and what you *didn't* tell them. Tell us, and we will get the information to those on the outside who need to know." Even prisoners who had managed to keep important secrets from Koubi spilled them to his birdies.

"The amazing thing is that by now the existence of the birdies is well known," Koubi says, "and yet the system still works. People come out of interrogation, go into the regular prison, and then tell their darkest secrets. I don't know why it still works, but it does."

BIG DADDY UPTOWN

Most professional interrogators work without the latitude given the CIA, the FBI, or the military in the war on terror. A policeman's subjects all have to be read their Miranda rights, and cops who physically threaten or abuse suspects—at least nowadays—may find themselves in jail. Jerry Giorgio, the legendary NYPD interrogator, has operated within these rules for nearly forty years. He may not know all the names of the CIA and military techniques, but he has probably seen most of them at work. Known as "Big Daddy Uptown," Giorgio now works for the New York County district attorney in a cramped office in Lower Manhattan that he shares with two others. He is a big man with a big voice, thinning gray hair, a broad belly, and wide, searching greenish-brown eyes. He is considered a wizard by his former colleagues in the NYPD. "All of us of a certain generation came out of the Jerry Giorgio school of interrogation," says John Bourges, a recently retired Manhattan homicide detective.

"Everybody knows the Good Cop/Bad Cop routine, right?" Giorgio says. "Well, I'm always the Good Cop. I don't work with a Bad Cop, either. Don't need it. You want to know the truth? The truth is—and this is important—everybody down deep *wants* to tell his or her story. It's true. No matter how damaging it is to them, no matter how important it is for them to keep quiet, they want to tell their story. If they feel guilty, they want to get it off their chest. If they feel justified in what they did, they want to explain themselves. I tell them, 'Hey, I know what you did and I can prove it. Now what are you going to do about it? If you show remorse, if you help me out, I'll go to bat for you.' I tell them that. And if you give them half a reason to do it, they'll tell you everything."

The most important thing is to get them talking. The toughest suspects are those who clam up and demand a lawyer right at the start. Giorgio believes that once he gets a suspect talking, the stream of words will eventually flow right to the truth. One murderer gave him three voluntary statements in a single day, each one signed, each one different, each one slightly closer to the truth.

The murderer was Carlos Martinez, a hulking former football player who in May of 1992 killed his girlfriend, Cheryl Maria Wright, and dumped her body in New York, right at the Coliseum overlook off the Henry Hudson Parkway. Since many young female murder victims are killed by their boyfriends, Giorgio started looking for Wright's. Martinez phoned Giorgio when he heard that the detective wanted to ask him some questions. Giorgio had pictures of Wright with Martinez, and in all the pictures the young beau had a giant head of Jheri curls. But he showed up in Giorgio's office bald. The detective was immediately more suspicious; a man who worries that somebody might have seen him commit a crime generally tries to alter his appearance.

Here is how Giorgio summarizes what turned out to be a very long and fruitful conversation:

"I was at home last night," Martinez said. "She did call me."

"Really, why?"

"She wanted me to pick her up. I told her, 'I'm watching the Mets game; I can't pick you up.'"

That was it. Giorgio acted very pleased with this statement, thanked Martinez, wrote it up, and asked the young man to sign it. Martinez did.

Then Giorgio stared at the statement and gave Martinez a quizzical look.

"You know, Carlos, something about this statement doesn't look right to me. You two had been going out for, what? Seven years? She calls you and asks you to pick her up at night where she's just gotten off work. It's not a safe neighborhood, and you tell her no? You mean a ball game on TV was more important to you?"

The question was cunning. The detective knew that Martinez

was trying to make a good impression; he definitely didn't want to leave Giorgio with any unresolved issues to play in his mind. So it concerned him that his first statement didn't sound right. Giorgio's question also touched Martinez's sense of chivalry, an important quality for many Hispanic men. It wouldn't do to be seen as ungentlemanly. Here was a young woman who had just been brutally killed. How would it look to her family and friends if he admitted that she had called and asked him for a ride and he had left her to her fate— for a ball game on TV? The question also subtly suggested an out: The neighborhood wasn't safe. People got hurt or killed in that neighborhood all the time. Maybe Martinez could admit that he had seen Cheryl on the night of the murder without directly implicating himself. No one ever accused the former footballer of being especially bright. He rose to Giorgio's bait immediately.

He said, "Jerry, let me tell you what really happened." ("Note," Giorgio says proudly, "already I'm *Jerry!*") Martinez now said that he had left his place to pick Wright up after work, but they had gotten into an argument. "She got mad at me and told me she didn't need a ride, so I waited until she got on the bus, and then I left." ("Look, now he's the picture of chivalry!" Giorgio says happily.)

"Let me take that down," Giorgio said, again acting pleased with the statement. He wrote it out neatly and asked Martinez to look it over and sign it. Martinez did.

Again Giorgio squinted at the paper. "You know, Carlos, something is still not right here. Cheryl was a strikingly beautiful girl. People who saw her remembered her. She's taken that bus home from work many nights, and people on that bus know who she is. And you know what? Nobody who rode that bus saw her on it last night."

(This was, in Giorgio's words, "pure bullshit." He hadn't talked to anybody who rode that bus. "Sometimes you have to just take a chance," he says.)

Again Martinez looked troubled. He had not allayed the detective's suspicions. So he tried again. "Okay, okay," he said. "This is really it. Let me tell you what really happened. Cheryl called, and I left to pick her up, but I ran into a friend of mine—I can't tell you his name—and we picked her up together. Then Cheryl and I got in this argument, a big fight. My friend got fed up. So we drove away, up Broadway to 181st Street, and stopped at the McDonald's there. He pulled out a gun, my friend, and he told me to get out of the car. 'Wait here,' he told me. 'I'm going to get rid of your problem.' Then he left. I waited. Then he came back. He said he had gotten rid of my problem."

Giorgio nodded happily and started to write up statement number three. He acted troubled over the fact that Martinez refused to name the friend, and the young man quickly coughed up a name. Giorgio's lieutenant, who had been watching the session through a one-way mirror, immediately got to work tracking down Martinez's friend. By the time the third statement had been written up, signed, and nestled neatly on top of the other two, Giorgio had a new problem to pose to Martinez: It seemed that his friend was in South Carolina, and had been for some time.

"We never did get to finish the fourth statement," Giorgio says. "Martinez's family had hired a lawyer, and he called the station forbidding us to further question his client." It was, of course, too late.

CAPTAIN CRUNCH VERSUS THE TREE HUGGERS

On a spring morning in the offices of Amnesty International, in Washington, D.C., Alistair Hodgett and Alexandra Arriaga were briefing me on their organization's noble efforts to combat torture wherever in the world it is found. They are bright, pleasant, smart, committed, attractive young people, filled with righteous purpose. Decent people everywhere agree on this: Torture is evil and indefensible.

But is it always?

I showed the two an article I had torn from that day's *New York Times*, which described the controversy over a tragic kidnapping case in Frankfurt, Germany. On September 27 of last year a Frankfurt law student kidnapped an eleven-year-old boy named Jakob von Metzler, whose smiling face appeared in a box alongside the story. The kidnapper had covered Jakob's mouth and nose with duct tape, wrapped the boy in plastic, and hidden him in a wooded area near a lake. The police captured the suspect when he tried to pick up ransom money, but the suspect wouldn't reveal where he had left the boy, who the police thought might still be alive. So the deputy police chief of Frankfurt, Wolfgang Daschner, told his subordinates to threaten the suspect with torture. According to the suspect, he was told that a "specialist" was being flown in who would "inflict pain on me of the sort I had never experienced." The suspect promptly told the police where he'd hidden Jakob, who, sadly, was found dead. The newspaper said that Daschner was under fire from Amnesty International, among other groups, for threatening torture.

"Under these circumstances," I asked, "do you honestly think it was wrong to even *threaten* torture?"

Hodgett and Arriaga squirmed in their chairs. "We recognize that there are difficult situations," said Arriaga, who is the group's director of government relations. "But we are opposed to torture under any and all circumstances, and threatening torture is inflicting mental pain. So we would be against it."

Few moral imperatives make such sense on a large scale but break down so dramatically in the particular. A way of sorting this one out is to consider two clashing sensibilities: the warrior and the civilian.

The civilian sensibility prizes above all else the rule of law. Whatever the difficulties posed by a particular situation, such as trying to find poor Jakob von Metzler before he suffocated, it sees abusive government power as a greater danger to society. Allowing an exception in one case (saving Jakob) would open the door to a greater evil.

The warrior sensibility requires doing what must be done to complete a mission. By definition, war exists because civil means have failed. What counts is winning, and preserving one's own troops. To a field commander in a combat zone, the life of an uncooperative enemy captive weighs very lightly against the lives of his own men. There are very few who, faced with a reluctant captive, would not in certain circumstances reach for the alligator clips, or something else.

"It isn't about getting mad, or payback," says Bill Cowan, the Vietnam interrogator. "It's strictly business. Torturing people doesn't fit my moral compass at all. But I don't think there's much of a gray area. Either the guy has information you need or not. Either it's vital or it's not. You know which guys you need to twist."

The official statements by President Bush and William Haynes reaffirming the U.S. government's opposition to torture have been applauded by human-rights groups—but again, the language in them is carefully chosen. What does the Bush administration mean by "torture"? Does it really share the activists' all-inclusive definition of the word? In his letter to the director of Human Rights Watch, Haynes used the term "enemy combatants" to describe those in custody. Calling detainees "prisoners of war" would entitle them to the protections of the Geneva Convention, which prohibits the "physical or mental torture" of POWs, and "any other form of coercion," even to the extent of "unpleasant or disadvantageous treatment of any kind." (In the contemptuous words of one military man, they "prohibit everything except three square meals, a warm bed, and access to a Harvard education.") Detainees who are American citizens have the advantage of constitutional protections against being held without charges, and have the right to legal counsel. They would also be protected from the worst abuses by the Eighth Amendment, which prohibits "cruel and unusual punishment." The one detainee at Guantánamo who was discovered to have been born in the United States has been transferred to a different facility, and legal battles rage over his status. But if the rest of the thousands of detainees are neither POWs (even though the bulk of them were captured during the fighting in Afghanistan) nor American citizens, they are fair game. They are protected only by this country's international promises—which are, in effect, unenforceable.

What are those promises? The most venerable are those in the Geneva Convention, but the United States has sidestepped this agreement in the case of those captured in the war on terror. The next most important would be those in the Universal Declaration of Human Rights, which asserts, in Article 5, "No one shall be subjected to torture or to cruel, inhuman or degrading treatment or punishment." There is also the Convention Against Torture, the agreement cited by Bush in June, which would seem to rule out any of the more aggressive methods of interrogation. It states, in Article I, "For the purposes of this Convention, torture means any act by which severe pain or suffering, whether physical or mental, is intentionally inflicted on a person." Again, note the word "severe." The United States is avoiding the brand "torturer" only by sleight of word.

The history of interrogation by U.S. armed forces and spy agencies is one of giving lip service to international agreements while vigorously using coercion whenever circumstances seem to warrant it. However, both the army and the CIA have been frank in their publications about the use of coercive methods. The *Kubark Manual* offers only a few nods in its 128 pages to qualms over what are referred to, in a rare euphemism, as "external techniques": "Moral considerations aside, the imposition of external techniques of manipulating people carries with it the grave risk of later lawsuits, adverse publicity, or other attempts to strike back." The use of the term "strike back" here is significant; it implies that criticism of such unseemly methods, whether legal, moral, or journalistic, would have no inherent validity but would be viewed as an enemy counterattack.

Bill Wagner, the former CIA agent, remembers going to the

Agency's three-week interrogation course at "the Farm," in Williamsburg, Virginia, in 1970. Until it was shut down, a few years later, it was considered the Agency's "premier course," Wagner says, and only the best recruits were invited to take it. "To say you had been through it was a real feather in your cap."

Volunteers played the role of captives in return for guaranteed space in a future session of the coveted course. They were deprived of sleep, kept doused with water in cold rooms, forced to sit or stand in uncomfortable positions for long periods, isolated from sunlight and social contacts, given food deliberately made unappetizing (oversalted, for instance, or tainted with a green dye), and subjected to mock executions. At least 10 percent of the volunteers dropped out, even though they knew it was just a training exercise. Wagner says that many of those who had served as victims later refused to take the course and victimize others. "They lost their stomach for it," he says.

Several years after Wagner took the course, he says, the Agency dropped it entirely. The scandals of the Nixon years put the CIA under unprecedented scrutiny. Over the next three decades spying schools and most human-intelligence networks were gradually dismantled. The United States itself was losing its stomach for hands-on intelligence gathering—and with it, interrogation.

Nobody experienced the effects of this shift more dramatically than Keith Hall, who earned the nickname Captain Crunch before he lost his job as a CIA agent. Now he describes himself as "a poster child for political correctness." He is a pugnacious brick of a man, who at age fifty-two is just a thicker (especially in the middle) version of the young man who joined the marines thirty years ago. After his discharge he earned a master's degree in history and international relations; he took a job as a police officer, because he craved a more physical brand of excitement than academia had to offer. His nickname comes from this craving.

The CIA hired Hall immediately after he applied, in 1979, because of his relatively rare combination of academic and real-world credentials. He was routed into the Investigation and Analysis Directorate, where he became one of the Agency's covert operators, a relatively small group ("about forty-eight guys, total," Hall says) known as the "knuckle-draggers." Most CIA agents, especially by the 1980s, were just deskmen.

Hall preferred traveling, training, and blowing things up, even though he felt that the rest of the Agency looked down its patrician nose at guys like him. When the U.S. Embassy in Beirut was bombed, on April 18, 1983, eight of the seventeen Americans killed were CIA employees. There were going to be plenty of official investigations, but the Agency wanted one of its own. Hall was selected to carry it out.

"They flew me to Langley on one of their private planes, and delivered me to the seventh floor," he says. "They told me, 'We want you to go to Beirut and find out who blew up the embassy and how they did it. The president himself is going to be reading your cables. There is going to be some retribution here.'"

Hall was honored, and excited. This was a mission of singular purpose, of the highest priority, and he knew he was expected to get results. Having been a police officer and a marine, he knew that the official investigations had to build a case that might someday stand up in court. His goal was not to build a case but just to find out who did it.

He slept on rooftops in Beirut, changing the location every two nights. It was a dangerous time to be an American—especially a CIA officer—there, and Hall kept moving. He worked with the Lebanese Special Security Force, and set up a computer in the police building.

Hall says he took part without hesitation in brutal questioning by the Lebanese, during which suspects were beaten with clubs and rubber hoses or wired up to electrical generators and doused with water. Such methods eventually led him to suspected "paymaster" of the embassy bombing, a man named Elias Nimr. "He was our biggest catch," Hall says—a man with powerful connections. "When I told the Lebanese minister of defense, I watched the blood drain out of his face."

Nimr was a fat, pampered-looking twenty-eight-year-old, used to living the good life, a young man of wealth, leisure, and power. He came to the police building wearing slacks, a shiny sport shirt, and Gucci shoes. He had a small, well-trimmed mustache at the center of his soft, round face, and wore gold on his neck, wrists, and fingers. When he was marched into the building, Hall says, some of the officers "tried to melt into the shadows" for fear of eventual retribution. Nimr was nonchalant and smirking in his initial interview, convinced that when word got back to his family and connections, he would promptly be released.

When Hall got a chance to talk to him, he set out to disabuse Nimr. "I'm an American intelligence officer," he said. "You really didn't think that you were going to blow up our embassy and we wouldn't do anything about it, did you? You really should be looking inside yourself and telling yourself that it's a good idea to talk to me. The best way to go is to be civilized. . . . I know you think you are going to walk right out of here in a few minutes. That's not going to happen. You're mine. I'm the one who will make the decisions about what happens to you. The only thing that will save your ass is to cooperate." Nimr smiled at him dismissively.

The next time they met, Nimr wasn't in such good shape. In this case his connections were failing him. No one had roughed him up, but he had been kept standing for two days. Hall placed him in a straight-backed metal chair, with hot floodlights in his face. The agent sat behind the light, so that Nimr couldn't see him. Nimr wasn't as cocky, but he was still silent.

At the third interrogation session, Hall says, he kicked Nimr out of his chair. It was the first time anyone had physically abused him, and he seemed stunned. He just stared at Hall. He hadn't eaten since his arrest, four days earlier. But he still had nothing to say.

"I sent him back to his cell, had water poured over him again and again while he sat under a big fan, kept him freezing for about twenty-four hours. He comes back after this, and you can see his mood is changing. He hasn't walked out of jail, and it's beginning to dawn on him that no one is going to spring him."

Over the next ten days Hall kept up the pressure. During the questioning sessions he again kicked Nimr out of his chair, and both he and the Lebanese captain involved cracked him occasionally across the shins with a wooden bat. Finally Nimr broke. According to Hall, he explained his role in the bombing, and in the assassination of Lebanon's president. He explained that Syrian intelligence agents had been behind the plan. (Not everyone in the CIA agrees with Hall's interpretation.)

Soon afterward Nimr died in his cell. Hall was back in Washington when he heard the news. He assumed that Nimr had been killed to prevent him from testifying and naming others involved in the plot. Armed with tapes of Nimr's confession, Hall felt he had accomplished his mission; but several months after finishing his report he was fired. As he understood it, word had leaked out about torture sessions conducted by a CIA agent, and the U.S. government was embarrassed.

None of the men charged was ever prosecuted for the bombing. Hall believes that the United States may have paid dearly for backing away from his investigation and letting the matter drop. William Buckley, who was Hall's station chief, was subsequently kidnapped, tortured, and killed. He was among the fourteen Western civilians kidnapped in Beirut in 1984. In October of the previous year, 241 American servicemen were killed in the bombing of their barracks at the Beirut airport. Some analysts believe that all these atrocities were committed by the same group, the one Hall believes he unearthed in his investigation. Still bitter about it nineteen years later, Hall says, "No one was punished for it, except me!"

Hall sees the loss of his career as dramatic proof that the CIA sold out to the "tree huggers" two decades ago, and points with scorn to a directive from President Bill Clinton that effectively barred intelligence agents from doing business with unsavory characters. The full-scale U.S. retreat from the uglier side of espionage is well documented—but has, by all accounts, been sharply reversed in the aftermath of 9/11.

"People are being very careful, very legal, and very sensible," one former top intelligence official says. "We are not inflicting intense pain, or doing anything damaging or life-threatening. We are once again asking, 'How do you take people down a series of steps in such a way that it has an impact?' That's the only game in town."

Despite the hue and cry over mistreatment of prisoners at Guantánamo, two former Pakistani inmates there—Shah Muhammad and Sahibzada Osman Ali—told me that except for some roughing up immediately after they were captured, they were not badly treated at Camp X-Ray. They both felt bored, lonely, frustrated, angry, and helpless (enough for Shah Muhammad to attempt suicide), but neither believed that he would be harmed by his American captors, and both regarded the extreme precautions (shackles, handcuffs, hoods) that so outraged the rest of the world as comical. "What did the American soldiers think I could do to them?" asked Sahibzada, who stands about five feet eight and weighs little more than 150 pounds. Indeed, the lack of fear at Camp X-Ray no doubt made it more difficult to sort out foot soldiers from dedicated terrorists.

The perfect model of an interrogation center would be a place where prisoners lived in fear and uncertainty, a place where they could be isolated or allowed to mingle freely, as the jailer wished, and where conversations anywhere could be overheard. Interrogators would be able to control the experience of their subjects completely, shutting down access to other people, or even to normal sensation and experience, or opening that access up. Subjects' lives could be made a misery of discomfort and confusion, or restored to an almost normal level of comfort and social interaction within the limitations of confinement. Hope could be dangled or removed. Cooperation would be rewarded, stubbornness punished. Interrogators would have ever growing files on their subjects, with each new fact or revelation yielding new leads and more information—drawn from field investigations (agents in the real world verifying and exploring facts gathered on the inside), the testimony of other subjects, collaborators spying inside the prison, and surreptitious recordings. The interrogators in this center would have the experience and the intuition of a Jerry Giorgio or a Michael Koubi.

Serious interrogation is clearly being reserved for only the most dangerous men, like Sheikh Mohammed. So why not lift the fig leaf covering the use of coercion? Why not eschew hypocrisy, clearly define what is meant by the word "severe," and amend bans on torture to allow interrogators to coerce information from would-be terrorists?

This is the crux of the problem. It may be clear that coercion is sometimes the right choice, but how does one allow it yet still control it? Sadism is deeply rooted in the human psyche. Every army has its share of soldiers who delight in kicking and beating bound captives. Men in authority tend to abuse it—not all men, but many. As a mass, they should be assumed to lean toward abuse. How does a country best regulate behavior in its dark and distant corners, in prisons, on battlefields, and in interrogation rooms, particularly when its forces number in the millions and are spread all over the globe? In considering a change in national policy, one is obliged to anticipate the practical consequences. So if we formally lift the ban on torture, even if only partially and in rare, specific cases (the attorney and author Alan Dershowitz has proposed issuing "torture warrants"), the question will be, How can we ensure that the practice does not become commonplace—not just a tool for extracting vital, life-saving information in rare cases but a routine tool of oppression?

As it happens, a pertinent case study exists. Israel has been a target of terror attacks for many years, and has wrestled openly with the dilemmas they pose for a democracy. In 1987 a commission led by the retired Israeli Supreme Court justice Moshe Landau wrote a series of recommendations for Michael Koubi and his agents, allowing them to use "moderate physical pressure" and "nonviolent psychological pressure" in interrogating prisoners who had information that could prevent impending terror attacks. The commission sought to allow such coercion only in "ticking-bomb scenarios"—that is, in cases like the kidnapping of Jakob von Metzler, when the information withheld by the suspect could save lives.

Twelve years later the Israeli Supreme Court effectively revoked this permission, banning the use of any and all forms of torture. In the years following the Landau Commission recommendations, the use of coercive methods had become widespread in the Occupied Territories. It was estimated that more than two thirds of the Palestinians taken into custody were subjected to them. Koubi says that only in rare instances, and with court permission, did he slap, pinch, or shake a prisoner—but he happens to be an especially gifted interrogator. What about the hundreds of men who worked for him? Koubi could not be present for all those interrogations. Every effort to regulate coercion failed. In the abstract it was easy to imagine a ticking-bomb situation, and a suspect who clearly warranted rough treatment. But in real life where was the line to be drawn? Should coercive methods be applied only to someone who knows of an immediately pending attack? What about one who might know of attacks planned for months or years in the future?

"Assuming you get useful information from torture, then why not always use torture?" asks Jessica Montell, the executive director of B'Tselem, a human-rights advocacy group in Jerusalem. "Why stop at the bomb that's already been planted and at people who know where explosives are? Why not people who are building the explosives, or people who are donating money, or transferring the funds for the explosives? Why stop at the victim himself? Why not torture the victims' families, their relatives, their neighbors? If the end justifies the means, then where would you draw the line?"

And how does one define "coercion," as opposed to "torture"? If making a man sit in a tiny chair that forces him to hang painfully by his bound hands when he slides forward is okay, then what about applying a little pressure to the base of his neck to aggravate that pain? When does shaking or pushing a prisoner, which can become violent enough to kill or seriously injure a man, cross the line from coercion to torture?

Montell has thought about these questions a lot. She is thirty-five, a slender woman with scruffy short brown hair, who seems in perpetual motion, directing B'Tselem and tending baby twins and a four-year-old at home. Born in California, she emigrated to Israel partly out of feelings of solidarity with the Jewish state and partly because she found a job she liked in the human-rights field. Raised with a kind of idealized notion of Israel, she now seems committed to making the country live up to her ideals. But those ideals are hard-headed. Although Montell and her organization have steadfastly opposed the use of coercion (which she considers torture), she recognizes that the moral issue involved is not a simple one.

She knows that the use of coercion interrogation did not end completely when the Israeli Supreme Court banned it in 1999. The difference is that when interrogators use "aggressive methods" now, they know they are breaking the law and could potentially be held responsible for doing so. This acts as a deterrent, and tends to limit the use of coercion to only the most defensible situations.

"If I as an interrogator feel that the person in front of me has information that can prevent a catastrophe from happening," she says, "I imagine that I would do what I would have to do in order to prevent that catastrophe from happening. The state's obligation is then to put me on trial, for breaking the law. Then I come and say these are the facts that I had at my disposal. This is what I believed at the time. This is what I thought necessary to do. I can evoke the defense of necessity, and then the court decides whether or not it's reasonable that I broke the law in order to avert this catastrophe. But it has to be that I broke the law. It can't be that there's some prior license for me to abuse people."

In other words, when the ban is lifted, there is no restraining lazy, incompetent, or sadistic interrogators. As long as it remains illegal to torture, the interrogator who employs coercion must accept the risk. He must be prepared to stand up in court, if necessary, and defend his actions. Interrogators will still use coercion because in some cases they will deem it worth the consequences. This does not mean they will necessarily be punished. In any nation the decision to prosecute a crime is an executive one. A prosecutor, a grand jury, or a judge must decide to press charges, and the chances that an interrogator in a genuine ticking-bomb case would be prosecuted, much less convicted, is very small. As of this writing, Wolfgang Daschner, the Frankfurt deputy police chief, has not been prosecuted for threatening to torture Jakob von Metzler's kidnapper, even though he clearly broke the law.

The Bush administration has adopted exactly the right posture on the matter. Candor and consistency are not always public virtues. Torture is a crime against humanity, but coercion is an issue that is rightly handled with a wink, or even a touch of hypocrisy; it should be banned but also quietly practiced. Those who protest coercive methods will exaggerate their horrors, which is good: It generates a useful climate of fear. It is wise of the president to reiterate U.S. support for international agreements banning torture, and it is wise for American interrogators to employ whatever coercive methods work. It is also smart not to discuss the matter with anyone.

If interrogators step over the line from coercion to outright torture, they should be held personally responsible. But no interrogator is ever going to be prosecuted for keeping Khalid Sheikh Mohammed awake, cold, alone, and uncomfortable. Nor should he be.

The image that kept coming to my mind as I was writing this story was the scene from Ang Lee's film The Hulk, *in which the monster's alter ego, Bruce Banner, is suspended inside a sensory-deprivation tank, tethered to computer monitors by wires from head to toe. Scientists arrayed around the tank are, in effect, peering inside his brain. It reminded me of the gap between what people think technology can do and what it can actually do. Hollywood does such a good job of building fantasies on half-truths that a surprising number of otherwise well-informed people walk around believing that, for instance, NASA has an antigravity machine for training astronauts, or that the CIA has ways of reading terrorists' minds. In real life, accomplishing these things is more difficult and a lot more interesting.*

I imagined that this story would be greeted by outrage from the human-rights community, but it sparked surprisingly little controversy. It turns out that almost everyone understands that in certain rare circumstances we are morally obligated to pry information from a person who does not want to share it. If the most effective way of getting information were to drill holes in prisoners' teeth—to summon another hair-raising cinematic moment—or to pull out toenails, we would be in an awful moral fix. So it comes as something of a relief to learn that the most effective methods are more subtle and less overtly cruel.

CONTRIBUTORS

CECILIA BALLI is a writer and columnist for *Texas Monthly*, covering the U.S.-Mexico border, South Texas, and Latinos in the state. She is working on a nonfiction book for Henry Holt about the murder of women and girls in Ciudad Juárez, Mexico. She lives in and around Texas.

CLARA BINGHAM, a former White House correspondent for *Newsweek* magazine, is the author of *Women on the Hill: Challenging the Culture of Congress* (Times Books, 1997) and co-author of *Class Action: The Landmark Case That Changed Sexual Harassment Law* (Doubleday, 2002).

CHARLES BOWDEN lives in Tucson, Arizona. His most recent book is *Down by the River: Drugs, Money, Murder and Family.*

MARK BOWDEN is the author of *Black Hawk Down* and *Killing Pablo* and is a national correspondent for *The Atlantic Monthly*. He lives in New London, Pennsylvania.

LUKE DITTRICH is a staff writer at *Atlanta* magazine. His articles have also appeared in *The Oxford American, Reader's Digest,* and *The Middle East Times.* Among the subjects he's written about in the last few years are a missing thermonuclear bomb, a Southern pornographer, an Egyptian faith healer, a dead pop star, and Jimmy Carter.

ROBERT DRAPER has been a writer at large for *GQ* for the past seven years, and previous to that he was a senior editor at *Texas Monthly* for six years. He is the author of *Rolling Stone Magazine: The Uncensored History* and of the novel *Hadrian's Walls* and is currently completing his second novel, *The Gleason Line.* He lives in Asheville, North Carolina.

JAMES ELLROY was born in Los Angeles in 1948. His L.A. quartet, *The Black Dahlia, The Big Nowhere, L.A. Confidential,* and *White Jazz* were international bestsellers. His novel *American Tabloid* was *Time* magazine's Best (Fiction) Book of the Year in 1995. He lives in Carmel, California.

SABRINA RUBIN ERDELY is a senior writer for *Philadelphia* magazine. Her work has appeared in *GQ, The New Yorker, Reader's Digest, Glamour,* and *Self,* among other publications. She has earned a number of awards for her feature writing and reporting, including a National Magazine Award nomination.

JAMES FALLOWS is national correspondent for *The Atlantic Monthly* and has reported for the magazine from many countries in the world since the late 1970s. His books include *Free Flight, Breaking the News,* and *National Defense,* which won the American Book Award in 1981. His writing about Iraq won the National Magazine Award in 2003. He lives in Washington, D.C.

ELISABETH FRANCK is a freelance journalist living in France.

DAVID GRANN is a staff writer at *The New Yorker.* His stories have appeared in *The New York Times Magazine, The Atlantic Monthly,* and *The New Republic,* where he previously served as managing editor. His work has also been excerpted in several collections, including most recently *The Best American Sports Writing 2003.*

PAT JORDAN is a freelance writer living in Fort Lauderdale, Florida. He writes regularly for *The New York Times Magazine* and other publications. His most recent book, a novel, is titled *a.k.a. Sheila Weinstein,* published by Carroll & Graf. It has a few murders in it and a few sex scenes that would be appropriate for Showtime's cable television series *The L Word.*

ROBERT F. KENNEDY JR. is President of the Waterkeeper Alliance, Senior Attorney for the Natural Resources Defense Council, and Clinical Professor and Supervising Attorney at the Pace Environmental Litigation Clinic, Pace University School of Law in New York. His editorials and articles have appeared in *The New York Times, The Atlantic Monthly, The Wall Street Journal, Esquire, The Village Voice, The Boston Globe, The Washington Post, Rolling Stone,* and *The Nation.* This year, Kennedy will publish two books, *Crimes Against Nature,* for HarperCollins, regarding the systematic attempt by the Bush administration to dismantle the nation's environmental laws, and *St. Francis of Assisi, A Life of Joy* for Hyperion Books for Children about the life of St. Francis.

JAY KIRK has written for *Harper's, The New York Times Magazine,* and the *Chicago Reader.* A story of his appeared in *Best American Crime Writing 2003.* He lives in Philadelphia.

JON KRAKAUER is the author of *Eiger Dreams, Into the Wild, Into Thin Air,* and *Under the Banner of Heaven.* In 1997 he received a National Magazine Award, in 1998 he was a finalist for the Pulitzer Prize in General Nonfiction, and in 1999 he was honored with an Academy Award in Literature from the American Academy of Arts and Letters.

HEATHER MAC DONALD is a fellow at the Manhattan Institute and a contributing editor of *City Journal.* Her most recent book is *Are Cops Racist?:*

How the War Against the Police Harms Black Americans (Ivan R. Dee, 2003). She was born in Los Angeles and now lives in New York City.

JOHN H. RICHARDSON is a writer at large for *Esquire* magazine and the author of two books, *The Vipers' Club* and *In the Little World: A True Story of Dwarfs, Love, and Trouble*. His third book is a mixture of history and memoir called *My Father the Spy*, scheduled for publication next year by HarperCollins.

BRENDAN RILEY is the pseudonym for an aspiring novelist no longer living in New Jersey. "Megan's Law and Me" was his first published article.

MARK SCHONE has been a senior contributing writer at *Spin* magazine since 1996. His investigative reporting has appeared in *Rolling Stone*, *Wired*, and *The Boston Globe*, among other publications, and his essays have aired on the Public Radio International show *This American Life*. In 2002, he received an Edgar Allan Poe award from the Mystery Writers of America for co-authoring the book *Son of a Grifter*, the true story of the mother-son con artists Sante and Kenny Kimes. He lives with his wife and daughter in Brooklyn, New York.

SCOTT TUROW is a writer and attorney. He is the author of six best-selling novels, including his first, *Presumed Innocent* (1987), and his most recent, *Reversible Errors*, published in 2002. He has also written two nonfiction books—*One L*, about his experience as a law student, and his newest book, *Ultimate Punishment*, a reflection on capital punishment. Mr. Turow has been a partner in the Chicago office of Sonnenschein, Nath, and Rosenthal, a national law firm, since 1986, concentrating on white-collar criminal defense, while also devoting a substantial part of his time to pro bono matters. He has served on a number of public bodies, including the Illinois Commission on Capital Punishment appointed by Governor George Ryan in 2000 to recommend reforms to the Illinois death penalty system. He is also a past president of the Authors Guild and is currently a trustee of Amherst College.

"The Professor and the Porn" by Elisabeth Franck (originally published in *New York* magazine, June 23, 2003), copyright © 2003 by *New York* magazine. Reprinted by permission of *New York* magazine.

"The Old Man and the Gun" by David Grann (originally published in *The New Yorker*, Jan. 27, 2003), copyright © 2003 by David Grann. Reprinted by permission of David Grann.

"CSC: Crime Scene Cleanup" by Pat Jordan (originally published in *Playboy* magazine, Aug. 2003), copyright © 2003 by Pat Jordan. Reprinted by permission of Pat Jordan.

"A Miscarriage of Justice" by Robert F. Kennedy Jr. (originally published in *The Atlantic Monthly*, Jan./Feb. 2003), copyright © 2003 by Robert F. Kennedy Jr. Reprinted by permission of International Creative Management, Inc.

"Watching the Detectives" by Jay Kirk (originally published in *Harper's* magazine, Aug. 2003), copyright © 2003 by Jay Kirk. Reprinted by permission of Jay Kirk.

"For the Love of God" by Jon Krakauer from *Under the Banner of Heaven: A Story of Violent Faith* by Jon Krakauer (originally published in different form in *GQ*, July 2003), copyright © 2003 by Jon Krakauer. Reprinted by permission of Doubleday, a division of Random House, Inc.

"Chief Bratton Takes on LA" by Heather Mac Donald (originally published in *City Journal*, Autumn 2003), copyright © 2003 by Heather Mac Donald/*City Journal*/Manhattan Institute. Reprinted by permission of *City Journal*.

"Not Guilty by Reason of Afghanistan" by John H. Richardson (originally published in *Esquire* magazine, Jan. 2003), copyright © 2003 by John H. Richardson. Reprinted by permission of *Esquire* magazine.

"Megan's Law and Me" by Brendan Riley (originally published in *Details*, April 2003), copyright © 2003 by Brendan Riley. Reprinted by permission of Brendan Riley.

"Unfortunate Con" by Mark E. Schone (originally published in *The Oxford American*, July/August 2003), copyright © 2003 by Mark E. Schone. Reprinted by permission of Mark E. Schone.

"To Kill or Not to Kill" by Scott Turow (originally published as "Annals of Law: To Kill or Not to Kill" in *The New Yorker*, Jan. 6, 2003), revised and published in *Ultimate Punishment* by Scott Turow, copyright © 2003 by Scott Turow. Reprinted by permission of Farrar, Straus and Giroux, LLC.

ABOUT THE EDITORS

THOMAS H. COOK is the author of eighteen books, including two works of true crime. His novels have been nominated for the Edgar Allan Poe Award, the Macavity Award, and the Dashiell Hammett Prize. *The Chatham School Affair* won the Edgar Allan Poe Award for Best Novel in 1996. His true-crime book, *Blood Echoes*, was nominated for the Edgar Allan Poe Award in 1992, and his story "Fatherhood" won the Herodotus Prize in 1998 and was included in *Best American Mystery Stories* of 1998, edited by Otto Penzler and Ed McBain. His works have been translated into fifteen languages.

OTTO PENZLER is the proprietor of the Mysterious Bookshop in New York City. He was the founder of the Mysterious Press and created the publishing firm Otto Penzler Books. He is a recipient of an Edgar Award for *The Encyclopedia of Mystery and Detection* and the Ellery Queen Award and a Raven by the Mystery Writers of America for his many contributions to the field. He is the series editor of *The Best America Mystery Stories of the Year*. His other anthologies include *Murder for Love, Murder for Revenge, Murder and Obsession, The 50 Greatest Mysteries of All Time*, and *The Best American Mystery Stories of the Century*. He wrote *101 Greatest Movies of Mystery and Suspense*. He lives in New York City.

JOSEPH WAMBAUGH was a member of the Los Angeles Police Department for fourteen years before becoming a full-time writer. Among his numerous best-selling novels are *The Choirboys, The New Centurions, The Glitter Dome*, and *Floaters*. He wrote the true story of two young cops and their encounter with two robbers in *The Onion Field* in 1974, for which he won the Edgar Allan Poe Award. One of the most chilling and heartbreaking books of its kind, it was later filmed and remains a classic. He also won an Edgar for best motion picture for *The Black Marble* (1981). His most recent book is *The Fire Lover*, the true story of a firefighter who was also an arsonist. He was recently given the Grand Master award by the Mystery Writers of America in recognition of lifetime achievement.